Fifth Edition

HUMAN RESOURCES LAW

John Remington

Richard Heiser

Cyrus F. Smythe

Kenneth L. Sovereign

Prentice Hall

Boston   Columbus   Indianapolis   New York   San Francisco   Upper Saddle River
Amsterdam   Cape Town   Dubai   London   Madrid   Milan   Munich   Paris   Montreal   Toronto
Delhi   Mexico City   Sao   Paulo   Sydney   Hong Kong   Seoul   Singapore   Taipei   Tokyo

Editorial Director: Sally Yagan
Editor in Chief: Donna Battista
AVP Executive Editor: Stephanie Wall
Director of Editorial Services: Ashley Santora
Sr Project Manager Editorial: Karen Kirincich
Director of Marketing: Patrice Jones
VP Director of Marketing: Kate Valentine
Marketing Assistant: Ian Gold
Sr Managing Editor: Cynthia Zonneveld

Project Manager: Renata Butera
Operations Specialist: Renata Butera
Creative Art Director: Jayne Conte
Cover Designer: Bruce Kenselaar
Full-Service Project Management: Hemalatha
Composition: Integra Software Services, Ltd.
Printer/Binder: LSC Communications, Inc.
Cover Printer: LSC Communications, Inc.
Text Font: 10/12, Palatino

Credits and acknowledgments borrowed from other sources and reproduced, with permission, in this textbook appear on appropriate page within text.

Many of the designations by manufacturers and seller to distinguish their products are claimed as trademarks. Where those designations appear in this book, and the publisher was aware of a trademark claim, the designations have been printed in initial caps or all caps.

Library of Congress Cataloging-in-Publication Data

Remington, John.
    Human resources law/John Remington . . . [et al.]—5th ed.
        p. cm.
    Revised ed. of: Personnel law/Kenneth L. Sovereign 4th ed. c1999.
    ISBN-13: 978-0-13-256889-0 (alk. paper)
    ISBN-10: 0-13-256889-6 (alk. paper)
    1. Labor laws and legislation—United States.   2. Employee rights—United States.
3. Discrimination in employment—Law and legislation—United States.   I. Sovereign,
Kenneth L. Personnel law.   II. Title.
KF3455.S68 2012
344.7301—dc22

                                                                    2010046291

Prentice Hall
is an imprint of

www.pearsonhighered.com

ISBN 10:   0-13-256889-6
ISBN 13: 978-0-13-256889-0

BRIEF CONTENTS

CONTENTS

Chapter 6 OCCUPATIONAL SAFETY AND HEALTH LAW 170

PREFACE

This text has been designed for undergraduate and beginning graduate students as well as practitioners in the area of human resources management. Although written primarily for business and management students, it should also be useful for students in other areas such as labor studies, political science, and American studies. It can also be utilized as an effective reference for practicing managers and workplace representatives.

Human Resources Law is an extensive revision of the Fourth Edition of *Personnel Law* by Kenneth L. Sovereign. The text revises and expands Sovereign's thorough coverage of at-will employment, basic labor and safety standards, and discrimination law, but it also includes new chapters on the development of employment law, public-sector labor relations, and the challenges of human resources management in the twenty-first century. The book provides an explanation of basic legal issues supplemented by case law examples and illustrative case studies. Specifically, this edition adds coverage of:

- Contemporary human resources issues, including privacy, globalization, and immigration
- Practical advice for employers to avoid litigation
- Development of employment law in the United States
- Coverage of new statutes and court decisions
- The environment for public-sector labor relations
- Employer obligations in communicating with employees

Human resources managers are increasingly being forced to deal with a multitude of employment law issues in the workplace and need a thorough knowledge of legal requirements and potential penalties to assist their employers in avoiding litigation and adverse employment relations outcomes. It is not sufficient simply to know the statutory requirements pertinent to the employment relationship. Rather, students and practitioners need to understand the ways in which the courts have interpreted these statutory requirements so that they can anticipate problems and develop strategies, policies, and processes to both maximize the productivity of an organization's human capital and avoid conflict and employee dissatisfaction.

To assist students in grasping basic legal concepts and their implications, *Human Resources Law:*

- **Presents the student with a layperson's explanation of basic employment law principles** Topics include discrimination, mandated employment practices, compensation, and labor relations together with relevant case citations.
- **Applies relevant employment law principles through case studies and citations** Chapter-ending practical cases illustrate key points and legal citations provide advanced students with fuller explanations.
- **Provides recommendations and advice for avoiding litigation** This includes utilization of alternative dispute resolution strategies and procedures.

ABOUT THE AUTHORS

John Remington is currently a Professor of Human Resources and Labor Studies in the University of Minnesota's Carlson School of Management. He has previously taught at West Virginia University, the University of Louisville, and Florida International University. He holds a Ph.D. from the University of Michigan and has done post-doctoral work at Stanford University and the University of Michigan.

Professor Remington has served as a labor arbitrator for over 35 years and is listed on the panels of the Federal Mediation and Conciliation Service, the American Arbitration Association, the Minnesota Bureau of Mediation Services, and numerous private panels. He teaches in the areas of labor and employment law, arbitration and alternative dispute resolution, and collective bargaining.

Dick Heiser's career spans more than 35 years in human resources management and education with private, public, and nonprofit organizations. His undergraduate and initial graduate study was at Western Michigan University followed by further study at the University of Minnesota, the Harvard Business School, and other institutions.

Beginning with job analysis and time and motion study at Deere & Company, Heiser advanced to human resources division management in two Fortune 500 firms. In Champion International Corporation, he served as compensation manager as well as plant and division personnel manager, and he negotiated union contracts. At Land O' Lakes, he served as division HR manager and undertook relocation and integration of an acquisition and the start- up of large manufacturing facilities. Years of consulting included auditing organizations for legal compliance, management training, out-placement, meeting facilitation, and appraisal program development. Heiser's writing includes publishing the first article about auditing human resources management compliance matters and the publication of a manual for supervisors and personnel specialists in 2011.

Cyrus F. Smythe Jr. received his Ph.D in Economics from University of Washington and is a Professor Emeritus at the University of Minnesota where he taught from 1961 to 1988. Professor Smythe has been a Labor Economics Consultant since 1958 and has also served as a consultant to U.S. government agencies and departments, state agencies, metropolitan commissions, and labor unions. In addition, he was an active labor arbitrator from 1961 to 1968, has been a labor relations representative for private and public employers since 1969, and the president of Labor Relations Associates, Inc., since 1969.

 **Kenneth L. Sovereign**, the original author, passed away in 2001. His personal philosophies on good safety programs and strong OSHA compliance are still included in this book. With over 18 years of experience as a safety director, 10 years of counsel representing management in OSHA cases, and more than 18 years as a member of the Minnesota OSHA Review Board, Sovereign shared his knowledge through the years by teaching personnel law to managers. His son, Jeffrey, is a key individual in pulling together the authors for this new edition. The publisher and authors are very grateful for his help and guidance.

ACKNOWLEDGMENTS

Our appreciation to Kenneth Sovereign for his effective, intelligent, and ethical writing of previous editions.

The authors wish to acknowledge Loel Kuehne and Courtney Thomas, both of whom provided valuable contributions to this edition.

Reviewers for the fifth edition:
Gerald E. Calvasina, *Southern Utah University*
Patrick D. Cullen, *Southern New Hampshire University*
Darlene Gerry, *Idaho State University*
Kimberly A. LaFevor, *Athens State University*
Marie Losquadro, *St. Joseph's College*
Mary Sheila E. McDonald, *Philadelphia University*
Neal Orkin, *Drexel University*
Gary Roberts, *Regent University*
Cindy W. Walter, *Antelope Valley College*
Ruth Ann Watry, *Northern Michigan University*

John Remington
Dick Heiser
Cyrus Smythe

CHAPTER 1

Human Resources and the Law

CHAPTER OUTLINE

Development of Employment
 Regulation

Employment at Will

Federal Legislative Action

State Action

Employment Relationship as a Contract

Public and Private Sectors

Guidelines for Human Resource
 Practitioners

Structure of the Courts

American society has typically viewed with suspicion attempts by governments, particularly the federal government, to discipline economic tendencies in general, and employment relationships in particular. Indeed, the nineteenth century liberal tradition was clearly hostile to any attempt by government to restrict the rights of private property or to dictate to any individual how his or her property might be utilized. To ignore the natural laws of the marketplace by controlling prices or wages or the terms and conditions of employment was considered to be neither wise nor prudent. This laissez-faire approach was supported both by the common-law doctrine that denied the existence of a **property right** to employment and by the classical economic theory that viewed labor as merely a factor of production. Indeed, the entire employment relationship was based on the common-law master and servant doctrine that legally placed the employee in a position subordinate to the employer.[1]

DEVELOPMENT OF EMPLOYMENT REGULATION

The impetus to challenge the nineteenth century status quo came largely from two separate but related developments: industrialization and urbanization. The unprecedented industrialization that occurred in the United States during the last decades of the nineteenth century created dramatic changes that affected patterns of work, employment relationships, and standards of living. This same period also witnessed a changeover in American society from a predominantly agrarian one to an urbanized one. Workers, particularly younger workers, were drawn from the farms to the cities in search of greater freedom and economic reward. According to census figures, there were only 141 cities of 8,000 persons or more in 1860. By 1900, there were 545 such cities with 160 of these exceeding 25,000 persons.[2]

The employment experience, if they had any at all, of these new urbanites had been primarily as family farmworkers, ranch hands, or rural storekeepers. In the city they were confronted with industrial employment in new and unfamiliar surroundings, found themselves in competition for jobs with recent immigrants, and experienced unregulated wages and working conditions, exploitation, submarginal living conditions, and a new kind of poverty. The plight of this new industrial worker was first addressed by Congress, motivated, in most instances reluctantly, by the **Progressive Movement** of the early twentieth century. Progressive attempts to remedy the most egregious symptoms of the labor problem resulted in the passage of worker-oriented reforms.[3] Child labor legislation regarding the restriction of the hours and types of work, protective laws for women in industrial employment, and workers' compensation statutes in individual states were examples of these early reforms.[4] Even the rights and status of organized labor were at least recognized, and in rare instances promoted, by the federal government in the early years of the twentieth century, beginning with Theodore Roosevelt's intervention in the 1902 coal strike and culminating with the passage of the Railway Labor Act in 1926.[5]

The latter part of the twentieth century saw government increase its level of influence in the private sector, although not systematically or always with sufficient knowledge of the problem it was attempting to address. Such influence was seen through expanded protective legislation that established the rights of employees in the workplace, principally through the adoption of the National Labor Relations Act in 1935, and much later through state legislation providing public employees with the right to collectively bargain. In the 1970s, federal legislation safeguarded pension funding, mandated minimum safety conditions, and provided employment rights following military service and family medical situations. The most powerful of these changes were statutes devised to provide equal opportunity and fair compensation practices.

EMPLOYMENT AT WILL

Fundamental to an understanding of the development of human resources law in the United States is the **employment-at-will** doctrine. This doctrine placed the courts fully in support of the employer's desire to dominate the employment relationship by controlling job security. The at-will doctrine holds that an employee can be terminated without legal liability for good cause, bad cause, or no cause at all. The doctrine is not applicable where there is an express statutory prohibition or formal contract (including collective bargaining agreements). This general rule of the common law is stated in the *American Law Reports (ALR)* as follows:

> Despite its sometimes harsh operation and the obvious opportunities for abuse it affords an unscrupulous employer, few legal principles would seem to be better settled than the broad generality that an employment for an indefinite term is regarded as an employment at will which may be terminated at any time by either party for any reason or for no reason at all.[6]

The at-will doctrine originated in the English common law and gained widespread acceptance in the U.S. courts. The unquestionable acceptance of the at-will rule is illustrated in the extreme case where an employee was discharged because his wife refused to sleep with his supervisor. The employee challenged the employer's right to discharge for this reason, but the court rejected his suit because the employment-at-will doctrine empowered his employer to discharge him at any time, for any reason, even if the reason was immoral.[7] The at-will doctrine was sustained by the U.S. Supreme Court in *Adair* v. *United States*, 208 U.S. 161 (1908), when the Court declared unconstitutional a statute that prohibited the discharge of a railroad employee because of his union membership. The Court said that since the duration of the employment was not specified, both the employer and the employee had equal rights to terminate for any reason. Few legal doctrines have been more firmly established than this common-law right of the employer to discharge employees without legal consequences. In another instance an employee was discharged for trading at a certain store that his employer decided to put out of business. The court found that the employer had a right to discharge even if it was morally wrong and held that "the law cannot compel them (employers) to employ workers nor keep them employed."[8] Even as late as 1949 a court held that an employer could discharge for no reason at all.[9]

Erosion of Employment at Will

With the migration of labor from farms to factory piece work and assembly lines, what was deemed simply a labor problem became viewed as more of a social problem. A worker's survival often depended on the whims of the employer, and the jobs of most American workers depended almost entirely on the continued goodwill of their employers. The employer's right to terminate without a legal risk first began to come under attack during the Progressive Era from social critics, economists, and legal scholars. The result was a beginning of a gradual erosion

of the employment-at-will doctrine through limiting legislation. Specifically, legislation concerning employees' rights, such as the Labor Management Relations Act as amended[10] and Title VII of the Civil Rights Act of 1964 as amended,[11] compelled the courts to adopt a changed view of this harsh doctrine. Some employees who challenged the at-will doctrine argued that their employment was for a fixed period, either expressed or implied. Others maintained that the employer had an obligation to evaluate job performance in good faith and therefore could terminate only for cause. Still others relied more on traditional legal arguments to justify their claims for relief, such as **due process,** the doctrine of good faith and fair dealing, or alleged malicious action by the employer. In a climate of employee rights created by Congress in other areas, the courts began to more favorably look at the **wrongfully discharged** employees' arguments. These cases almost always involved breach of contract or violation of state statute and were therefore typically brought in state courts. Accordingly, there has been, and continues to be, some variation in the application of the at-will principle across the states.

The early 1980s witnessed the further erosion of the common-law doctrine of employment-at-will as federal legislation regulating the American workplace expanded. As one court stated, "it represents an area of the law undergoing dynamic development."[12] As a result, employees and lawyers were more willing to pursue discharge cases that they might have rejected in the past. Further, the reporting of court verdicts and settlements by the news media resulted in greater **exposure** of the employer to litigation related to discharges. The proponents of eliminating the at-will doctrine are quick to point out that the United States is the only industrialized country that does not provide employees with some form of comprehensive protection against wrongful discharge. The just-cause provisions of labor agreements cover some employees, but union membership has failed to keep pace with the growing workforce and today only about 13 percent of the workforce is covered by labor agreements. However, employers have not been deceived into believing that the at-will doctrine has been abolished by the courts[13] or accepted the premise that they must show **just cause** in all cases of discharge.

FEDERAL LEGISLATIVE ACTION

Statutory restriction not only limited the at-will doctrine but it also provided employees with the right to negotiate with employers over wages, hours, and the terms and conditions of employment as well as established minimum standards for wages and hours. These restrictions were first established in the provisions of the National Railway Labor Act in 1926, which recognized unionization and collective bargaining in the railway industry and provided for "boards of adjustment" through which employees could challenge terminations. These encroachments on the employment relationship were upheld by the Supreme Court.[14] The Railway Labor Act was followed in 1935 by the National Labor Relations Act, which will be discussed in Chapter 8. Originally known as the Wagner Act, this statute covers many, but not all, private-sector employees and protects them from discharge when engaged in concerted activities for the purpose of mutual aid and protection. Protection from discharge because of **concerted activity** includes union-organizing activity and extends to verbal complaints about working conditions as well as dissatisfaction because of wages.[15] Most union collective bargaining agreements include a provision that requires the employer to demonstrate "just cause" when disciplining or discharging an employee. The contract terms remove the employee from at-will status.

The Fair Labor Standards Act, discussed in Chapter 5, provides for minimum wages and requires premium payments for overtime hours but also prohibits discharge for exercising rights guaranteed by the minimum wage and overtime provisions of the Act.[16] Title VII of the Civil Rights Act of 1964 and its 1991 Amendments, 42 U.S.C. §§ 2000e-2, 2000e-3(a) (1981), prohibits discharge and other job actions based on race, color, religion, gender, or national origin, and reprisal for exercising Title VII rights. This legislation is addressed in Chapter 2. Protection against termination or reprisal for employees between the ages of 40 and 70 is provided by the Age Discrimination in Employment Act of 1967, 29 U.S.C. §§ 623, 631, and 633. This statute is also covered in Chapter 2. The Occupational Safety and Health Act of 1970, 29 U.S.C. § 66 (1975), discussed in Chapter 6, provides for workplace safety standards, authorizes procedures for employees to enforce these standards, and prohibits the discharge of employees in reprisal for exercising rights under the Act. The Rehabilitation Act of 1973, 29 U.S.C. §§ 793, 794 (1975), addressed in Chapter 4, prohibits federal contractors or any program receiving federal financial assistance from discriminating against handicapped persons. The Americans With Disabilities Act, 42 U.S.C. § 12112, also considered in Chapter 4, prohibits the discharge of, or discrimination against, persons because of certain disabilities. The Family and Medical Leave Act of 1993, Public Law No. 1033 (107 § 6), discussed in Chapter 4, prohibits discharge or adverse action against employees who exercise their statutory right to take leave for personal or family medical reasons, or to provide care needed by family members as a result of their military service.

Other regulatory legislation not given extensive coverage in this text includes, but is not limited to:

- Employee Retirement Income Security Act of 1974, as amended by the Pension Reform Act of 2006, 29 U.S.C. §§ 1140, 1141 (1975) (prohibits discharge of employees in order to prevent them from attaining vested pension rights)

- Consumer Credit Protection Act, 15 U.S.C. § 1674(a) (1982) (prohibits discharge of employees because of garnishment of wages for any one indebtedness)
- Civil Service Reform Act of 1978, 5 U.S.C. § 7513(a) (1980) (permits removal of federal civil service employees "only for such cause as will promote the efficiency of the service")
- Judiciary and Judicial Procedure Act, 28 U.S.C. § 1875 (Supp. 1982) (prohibits discharge of employees for service on grand or petit jury)
- Federal Worker Adjustment and Retraining Notification (WARN) Act, 29 U.S.C. § 2101 (1988) (prohibits discharge of employees in connection with plant closings without specified notice and/or severance pay)

This list is not exhaustive. For a complete listing, see Richard Carlson, *Carlson's Federal Labor Law Annotated* (Rochester, NY: West Publishing Co., 2009).

STATE ACTION

Whistle-Blower Laws

Various states have also regulated the employment relationship through so-called **whistle-blower** statutes and applying **public policy** exceptions to the at-will doctrine through the courts.[17] Although the first state whistle-blower statute was not adopted until 1981, a majority of states have since adopted one. These statutes apply to the private sector as well as the public sector (almost all public employees are protected by whistle-blower statutes). The various statutes have some degree of uniformity, but beyond the basics they are widely diverse.[18] The objective of all these statutes is to provide protection for an employee who, in the public interest, discloses a violation of the law by an employer, superior, or co-worker.[19]

These statutes also give protection to the employer in providing penalties for false or unwarranted disclosures. Most statutes include a very broad protection for employees and prohibit retaliatory action against any employee who testifies or provides information to a public body. In some states the statute requires that there must be an objective belief on the part of the whistle-blower that the employer violated the law, whereas in other states the employee must make an attempt to verify the accuracy of the information. There is also a wide variation in the statutes concerning to whom the disclosure must be made. Some laws require disclosure to any local, federal, or state agency, whereas other states permit it to be made internally to the attorney general or other official of that state. Various forms of notice provisions also appear in the statutes. Some of these notice provisions require that the employer be put on notice before the disclosure, but others do not. The remedies for violation of whistle-blower protection also differ across states. Some of these statutes require that the whistle-blowing employee be made whole, whereas others provide for punitive damages. Some statutes even provide for criminal penalties as well as a civil penalty.

The employer's defense against potential violation of whistle-blower statutes is to establish procedures and policies that require the employee to report to the company any belief of company misconduct. This allows opportunity and time for the employer to correct any wrongdoing or to explain to the employee why the company has taken a particular course of action.

The Public Policy Exception

The public policy exception to the employment-at-will doctrine has been adopted by a majority of state courts. This exception declares that the employer should not be permitted to discipline or discharge an employee for reasons that are violative of public policy. *Public policy* is a broad and less than clearly defined term used by the courts as the basis for an exception to an otherwise well-accepted principle of law. Under this exception, the employee's cause of action is based on the harm that society suffers as a result of the employer's conduct. The employee is not alleging that there is an injury to himself or herself, but rather an injury to society.[20]

Some law textbooks define *public policy* as a private dealing that is restricted by law for the good of the community. Another definition is "whatever contravenes good morals or established interests of society." Public policy is decided on a case-by-case basis and often is not defined by the court until after a violation has occurred. For example, the courts have held that a gambling contract, although it complies with all the necessary elements of a contract, cannot be enforced because the contract is not for the benefit or for the convenience of the public. Other exceptions to principles of law are not as widely accepted as the enforcement of gambling contracts. The common-law exception of public policy to employment-at-will is one of them. Where a discharge has been held to be a violation of public policy, the basis for the discharge is also likely to reveal poor employee relations practice. Three distinctly different reasons for discharge have been held to be contrary to public policy. These include exercising a right under a statute; refusing to disobey a law when requested to do so by the employer; and disclosing violations of the law by the employer to authorities, commonly called whistle-blower cases.[21]

Under the public policy exception theory, the employee alleges that a public policy issue exists; that the employer failed to observe the public policy; and that the employee was discharged in retaliation for following the policy. The basis for the public policy violation concept is founded in **tort** law. *Tort law,* as applied to this concept, is based on the premise that each member of

society owes an obligation to every other member to be treated fairly. Public policy is therefore violated when the employee is treated unfairly.

A violation of an explicit provision in a statute is not considered an exception to employment-at-will but simply a violation of the statute. The remedy is normally provided for in the statute. One of the statutory rights that employers sometimes object to is the employee's right to file for and receive workers' compensation benefits. In one case, a local gas company discharged an employee without giving a reason after the employee obtained a settlement on a workers' compensation claim.[22] In this landmark case the court explained the reasoning underlying this and other situations where an employee exercises a right under the statute when it said :

> If employers are permitted to penalize employees for filing workmens compensation claims, a most important public policy will be undermined. The fear of being discharged would have a deleterious effect on the exercise of a statutory right. Employees will not file claims for justly deserved compensation—opting, instead, to continue their employment without incident. The end result, of course, is that the employer is effectively relieved of his obligation.

Termination of employment is often the retaliatory measure chosen by employers in response to employees' filing workers' compensation claims or exercising other rights based on statute. The issue in all of these cases is whether the discharge is actually because the employee filed a claim under statutory law or because he or she violated the employer's rule or policy.

A more serious situation arises when an employee refuses to break the law and is discharged. Most courts consider it as contrary to public policy to force an employee to choose between violating the law and keeping a job.

Making continued employment contingent on the commission of a felony is a tortious violation of public policy and an exception to the at-will doctrine. Other public policy exceptions to common law employment-at-will doctrine include discharge for performing jury duty, reporting to authorities any violation of the law by the employer, reporting a health hazard, and a showing of **malice** or bad faith on the part of the employer.

Some state courts have protected at-will employees when discharged for reason of malice and bad faith.[23] These jurisdictions hold that an employee must be protected from the unrestricted discretion of the employer to be discharged. State courts allow malice and bad faith as cause of action but may not find the violation severe enough for the plaintiff to obtain reinstatement or receive monetary damages. Choosing to seek damages in a state court rather than seeking a remedy under arbitration has been approved by the Supreme court in *Lingle* v. *Norge Div. of Magic Chef, Inc.*, 108 S.Ct. 1877 (1988), where the Court held that union-represented employees can sue the employer in state court over a dismissal, even when the contract provides a grievance procedure and arbitration.[24]

Finally, it should be noted that one state, Montana, has adopted a wrongful discharge statute. This 2001 statute provides that employers must show cause to terminate employees who have completed a probationary period. Although a Model Employment Termination Act (META) was proposed in 1991 as a standard for states to modify employment at-will by requiring "good cause" for termination, no other states have adopted such legislation.[25]

EMPLOYMENT RELATIONSHIP AS A CONTRACT

Contractual relationships are at the heart of English common law and employment contracts, as noted earlier, modify the employment at-will doctrine. However, unlike collective bargaining contracts, individual written employment contracts are relatively rare, although many courts will find an **implied contract** in the employment relationship. Under contract law there must be an offer, an acceptance, and consideration. The courts will hold that the offer of employment is an offer under contract law. The acceptance is coming to work at a certain time. The consideration is the wages paid for services. Since there is usually nothing in writing, the courts are inclined to find that the statute of frauds[26] does not apply because the contract of employment can be performed within one year. The employee can quit or the employer can discharge within one year without exposure.

Where companies have positive human resource policies, the common-law exceptions of public policy, whistle-blowing, and malice and bad faith are academic, but this is not necessarily so with the implied contract exception. Well-intended human resources policy could actually increase exposure to the implied contract exception. For example, aggressive recruiting and promotion that result in promises being made at the time of hiring, handbooks that promote the company as a place of continuous employment, and salaries quoted as annual salaries, which may imply a contract of employment for one year—all are positive programs that could result in the courts finding that an implied contract has been created.[27]

The Implied Contract

The employer and its representatives are most vulnerable where, in the interest of selling the company or promoting good employee relations, a certain promise is made. In determining whether such a promise is an implied contract of continuous employment, the courts look at the surrounding circumstances at the time of hiring to determine whether a promise was in fact made.[28] Where a promise is considered an implied contract, the employee must show some reliance on the promise. One example would be a long-distance move where the employee left a secure job with a competitor and at a later date was discharged without cause or where there was a reliance on a promise of a better opportunity that never materialized. Promises of this kind are not uncommon when an aggressive recruiter is operating in a tight labor market. The reason that the job does not materialize or that the employee is laid off may be legitimate, but the employee is still emotionally and financially harmed. In this situation the courts often allow punitive damages.

One of the more definitive statements from a court that adopted the implied contract approach is found in *Pugh* v. *See's Candies, Inc.*, 116 Cal. App. 3rd 311 (1981), where a vice-president of employee relations with 32 years of service was terminated. When he asked why, he was told, "Look deep within yourself." The jury determined that length of service, a series of promotions and commendations, the lack of direct criticism of his work, and the assurance by his superior that if he did a good job his future would be secure established an implied contract.[29] The company violated that contract by the discharge.

A common practice that can result in an exposure is quoting an annual salary in a job offer. This a good selling point but it can often backfire. An annual salary figure impresses the applicant because it looks much larger than a weekly or a monthly figure. However, after the employee is terminated, the courts consider how the annual salary offer was interpreted by the employee rather than the intent of the person who orginated it. In *Berand* v. *IMI Systems, Inc.*, 8 IER Cases 325 (BNA 1993), the court, in reversing a long-established precedent, said that an employee expects to be employed at will when hired and an annual salary quote does not mean a one-year contract. The few

state courts that have had the issue before them are split on whether a one-year contract is formed by quoting an annual salary. For example, South Dakota has a statute stating that when an annual salary is quoted, it results in a contract for one year [S.D. Codified Laws Sec. 60(1)(3)].[30] The concept that a contract is created by quoting a salary for a fixed period of time is not the law in all jurisdictions and only a few state courts have directly addressed the issue through legislation. The problem in the use of "annual salary" is that it may create exposure to a lawsuit, win or lose.[31] Quoting a monthly salary does not create the same exposure. *Annual salary* is a term that probably should be deleted from the human resource recruiter's vocabulary.

Some jurisdictions have held that employee handbooks or policy manuals may also create an implied contract. The Michigan court, in a leading case involving Blue Cross and Blue Shield, held that guidelines and the supervisor's manual were an expressed contract.[32] The clauses that were especially troublesome were where a supervisor's manual stated that an employee could be discharged only for just cause and "could work until 65 as long as he did his job." In a companion case the employee testified that he was promised at the time of hiring he could work for the company "as long as I did my job." The court said that was a contract that changed the at-will doctrine, although it was an oral promise.[33]

In a New York case an employee handbook stated that an employee would be discharged only for just cause. When hired, the employee signed the application form, which stated that employment would be subject to the *Handbook on Personnel Policy*. Eight years later he was discharged. The court held that the handbook was a contract and that the employer had to demonstrate just cause to terminate. However, in reaching this conclusion the court held that this was an expressed contract.[34]

A Minnesota case where a handbook was deemed an implied contract involved a loan officer in a bank who was in default on his personal loan and had approved 56 out of 57 loans in violation of the loan policy. Nonetheless, his subsequent discharge was held to be a breach of contract because the employer failed to follow the discharge procedure outlined in the handbook, even though it had a legitimate reason to terminate the loan officer.[35]

The two Michigan cases and the Minnesota case cited here were subsequently accepted by several other jurisdictions, which many employers interpreted as a warning. Some became "gun-shy" and discarded their handbooks. By 1985, the vast majority of states held that a handbook could be deemed a contract under certain circumstances, although some industrial states such as New York, Illinois, and Indiana still required a written contract before the at-will status could be changed.[36] Practitioners should also be aware of another common practice: flexible application of human resource policies to certain individuals, which the courts may well construe as disparate treatment and a breach of contract.

PUBLIC AND PRIVATE SECTORS

Whatever slight regulation of the employment relationship existed in the private sector prior to the twentieth century, was absent in the public sector. Although the employment-at-will doctrine was technically applicable to both public and private employment, the vast majority of public employment was based on political **patronage** and an understanding that the government employer was unchallengeable in personnel matters and immune from lawsuit under the Doctrine of Sovereignty. The Pendleton Civil Service Act, enacted in 1883, although generally viewed as a reform designed to curb perceived public employment abuses, was designed as much to wrest patronage from the hands of local politicians

as it was to establish a merit selection and retention system. The original Civil Service Commission created by the Act was given jurisdiction only over public employment in Washington DC, the federal customshouses, and post offices in larger cities.[37] The coverage of the Pendleton Act was expanded by subsequent administrations, but this expansion was primarily intended to protect incumbent patronage jobholders appointed by new administrations. Perhaps for the same reason many states and municipalities adopted merit appointment and retention systems of their own.

Political patronage continued to dominate government employment throughout the early part of the twentieth century. This was of little significance to anyone other than public employees, since total employment at all levels of government reached only 3 million by 1934. However, government employment nearly doubled by 1944, spurred by both New Deal public service employment opportunities and the demands of World War II. Public employment continued to grow after the war as municipalities and school districts expanded their size, tax base, and employment levels. The growth in public employment led career employees to seek greater control over their tenure, wages, and working conditions through collective bargaining.

Wisconsin established the first state public-sector collective bargaining statute in 1958, and federal employees obtained limited rights to bargain in 1962 when President Kennedy issued **Executive Order** 10988.[38] These rights were expanded by Presidents Nixon and Ford in subsequent executive orders. The Nixon and Ford executive orders provided comparable organizational and recognition rights to those rights enjoyed by private-sector employees under the National Labor Relations Act.[39] The major difference was that federal employees, unlike their private-sector counterparts, were not permitted to bargain over wages or to strike. In 1972, the Postal Reorganization Act created the United States Postal Service to replace the Federal Department of the Post Office and placed postal employees under the jurisdiction of the National Labor Relations Act, limiting only the right of those employees to strike.[40]

Following the passage of the Wisconsin statute, many eastern, midwestern, and West Coast states adopted public employee labor relations legislation in the 1960s and 70s. Currently, most states have created some type of legislation permitting state and municipal employees to organize and bargain. This state legislation varies substantially, granting public employees in some jurisdictions rights comparable to those provided by the National Labor Relations Act, whereas employees in other jurisdictions enjoy only limited rights. For federal employees, the Executive Orders (previously mentioned) were supplanted by the Federal Service Labor-Management Relations statute, a part of the Civil Service Reform Act of 1979. The statute continued the prohibition of strikes and bargaining over economic issues.[41]

Protections for Public Employees

The courts have also had a role in differentiating the employment environment for public employees. Most significantly, they have held that a public employee, unlike a private employee, has a property right in his or her job. Since a public employee's job is necessary to maintain self and family, it was argued that she or he should receive the protection of the government. The Supreme Court took this position in *Perry* v. *Sindermann* when a school board failed to renew a teacher's contract and did not provide an official statement as to the reason for his termination or allow an opportunity for a hearing. The teacher alleged that this denied him due process as required by the Fourth Amendment. The Supreme Court held that job security, whether it was expressed or implied, was a property right that could not

be abridged without a procedural due process.[42] A similar argument has also been raised by legal theorists who argue that even in the private sector, state and federal government should intervene in the employment relationship because private employees are also entitled to receive constitutional protection.[43]

The courts have also protected the rights of public employees in investigatory interviews when potential criminal charges are involved. In 1967, the United States Supreme Court ruled that public employees could not be forced to choose between losing their job and giving up their Fifth Amendment rights—the "right to remain silent."[44] Ordinarily, if questioned about committing a crime, any individual is given a *Miranda* warning; the person has the right to remain silent, but anything that is volunteered can be used against that person in a court of law. The right to remain silent when questioned by a government authority and not self-incriminate is guaranteed under the Fifth Amendment of the U.S. Constitution. Accordingly, public employees face a dilemma. On the one hand, they have the right to remain silent under the Constitution; on the other, since the employer is the government, a refusal to answer a public employer's question could constitute insubordination and grounds for termination. The Supreme Court resolved this dilemma by creating what has become known as a *Garrity warning*. This warning informs the employee that he or she will be questioned as part of an official investigation. It guarantees the employee that anything he or she says *cannot* be used later in a court of law to prosecute the employee. Once a Garrity warning is issued, the employee *must* answer the employer questions or face disciplinary action. These answers can be used in disciplinary proceedings but not in criminal proceedings.

The existence of a property right to a public job has also afforded public employees expanded due process rights. Under a 1985 court decision, every public employee is entitled to a hearing prior to termination. This right was established in a case filed by James Loudermill, a Cleveland school district security guard who was not permitted to respond to or challenge his dismissal for alleged dishonesty in completing his job application. The court ruled that "an essential principle of due process is that a deprivation of life, liberty, or property [job] be preceded by notice and an opportunity for hearing appropriate to the nature of the case." Public employees now have a right to respond to the employer's allegations of misconduct through a so-called *Loudermill hearing* before they can be terminated.[45]

GUIDELINES FOR HUMAN RESOURCES PRACTITIONERS

As government mandates and court decisions have intruded on the employment relationship, it would appear that society has accepted, indeed embraced, the external regulation of workplace standards and conditions. The human resource (HR) practitioner may be aware of the legal consequences of an employment decision, but often other members of management are not. In fact, management may well be hostile to the changes necessary to comply with government regulations. Hostile management often considers these regulations to be an interference with its employment decisions. It is therefore the duty of the HR practitioner to make other managers aware of the legal consequences of regulations and applicable laws, and obtain legal counsel when necessary. As the human resource function of management attempts to solve legal problems, solutions must be weighed in light of employee relations consequences.

Exposure to Lawsuits

Throughout this book the text will often refer to *exposure* to a lawsuit. Nothing can stop an employee from seeking a lawyer to represent him or her in a lawsuit. If the facts of the case indicate that the employee has some likelihood of prevailing, the lawyer may take the case on a contingency basis. If the facts show it will be a difficult case to win, the lawyer either may refuse to take the case or will demand an up-front fee before taking it. *Exposure,* as used in this book, means that the employer's actions have developed facts that give the employee a good chance of prevailing in court. When appropriate policies and procedures of the employer are in place, there is reduced exposure and little chance of the employee prevailing. This may cause the lawyer to demand a fee that may, in turn, result in averting the lawsuit, since the employee may not take the risk of losing and paying a fee. This is common in discharge cases where the employee's income has stopped. It should be remembered, however, that the only person who wins a lawsuit is the person who avoids it.

The employer must prevent exposure to lawsuits by putting policies and practices in place so that the employee is discouraged from initiating a lawsuit. Once the lawsuit is started, it is too late to reconsider, because time and legal fees must be expended in defense of the employer. The HR practitioner must, therefore, find a way to communicate to operating management that the employer may not have a full range of choices at its disposal when dealing with employees.

The use of such terms as *probationary period, permanent employee, merit increases, white collar, gold collar,* or *annual salary* in a job offer, and *personality problems* on a termination form may well create exposure to a lawsuit. The use of these terms should be avoided. Human resources administrators are faced with an increasing number of seemingly conflicting legal and employee relations issues. Therefore, they must have enough knowledge of the law to be aware of the legal implications and when to seek legal counsel. A vital part of human resource administration involves advising management personnel of the consequences of failure to apply the law as interpreted by a regulatory agency. As new laws are enacted and government agencies created to enforce them, challengeable gray areas are also created.

STRUCTURE OF THE COURTS

It is important for the reader to have a basic understanding of the court structure in the United States as well as a knowledge of legal citations and references. Not only will this assist in understanding the references in this text but it will also aid the practitioner in dealing with legal documents and legal counsel. Human resources professionals will frequently be required to respond to legal documents and inquiries from attorneys. Some of these documents and inquiries may be routine, but if the practitioner is uncertain concerning the appropriate response, at attorney should be consulted.

Some HR professionals may have the luxury of an in-house attorney available for consultation; others may be required to involve a superior before the decision to contact outside counsel is made. Whatever the case, there is no substitute for competent legal advice when a legal question arises.

The court structure for both state and federal governments is as follows:

Federal	State
District Court	District Court
Appeals Court	Appeals Court
Supreme Court	Supreme Court

The Supreme Court in both federal and state structure is the last court of appeal.

Some statutes allow an administrative ruling to be appealed. If so, most of them provide for the district court to hear the matter first, with appropriate appeals to the appellate court. Some statutes allow the appellate court or Supreme Court to hear the dispute initially, thereby omitting the lower courts.[46] The federal courts of the United States are structured at three levels: district court, appellate courts, and Supreme Court. The *district court* is where the case normally begins. All the evidence is recorded and witnesses testify. In certain cases the jury will participate, but in other cases the judge makes the decision. The federal district court decisions are cited in this text as West's Federal Supplement Reports. (Sometimes they are cited as, for example, 1995 D.C. Mont. Lexis 560.) An example of citation would be 560 F. Supp. 820 (D.C. Mont. 1995). In this example, 560 is the volume number, F. Supp. is Federal Supplement Reports, and 820 is the page number. D.C. Mont. is the district court of Montana (where the case was decided), and 1995 is the year of the decision.

Although district court decisions are important, they are not considered precedent setting. If not appealed, they apply only to the area where the court has jurisdiction. The employer must decide, after consulting an attorney, whether the district court decision necessitates changing a policy. Within a certain time after a decision is rendered (usually 30 days), either party may appeal the decision to the next higher court. This court must consider the appeal. The *appellate court* considers whether the decision of the lower court was proper as to the law and the facts presented. The appellate court will usually not hear new evidence. These cases are cited in this text as_F.2d_(5th Cir. 2010). The F.2d stands for West's Publishing Federal Reporter 2d series, the 5th circuit is where the case was decided, and the year of the decision was 2010. Lexis is another reporting system, similar to West, so it would cite as 2010 US App. L.___. There are 11 circuit courts of appeal in the United States, and nine federal courts that are divided into geographic areas. The D.C. (district court) circuit is the 12th appellate court and has jurisdiction over the entire country.

Most lawyers respect circuit court opinions because few are appealed to the U.S. Supreme Court, the highest court in the system, which hears a little over 1 percent of the appeals filed.

Supreme Court

The Supreme Court doesn't have to grant review of the appellate court decision. Appeal for such a review is called a *writ of certiorari*. If the Supreme Court refuses to review, the decision of the appellate court becomes the law in the circuit where it was decided. The Supreme Court will not hear any new evidence but will make its decision based on the oral arguments, case law, statutes, and legal reasoning of the lower courts. Both the appellate court and the Supreme Court review whether the rules of procedure were followed in the district court.

All federal judges are appointed for life by the President of the United States with the consent of the Senate. Presidents tend to appoint judges of their own political philosophy, so one president in office may appoint most of the judges in a certain court and another president of a different philosophy may appoint those in a higher court. Often the philosophy influences the interpretation of the law. As a result upper courts will often reverse lower courts.

Most state courts have basically the same structure as the federal court, only they interpret the state laws. The court where the case starts is the state district court, then there is the appellate court and the state Supreme Court. As in the federal system, the appellate court must consider the appeals from the district court, but the Supreme Court can decide what cases it will hear.

Explanation of Legal Documents

The human resources professional should become familiar with basic legal terms. Often servicing of court proceedings against the company is made to the persons in the HR office when the matter involves employees. Most legal documents have a time limit in which they have to be acted on; it is highly important that the documents are expedited promptly. Failure to act within the time limits can result in liability by default or other serious legal consequences. In all legal documents the time limits are clearly stated. The court serving the papers and the attorneys involved are clearly stated on the documents.

INTERROGATORY Interrogatories are a set or series of written questions served on one party in a proceeding. The purpose is a factual examination of a prospective witness. They are used mostly in pretrial *discovery* to obtain information, to aid the attorney in preparing the case, and to help in selecting witnesses. The personnel practitioner will sometimes receive the interrogatories from an opposing attorney to obtain information about employees. An attorney should always review the information before it is released. Answers to interrogatory questions are not done under oath but are often used as a basis for questions that are answered under oath. Answers can also determine how the attorney will try the case.

The request for interrogatories comes directly from the attorney requesting them; they do not need court approval unless objected to by the opposing party. Exhibit 1.1 is an interrogatory served on a company where the personnel department would supply the answers. In the interest of brevity, only enough questions are included to show a typical interrogatory.

DEPOSITION The *deposition* is a pretrial discovery procedure whereby the testimony of a witness is taken outside of open court, pursuant to permission by the court to take testimony from a witness. Most questions during depositions are based on, but not restricted to, the interrogatories. A deposition differs from interrogatories in that it is taken under oath and is used under certain

| STATE OF _____ | DISTRICT COURT |
| COUNTY OF _____ | SECOND JUDICIAL DISTRICT |

LEO SMITH,

      Plaintiff,

    v.   <u>INTERROGATORIES</u>

ABC COMPANY

      Defendant.

TO: DEFENDANT ABC COMPANY AND ITS ATTORNEY JOHN ROE, (ATTORNEY'S ADDRESS)

    PLEASE TAKE NOTICE that Plaintiff, Leo Smith, requests, pursuant to Rule 33 of the Rules of Civil Procedure, that the Defendant ABC Company answer the following Interrogatories within the time prescribed by law. These Interrogatories shall be deemed continuing in nature and should the answers require modification or supplementation it is demanded that you so advise Plaintiff and his attorney.

DEFINITIONS

    Unless conclusively altered by the context of a specific Interrogatory, the following definitions are to be considered to apply to all the Interrogatories contained herein.

  A. <u>You</u> and <u>Your</u> means ABC Company, Present and former directors, officers, employees, attorneys, agents, representatives, and any and all other persons, firms, corporations, or entities acting or purporting to act on behalf of ABC Company.

  B. <u>Identify</u> or <u>Identification</u>

      1. When used in reference to a <u>person</u>, means her or his:

        a. Full name

        b. Present or last known residence address

        c. Position and job description at the time in question

INTERROGATORIES

1. Describe the nature of the supervision of your premises employed to maintain control over employees on the job, in the cafeterias, and in any other areas of the premises to which the employees have access.
2. Had you received any complaints in 2010 by nonunion workers that they were being harassed by union workers?
3. If the answer to interrogatory No. 2 is yes, identify all persons who made such complaints.
4. Did any security unit, the foreman, or any other of your employees investigate such complaints?

                         LAW OFFICES OF RICHARD ANDERSON

                         By _____

                         Richard Anderson

                         (Address)

Dated _____   (Telephone)

EXHIBIT 1.1

conditions in court proceedings for questioning the witness.

When a deposition is taken, it is contemplated that the person will be a witness in the trial, but this is not always the case. When an employee is requested to give a deposition, often there is a sense of insecurity; although the other attorneys may be present, the employee should request the legal counsel from the company to be present. This is a policy matter for management and legal counsel to determine. Some companies consider it good employee relations to give security to an employee when giving a deposition; others feel that the presence of one attorney representing the employee's interest is sufficient.

SUBPOENA   The *subpoena* is an order directed to a certain person to appear and at a certain time and give testimony on a certain matter.[47] The most common subpoena in the personnel department is to appear and bring all documents and written materials related to the subject matter of the case. This is called a *subpoena duces tecum*. Often the records are all that the attorney wants. Production of the records satisfies the subpoena. It is not necessary for the person in charge of the records to testify. However, permission from the attorney signing the subpoena not to appear is required. When receiving a subpoena *duces tecum*, the attorney requesting the documents should always be asked whether only the records are wanted or whether the person subpoenaed has to testify. A lot of time will be saved if only the documents must be produced. Also, it is not advisable for the HR practitioner to appear in the courtroom and be called as a witness. He or she will be subject to cross-examination. Any personnel document marked confidential, as between company counsel and the employee, need not be produced.

Exhibit 1.2 is a typical subpoena *duces tecum*, often received in workers compensation

and divorce suits. Subpoena *duces tecum* is also used in criminal proceedings.

SUMMONS   A *summons* is an order served on the defendant to appear in court, to give an answer within a specified time. The nature of the lawsuit is stated in the complaint. It is important to note the time and date when the summons is received, as the answer must be within a specified time (usually 20 or 30 days).

COMPLAINT   A *complaint* in a civil proceeding is the first or initial pleading by the plaintiff. The complaint is usually served with the summons. Under the rules of civil procedure, it must contain certain information about the case, such as the alleged wrong, the names of the parties, the county and name of the court where the action is brought, and the relief sought by the plaintiff. The HR department should not respond to a complaint but refer it to legal counsel.

Increase in Litigation

The entry of the law into the management function is not a phenomenon exclusive to human resources, but it is indicative of the growth of law in all business and social activities. Beginning in the early 1970s there was a growing concern for people to be protected legally from every problem, even from their own gullibility. Accordingly, litigation has grown so rapidly that it is difficult to know the total number of pending cases on the dockets of the courts. Indeed, the stigma associated with a lawsuit has almost disappeared. Doctors are sued by patients, lawyers by clients, parents by their children; brothers sue brothers and sellers sue customers. Social legislation such as antidiscrimination laws, the Occupational Safety and health Act, the Civil Rights Act of 1991, the Employee Retirement Insurance Act, the Immigration Reform and Control Act, Consolidated Omnibus Budget

State of Minnesota,

County of ___Smithson___

DISTRICT COURT

___1st___ _Judicial District_

John Doe

Plaintiff

SUBPOENA
DUCES TECUM

_vs._

Homer Smith

Defendant

THE STATE OF MINNESOTA TO ___ABC Corp., Milltown, Minnesota___:

You are hereby commanded to appear in the above named court at the Court House, in the County ___of___ ___Smithson___, on the ___22nd___ day of ___August___, 19 ___92___, at ___9:00___ o'clock ___fore___ noon, then and there to testify on behalf of ___John Doe___ in above entitled proceeding.

You are further directed and commanded to bring with you the following papers and documents now in your possession or under your control, viz.:

   All Personnel Records, including wages paid during the last two years,

   days absent during said period, all medical records and work performance

   records and appraisals.

WITNESS, The Honorable ___RONALD E. HACH___ Judge of said Court, and the seal thereof this ___2nd___ day of ___July___, 19 ___92___.

___HAZEL G. ART___

Clerk

By ___Wallu Meadow___

Deputy

State of Minnesota,

County of ___Smithson___

I hereby certify and return that I served the within Subpoena on the within named ___Personnel Director___ by reading the same to him and delivering to him a true copy thereof, at ___ABC Corp., 415 Jones St., Milltown, Minnesota___ in said County and State, on this ___15___ day of ___Aug.___, 19 ___92___.

SHERIFF'S FEES:

Service, ___15.00___

Mileage, $ ___12.00___

___Arnold Anderson___

Sheriff of said County

By ___M. Johnson___

(All names and places are fictitious)

EXHIBIT 1.2

Reconciliation Act, Family and Medical Leave Act, and Americans with Disabilities Act have given added legal opportunities to individuals never before experienced in judicial history. The alphabet-soup of government regulatory agencies creates a thriving climate for those who would redress their grievances in a court of law.

When to Use Legal Counsel

When legal documents are received that require an answer, they should be referred to legal counsel. Sometimes these documents can be interpreted as admitting liability, which should never be admitted without advice of counsel. Once liability is admitted or implied, there is nothing left to mitigate. The company is at the mercy of the court or regulatory agency.

Written agreements that can be interpreted as enforceable contracts should be either drafted or reviewed by an attorney. If a layperson drafts a contract, it is more likely to be challenged. In the event of latent liability, the drafter is protected if the contract is reviewed by an attorney. No document should be signed without understanding the terms or having it explained by counsel. When the employer is involved, there should be some control on who has authority to sign, because any member of management can bind the corporation if there is reason to believe that the person signing has authority to do so. The erosion of the at-will doctrine has caused many astute employers to have legal counsel review all discharges. The lawyer will determine whether there is a possible exposure to a lawsuit. This is a good procedure when there is any doubt. Voluntary "quits" in some situations can be constructive discharge, and if that possibility exists, it should be reviewed by counsel. [48]

CASE 1.1

The Discharged Executive

Dan was a self-employed 62-year-old financial advisor with a long history of administrative and leadership experience. Due to health issues, he had left his prior employment and was working part time. At various times during his career Dan had served as the controller of a small company, a local elected official, a city manager, and the owner and CEO of a consulting company. When the small suburban city in which he resided approached him about becoming the city finance director, he saw a good opportunity to acquire employer subsidized health insurance, enhance his pension plan, and earn a comfortable salary until full retirement. He planned to work for the city four or five years and fully retire by age 68.

Prior to assuming the finance director's job, Dan advised his supervisor, the city ,manager, about his health problems, which would require him to work from home frequently and possibly take extended leave. The city manager had no objection to this and assured Dan that he was being employed in an executive position and would not be subject to regular attendance at the city's office so long as he completed his work.

During his second year of employment with the city Dan experienced heart problems that caused him to be hospitalized followed by an extended period of recuperation at home. Although his health improved somewhat, he had difficulty walking and continued to work extensively at home. His prolonged absence from the office was noticed by city officials, and the manager became increasingly uncomfortable about the fact that Dan was rarely in the office, even though his work was always up to date. After several unproductive conversations with Dan about his work schedule and continued absence from the office, the city manager told Dan he would have to return to work in the office on a regular basis. When Dan failed to comply, he was terminated.

What exposure to legal action does the city have? Assuming that Dan was an employee-at-will, does he have grounds for a wrongful discharge suit? Does the city have exposure to an age discrimination complaint? ▨

CASE 1.2

The Injured Driver

Ken was a truck driver for a regional freight carrier. He was paid $12 an hour and typically worked a 40-hour week, although when work was light he was sent home early and his hours and pay were accordingly reduced. One day he injured his back while unloading his truck at a delivery point. When he returned to the terminal, he notified the employer of his injury. Because Ken lived in a state adjacent to the employer's terminal, he had been omitted (the employer claimed unintentionally) from the list of drivers that the employer had submitted and paid on for workers' compensation insurance. Since the employer was unsure if Ken was covered, he told Ken not to file a workers' compensation claim but to go to the employer's doctor for treatment. Ken did as he was told, was treated by the employer's doctor who sent the bill to the employer, and felt that his back was much better after a week of treatment and rest.

Ken returned to work the following week but was told that business was slow and that he wasn't needed. The employer promised to schedule Ken for work as soon as work picked up and his back injury was fully healed. Ken waited for two weeks, checking regularly with the employer to see if he was scheduled, but the employer continued to put him off. At this point Ken filed a workers' compensation claim only to discover that the employer had no workers' compensation coverage in the state where Ken resided. When the employer continued to refuse to schedule him for work, Ken went to an attorney who filed a wrongful discharge suit against the employer on Ken's behalf.

What is the likelihood that Ken will prevail? What arguments is he likely to present in court? ■

CASE 1.3

The Disgruntled Secretary

Sharon was a secretary for a small company. She wanted to return to college and complete the requirements for a degree but was unable to do so because of her work schedule. She mentioned this to her roommate Marcia who suggested that she apply for an open secretarial position at the candy company where Marcia worked. Marcia showed Sharon the candy company's handbook that listed their employment benefits. Although the hourly wages at the two companies were comparable, Sharon was very interested in the flex-time arrangement described in the handbook. It allowed clerical employees to work any 8-hour period between 6:00 a.m. and 6:00 p.m. The handbook also included a provision that employees would be terminated only for cause.

Sharon applied for the open position at the candy company and was hired. However, her new supervisor wanted Sharon to work the same hours that she did and refused to allow Sharon to leave before 4:30 p.m. to attend classes. When Sharon complained, the supervisor told her that she would have to wait until she was more familiar with her work before she could utilize the flex-time provision. Several months later Sharon again complained about her inflexible work schedule. She was instructed to "stop complaining and do as you are told." When she went over the supervisor's head and complained to the HR department, her supervisor terminated her for being "uncooperative and insubordinate."

On what basis might Sharon contest her discharge? What is an implied contract? What might the employer have done to reduce its exposure in this case? ■

Summary

Chapter 1 introduces the concept of employment regulation together with the factors that influenced its growth in the United States, and traces the development of federal and state legislation and regulations from the late nineteenth through twentieth centuries.

It also discusses the impact of the common-law doctrine of employment-at-will and describes the erosion of that doctrine through legislation and court decisions. The chapter goes on to explain the impact of contract law on court decisions concerning the employment relationship and to examine the notion of implied contracts.

Chapter 1 continues with an explanation of the differences in the way the courts view public- versus private-sector employees, suggests some guidelines for human resources practitioners, and concludes with an explanation of the federal and state court structure in the United States.

Key Terms

property right *1*
Progressive Movement *2*
employment-at-will *2*
due process *3*
wrongful discharge *3*
exposure *3*
just cause *4*
concerted activity *4*

whistle-blower *5*
public policy *5*
tort *6*
malice *7*
implied contract *7*
patronage *9*
executive order *9*
Garrity warning *10*

Loudermill hearing *11*
writ of *certiorari 13*
interrogatories *13*
discovery *13*
deposition *13*
subpoena *15*
summons *15*
complaint *15*

Questions for Discussion

1. Explain how the industrialization and urbanization of the United States in the late nineteenth century changed the nature of employment.
2. Identify three (3) reforms initiated during the Progressive Era.
3. Define employment-at-will in your own words. Why did this doctrine become viewed as harsh, immoral, or unfair, from an employee's perspective?
4. Why are employers likely to resist or attempt to avoid requirements to demonstrate "just cause" before terminating an employee?
5. How does a "Whistle-Blower Law" serve to effectuate good public policy?
6. What is a retaliatory discharge?
7. Only one state, Montana, has adopted a so-called wrongful discharge statute. What is the intent of such a statute and why do you think no other states or the federal government have passed wrongful discharge legislation?

8. Why are collective contracts of employment (collective bargaining agreements) relatively common, yet individual employment contracts are rare?
9. Give an example of a situation in which a court is likely to find the existence of an implied contract of employment.
10. What were the main purposes of the Pendleton Act?
11. Why were public employees excluded from coverage under the National Labor Relations Act in 1935?
12. Why are public employees considered to have property rights in employment whereas private-sector employees are not considered to have such rights?
13. What is the purpose of an interrogatory?
14. Where is a lawsuit alleging wrongful discharge most likely to be filed?
15. As a human resources representative, what may you be required to do if you are served with a *subpoena duces tecum*?

Notes to Chapter 1

1. The master servant doctrine is the basis for the more contemporary law of agency.
2. Henry W. Ruoff, ed., *The Century Book of Facts* (Springfield, MA: King-Richardson Co., 1908).
3. E. E. Cummins, *The Labor Problem in the United States* (New York: Van Nostrand, 1932). For a more recent discussion, see John W. Budd, *Labor Relations: Striking a Balance,* 3rd ed. (New York: McGraw-Hill, 2010), pp. 37–41, and Bruce E. Kaufman, *The Origins & Evolution of the Field of Industrial Relations in the United States* (Ithaca, NY: ILR Press, 1993), pp. 4–8.
4. Thomas N. Bonner, *Our Recent Past* (Englewood Cliffs, NJ: Prentice-Hall, 1963), p. 52.
5. 45 U.S.C. § 1456.
6. 62 ALR 3rd 271 (1975, 1992 suppl).
7. *Comerford* v. *International Harvester Co.,* 178 So.2d 894 (Ala. 1932). See also *Tomkins* v. *Public Service Electric & Gas Co.,* 568 F.2d 1044 (3rd Cir. 1977), where there was a discharge over refusal to have sexual relations with the supervisor.
8. *Payne* v. *Western and Atlantic R.R. Co.,* 81 Tenn. 507 (1884).
9. *Lewis* v. *Minnesota Mutual Life Insurance Co.,* 37 N.W. 2d 316 (Iowa 1949)
10. 29 USC § 158 et seq.
11. 42 USC § 2000 et seq.
12. *Savodnik* v. *Korvettes, Inc.,* 488 F. Supp. 822 (E.D. N.Y. 1980), p. 824.
13. *Adzick* v. *AGS Computers,* 554 N.Y.S.2d 182 (1990).
14. *Texas & New Orleans Railroad Company* v. *Brotherhood of Railway and Steamship Clerks,* 281 U.S. 548 (1930).
15. 29 U.S.C. § 158(a)(1),(3),(4) (1975).
16. 29 U.S.C. § 215(a)(3), 216(b) (1975 and Supp. 1982).
17. S. C. Gertz, "At-Will Employment: Origins, Applications, Exceptions and Expansions in the Public Service," *International Journal of Public Administration,* 31(2008): 489–514.
18. For a more complete review of whistle-blower statutes, see R. Boyle, "Review of Whistle-Blower Protections and Suggestions for a Change," *Labor Law Journal,* 41:12 (December 1990): 821.
19. See Section 181.93 Minnesota Statutes as amended.
20. See James A. Bryant and Michael Giallourakis, "Employment at Will: Where Is It Going and What Can Be Done?" *SAM Advanced Management Journal* (Autumn 1984): 12–21.
21. *Smith* v. *Calgon Carbon Corp.,* 917 F.2d 1338 (1990); *Adzick* v. *AGS Computers,* 554 N.Y.S.2d 182 (1990).
22. *Frampton* v. *Central Indiana Gas Co.,* 297 N.E.2d 425 (Ind. 1973).
23. Alaska, Arizona, California, Connecticut, Massachusetts, Minnesota, and Montana are a few states where this has occurred.
24. If the labor agreement did not provide for arbitration, the union could still sue under Section 301 of NLRA to enforce the agreement. It is not necessary to strike to enforce a labor agreement: *Groves* v. *Ring Screw Workers, Ferndale Fastener Div.,* 111 S.Ct. 498 (1990).
25. Uniform Law Commission. "Model Employment Termination Act," in *Uniform Law Commissioners* [Summary] Retrieved 4/2009 from www.nccusl.uniformact_summaries/uniformacts-s-meta.asp
26. The Statute of Frauds is a state law; however, all states have passed a statute of frauds in some form. These laws are patterned after the English statute (29 Car. II, c.3) dating back to 1677. They provide that no suit or action shall be maintained on certain classes of contracts or engagements unless there is a note or memorandum in writing signed by the party to be charged, or, by an authorized person. If the contract can be performed within one year the statute doesn't apply. Some states put this in the statute, while others leave it to court interpretation, but the result is the same: Employment relationships do not come under the statute.
27. M. R. Wallace, "Employee Manuals as Implied Contracts: The Guidelines That Bind" (comment), *Tulsa Law Journal,* 27 (1991): 263.

28. *Rognlien* v. *Carter,* 443 N.W.2d 217 (Minn. App. 1989). In a recent case an employer refused to hire a prospective employee after implying a contract offer. The prospective employee sued under a negligent misrepresentation theory. *Williams* v. *Board of Regents of the University of Minnesota* No. A08-0765 (Minn. 2009).

29. F. Vickory, "The Erosion of the Employment-at-Will Doctrine and the Statute of Frauds: Time to Amend the Statute," *American Business Law Journal,* 30 (May 1992): 97–122; see also Axel R. Granholm, *Handbook of Employee Termination* (New York: John Wiley & Sons, 1991), p. 19.

30. In *Goodwyn* v. *Sencore, Inc.,* 389 F.Supp. 824 (D.S.D. 1975), the court held that an annual salary formed a one-year contract. This was before the statute was adopted.

31. In *Tipton* v. *Canadian Imperial Bank of Commerce,* 872 F.2d 149 (11th Cir. 1989), the court rejected the concept. Some courts will reject but hold that annual salary is an inducement to accept the job.

32. *Toussaint* v. *Blue Cross and Blue Shield of Michigan,* 292 N.W.2d 880 (Mich. 1980); also *Bullock* v. *Auto Club of Michigan,* 444 N.W.2d 114 (Mich. S.Ct. 1989). Michigan is an employee-at-will state.

33. *Ebling* v. *Masco Corp.,* 292 N.W.2d 801 (Mich. 1980).

34. *Weiner* v. *McGraw-Hill,* 443 N.E.2d 441 (N.Y. 1982). However, in *LeNeave* v. *North American Life Assurance Co.,* 854 F.2d 317 (8th Cir. 1988), the court held that the same language did not always imply a contract.

35. *Pine River State Bank* v. *Richard F. Mettille Sr.,* 333 N.W.2d 622 (Minn. 1983).

36. *Enis* v. *Continental Ill. Nat. Bank & Trust,* 582 F.Supp. 876 (N.D. Ill. E.D. 1984); *Mead Johnson and Co.* v. *Openheimer,* 458 N.E.2d 668 (Ind. App. 1 Dist. 1984). See *Fleming* v. *Kids and Kin Head Start,* 693 . P.2d 1363 (Ore. App. 1965) for the majority rule. For purposes of this discussion, a policy manual is the equivalent of a handbook.

37. Ray Ginger, *The Age of Excess* (New York: Macmillan, 1965), p. 104.

38. E.O. 10988.

39. E.O. 11491; E.O. 11616; E.O. 11838.

40. 39 U.S.C. § 1207-1209.

41. 5 U.S.C. § 7101-7135.

42. *Perry* v. *Sinderman,* 408 U.S. 593 (1972). See also *Franklin* v. *Marshall College,* 775 F.2d 110 (3rd Cir. 1985), cert. den. 1986; see also *University of Pennsylvania* v. *EEOC,* 850 F.2d 969 (3rd Cir. 1988), aff'd 110 S.Ct. 577 (1990). Private-sector employees do not have this protection.

43. See C. Peck, "Unjust Discharges from Employment: A Necessary Change in the Law," *Ohio State Law Journal,* 40, no. 1 (1979): 25–35; "The Employment-at-Will Doctrine: Time to Collapse Another Citadel," *University of Dayton Law Review,* 2, no. 2 (1985), p. 399; For state-by-state comparisons, see C. J. Muhl, "The Employment at Will Doctrine: Three Major Exceptions" *Monthly Labor Review,* 3, no. 11 (January 2001).

44. *Garrity* v. *New Jersey* 385 U.S. 493 (1967)

45. *Cleveland Board of Education* v. *Loudermill* 470 U.S. 532 (1985)

46. See *Wicken* v. *Morris,* 523 N.W.2d 415 (Minn. 1995). See also *Malley* v. *Ulland Bros.,* 529 N.W.2d 735 (Minn. Ct. Appl. 1995) MSA 26 et seq. as amended in 1995.

47. *Black's Law Dictionary,* 6th ed. (St. Paul, MN: West, 1990), p. 1026.

48. This doctrine is explained in Chapter 10.

CHAPTER 2

Discriminatory Conduct

CHAPTER OUTLINE

Recent Developments

The Civil Rights Act of 1866 and Its
    Amendments

Title VII and the Civil Rights Act of 1991

Harassment in the Workplace

Age Discrimination in Employment Act

Avoiding Litigation

Chapter 1 described how the law impinged on the human resources function and drastically changed human resources management. Traditional practices of adopting attitudes, beliefs, and ideas about political or ethnic background in employment decisions became restricted by antidiscrimination laws. Many formerly accepted practices and policies are simply no longer advisable. A primary reason for this change has been the impact of antidiscrimination legislation.[1] This legislation prohibits policies and practices that result in **disparate treatment** of or **disparate impact** on any protected class of applicants or employees.

State and federal statutes affect all phases of the employment process, from initial advertising of a job vacancy through hiring, promotion, discipline, discharge, and retirement of the employee. **Title VII** of the Civil Rights Act was the first major antidiscrimination legislation that drastically affected employment decisions. If the employment decisions resulted in a person being treated differently because of race, color, religion, gender, or national origin, Title VII would require the employer to restore the employee to his or her original status, including reimbursement for any monetary losses. Although Title VII had the greatest impact on the employment relationship, it was not the first antidiscrimination statute passed by Congress. In 1866, Congress passed a civil rights act that prohibited discrimination because of race. In 1870 and 1871, the act was amended to plug the loopholes in the 1866 statute. This statute was not applied to the employment relationship until 1971, but it is now used in discrimination cases as much as Title VII.

This chapter will discuss the application to the employment relationship of Title VII, the 1866 statute (42 U.S.C § 1981–83), and the **Civil Rights Act of 1991 (CRA91)**. The CRA91 amended Title VII, the 1866 statute, the Age Discrimination in Employment Act (ADEA), and the **Americans with Disabilities Act (ADA)** and voided several state statutes. The ADA, as amended, will be given consideration in subsequent chapters. The concept of equal pay for equal work as embodied in the Equal Pay Act of 1963 is discussed in Chapter 5. The effect of CRA91 on state statutes will be referred to when applicable.

RECENT DEVELOPMENTS

Since 1992, two modifications to Civil Rights legislation have been made by Congress. In 2008, President George W. Bush signed the **Genetic Information Nondiscrimination Act (GINA)** designed to protect Americans from discrimination based on their genetic information with regard to health insurance and employment. The Act also amends the **Employee Retirement Insurance Security Act of 1974 (ERISA)** and the Internal Revenue Code. Early in 2009, President Barack Obama signed the "Lilly Ledbetter" **Fair Pay Act** extending the filing period for pay discrimination lawsuits.

The Law of Discrimination

It is a violation of antidiscrimination statutes if by some employment action or inaction an employee is treated less favorably than another because of gender, race, age, disability, national origin, or religion. The mere showing of a difference in treatment does not prove discrimination. There must be a discriminatory purpose or result to demonstrate illegal discrimination. The action taken by the employer must be based on a prohibitive

provision of the statute. In *St. Mary's Honor Ctr. v. Hicks*, 113 S.Ct. 2742 (1993), the United States Supreme Court held that a plaintiff who establishes a *prima facie* case of intentional discrimination is not entitled to judgment as a matter of law, even if the fact-finder rejects the employer's nondiscriminatory reasons for the adverse employment action. Instead, the plaintiff must still prove that the adverse action was based on discriminatory conduct prohibited by Title VII.

When the employee alleges discrimination, she or he must show that a statute has been violated. This is done by showing that:

1. The employee is protected by a statute.
2. The action was taken because the employee was a member of the protected class.
3. The employee was qualified, but was replaced by someone else.[2]

The procedure in court is that the employee alleges discrimination. The employer states that the action was nondiscriminatory and that there was no violation of a statute. The employee then alleges that this is pretext and the real reason for the action was discrimination. This raises the issue for the court or a jury to decide.

THE CIVIL RIGHTS ACT OF 1866 AND ITS AMENDMENTS

The original Civil Rights statute was passed shortly after the Civil War to support the Thirteenth Amendment. It gave nonwhites the same rights under the law as whites. Since it did not cover all activities—such as the right to sell, purchase, lease, or inherit real and personal property where the state has jurisdiction—the act had to be amended. The 1871 amendment, which is presently the most widely used statute, asserts that when acting under the "color of the state" (this includes any local, state, or federal governmental units or government officials) all persons must be given the same rights.[3] The 1871 amendment made the employer or the employee acting in behalf of the employer personally liable for violating the act.[4]

Personal Liability

The precedent in personal liability was clearly established in *Vinyard* v. *King*, 728 F.2d 428 (10th Cir. 1984), where the director of a municipal-owned hospital, contrary to the procedure in the employer's handbook, discharged an employee without a hearing. The court held the director personally liable but not the hospital, since it was part of the municipality, which couldn't be sued under the Doctrine of Sovereignty. Even if it could have been sued, the city could only have been held liable if an employee's action was based on policy that is unconstitutional. This made it much harder for employees who were wrongfully discharged to sue a governmental unit. Similarly, when a prison guard placed an inmate in a cell with another inmate whom he knew to be dangerous, and the plaintiff was assaulted, the guard was held personally liable. This personal liability extends to judges of state courts who, in an administrative action, violate the statute.

A difference between the 1866 statute and Title VII, in addition to individual liability, is that the plaintiff does not have to show intent[5] under Title VII and the CRA91 amendment when punitive or compensatory damages are asserted.[6] If the plaintiff's attorney uses both statutes and intent cannot be shown, it is still a violation of Title VII, where the only remedy is to make the employee whole (unless compensatory or punitive damages can be shown under CRA91). (Making an employee "whole" is to return the employee to his or her former status that he or she would have been in but for the employer's wrongful conduct.) Another difference between the 1866 statute and most other antidiscrimination statutes is that there is no limitation on retroactivity.

The act goes back to the date of the incident. Still another distinction is exclusive remedy. The plaintiff does not have to go through the Equal Employment Opportunity Commission (EEOC) or other administrative agencies, but can go directly into court. This is sometimes a great advantage when the plaintiff desires to have the case adjudicated quickly. Since it is an exclusive remedy, if the plaintiff falls under other antidiscrimination statutes, he or she can still bring an action under the 1866 statute.[7] Although the 1866 statute does not cover gender discrimination, the statute was amended by CRA91 to include all members of a protected class. Previously, intent was not required in a Title VII action as it was under Section 1981. The Civil Rights Act of 1991 somewhat narrowed this major difference by requiring a showing of intent[8] under Title VII if compensatory or punitive damages are sought. This is also true of trial by jury. Before the CRA91 amendment, jury trial was allowed and intent had to be shown in any action under the 1866 statute.

If possible, the employee will always choose a jury trial over a judge's decision. Juries are more sympathetic to employees (most of them are employees or have been at one time) than a judge who must follow the law more closely and is not as emotionally influenced as a jury. The unequivocal right to a jury trial and the ability to hold an individual personally liable are two great incentives for the plaintiff to sue under the 1866 act and CRA91.

TITLE VII AND THE CIVIL RIGHTS ACT OF 1991

The broadest antidiscrimination statute is the 1964 Civil Rights Act together with the CRA91 Amendment (commonly called Title VII). The Act and its amendments prohibit discrimination in all employment decisions on the basis of race, color, religion, national origin, disability, or gender, including pregnancy, childbirth, or abortion. Title VII applies to employers, labor unions, apprenticeship committees, employment agencies, and federal, state, and local governments. It covers all employees from the part-time office worker to the chief executive officer of the company. Before an employer is subject to the act, it must affect interstate commerce and employ 15 or more individuals for at least 20 weeks during the current or preceding calendar year.[9]

Section 101 of CRA91 specifically amended Section 1981. The old clause in Section 1981 that referred to making and enforcing contracts now includes making, performing, modifying, and terminating contracts. It also includes the enjoyment of all benefits, privileges, and terms and conditions of a contractual relationship. The effect of this amendment is to allow more individuals complaining of discrimination to sue for actual compensatory and punitive damages for alleged violation of their rights. Section 3 of CRA91 states the purposes of the amendments to the various antidiscrimination statutes, as follows:

1. To provide appropriate remedies for intentional discrimination and unlawful harassment in the workplace
2. To codify **business necessity** and job-related concepts
3. To reinstate the Griggs doctrine (discussed later in this chapter) and reverse *Wards Cove Packing Co. v. Atonio*, 409 U.S. 642 (1989)
4. To confirm statutory authority and provide statutory guidelines for adjudication of disparate impact suits under Title VII

Accordingly, the effect of the CRA91 amendment was to invalidate the holding of the Supreme Court in six significant cases. These cases are discussed next.

The Impact of CRA91

In *EEOC v. American Arabian Oil Co.*, 111 S.Ct. 1227 (1991), the court held that Title VII does not apply to American companies that employ U.S. citizens abroad. Under Section 109 of CRA91 such workers are now covered. In *West Virginia University Hospitals, Inc. v. Casey*, 111 S.Ct. 1138 (1991), the court held that expert witness fees could not be collected by the losing party. Under Section 113 of CRA91 expert witness fees are now included within the definition of attorney's fees. In *Patterson v. McLean Credit Union*, 491 U.S. 164 (1989), the court held that adverse employment actions, including racial harassment, were not covered by Section 1981 of the Civil Rights Act of 1866. Section 101 of CRA91 allows coverage for all aspects of the contractual employment relationship as well as covering termination of that relationship. In *Wards Cove Packing Co. v. Atonio*, 409 U.S. 642 (1989), the court increased the burden on the plaintiff in disparate impact cases. It stated that statistical imbalance does not necessarily establish a *prima facie* case to allow the plaintiff standing to sue. The controlling factor was the relevant labor market rather than an apparent statistical imbalance. Section 105 of CRA91 overturns this decision and returns to the doctrine set forth in *Griggs v. Duke Power Co.*, 401 U.S. 424 (1971), which requires that once the plaintiff has shown a practice or policy to be discriminatory, the burden of proof shifts to the defendant to prove business necessity or to demonstrate that the policy was not discriminatory.

Section 107 of CRA91 has proven to be one of the most contentious areas of discrimination law. Section 107 changes the legal standard in mixed motive discharge cases. Under current interpretation of the law, if the plaintiff can show that a prohibited motive led to an employment action even though a nonprohibited motive was also involved, the plaintiff is entitled to recover. This abandoned the standard established in *Price Waterhouse v. Hopkins*, 409 U.S. 228 (1989), and many subsequent mixed discharge cases, such as *NLRB v. Transportation Management Corp.*, 103 S.Ct. 2469 (1983), and the NLRB precedent found in *NLRB v. Wright*

Lines, 662 F.2d 899 (1st Cir. 1981). Under the old standard, a defendant employer only had to prove that it would have taken the same action if the employee was not a member of a protected class.

The question before the court in a mixed-motive, age-discrimination case is whether or not the employer should be allowed to avoid liability if it proves that it would have taken the same action irrespective of the alleged discriminatory motivation. In contention are the types of evidence (direct or circumstantial); whether or not the discriminatory reason was "substantial" or motivating in the employer's decision; and which party shoulders the burden of proof. This uncertainty previously allowed employers considerable latitude in defense. As a result, Congress lowered the standards for employees when it enacted CRA91. The ambiguity over the type of evidence required was apparently resolved when the court held that a preponderance of either direct or circumstantial evidence was sufficient.[10] However, the Court removed the burden-shifting requirement in the **Age Discrimination in Employment Act (ADEA)** cases when it held in *Gross* v. *FBL Financial Services,* 129 S.Ct. 2343 (2009), that the plaintiff must prove that the alleged age discrimination was the "but for" cause of the defendant employer's action.

The Supreme Court prevented a challenge to an **affirmative action** seniority system if it was not challenged when the system was adopted in *Lorance* v. *AT&T Technologies, Inc.,* 490 U.S. 900 (1989). Section 112 of CRA91 expressly overrules this doctrine and allows a challenge at any relevant time.[11] Similarly, the Fair Pay Act of 2009 expressly overrules the court's determination in *Ledbetter* v. *Goodyear Tire & Rubber Co.,* 550 U.S. 618 (2007), that the 180-day statute of limitations for suits under the Civil Rights Act begins to run after the initial act of discrimination and not any subsequent or continuing act.

Despite assertions to the contrary, Section 107 of the CRA91 does not require

quotas.[12] This section has, however, made it more difficult for employers to defend themselves against discrimination charges. Jury trial and punitive and compensatory damages tend to increase the exposure to lawsuits and raise the price that employers will pay for intentional discrimination. The cost-conscious employer will not overreact and rush into major policy changes. This would likely result in exposure to litigation.

There are several guidelines that the employer can follow to avoid exposure to litigation as a party to an expensive lawsuit:

1. Do not in any way indicate or even suggest an intent to discriminate. You can treat employees differently, but don't discriminate.
2. Be knowledgeable concerning the provisions of Title VII, as amended, and draft policies and procedures accordingly.
3. Have accurate and current job descriptions. These will document your business necessity.
4. Always investigate an alternative practice that is practicable but has less discriminatory implications.
5. Make sure that practices and procedures as well as business-necessity beliefs are not based on stereotyped thinking.
6. Document everything that is questionable, and maintain objective records.

How Discrimination Is Defined under Title VII

The EEOC enforces the provisions of all civil rights legislation. All charges under Title VII must begin with the EEOC or a state referral agency whose decision is not binding on the EEOC. Since Title VII did not define discrimination, one of the first tasks of the courts was to define it. Discrimination exists, according to the Supreme Court, if there was disparate treatment of the protected class.[13] If an employment policy resulted in the treatment of employees or individuals in the protected class differently from those in another class, the result is discrimination because of *disparate impact*. The term *disparate treatment* is usually used when less than the entire class is affected. Business necessity is a common defense for both allegations.[14]

In order for an employer to determine whether employment practices would result in discrimination on a member of the protected class, the EEOC issued guidelines since Title VII does not address disparate impact. These guidelines resulted in the widespread adoption of the so-called **four-fifths rule**, a formula that enables the employer to determine mathematically whether a disparate impact on a certain class of employees exists. This formula is not a statutory definition of a violation but only evidence of violation.[15] When discrimination is found, the employer must provide a nondiscriminatory reason why it exists. Exhibit 2.1 illustrates how an employer can determine whether a disparate impact exists.

If the selection rate for minorities is less than 80 percent of the selection rate for the remaining applicants, a disparate impact is demonstrated. To make this computation, divide the selection rate for the minorities (or covered group) by the selection rate for the remaining applicants. In this example 67 percent is below 80 percent; therefore a disparate impact would exist.[16]

Disparate Impact

Disparate impact is a term used when the plaintiff challenges the policies of management as being discriminatory toward a group of employees who are members of the protected class. The employer's intent to discriminate is irrelevant. The disparate impact theory was defined in *Griggs* v. *Duke Power Co.* The distinction is important to employers because if the complaint is disparate treatment, and only one person is involved, intent or unlawful motive must be shown. Often employers become concerned about treating one employee differently from another. These concerns are not well founded because many times the person involved is not a member of a protected class. Even if he or she is, if a nondiscriminatory reason can be shown and there is no intent to discriminate, the action is not discriminatory within the meaning of the act.

Under disparate impact, although the plaintiff does not have to show intent, the plaintiff must show by statistical evidence that the policy or procedure had the effect of discriminating against several members of the protected class. In *Watson* v. *Fort Worth Bank & Trust,* 108 S.Ct. 2777 (1988), the court held that although there may have been disparate treatment of a black female (who was refused four promotions by subjective decisions of white males), the

Applicants	Number of Minority Rejected	Number of Nonminority Rejected
100	53	30

Rate of selection = 100 − rate of rejection

Selection rate for minorities (47%)

Selection rate for nonminorities (70%) = 67%

EXHIBIT 2.1   Computation of Rates of Selection

plaintiff failed because she brought the suit under the disparate impact theory. She could not prove that a protected class was intentionally affected by an employer's policy. However, under the disparate treatment theory she would have had a strong case for individually being treated differently as a member of the protected class. It must be remembered that an employer can always treat a member of the protected class differently (although it may be disparate treatment) as long as there is no intent to discriminate, a nondiscriminatory reason can be shown, and there is no alternative that is less objectionable.

However, in *Ricci v. DeStefano,* 129 S.Ct. 2658 (2009), a controversial race discrimination case that many view as a retreat from the principles of Title VII, the court held that the city of New Haven (CT) had discriminated against white firefighters when it rejected the results of a promotional examination that failed to qualify any black applicants but did qualify 18 white and Hispanic applicants for promotion.

Disparate Treatment

When the term *disparate treatment* is used, an employee alleges that she or he has been treated less favorably than others because of gender, race, and so on. Sometimes the term *disparate impact* is used in place of the term *disparate treatment,* but the meaning is not the same. Disparate treatment is a term used when the employer has treated one person differently from another because of that employee's inclusion in a protected class. The disparate treatment complaints are individual cases, and the plaintiff must show that the employer had an unlawful motive or intended to discriminate. The basis for a violation under this theory can be found in *Furnco Construction Co. v. Waters,* 438 U.S. 567 (1978), and *Texas Community Affairs v. Burdine,* 450 U.S. 248 (1981).

Affirmative Action

Ricci v. *DeStefano,* also known as the New Haven firefighters' decision, further clouded the affirmative action picture for employers. The city of New Haven's decision to invalidate the results of a promotional examination was based primarily on its attempt to avoid exposure to a disparate impact discrimination claim. One of the difficulties with affirmative action is that there is no agreement as to the legitimate objectives of such a program. Some believe that, within reason, a preference should be given to those members of a protected class who have been discriminated against in the past. They believe that it is irrelevant that individuals within the class have not themselves been victims of discrimination. This view contends that there should be set-aside goals or preferences to correct the past discrimination.

Others believe that affirmative action should not favor one class over another. They argue that affirmative action should not be used to remedy the effects of either actual or historical discrimination that benefits individual nonvictims to the detriment of the nonprotected classes. They contend that only those who have actually been discriminated against should be given a remedy through affirmative action preference.[17]

The scope of affirmative action is broad. The existence of an affirmative action program does not prevent the Office of Federal Contract Compliance (OFCC) from reporting violations to the EEOC or Justice Department for enforcement of Title VII or any other antidiscrimination statute. Executive Order 11246, the order mandating affirmative action for federal agencies and contractors, does not require the employer to hire an applicant who is not the best qualified. The courts simply require the employer to make a good faith effort to find and hire qualified applicants who are members of the protected class.

Implementation of an Affirmative Action Plan

If affirmative action programs are realistic, honest, and current, compliance should not be a problem. The first step in determining whether one can improve employment opportunities is to determine whether there will be any employment or promotion opportunities in a given period. The next step is to determine whether there has been a denial of job opportunities for a protected class. If there is a possibility to improve the balance of a job category through the promotion of a member of a protected class, then it is considered an underutilized job category in which improvement can be made. Affirmative action does not demand that underutilization be corrected immediately, but that a good faith effort be made to improve the number of the protected class in the underutilized job category.

Affirmative Action in Promotion

The proper determination of whom to promote is a primary consideration in the successful management of any organization. It is a commonly accepted human resources doctrine that one determines promotion on the basis of ability to perform the job. No other criteria should be used, with the exception of seniority. This usually supersedes minority interests or any affirmative action plan.[18]

In 1972, a lower court found the State of Alabama guilty of systematically excluding blacks from state trooper jobs. They were ordered to follow a quota for hiring and promotion. By 1979, no blacks had been promoted to the upper ranks. The court then approved a plan whereby the state would develop a program within one year for promotion of blacks to the rank of corporal. The lower court found the state in contempt and the Supreme Court affirmed EEOC guidelines in all other respects. Two more years passed without a single black person

promoted. The state then agreed to develop a test, which proved to have an adverse impact on minorities. The court ordered the state to promote to the rank of corporal 50 percent blacks if a vacancy existed. The order was given based on the theory that an affirmative action plan can be designed to increase participation of blacks as state troopers. The state appealed to the Supreme Court.

The Supreme Court in *United States* v. *Paradise et al.,* 107 S.Ct. 1063 (1987), by a 5-4 vote affirmed the lower court's order, stating that the court had wide discretion in ordering remedies where discrimination had been found. The plan was temporary and whites had an equal chance to be promoted. To some extent, the Court followed *Weber, City of Cleveland,* and *Fullilove* in affirming that racial preference can be given under certain conditions.[19]

The real uncertainty of affirmative action programs that result in reverse discrimination was created by *Johnson* v. *Transportation Agency, Santa Clara County,* 107 S.Ct. 1442 (1987). The facts of the case lacked the requirements of previous decisions that upheld racial preference to correct past discrimination in affirmative action plans. In *Johnson,* there was no previous court determination of discrimination and there was no record of past discrimination against women, although an imbalance existed. The court stated that promoting women over men for a nondiscriminatory reason is acceptable where there is an imbalance. Gender was one of numerous factors taken into account, and the facts indicate that it was the major factor.

In a 6-3 decision, the Court held that Title VII permits the employer the right to voluntarily rectify a manifest imbalance in the workforce by an affirmative action program. The Court didn't overrule the previous cases of *Bakke, Wygant,* or *Stotts*[20] but relied heavily on *Weber* because the facts in *Weber* and *Johnson* were similar.

The affirmative action plan was permanent and allowed the exclusion of whites who were better qualified. The holding in the case is that a bona fide affirmative action plan can use race, gender, or ethnic background as a factor in hiring or promotion. The Court's decision in the New Haven Firefighters' case would appear to reject *Johnson* and perhaps *Weber* and limit the use of affirmative actions programs.

Business Necessity as a Defense

Business necessity is a term originated by the Supreme Court in the *Griggs* case noted earlier. The employer's burden to prove the existence of a business necessity was reinstated in CRA91. In the *Griggs* case the court held that business necessity is justification for a policy that discriminates against a member of a protected class. *Business necessity* has been defined as that which is reasonably necessary to the safe and efficient operation of the business. Business necessity has not been as useful as a defense to the employers as it might appear because of the narrow interpretation by the courts of what constitutes efficient and safe operation of the business.

The courts have held that business necessity cannot be used as a defense unless there is a showing that no other acceptable alternative will serve the employer equally well with a lesser impact on members of protected groups. With a defense of business necessity, the employer admits discrimination but argues that there is a legitimate reason for discriminating.

Bona fide occupational qualification (BFOQ) differs from business necessity in that it is defined by 703(e) of Title VII and originally referred only to gender. Section 703(e) states that gender discrimination is valid in certain circumstances where sex is "a bona fide occupational qualification reasonably necessary to meet the normal operation of that particular business or enterprise." As a practical matter there is

very little difference between the two, and often they are interchanged when used as a defense for discrimination in an employment decision. If the employer's perception of business necessity is not supported by objective data, the courts will reject it. The objective data must show that the discriminatory action was necessary for the efficient operation of the business. The courts demand evidence that the traditional qualifications for hiring or promotion are necessary to the safe and efficient performance of the job. The employer often fails to sustain this burden because of subjective beliefs of what is necessary for the safe and efficient operation of the business.

Where the employer alleged business necessity in promoting a white over a black because the white had supervisory experience, the court found that the need for supervisory experience in order to perform the job was subjective. The one area in which the employer has consistently been able to show business necessity is where the safety of the employee or safety of others is involved. Business necessity has been accepted as a good reason for discrimination in airline cases where flight attendants become pregnant and are removed from duty.[21] In *Levin* v. *Delta Airlines*, 730 F.2d 994 (5th Cir. 1984), the court had little trouble in holding that removal of flight attendants as soon as it was known that they were pregnant was a business necessity. However, the employees argued that there was available a less-discriminatory alternative that would cushion the adverse consequences of the discriminatory policy. The court held that the employer need only adopt the alternative when it is a customary practice in similar situations. Failure to use the customary alternative does not indicate that the policy was a pretext.

The safety factor excepted, business necessity is very difficult to prove. When customers in South America would not deal with a female sales representative and so the employer removed her, the court said as a matter of law the reason was insufficient defense of business necessity for the gender discrimination.[22] Since discrimination is admitted when using business necessity, the employer should not use this defense unless there are very strong facts to support it. In *Latuga* v. *Hooters, Inc.,* 1996 WL 164427 (N.D. Ill., 1996), a prospective male waiter claimed discrimination based on gender. The employer utilized the BFOQ defense in claiming that its "restaurant concept includes certain ambience requirements and a female waitstaff wearing cutoff t-shirts, tanktops and orange jogging shorts." It argued that this concept permitted its restaurants to compete with any casual dining place, particularly those featuring female sex appeal. The court refused to certify the case as a class action. Subsequently, three other males sued Hooters in Illinois and four others sued Hooters in Maryland when all were denied employment. The cases were settled with the plaintiffs receiving damages, and Hooters continuing to employ an all-female waitstaff. However, Hooters agreed to create other support jobs such as bartenders and hosts that could be filled irrespective of the applicant's gender.

It is well-settled law that when an employee alleges that she or he has been discriminated against, the employee must establish a *prima facie* case as discussed later in this chapter. Once the court finds that such a case exists, the employer has to show a nondiscriminatory reason for the employment decision. This principle was established by the Supreme Court in two landmark decisions. In the first, *Furnco Construction Corp.* v. *Waters* (noted earlier), the employer had to defend what appeared to be a discriminatory action of refusing to hire three black bricklayers who were fully qualified. The firm had a policy of hiring only bricklayers known to be experienced and competent or recommended by other contractors as skilled workers. The evidence showed that this policy was consistently followed with all applicants. Under this policy

some blacks were hired. The court held that the employer only had to give a legitimate nondiscriminatory reason for not hiring the blacks and that there is no requirement for the hiring procedure to maximize the hiring of minorities.

In the second case, a female alleged that she was discharged because of her gender and a male was hired in her place.[23] The issue before the court was what kind of proof was necessary to prove to the court that the action was nondiscriminatory. The court held that once a *prima facie* case was established, the employer had to articulate a nondiscriminatory reason for the action. The employee could rebut that reason as being a pretext. It then became a question of fact for the trial court to decide. The court held that there was no burden on the employer to persuade the court that the reason was not a pretext. This was up to the employee.

It is now well-settled law that in any situation where the employer's action is alleged to be discriminatory, this action can be defended by showing a nondiscriminatory reason. The burden is on the employee to show that the nondiscrimatory reason was a pretext. The Supreme Court unanimously held in *Reeves* v. *Sanderson Plumbing Products,* a 2000 decision, that once a reasonable factfinder (judge or jury) has found that the employer's nondiscriminatory reason is pretext, it may be adequate to sustain a finding of intentional discrimination.[24]

To prevent exposure to lawsuits under Title VII or any other antidiscrimination statute, the employer should always ask the question: Was the reason for the action a nondiscriminatory one? If the answer is in the affirmative, then there is a good defense available.

Prima Facie Evidence

It is a legal principle that before a person can go to court, it must be shown that a wrong has been committed by stating certain facts. In discrimination lawsuits this is called a *prima facie* case (a fact that will be established until rebutted). In alleging discrimination in employment, the Supreme Court stated that the charging party (plaintiff) must establish a *prima facie* case by showing the following:[25]

1. The applicant is a member of a class protected by the statute.
2. The applicant applied for the vacancy and is qualified to perform the job. (Where the employer requested specific questions be answered in a résumé and the applicant refused to answer those questions, the court held that the plaintiff had not completed the application process and therefore was not an applicant and failed to establish a prima facie case.)[26]
3. Minimally qualified, the applicant was rejected.
4. After rejection, the job vacancy remained open. The employer continued to seek applications from persons of equal qualifications.

It is a common, and often erroneous, belief among human resource managers that there is no discrimination when a minority is rejected and another minority is selected. This issue was presented in *Connecticut* v. *Teal*, 102 S.Ct. 2525 (1982). The court stated that Title VII is designed not only to protect groups but also to protect individuals. In this particular case, the selection procedures revealed no disparate impact on the group, but individuals were denied an equal opportunity to be employed because of an identifiable pass/fail test barrier. Those individuals were entitled to protection under Title VII. If the individuals are deprived of employment opportunities or if their status is affected, then Title VII is violated. The law guarantees members of a protected class the opportunity to compete equally on the basis of job-related criteria. The fact that some members of a protected class were not discriminated against in the hiring process does not mean that certain other individuals were not subject to discrimination.

Equal Employment versus Equal Opportunity

It is clear from the *Teal* decision that there is a difference between equal employment and equal opportunity. Title VII requires that an employee be given an equal opportunity to be employed. Prior to the *Teal* decision, employers could review their hiring and promotion procedures according to the number hired. The procedures would pass scrutiny by EEOC if the final result did not show a disparate impact. The courts and EEOC did not inquire into the disparate impact or disparate treatment of the process, however.

The Supreme Court in the *Teal* decision stated that the "bottom-line" approach is not a defense if, during the process, individuals have been adversely affected. In this case certain individuals were disqualified for promotion because they failed to pass a test that had not been validated. The results of the test had a disparate impact; therefore, business necessity had to be shown by validating the test. The fact that the final selection rate did not show a disparate impact was immaterial. The *Teal* decision clearly establishes the difference between **equal employment** and equal opportunity in the eyes of the courts.

Discrimination can take place at any step in the employment process. The individual must be given an opportunity to demonstrate that she or he is qualified to perform the job. Elimination from consideration for a promotion or to fill a vacancy for non-job-related reasons denies the opportunity to be considered according to qualifications. An equal opportunity employer is one who provides a full and fair opportunity to become employed. Any barrier that is not job related or a business necessity is discrimination under Title VII.[27]

Protection from Retaliation

Discrimination statutes include a provision that prohibits the employer from retaliating against an employee who attempts to aid in the enforcement of a statute. The legislative purpose of these provisions is to encourage the employee to use the protection of the statute by reporting a violation and enhancing its enforcement.[28] Title VII has a retaliation provision that is similar to those of other statutes.[29] *Retaliation* is defined by the courts as an unlawful practice of an employer whereby the employer discriminates against the employee for participating in the enforcement of a statute or a right.[30]

The application of these principles can be found in *Donnellon* v. *Fruehauf Corp.*, 794 F.2d 598 (11th Cir. 1986). The employee filed a discrimination complaint with the EEOC alleging that she was denied the sales representative position because of her sex. Three weeks later she was discharged. Four days after her discharge she filed an additional retaliation charge with the EEOC alleging that she was discharged in retaliation for filing her original claim. The court held that there was no gender discrimination but that she was discharged in retaliation for filing a claim.[31] In order to demonstrate *prima facie* proof of retaliation, the employee must show that:

1. She or he has engaged in statutorily protected activity.
2. The employer has taken an adverse employment action.
3. There is a causal connection between the protected activity and adverse action.
4. The employer would not have taken the adverse action, "but for" the employee's good faith belief that the practice under the law was wrongful, and he or she was seeking to enforce it.

It is then the employer's burden to show that the adverse action had nothing to do with the filing of the charge. If the employee's conduct was unlawful, excessively disloyal, hostile, disruptive, or damaging to the employer's business, then she or he will have difficulty claiming protection under the statute's retaliation clause. In *Donnellon* there was no question that the plaintiff could meet the requirements to get into court. It then became a question of why she was discharged. The employer, according to the court, could not give an articulated, clear, and consistent reason for the discharge. Each witness gave a different reason. Inconsistency on the part of the employer is always damaging in a discharge case. The court put great weight on the fact that the plaintiff was discharged a month after filing the gender discrimination charge.

The Supreme Court extended the reach of Title VII's prohibition against retaliation beyond the workplace in *Burlington Northern Santa Fe Railway Co.* v. *White,* 126 S.Ct. 2405 (2006), when it found that the employer had retaliated against White, a female track laborer, by reassigning her to a less desirable job following her complaints of sexual harassment, and later suspending her for alleged insubordination. The Court determined that the anti-retaliation provision "does not confine the actions and harms it forbids to those that are related to employment or occur at the workplace" and that the employer can retaliate by causing the employee harm outside the workplace. In another case an appellate court found an employer guilty of retaliation when it filed false criminal charges against a former employee who had complained of discrimination.[32]

Sometimes the employer will give clear reasons for discharge but they are not very persuasive. Reasons such as "generally poor work performance," "failure to cooperate," and "gross insubordination" usually will not be accepted by the court as legitimate, nondiscriminatory reasons, but will be considered a pretext for retaliation. The reason for the discharge must stand on its own. If the employee would not normally have been discharged for the offenses committed or if other employees committed the same offenses and were not discharged, then the courts could conclude it was retaliation. This also applies to former employees under Title VII.[33]

It must be established that the employer's treatment was intentional in order to show that retaliation has occurred. Showing that the employer treated the plaintiff differently from the way the firm would have treated other employees under similar circumstances is usually considered intentional.[34] The most important element in the defense of retaliation cases is that the discipline or employment decision is applied to all employees when the situation is the same. The mistake that employers often make is to treat a person who has filed a charge either more leniently or more strictly. Either policy is troublesome in retaliation charges. The more lenient policy reaches the point of no return; when enforcement takes place, retaliation is alleged. The overly strict policy will cause retaliation charges unless it is consistent. Proper procedures for discharge are the best defenses to retaliation charges. If the employer's discipline, grievance, and discharge procedures are uniformly applied, violation of a statutory retaliation provision will seldom be found.

Labor Unions

Labor organizations are also covered by the provisions of Section VII and fall under the jurisdiction of the EEOC. A *labor organization* is defined under Title VII as any organization, agency, or employee representation committee that exists to deal with the employer.[35] Any union conference or joint board that is subordinate to a national or international labor organization is also subject to the act. The labor organization must have at least 15 members for coverage under Title VII. The union cannot exclude from membership or otherwise discriminate against members because of race, color, religion, disability, gender, national origin, or age.[36] It cannot cause or encourage the employer to discriminate against an individual. A labor organization cannot maintain segregated locals or discriminate as to referrals for acceptance in apprenticeship training programs. Labor unions have a special duty under Title VII to represent fairly all employees apart from the requirements of the National Labor Relations Act (NLRA). They must attempt to eradicate any discriminatory practices. For more than 30 years the NLRA was the only legislation concerned with labor–management relationships except for some occasional disputes under the Fair Labor Standards Act. In 1972, when Title VII was amended, a third party entered the relationship. The EEOC could sue both the union and the employer for discrimination. The problem immediately arose as to who had jurisdiction, the NLRB or the EEOC. For example, the National Labor Relations Board (NLRB) that enforces the NLRA will refuse to hold a representation election if a union has discriminated under Title VII. The employee's right to strike over discriminatory practices of both the company and the union is supported by the NLRB after a grievance is processed.

For the purpose of this section it is important to review only two basic principles concerning the role of the union in discrimination cases.

1. The Supreme Court, long before Title VII, held that a collective bargaining agreement between a union and an employer that discriminated against blacks is a violation of the union's duty of fair representation. All classes of employees must be represented.[37] Indeed, the courts have refused to enforce an unfair labor practice when a union discriminates.[38]

2. Since the employees have elected the union to be their bargaining representative, they cannot discuss discrimination matters directly with the employer but must go through the union. If there is evidence that the union approves of employer discriminatory practices, the employees must still go through the union before going to the EEOC. When the employees went out on strike over discriminatory practices without going through the grievance procedure, it was not considered protected activity; therefore, discharging the employees was not an unfair labor practice.[39] The court said that although employees have a right to be free from discrimination under Title VII, the right cannot be pursued at the expense of orderly collective bargaining.

When employees are represented by a union, the employer should not entertain complaints about discrimination unless they are discussed with the union first. The NLRB, NLRA and the courts strictly hold the employer to this rule. Regardless of whether the union is discriminating, the employees are represented by the union and therefore they must act through their chosen representative.

HARASSMENT IN THE WORKPLACE

Closely related to the problem of overt discrimition in the workplace is the matter of the harassment of employees based on their gender, race, national origin, and so on, by employer representatives or fellow employees. Sexual harassment in the workplace arose as a legal issue in the 1970s and by the end of the decade became recognized by the courts as discrimination prohibited by Title VII.[40] In 1980, the EEOC issued guidelines concerning the problem of sexual harassment. More recently, racial harassment in the workplace has been identified as a problem area by the EEOC.

Definition and Control

Harassment in the workplace is a violation of Title VII when a member of a protected class is subjected to a **hostile environment** or unwelcome attention unrelated to job performance. Title VII does not have a specific provision prohibiting harassment as such, but the courts and the EEOC have so interpreted the statute.[41] For example, racial harassment would be found where a black employee is subjected to racial slurs and pranks or other bigoted acts such as the display of a hangman's noose by other employees or supervisors;[42] age-based harassment where a supervisor consistently makes derogatory statements about older workers;[43] and disability-based harassment where an injured employee is teased and ridiculed by a supervisor.[44] An employer's attention solely to sexual harassment is short-sighted. The ridiculing, bullying, or abuse of employees in any protected class increasingly creates legal exposure.[45]

Reluctance of Management

Harassment situations often involve sexual harassment or sexual relations. Until recently, most managers preferred to avoid interference or involvement with sexual relations between employees, either within or outside the working relationship, so long as they did not interfere with work performance or did not occur on company time.[46] If management became aware of sexual advances, it would often attribute them to simple attraction between the sexes, allowing the parties involved to resolve the matter. If, in extreme cases, correction was needed, the matter was handled on a confidential and individual basis. Many managers reasoned that, because of the personal nature of sexual matters, dealing with the matter openly could create more problems than it would solve. Another reason for management's reluctance is that sexual advances are often difficult to define or prove. Further, female employees are frequently reluctant to bring the matter to the attention of the employer for fear of embarrassment or provoking an adverse reaction from a supervisor or co-worker.[47]

On May 7, 2009, the *Los Angeles Times* reported that, due to unresolved charges of misconduct, 160 teachers and staff were suspended with pay. These charges included allegations of drug abuse, sexual contact with students, harassment, and drug possession. The article highlighted one teacher who stayed home and collected $68,000 a year in salary after allegedly harassing both students and teachers. The school district had already spent $2 million in legal fees. The Superintendent has since retired— "Exhausted," he said, "by the battle to fire" the teacher. In fiscal year 2008, the EEOC received 13,867 charges of sexual harassment. Males filed 15.9 percent of those charges. The EEOC resolved 11,731 sexual harassment charges in fiscal year 2008 and recovered $47.4 million in monetary benefits for charging parties and other aggrieved individuals (not including monetary benefits obtained through litigation).[48]

Legal Basis

Sexual harassment is a form of gender discrimination, but it is distinguishable in that the conduct involves pressure to provide sexual favors, or the creation of an environment that tolerates unwelcome sexual advances or language. Where discrimination because of an employee's sex involves an adverse employment decision, it is a violation of Title VII.[49] Discrimination based on gender and sexual harassment can be distinguished in that discrimination is usually a single act, whereas sexual harassment usually involves continual conduct.[50]

The reason sexual harassment is unlawful is that Title VII prevents one sex from being favored over another; when a male favors a female and not other males, there is a violation.[51] By the same principle, a female can sexually harass a male, and the courts have so held. A male sexually harassing a male is unlawful because females are not given the same attention.[52] The same would apply to females harassing females.

The question of same-sex harassment was directly addressed by the court in *Oncale* v. *Sundowner Offshore Services* 523 U.S. 75 (1998). In *Oncale*, a male oil platform roustabout was forcibly subjected to sex-related humiliating actions by other employees, two of whom were supervisors. Oncale reported these actions but the employer was unresponsive to his complaints. He eventually quit because of this harassment and filed a complaint under Title VII. The Court held, in citing *Harris* v. *Forklift Systems, Inc.,* 114 S.Ct. 376 (1993), that the critical issue is whether members of one sex are exposed to disadvantageous terms and conditions of employment that members of the other sex are not exposed to. Accordingly, the statute covers sexual harassment of any kind and that same sex harassment is actionable under Title VII.

Bisexuals and transsexuals are unlikely to be protected by Title VII because of the difficulty in determining which sex is being favored.[53] Where a transsexual, who claimed to be a female at the time of hire, was denied use of female restroom facilities, the employer discharged for misrepresentation. Because the employee was a male in the employer's opinion, the court said discharge was not a violation of Title VII. The Act is not intended to cover transsexuals.[54] If the harassment would not have occurred "but for" the employee's sex, it is harassment because it constitutes an unequal condition of employment.[55] However, the conduct must be sufficiently persuasive to alter the conditions of employment. In deciding whether there has been sexual harassment, the EEOC and the courts will look at the facts as a whole and the totality of the circumstances.[56] Some courts will consider evidence of the complainant's sex life to determine whether the conduct constitutes sexual harassment.[57]

Reverse Sexual Harassment

The EEOC guidelines [29 CFR § 1604.11] also deal with what might be called *sexual harassment in reverse*. In this type of case, an employee climbs the corporate ladder at the expense of other qualified persons by giving sexual favors to the decision maker. The qualified employees passed over for promotion have a claim for sexual discrimination.[58] The employer may avoid litigation from the person promoted but has an exposure from those who were passed over.

Third-Party Actions

Third parties who have been affected by sexual harassment normally cannot sue,[59] although some courts have found an exception in hostile environment cases. In *Broderick v. Ruder*, 685 F. Supp. 1269 (D.C. 1988), a female attorney was allowed to sue, although little of the harassment was directed at her. Several federal courts have found strict liability for third-party complaints if management creates the hostile environment,[60] whereas other courts limit strict liability to **quid pro quo** cases.[61]

The Civil Rights Act of 1991 amended Title VII to provide for compensatory and punitive damages as well as jury trial. In addition, the plaintiffs can recover expert witness fees. Damages in sexual harassment cases are expressly limited by statute. If there is a conflict with a state statute, the federal statutes will prevail. When the employer has knowledge of harassment and fails to do anything about it, the courts have overwhelmingly held the employer liable under Title VII. If courts find a blatant example of inaction, they will allow a negligence action before a jury and permit the jury to award punitive damages.[62]

The *Meritor* Case

Many questions about what is or is not sexual harassment were cleared up in the first case on the subject to come before the Supreme Court. In the landmark case of *Meritor Savings Bank, FSB* v. *Vinson* (hereinafter called *Meritor*), 106 S.Ct. 2399 (1986),[63] the plaintiff alleged that Taylor, a vice-president of the

bank, had asked for sexual relations with her. At first she refused, but later she yielded out of fear of losing her job. She testified that she had sexual relations with the manager from 40 to 50 times in the previous four years, both during and after business hours. She never reported her action to any of the manager's supervisors, nor did she attempt to use the complaint procedure that the employer had established. She also alleged that Taylor had fondled her in front of other employees, and had followed her into the women's restroom when she went there alone. He exposed himself to her, and even on occasion forcibly raped her. These activities ceased after she became involved with another man. About a year later, the plaintiff took sick leave for an indefinite period. Three months later, the employer fired her for excessive sick leave.

She brought suit, alleging sexual harassment during the four years of employment. The district court held that she was not subjected to sexual harassment, but merely was involved in a broken love affair. The appellate court reversed the decision, holding that the action was a violation of Title VII even though no job opportunities were involved. The court imputed notice to the employer because the manager obviously knew about the harassment. The manager was the representative of the employer; therefore, the employer knew or should have known about the sexual conduct.

The Supreme Court, in a unanimous decision for the plaintiff, held that a violation of Title VII is predicated on two types of harassment:

1. Those involving economic benefits (quid pro quo)
2. Those where a hostile environment is created

The provocative dress and speech of the alleged victim, and the voluntary participation in sexual affairs, did not preclude a finding that the episodes were unwanted and therefore unlawful.[64] The Court said that the employer is not relieved of liability in all situations, even though there is an announced policy against sexual harassment or by the failure of the victim to utilize existing grievance procedures. The Court was not willing to impute knowledge in all cases in which a supervisor was involved, as had been determined by the appellate court and the EEOC guidelines.[65] Rather, it stated that the facts and circumstances in each case should determine whether the employer had notice, but that the absence of notice did not necessarily insulate the employer from liability. Many state courts impute knowledge under the common-law doctrine of *respondent superior.*[66]

The *Meritor* decision summarizes all previous appellate court decisions on sexual harassment and clearly defines sexual harassment as unwelcome. It goes further in saying that voluntary participation in sexual activity does not necessarily mean that the activity is welcome. The Court invalidated prior EEOC guidelines that stated that knowledge can be imputed where the supervisor is involved. The Court thus reversed several appellate court decisions that had upheld the imputed knowledge guidelines. However, the employer can still be liable based on imputed knowledge.

This landmark decision stated that in order to find sexual harassment there must be three elements:

1. The conduct must be unwelcome.
2. The employer must have knowledge, either actual or imputed.
3. The outcome must either involve job opportunities or the creation of a hostile environment.[67]

Tangible Employment Action

Subsequent to its *Meritor* decision, the Supreme Court further defined the distinction between hostile environment and quid pro quo harassment in two 1998 cases—*Burlington Industries* v. *Ellerth,* 524 U.S. 742 (1998), and

Faragher v. *City of Boca Raton,* 524 U.S. 775 (1998)—both involving sexual harassment by supervisors. In these cases the Court found that a quid pro quo "tangible employment action" occurs when an employer takes a significant adverse employment action such as termination, demotion, or undesirable transfer against an employee based on the employee's refusal to submit to an employer's request for sexual favors. In these situations the employer is always responsible for the acts of its supervisors and is barred from raising an affirmative defense such as lack of knowledge of the request for sexual favors or the existence of a no harassment policy.

Hostile Environment: A Definition

The court, in considering whether there is a hostile environment, must evaluate the conditions existing before the plaintiff was hired;[68] the background and experience of the plaintiff as well as his or her co-workers and supervisors; and the totality of the physical environment. However, if anti-female animus is found, the court will usually find hostile environment.[69]

Whether a hostile environment exists must be evaluated on a case-by-case basis. The court in *Rabidue* v. *Osceola Refining Co.,* 107 S.Ct. 1983 (1987), noted that in some work environments, sexual jokes and vulgarity are extremely common; and Title VII was not meant to bring about "a transformation in the social mores of American workers." The remarks may be annoying, but if they are not so offensive as to have seriously affected the plaintiff, there is no hostile environment. In *Davis* v. *Monsanto Chemical Co.,* 858 F.2d 345 (6th Cir. 1988), the court rejected *Rabidue* by stating that there are only two requirements for hostile environment:

1. Repeated activity
2. Management tolerance

No interference with work performance was shown. Some courts say that sexy posters create a hostile environment, whereas others disagree.[70]

In summary, there is no clear-cut definition of *hostile environment*.[71] The necessary elements of the definition are the employee's declaration that the environment is hostile and unwelcome, and the employer's knowledge of that declaration. The employer can usually be relieved of liability by directly addressing the problem.

Hostile Work Environment

Absent tangible employment action, allegations of sexual harassment are considered to be hostile work environment cases. The significance of this distinction is that in hostile work environment cases the plaintiff must prove pervasive conduct on the part of the employer. The employer may raise affirmative defenses by showing that it exercised reasonable care to prevent sexually harassing behavior in the workplace through its policies and procedures, and that the plaintiff failed to avail herself or himself of those procedures.[72]

Unwelcome Conduct

The court recognized that a person might be the victim of sexual harassment, even though he or she participated in or condoned acts of a sexual nature.[73] It is difficult for an employer to know whether an intimate relationship is unwelcome, or at what point it will be welcomed.[74] It appears the only way the employer will know, is if the employee reports that advances are presently unwelcome. The ruling on admissibility of evidence concerning a complainant's sexual behavior may help, because the employer can argue that due to the behavior, a reasonable person would believe that the conditions were not entirely unwelcome.[75]

The more evidence that there is of a personal relationship between the plaintiff and the alleged harasser, the more difficulty the plaintiff will have in showing that the conduct was unwelcome. The Supreme Court in *Harris* v. *Forklift System, Inc.*, used a "reasonable person" test now found in a majority of courts.

Opportunity or Hostile Environment

Again, there are two types of sexual harassment: quid pro quo harassment resulting in a tangible employment action and hostile work environment. *Quid pro quo tangible employment action* occurs when an employee is forced to choose between agreeing to a superior's sexual demands or forfeiting a tangible employment benefit, such as promotion, wage increase, leave of absence, or continued employment. Because the quid pro quo version is easily identified by its objectivity, there is little problem in determining whether or not it has occurred. Hostile environment claims are more difficult to prove.[76] They are more subjective, in that they do not involve a specific employment benefit and can involve a co-worker. *Hostile environment* is defined by the EEOC guidelines as an interference with the employee's work behavior or a creation of an offensive work environment.[77] The *Meritor* case merely reaffirmed the appellate court's position that hostile environment is a violation of Title VII; and that both provocative dress requirements and verbal statements could create a hostile environment. It did not specifically define hostile environment.

The Supreme Court's finding in *Harris* that a "reasonable person" standard should be used, resolved a conflict among the circuits where both the "reasonable person" and "reasonable woman" standard were used to find that a hostile environment existed. The employer, to be safe, uses the "reasonable woman" standard. A *hostile environment* can be defined as one that a "reasonable woman" would find unwelcome. The court further held that it is not necessary that the plaintiff show a tangible psychological injury, although some prior decisions had indicated that it was necessary.[78] It said, beginning at 63 FEP Cases 227:

> Conduct that is not severe or pervasive enough to create an objectively hostile or abusive work environment, an environment that a reasonable person would find hostile or abusive, is beyond Title VII's purview. Likewise, if the victim does not subjectively perceive the environment to be abusive, the conduct has not actually altered the conditions of the victim's employment, and there is no Title VII violation.

But Title VII comes into play before the harassing conduct leads to a nervous breakdown so long as the environment would reasonably be perceived, and is perceived, as hostile or abusive.[79]

The Supreme Court took a middle ground in *Harris*. It reaffirmed its earlier holding in the *Meritor* case and did not reverse any case. However, it took a later Eighth Circuit case to clear up confusion over the plaintiff's burden. In *Kopp* v. *Samaritan Health Systems*, 13 F.3d 264 at 269, the court outlined the five elements in a plaintiff's burden:

1. The plaintiff has membership in a protected group or class.
2. The plaintiff was subject to unwelcome sexual harassment.
3. The harassment was based on sex.
4. The harassment affected a term, condition, or privilege of employment.
5. The employer knew or should have known of the harassment and failed to take proper remedial action.

The plaintiff in *Meritor* was not specifically required or asked to give sexual favors as a condition of promotion. From the testimony, her promotions were based on merit; the employer liability was therefore based on hostile environment, and not quid pro quo

harassment. The court held in this situation that the manager's behavior constituted a hostile environment.[80]

Management Cognizance

Imputed (employer) knowledge is one of the cloudiest areas of the *Meritor* decision. Surveys show that only a small percentage of employees who are being harassed will report it to the employer. The EEOC-proposed guidelines[81] explicitly state that employers are responsible for all acts of sexual harassment in the workplace where a supervisor is involved, unless it can be shown that the employer took immediate action to correct the problem. The Supreme Court was widely split on whether they should adopt the EEOC guidelines,[82] but the majority held in *Meritor* that employers are not strictly liable for acts of supervisors. That interpretation has been modified by the *Ellerth* and *Faragher* decisions as noted earlier. In *Meritor*, the Court had no trouble in finding that knowledge was imputed, because the grievance procedure required the plaintiff to go to the person involved. The employee was not encouraged to complain; the Court imputed knowledge.[83] From the dictum in the case, the Court indicated that if there had been a different grievance procedure and a policy, knowledge would not have been imputed.

The *Meritor* case cleared up many issues; a hostile environment is a violation under Title VII; sexual harassment must be unwelcome; acquiescence does not always mean that it is welcome; and unless the employee can report to a member of management other than the person involved, knowledge will be imputed. However, if there is a hostile environment without specific proof that work performance is affected, and if proof is required that the employee is actually offended by the environment, the determination of a hostile environment will be made by the totality of circumstances, on a case-by-case basis.[84]

AGE DISCRIMINATION IN EMPLOYMENT ACT

The Age Discrimination in Employment Act (ADEA) of 1967 makes it unlawful for employers to discriminate based on age with respect to compensation and terms, conditions, and privileges of employment.[85] Additional unlawful acts under ADEA include discrimination or retaliation based on the assertion of rights under the Act, publication of notices or advertisements related to employment that express an age preference or limitation, and the forced retirement of nonfederal employees.[86]

The Act and its amendments contain the following basic provisions:

1. It forbids employers with 20 or more employees—including public employers, employment agencies, and labor organizations (with 25 or more members)—to make employment decisions based on a person's age when that person is over 40 years old. This is interpreted to mean that preference cannot be shown within the protected group. An employer could not express preference of a 45- to 55-year-old person, as this would discriminate because of age.

2. It invalidates compulsory retirement for pension plans in the private and public sectors. If the inability to perform the job can be shown, or if an executive in a policy-making position, or if the person has a pension above $44,000 without Social Security, the employee could be subjected to compulsory retirement.

3. It authorizes a jury trial of any issue of fact.

4. It expressly authorizes employers to discriminate against older employees under certain circumstances.

Overt age discrimination in employment and mandatory age-based retirement has largely disappeared in the private sector since the passage of ADEA.[87]

Exemptions

Under ADEA an employee is subject to compulsory retirement if he or she is an executive in a policy-making position or has a pension over $44,000, or if unsatisfactory performance can be shown. The ADEA provides that if an employee has been employed for two years preceding the retirement date in a "high policy-making position" this employee would be exempt from the compulsory retirement restrictions of the ADEA. The issue in all these cases is what constitutes a policy-making decision. The leading cases state that the person must perform policy-making duties for at least two years before termination. Level of salary is not the determining factor. The court looks at the duties that the employee performs.[88] When considering whether or not an executive can be retired at age 65, the employer must consider the job content, the reporting relationship, and whether or not the employee participated in policy-making decisions and had discretionary powers. Also, ADEA does not cover the total employee relationship.[89]

Defending Employment Decisions

Since ADEA is concerned with workers who are over age 40, many unique problems are created that are not found in other antidiscrimination laws. For example, ADEA is the only antidiscrimination law that allows jury trial.[90] Since the average age of people selected to serve on a jury is over 40 years old, and almost all jurors are now or were at one time employees, there isn't much sympathy for the employer. It is also "human" for a judge to sympathize with the older worker since his or her age is usually over 40. The employer has another "built-in head wind" when dealing with the older worker. Due to the length of service, the worker's salary is usually higher than the market price for the same skills, and these skills may decrease with age.[91] When the labor costs have to be reduced, the older worker can be replaced by a younger person, who may be as well qualified, at less cost. The Age Discrimination in Employment Act inhibits management's desire to perpetuate the company by training and promoting younger workers. At one time the older worker could be retired at 70 so at least there was some room to move up the younger worker, but with the age 70 limitation removed, management must now prove poor performance before the older worker can be replaced. This is often difficult to do involving a worker with 30 years of service.

It should be noted that the burden of proof requirement for showing a *prima facie* case is similar to the burden required in other disparate treatment cases. However, a showing of age discrimination does not require that the individual replacing the older worker be younger than 40 years.[92]

Some companies are still using subjective evaluations such as personality traits to measure performance. It is therefore not surprising that age discrimination lawsuits are the second largest type of all antidiscrimination lawsuits filed with the EEOC.[93] Bringing in "new blood" is considered a violation of ADEA when it is accompanied by age-related comments. In *Wilson* v. *Monarch Paper Co.*, 939 F.2d 1138 (5th Cir. 1991), such an action was considered constructive discharge. The court upheld a jury award for punitive damages.

Age as a Factor in Decision Making

The ADEA affects every employment decision where the employee involved is over age 40.[94] To establish a *prima facie* case under ADEA, the employee must show that the job was performed satisfactorily and that he or she was dismissed and replaced by a younger person (not necessarily under age 40).[95] The employer must then show that age was not a contributing factor.[96] Disparate treatment claims under ADEA have been

interpreted identically to claims brought under Title VII.[97] The Court has held that disparate impact theory may be applicable under ADEA, but an employer may defend against such claims by showing that reasonable factors other than age created an apparently disparate impact.[98]

A unanimous United States Supreme Court decision held that an employer does not violate the ADEA by firing an older employee to avoid pension benefits that would have vested by virtue of the employee's years of service. The plaintiff had been employed by Hazen Paper since 1977 as its technical director. In 1986, at the age of 62, and a few weeks before his pension would have been vested, the plaintiff was terminated for doing business with competitors of Hazen Paper. The plaintiff sued Hazen Paper for violating the ADEA and the Employee Retirement Income Security Act of 1974 (ERISA).[99] On his ADEA claim, the plaintiff claimed that age had been a determinative factor in the decision to fire him. A jury rendered a verdict in favor of the plaintiff on his ADEA claim, and specifically found that the company had acted "willfully" so as to be liable for liquidated damages under 29 U.S.C. § 626(b).

The district court, however, granted the company's motion for judgment notwithstanding the verdict as to the finding of willfulness. In upholding ADEA liability, the appeals court considered evidence that Hazen Paper had fired the plaintiff in order to prevent his pension benefits from vesting. The appeals court also reversed the district court's judgment with respect to willfulness, finding sufficient evidence to establish that the company knew that its action violated the ADEA or showed reckless disregard for the matter. However, the United States Supreme Court reversed the appellate court, holding that an employer does not violate the ADEA by interfering with an older employee's pension benefits that would have vested by virtue of the employee's years of service. The court reasoned that the employer's decision was wholly motivated by factors other than age.[100]

Age may be ignored if the employer can demonstrate just cause for discharge. In a case where a 56-year-old repeatedly ignored specific directions of his supervisors, the court held that discharge was not because of age but for insubordination. The inability to satisfactorily perform a particular job and demonstrated lack of competence in performing a job are other factors[101] that could justify a discharge or transfer. However, performance and incompetency determinations are often subjective when age is involved. Therefore, the burden of proof is greater than in traditional misconduct situations where objective facts are more easily obtainable.[102] It is advisable in incompetency situations to have objective measurements of unsatisfactory performance before a decision is made involving an older worker's performance. When an employee is not performing satisfactorily, the company has to either transfer, terminate, or tolerate the unsatisfactory performance. Given the possibility of prevailing in a lawsuit or at least gaining a sizeable settlement, employees may allege age discrimination where none exists.

Jury awards in age discrimination cases can be substantial. In *Wilson* v. *Monarch Paper Co.,* cited earlier, the jury awarded a plaintiff more than $3 million, mostly for pain and intentional infliction of emotional distress for age discrimination. The company reduced the job of a vice-president and assistant to the president to janitor. This precipitous demotion was apparently intended to humiliate the plaintiff. The court noted that age-related comments ("bring in new blood") made about the plaintiff by the defendant's officials and absence of criticism of the work performance caused them to affirm the age discrimination verdict.

When the employer can show that the decision to terminate was not based on age, that termination can be defended.[103] Employer actions do not always create an inference of age discrimination. Assignment of work to younger employees, hiring a younger person to replace an older person, and comments about age by persons in a non-decision-making position are not per se a violation.[104] Evidence that there were attempts to improve performance, and that the plaintiff was warned about unsatisfactory performance, is a strong defense to rebut the employee's contention that the decision was based on age. In *Bohrer* v. *Hanes Corp.,* 715 F.2d 213 (5th Cir. 1985), the plaintiff had been a salesman for 20 years. He was moderately successful in meeting his sales quotas but according to the company was deficient in other aspects of his job. Performance, not age, was the company's justification. The company offered subjective evidence that the employee did not institute merchandising techniques with his customers and would not follow management policy or instructions. The evidence showed that supervision had several meetings with the employee in order to correct the problem. The employee acknowledged the criticisms and expressly resolved to do better, but he didn't. This evidence lent credibility to the subjective evaluation. The employee was terminated and replaced with a 28-year-old person. The jury found for the plaintiff; the employer moved for a judgment notwithstanding the verdict. The lower court granted the employer's motion, and the circuit court, in affirming, stated that there was substantial evidence of poor performance so that if allowed to stand the jury verdict would be miscarriage of justice. The U.S. Supreme Court denied review. This is a good example of a case in which there was evidence of trying to correct the poor performance, age could not have been a factor in terminating, and the jury had no basis for the award. Nonetheless, the employer still likely had substantial legal fees in defending its actions. Sometimes an employer will argue that an older worker was replaced by a younger worker to reduce costs.[105] The courts will consider this as a factor if there would be severe economic consequences by retaining the older worker.[106]

Early Retirement Programs

It is not a violation of ADEA if the employee voluntarily retires.[107] Many companies offer early retirement incentives to employees over 55 years of age and with a specified length of service (10 or more years being the most popular). Early retirement options have even been presented to workers younger than age 55 during economic downturns since early retirement programs avoid layoffs or involuntary terminations. Early retirement plans have gained wide acceptance among employers, and employees also like them. Most employers underestimate the number of employees who will accept the incentives and take early retirement. In making early retirement offers, the employer often faces the loss of skills and management know-how that cannot quickly be replaced.[108] One way to bridge the gap between training new employees and the loss of the old is to make a consulting agreement with early retirees. Consulting agreements are very popular, not only to bridge the gap but also to provide the retiree with additional income while the adjustment is being made from full salary to retirement income.

Employers often try to cap exposure to ADEA lawsuits by the use of waivers and releases.[109] The **Older Workers Benefit Protection Act of 1990 (OWBPA)** was designed, in part, to put to rest the judicial confusion over waivers and releases.[110] Almost all early retirement programs require the employee to sign a waiver or a release.[111] The legal status of a waiver is not identical to that of a release. In a waiver, the employee waives all rights. In a release, the employer is relieved of liability, but no rights are given up. A waiver under ADEA is enforceable in the courts if there is no showing of coercion.

Enforceability is uncertain in the case of a release; it depends on how the release is worded.[112]

Waivers under the Older Workers Benefit Protection Act

The following requirements apply to waivers under the OWBPA:

1. The agreement must be in clear, concise language, signed by the employee.
2. The agreement must clearly state that the employee is waiving all rights under ADEA.
3. The employee has 21 days to decide whether to accept the waiver and one week to rescind after signing.
4. The waiver must state that the employee has consulted an attorney.
5. The employee can waive rights or claims only in exchange for something he or she does not already have.
6. Although not required, there should be evidence of negotiations as to the benefits of retirement.

The Older Workers Benefit Protection Act provides that no waiver agreement may affect the EEOC's rights and responsibilities to enforce ADEA, and an employee may not waive the right to file a complaint under ADEA unless the employer strictly complies with the statute.[113] These requirements are designed to assure the EEOC that the early retirement was "knowingly voluntary." Signing a waiver does not prevent the employee from later filing a charge, although his or her right to recover any damages may have been compromised by signing. When signing a release, the employee is prevented from recovering damages.

The employer must be cautious not to imply any form of coercion when an early retirement plan is accepted by the employee.[114] In one case the employee stated that he would not have signed the agreement had he thought the waiver was enforceable.

The court considered the testimony credible, but enforced the waiver because the employee had consulted an attorney. Any evidence that age is a factor and that retirement was not voluntary would result in an exposure to a lawsuit. An option of early retirement or termination, for whatever reason, could be construed as an involuntary discharge. One court held that the employer was required to pay severance pay to employees who elected early retirement because it was paid to employees discharged as a result of reduction in force. It would be a violation of ADEA to give a smaller amount to those who retire at age 65 than to those who retired early, but not a violation of ADEA if the same amount is given to early retirees.[115] An employer who is convinced that a release or waiver will eliminate all exposure to employment litigation needs a good lawyer. Sometimes a release is more costly to defend than the employment decision at issue.[116]

Lawsuits following the acceptance of voluntary retirement incentives normally result because the retiree alleges that he or she was coerced into accepting these incentives. In other words, the person must claim that the "voluntary" retirement incentives were not, in fact, voluntary. Because of the potential exposure, employers need to be sure that certain conditions are understood and are well documented, for example:

1. Inducements for the employee to retire should be clearly communicated. Some of the most popular early retirement incentives include early vesting of pension benefits, continuation of health care insurance, severance pay above the normal amount, maintaining an employee on a consulting basis, and retraining for a retirement vocation.
2. A frank discussion of the benefits the employee would receive if he or she continued working and retired at a later date should be held. Some negotiation may be helpful.
3. The employees must agree to sign a statement that the early retirement option was absolutely voluntary. This is the key to avoid exposure.

Early retirement can be a useful tool in avoiding age discrimination charges, but it also can cause litigation if not properly administered.[117]

Reductions in Force

One of the areas that has been given particular attention under ADEA is termination as a result of a reduction in force (RIF).[118] There are several reasons for this. Often the older worker's performance has not been objectively evaluated for a long period of time, yet she or he continues to be employed and receives periodic wage increases. However, when a RIF becomes necessary the employer may consider the advantages in having a younger workforce and looks for reasons to reduce the force by terminating the older workers. This practice runs head-on into ADEA. In any RIF program care must be taken to be sure that age is not a factor in selecting the employees to be reduced.[119] Discrimination claims arising from a RIF can be premised on either disparate treatment or disparate impact theories. The premise of a disparate treatment claim is that the reduction in force was simply a subterfuge or pretext for the employer's actual objective to rid itself of certain employees, such as older workers, members of a minority group, women, and so on. The premise of a disparate impact claim is that the RIF, although having a bona fide business rationale and factually-neutral criteria for job elimination, resulted in a disproportionately adverse impact on protected categories of employees. Common to both arguments is the claim that the employees were terminated *because* they were members of a group protected from employment discrimination by state or federal law.

A legitimate RIF is motivated by business considerations. Because these justifications are the employer's best defense in the event terminated workers claim discrimination, it is absolutely essential for the employer to fully explain why it is downsizing, reorganizing, and eliminating jobs. The business rationale should be explicit and well defined. The courts have emphasized that in most reduction-in-force cases the evidence demonstrates that the company had some kind of plan to reduce expenses by eliminating jobs. These plans generally include objective criteria by which to determine which jobs will be eliminated and often include objective evidence of a business decline.[120] In the absence of a "smoking gun" or foolish admissions by corporate managers, statistics are frequently the most powerful, and in some instances the only, evidence supporting the plaintiff's claim of discrimination. One of the most difficult challenges for the employer involving RIFs is demonstrating statistically that the reductions did not have a discriminatory impact.[121] No matter what method a company uses and what review is done by line manager decisions, an analysis that shows the reductions had a discriminatory effect can expose the company to age discrimination collective actions or race and gender class actions. The employer can reduce the exposure associated with selecting employees for RIF through the following strategies:

1. Adopting an objective business criterion
2. Providing supervisory training in the use of that criterion
3. Eliminating any words, such as a code, that might suggest age was a factor
4. Analyzing statistical data of the employees selected for RIF, and having more than one person rate the employees without knowing their age[122]
5. Providing any employee with assistance in job transition
6. Being sensitive, but not apologetic, when informing employees selected for RIF

The selection of the person to be terminated should never be subjective. There must be objective criteria for selection that leaves no doubt that a protected class was not a factor in the selection process.[123] The courts are clear that ADEA is not a guarantee of employment beyond age 40, but "shabby employment practices" often indicate that age might be a factor.[124] When the employer used a supervisor peer committee and a number of rating systems, which were sent to the personnel department and objectively reviewed, and some of the senior older workers were terminated, the court held that the employer had proved the nondiscriminatory basis for its decision.[125]

Severance Pay as an Exposure

Severance pay is often provided to employees who are permanently laid off due to a reduction in force. The principle behind severance pay is that the employee needs temporary financial support until he or she finds another job. When employers apply this principle to older workers, it may be interpreted as age discrimination. Any time decisions are made that will have a disproportionate impact on a protected class of employees, there is an exposure to a lawsuit. This exposure under ADEA has been reduced, at least in the case of unionized workers, by a recent decision of the Supreme Court. Under a long-standing precedent, the court has held that workers covered by a collective agreement that included an arbitration provision were not foreclosed by that provision from filing a claim of discrimination with the EEOC.[126] However, in *14 Penn Plaza LLC* v. *Pyett*, 556 U.S.___ (2009), the court ruled that collective bargaining language that establishes arbitration as the exclusive mechanism for the resolution of disputes waives the right of workers covered by that agreement to sue under Federal antidiscrimination laws. This decision reveals the court's preference for the arbitration of statutory rights in both the union and nonunion sector. The court had previously held that arbitration clauses included in employment contracts were enforceable under the Federal Arbitration Act (FAA).[127]

Punitive Damages

Originally the courts were reluctant to allow punitive damages under the Age Discrimination Employment Act. The CRA91 amendment to the ADEA allows punitive damages under certain conditions, but imposes a cap of $300,000. The ADEA also incorporates the enforcement powers of the Fair Labor Standards Act. In punitive damages requests, the plaintiff is required to prove the violation to be a willful violation. The ADEA allows for the doubling of damages where the court finds a willful violation. In *Trans World Airlines, Inc.* v. *Thurston,* 105 S.Ct. 613 (1985), the U.S. Supreme Court stated that under ADEA, it was willful if the employer either knew or showed reckless disregard for the statute concerning whether its conduct was prohibited by the ADEA. If the employer did not know that the Act was being violated or did not recklessly disregard the ADEA, the action could not be willful.[128]

Punitive damages continue to be difficult to obtain apart from CRA91 if the ruling in *Foley* v. *Interactive Data,* 765 P.2d 373 (Cal. S.Ct. 1988), is followed in other jurisdictions. In *Foley,* the court reversed all previous California decisions and held that in discharge cases damages are limited to contract damages where a breach is shown. If CRA91 applies, this will end the punitive damages issue in ADEA cases. When the jury or the court does not like the way the employer discharges, it may award large punitive damages for the abuse. If CRA91 applies, there will be a cap of $300,000 on punitive damages. If CRA91 doesn't apply, then punitive damages are unlimited.

AVOIDING LITIGATION

Today employers need to be proactive in monitoring for potential discrimination problems and developing practices and policies to avoid the litigation of discrimination complaints. Litigation over employment issues can be extremely expensive and time consuming. A successful plaintiff can recover both damages and legal fees from the employer. In some instances the legal fees can be larger than the damages because legal fees are based on the extent of legal services provided and not on the amount of damages awarded.[129]

Charges to the EEOC, particularly under the ADEA, have been increasing, and the employer must develop positive programs to halt or reverse this trend. One of the most popular methods to prevent litigation of age discrimination claims is the early retirement program. As discussed earlier in this chapter, the key to these programs is to obtain a voluntary decision to retire under OWBPA. Since it is very easy to get into court and allege coercion, the signing must be absolutely voluntary. The employer must show that an analysis was made of selection in a reduction of force or that performance was measured objectively and that factors other than age were used in making a decision. If the employer is not certain that a factor other than age can be defended, an individual agreement to voluntarily retire or a general early retirement program should be considered. If nothing else works, make a deal with the employee. It may not work, but it is worth the effort in most instances. Employer procedures can aid in encouraging retirement. These procedures should be designed to mitigate the impact of retiring and prevent adversity when the employee is faced with a retirement decision.

Probably the most effective practice in avoiding discrimination lawsuits of all types is for the employer to adopt an employment arbitration provision.[130] These provisions waive an employee's right to sue and substitute final and binding arbitration as an alternative dispute resolution mechanism. The courts have been increasingly supportive of these arbitration procedures, particularly in cases involving allegations of age discrimination.[131] Existing employees can be encouraged or incented to sign these provisions, and arbitration clauses can be mandated in agreements with new employees.

The following recommended procedures will aid in preventing exposure to litigation:

1. Objective, written standards of performance for employees in all job categories must be established. The essential functions of the job must be clearly defined.
2. Employment decisions must be based on performance and competence. Performance must be gauged by a fair and accurate performance evaluation that is conducted regularly. Results of this evaluation must be shared with the employee in a timely manner.
3. Termination policies or practices must make it clear that failure to meet the standards of performance is just cause for discharge.
4. Appropriate responses to employee complaints must be made in a timely manner. An individual or entity that is viewed as neutral by employees should be designated to receive and respond to these complaints.

The practice of supporting only job-related training programs backfires when early retirement is encouraged. Educational programs must be expanded in order to provide related skills for the second career or a transfer to other jobs in the organization.[132]

Settlements

Out-of-court settlement is always an alternative when allegations of discriminatory conduct are raised by employees. A high percentage of claims are resolved without trial or alternative hearing. A settlement in a civil rights case is a compromise that is voluntarily agreed on by the parties. Both parties accept a little less than they believe they are entitled to. The incentive to settle is that each party believes that the compromise is more advantageous than taking the risks and costs involved in pursuing the claim. Before either party agrees to enter into a settlement, the disadvantages and advantages should be carefully considered. The courts encourage settlements without consideration of the consequences. It must be shown that the parties have had opportunity to read and understand the contents of the settlement agreement that is usually drafted by a lawyer. If these facts are present, the courts have little sympathy with a person who wants to rescind or modify the settlement.

Prior to approaching a complainant about settlement, the employer should review the following factors:

1. *The problems created by administrative and/or judicial proceedings:* the length of time it takes to get a decision, the necessity for witnesses to testify who later have to work with the employee, the emotional stress for some management members, and the management time to process the case. This is a hidden cost of litigation and is seldom considered.
2. *The chances of prevailing:* This is a judgment factor that should be determined in conjunction with legal counsel, who can only make an educated guess. Some cases that should never be lost *are* lost, and sometimes all the facts point to losing and the case is won. If there are "grey areas" in the law, it becomes more difficult to assess the case.
3. *The out-of-pocket cost of taking the charge through the judicial process:* In discrimination cases, if the employer loses he or she must pay the employee's attorney's fees, which are sometimes more than the damages.[133]

These factors should be considered in the early stages of the case. As the case progresses, these factors become less important, and if the case is settled "on the courtroom steps," most of the economic advantages of settlement are gone.

Considerations concerning out-of-court settlements should contain legal as well as employee consequences. One such consideration is that a settlement does not prevent a retaliation charge if the employee has been reinstated. Therefore, in the settlement negotiations, whether reinstatement is a "must position of the employee" has considerable influence on the decision. The employee will often propose reinstatement along with full back pay, but that is sometimes a starting point for negotiations. To accept would be capitulation.

Consideration must also be given to the impact of the proposed settlement on the manager or supervisor involved. Any monetary settlement implies discrimination regardless of the settlement agreement. With some managers and supervisors, this stigma is difficult to overcome and can create new problems, especially in a gender discrimination case involving married managers. Often a member of management feels that settlement is an admission of guilt. Settlement can cause internal problems, especially when management strongly believes that no discrimination has occurred. Settlement for economic reasons alone is often a mistake, unless management determines that economic reasons override all other considerations.[134]

The effect of lump-sum payment on other employees is also a consideration. It has little effect unless the employee is reinstated. If reinstated, the exposure to adverse employee relations is present, but it does not always have an adverse effect on employee relations. One way to mitigate an adverse effect on employee relations is to prohibit disclosure of the terms in the settlement agreement.

Settling a case where there is little evidence of discrimination is not advisable when consideration is given to the long-range economic and employee relations consequences. In situations where the legal assessment of winning in the courts is assessed at greater than 50 percent, the long-range economic and employee relations benefits may be worth risking a court decision, although the immediate cost may not justify it.

When it appears that both parties want to settle, no final agreement should be reached until a settlement agreement is drafted. The language of the settlement agreement is as important as the agreed-on award. This written agreement should be reviewed by an attorney. When the attorney drafts the agreement, the practitioner should be certain that it contains certain nonmonetary elements, including the following:

1. The charging party or regulatory agency (if involved) should release any and all rights it has to further pursue the case, including participating in a class action. In some cases the parties involved may want to get releases from other possible members of the class.
2. The parties should agree to keep the terms of the settlement confidential.
3. There should be no determination of who is right or wrong.
4. Payment of the claimant's attorney's fees should be agreed on. A settlement agreement does not prevent the prevailing party from later collecting attorney's fees unless there is previous agreement.
5. In regard to conduct after the case is closed, the employer should agree to take steps so the situation will not be repeated. However, nothing should be agreed on that will interfere with the economical operation of the business or that is administratively burdensome.
6. Since retaliation is always a possibility, there should be a clause that states that settlement terms will not prevent the employer from treating the charging party any differently from other employees.

Unreasonable provisions can be prevented by hard negotiations. Usually the parties will agree rather than not settle when there is disagreement over language. It is the amount of the award and demands for reinstatement that often prevent a settlement.

CASE 2.1

Discrimination Exposure

You are the human resources manager at Gopher Products, a company that manufactures and distributes home security products. Gopher employs a regional sales force under the supervision of a vice-president for sales and 12 regional sales managers. Ben Green, a 55-year-old black male is the only minority regional sales manager employed by the company. Green was hired 15 years ago and left another position as sales manager with another company to join Gopher. The company has a nondiscrimination statement and an affirmative action policy in its handbook There is no indication of past discrimination on the part of the company and the company has never had a discrimination complaint or a lawsuit alleging racial discrimination filed against it.

Over the past three years the productivity of Green's sales force has declined markedly each year. Two years ago the company realigned its sales force and replaced half of Green's sales force with a combination of new and experienced salespersons. Last year Green was reassigned to a new region with an existing sales force. Despite these changes, the productivity of Green's sales force has dropped 30 percent over the three-year period. No other regional sales manager has experienced consecutive annual losses during this period and none has seen her or his overall productivity drop more than 5 percent over the same three-year period.

The company has utilized the Minnesota Multiphasic Personality Inventory (MMPI) as an aptitude test to select sales personnel for the past 10 years and has records to show that there has been a high correlation between the MMPI test and sales manager productivity. (The MMPI has predicted high performance.) Green was hired before the test was adopted and has never taken it.

The vice-president for sales has approached you and indicated that he plans to terminate Green for poor performance. He further plans to advance the salesperson with the highest score on the MMPI to Green's position. The five high scorers on the MMPI currently employed in sales by the company are all white males.

What would you advise? What is the relative exposure to a discrimination claim under ADEA and/or Title VII? Specifically, discuss the extent of the company's potential exposure under disparate impact or reverse discrimination decisions by the courts. ■

CASE 2.2

Discrimination in Selection

The ABC University offered an Advanced Technology Internship Program to graduates of a medical technology baccalaureate program. In 2008, the University graduated 77 students and there were five positions available (three full time and two part time) in the internship program. Iris was a 2008 graduate of the University and one of 32 applicants who applied for the Advanced Technology Program. The positions were posted on the University's website with the following qualifications:

Requires a graduate of an accredited medical technology program. Technologist experience preferred.

Organized, efficient, and multifunctional. Ability to work independently. Requires excellent interpersonal skills and demonstrates effective communication. . . .

Candidates were selected to interview based on their job application, school/program attended, prior technologist experience, prior patient care experience, prior application or interview at the medical center, and desire to work at the medical center as demonstrated in their cover letter. Iris was one of 20 applicants interviewed for the five openings. The group of candidates interviewed also included graduates from previous years as well as graduates from other outside programs.

The interview process consisted of a one-hour panel interview with two supervisors and one staff technologist. During the interviews, 10 behavioral interview questions were asked. Each panel member rated the candidates on their own and then discussed with the team to reach a consensus. The factors used to make the final hiring decisions were the candidates' interview ratings and reference information from the University (for the 2008 graduating class only).

Iris was ranked in the top one-third of candidates interviewed by the panel, but was ultimately not selected for any of the five openings. Because Iris was well qualified, the HR representative encouraged her to continue to apply for future technologist positions.

Following her denial, Iris submitted an EEOC claim alleging race and national origin discrimination. The complaint stated:

I applied for a Technologist position with the above named respondent and was informed that I would not be hired for the job on July 29, 2008. I believe I was not offered the position due to my race (black) and national origin (Somalian). My white American classmates who had also participated in the respondent's program were treated preferentially and were hired into the positions. I was told I did not have specific job experience. I do not believe any of my classmates had such experience.

For the three full-time positions, the employer had determined that Iris was not a top candidate, as there were two unanimous top candidates with technologist experience and a strong third-choice candidate. Iris had no technologist experience.

What type of *prima facie* evidence must Iris submit to shift the burden to the employer? How do you anticipate the employer will respond to the EEOC? ■

CASE 2.3

Gender Discrimination

Bob Johnson worked as a canning machine operator at West Coast Fisheries. As part of his job description and assigned duties, Bob was responsible for both operating and making minor repairs to the canning machine. The job required some mechanical ability and significant physical strength and agility because the design of the canning machines regularly required the operator/repairperson to climb 12 to 15 feet on a ladder attached to the machine, carrying tools and materials. The operator then fed sheet metal stacks into the mechanism and/or effected repairs or replaced parts that also had to be hand carried. The job was both arduous and dangerous. Accordingly, it was the highest paid job in the cannery.

Although 90 percent of the cannery production employees were female, all of the six (6) canning machine operator positions were held by men. Only men had worked as canning machine operators since the plant was opened 25 years ago. Promotions at West Coast Fisheries were based both on qualifications and seniority. Qualifications were demonstrated either through formal training or on-the-job experience. The company credited both experience with other employers or temporary performance in the same or similar job with the company. When qualifications were determined by West Coast Fisheries to be equivalent, seniority with the company was the deciding factor in selection.

When Bob announced his anticipated retirement, Joyce Brown approached her supervisor about replacing Bob as a canning machine operator. Joyce was 25 years old, was 5 feet 7 inches tall, and weighed approximately 140 pounds. She had worked at the company for six years as a packer, the lowest paid production job. She told the supervisor that she had grown up on a farm and had experience repairing tractors, combines, and other farm equipment. The supervisor expressed doubt about Joyce's ability to perform the operator's job but said he would let her know when the job was posted.

A few days before Bob retired and the day after the job was posted, the company announced that it had hired Harry Brandt, a laid-off aircraft mechanic, as a canning machine operator to replace Bob. When Joyce went in to apply for the job she was told that Harry had been referred by a local employment agency (the agency had received advance notice of the posting), that he was extremely well qualified, and that the company didn't want to lose an opportunity to hire him. The HR director indicated that Joyce had never demonstrated her ability to perform the work and he felt that the operator's job was too physically taxing and dangerous for a woman.

What exposure does the company have to a discrimination complaint?

How would you expect the company to defend its position?

Is there a bona fide occupational qualification here? Does the fact that a canning machine operator has always been a male job make a difference?

What factors would the EEOC or a state agency consider in evaluating a complaint? ▪

Summary

This chapter discusses the development of antidiscrimination legislation that governs and applies to most employment relationships in the United States. All phases of the employment relationship, from job postings, promotions, layoffs, and discipline, are affected by these statues. The Civil Rights Act of 1991 is significant in that it provides that any decision affecting employment based on race, color, religion, national origin, or gender is unlawful. Other antidiscrimination legislation, including Title VII, ADEA, and ADA, are addressed. Equal employment and affirmative action are addressed briefly, as is harassment in the workplace and the business necessity defense. Finally, tips for employers and managers on how to avoid litigation are presented.

Key Terms

disparate treatment   22
disparate impact   22
Title VII   22
Civil Rights Act of 1991
   (CRA91)   23
Americans with Disabilities
   Act (ADA)   23
Genetic Information
   Nondiscrimination Act
   (GINA)   23

Employee Retirement
   Insurance Security Act of
   1974 (ERISA)   23
Fair Pay Act   23
business necessity   25
Age Discrimination in
   Employment Act
   (ADEA)   26
affirmative action   26
equal employment   32

hostile environment   35
quid pro quo   37
Older Workers Benefit
   Protection Act of 1990
   (OWBPA)   44

Questions for Discussion

1. What is the difference between disparate impact and disparate treatment? Explain how they are similar and different and give an example of each.
2. A 43-year-old male, Mike, applied for a job promotion at a marketing firm, along with four other employees. He is notified that he did not get the job, but his 32-year-old female co-worker, JoAnn, will be promoted. Mike feels he was equally qualified for the job and should have been promoted. Assume you are Mike. What statutes are in place you may be able to apply to this scenario? What are the next steps you will need to take to prove discrimination in the workplace?
3. As an employer, what are steps you can take to avoid discrimination litigation?
4. Are unionized workers covered under antidiscrimination legislation? Are there are differences in how employees in a collective bargaining unit can be treated compared to at-will employees? Explain.

5. What was the impact of the *Griggs* v. *Duke Power Co.*, decision on the employer? What would you be concerned about as an employer or HR professional?

6. You are a new employee at a large corporation and have been put under a lot of pressure lately to impress the boss. At your weekly review meeting, your boss informs you that you are meeting your performance expectations and he hopes you can continue to deliver, despite the heavy workload. At the end of the meeting, your boss invites you out to dinner and a movie Friday night. You let your boss know that are unavailable and feel it would be inappropriate. The next day, your HR representative asks to speak with you about your poor performance. What are your next steps? Have you or your boss violated any laws?

7. In *Connecticut* v. *Teal*, the Supreme Court ruled that even though disparate impact was not shown in the employment decision numbers, an employer may still be found guilty of discrimination. Should this be allowed? What are your concerns as an employer in light of this decision? How can you ensure your employment practices are nondiscriminatory?

8. Explain how severance pay can result in exposing the employer to a discrimination suit.

9. Under what circumstances will the courts award punitive damages in discrimination claims?

10. What is the Older Workers Benefit Protection Act? How does this legislation complicate age discrimination claims?

Notes to Chapter 2

1. It has been argued that Title VII has been hampered by the enduring doctrine of employment-at-will. See J. C. Suk, "Discrimination at will: Job security provisions and Equal Employment Opportunity in conflict," *Stanford Law Review* 60, no. 1 (October 2007): 73–113.

2. Whether the employee is qualified is a factual matter. A court will not force an employer to tolerate a low-level performer: *Lucero* v. *Hart*, 915 F.2d. 1367 (9th Cir. 1990).

3. 42 U.S.C § 1981–83.

4. See Shari Weinman, "Supervisory liability under 42 U.S.C., § 1983: Searching for the deep pocket," 56 Missouri: L. Rev. 1041(1991).

5. Under Americans with Disabilities Act no intent is required, but discrmination has to be shown: *Mayberrey* v. *von Valtier*, 62 N.W.252 D.C. E. Mich. (1994).

6. *Compensatory damages* as used in this text means an actual loss has been suffered. *Punitive damages* (sometimes called *exemplary*) are punishment for outrageous conduct and are given to deter future wrongdoing; they are often in addition to compensatory damages.

7. *Johnson* v. *Railway Agency*, 421 U.S. 454 (1975).

8. Under ADA intent is required.

9. If an employer is not covered by federal law, state or municipal laws fill in the void. Employers should not seek jurisdictional shelter under federal law because it is likely that some other law will cover them.

10. *Desert Palace Inc.* v. *Costa*, 539 U.S. 90 (2003). See also: *United States Postal Service Board of Governors* v. *Aikens*, 460 U.S. 711 (1983).

11. ADEA and Section 1981 cases are not protected: *EEOC* v. *City Colleges of Chicago*, 944 F.2d 339 (7th Cir. 1991).

12. William W. Van Alstyne, "Affirmative action and racial discrimination," in *Foundations of employment discrimination law*, 2nd ed. (New York: Foundation Press (Thompson-West), 2003).

13. *Griggs* v. *Duke Power Co.*, 401 U.S. 424 (1971)

14. For a discussion of the various legal issues concerning employment discrimination see John J. Donohue III, *Foundations of employment discrimination law*, 2nd ed. (New York: Foundation Press (Thompson-West), 2003).

15. *Watson* v. *Ft. Worth Bank and Trust*, 108 S.Ct. 2777 (1988).

16. The court in *Albemarle Paper Co.* v. *Moody*, 422 U.S. 1343 (1975), gave judicial approval to the formula.

17. This was the position of the Reagan and Bush administrations; see also *City of Richmond* v. *J. A. Croson Co.*, 109 S.Ct. 706 (1989).

18. *Ricci* v. *DeStefano*, 129 S.Ct. 2658 (2009).

19. However, see *Rogers* v. *Haley* (M.D. Ala. 2006).

20. *Regents of Univ. of Cal.* v. *Bakke*, 348 U.S. 267 (1986); *Wygant* v. *Jackson Bd. of Education* 476 U.S. 267 (1986); *Firefighters Local Union No. 1784* v. *Stotts et al* 467 U.S. 561 (1984). The *Wygant* and *Stotts* decisions are discussed in Chapter 10.

21. In *International Union UAW* v. *Johnson Controls*, 111 S.Ct. 1196 (1991), the Court held that an EEOC directive is not a BFOQ and that employer action was discriminatory.

22. *Fernandes* v. *Wynn Oil Co.*, 653 F.2d 1275 (9th Cir. 1982).

23. *Texas Department of Community Affairs* v. *Burdine*, 450 U.S. 248 (1981).

24. *Reeves* v. *Sanderson Plumbing Products*, 530 U.S. 133 (2000).

25. *McDonnell Douglas Corp.* v. *Green*, 411 U.S. 792 (1973).

26. *Tagupa* v. *Board of Directors Research Corp.*, U. *of Hawaii*, 633 F.2d 1309 (9th Cir. 1980).

27. Feminist remarks were given great weight by the court in *Price Waterhouse* v. *Hopkins*, 109 S.Ct. 1775 (1989). See also *Sherman* v. *Burke Contracting*, 891 F.2d 1527 (11th Cir. 1990).

28. *EEOC* v. *Ohio Edison*, 1 F.3d 541 (6th Cir. 1993).

29. 42 U.S.C § 2000(e)(3) provides that an employer cannot discriminate against an employee "because he has opposed any practice made an unlawful employment practice by this subchapter or because he has made a charge, testified, assisted, or participated in any manner in an investigation or hearing under this chapter."

30. *Tartaglia* v. *Paine Webber Inc.*, 350 N.J. Super. 142, 794 A.2d 816 (2002). A retaliatory discharge of an at-will employee is a tort action in state courts as contrary to public policy, although other statutory remedies are available: *Tate* v. *Browning-Ferris Inc.*, 833 P.2d 1218 (Okla Sup. Ct. 1992).

31. *Ayoub* v. *Texas A&M University*, 927 F.2d 834 (5th Cir. 1991). Also, in *Alberty* v. *Tyson Foods*, 286 F.2d 1428 (1992), the court found retaliation in a workers' compensation claim.

32. *Berry* v. *Stevinson*, 74 F.3d 980 (10th Cir. 1996).

33. *Robeson* v. *Shell Oil Co.*, 66 FEP Cases (BN) 1284 (1994).

34. The employee is adversely treated when a right is asserted; there does not have to be a statute involved. *Quiroga* v. *Hasbro, Inc.*, 934 F.2d 497 (3rd Cir. 1991), cert. denied.

35. See *EEOC Compliance Manual*, § 1.89, Part III.

36. Labor organizations are specifically covered under the ADEA at 29 U.S.C. §§ 623(c), 630(d), (e).

37. *Steele* v. *Louisville & Nashville Co.*, 323 U.S. 192 (1944).

38. In *Chicago Tribune Co.* v. *NLRB*, 943 F.2d 791 (7th Cir. 1992) the court refused to enforce an NLRB order to bargain with a union that was guilty of racial discrimination.

39. *Emporium Capwell Co. and Western Addition Community Organization* v. *NLRB*, 420 U.S. 50 (1973).

40. *Barnes* v. *Costle*, 561 F.2d 983 (D.C. Cir. 1977). See also *Gerber* v. *Saxon Bus. Prod., Inc.*, 552 F.2d 1032 (4th Cir. 1977).

41. Harassment received its first formal judicial recognition in *Williams* v. *Saxbe*, 413 F.Supp. 654 (D.C. 1976), where the court held that Title VII's prohibition against sex discrimination includes a prohibition against sexual harassment.

42. For the EEOC position on sexual harassment, see "Policy Guidance of Sexual Harassment," Equal Opportunity Commission, 1801 L Street NW, Washington, DC 20507. See also *Goldsmith* v. *Bagley Elevator Co., Inc.*, 11 Cir. OH. 06-14440 – 1/17/00, where a racial slur cost the company $550,000.

43. *Crawford* v. *Medina General Hospital*, 96 F.3d 830 (6th Cir. 1996).

44. *Fox* v. *General Motors Corp.*, 247 F.3d 169 (4th Cir. 2001).

45. Can be based on race, national origin, or religion if it is "sufficiently patterned or pervasive" and directed at employees because of their sex. *Hicks* v. *Gates Rubber Co.*, 833 F.2d at 1416; *McKinney* v. *Dole*, 765 F.2d 1129, 1138, 37 EPD 35,339 (D.C. Cir. 1985).

46. Rules against sexual relations at the workplace are difficult to enforce because they are rarely witnessed.

47. See J. Pollack, "Sexual harassment: Until then it didn't have a name, it just happened," *Women*, 41, no. 11 (1991).

48. EEOC Charge Statistics: Sexual Harassment.

49. See "Policy Guideline on Current Issue of Sexual Harassment," EEOC Policy Statement No. 925.035.

50. In *Shore* v. *Federal Express*, 777 F.2d 1155 (6th Cir. 1985), a female employee was involved in an intimate relationship with a male. The male was promoted to an executive position and, as a supervisor, terminated the female because the relationship interfered with office operations. This was sex discrimination but not harassment, because the conduct did not involve favors and was not continual, and because an unpleasant, sexually unacceptable working environment was not created. Also see *De Cintio* v. *Westchester County Medical Center,* 807 F.2d 304 (2nd Cir. 1986).

51. It is considered rare when a female harasses a male. Less than 10 percent of complaints involve females harassing males.

52. *Wright* v. *Methodist Youth Services,* 511 F.Supp. 307 (I11. 1981); *Joyner* v. *AAA Cooper Transportation,* 597 F.Supp. 537 (Ala. 1983).

53. A *transsexual* is described as an individual who is mentally of one sex but physically of another. 63 ALR3d 1199 (1975).

54. *Sommers* v. *Budget Marketing, Inc.,* 667 F.2d 748 (8th Cir. 1982).

55. *McKinney* v. *Dole,* 765 F.2d 1129 (D.C. Cir. 1985).

56. "Totality of circumstances" can result in unpredictable outcomes.

57. *Burns* v. *McGregor Electric Industries, Inc.,* 955 F.2d 559 (8th Cir. 1992).

58. See *DeCinito* v. *Westchester Medical Center,* 807 F.2d 304 (2d. Cir. 1986), cert. denied (1987), and *Broderick* v. *Ruder,* 685 F.Supp 1269 (D.C. 1988), for different views.

59. *Blaw-Knox Foundry and Mill* v. *NLRB,* 646 F.2d 113 (4th Cir. 1981).

60. *Katx* v. *Dole,* 790 F.2d 251, 255 (4th Cir. 1983).

61. *Steel* v. *Offshore Shipbuilding, Inc.,* 867 F.2d 1311, 1316 (11th Cir. 1989). See also William L. Kandell, "Mixed motives: Sexual harassment and CRA91," *Employee Relations Law Journal,* 17 (Spring 1992).

62. This is still good law, but the CRA91 limitations will apply, unless a different statute is used.

63. This is a landmark case and is duly studied by legal scholars. See "Employer liability under Title VII for sexual harassment after Vinson," *Columbia Law Review,* 87 (1987): 1258; J. Sweeney, "Meritor slaps at competition," *Bankers Monthly,* 105 (July 1988); M. Morlacci, "Sexual harassment and impact of Vinson," *Employee Relations Law Journal* (Winter 1987–1988): 501.

64. Appeal courts hold that such evidence can be used to determine that the activity was unwelcome. Also see *Burne* v. *McGregor Electronics, Inc.,* 989 F.2d 959 (8th Cir. 1989).

65. *Vinson* v. *Taylor,* 753 F.2d 141 (D.C. 1985).

66. See *Heaser* v. *Lerch, Bates & Associates,* 467 N.W.2d 833 (Minn. App. 1991).

67. *Meritor Savings Bank, FSB* v. *Vinson,* 106 S.Ct. 2399, 477 U.S. 57 (1986).

68. In *Burns* v. *McGregor Electric,* 989 F.2d 939 (8th Cir. 1993) the court said, "This is not a case where Burns posed in provocative and suggestive ways at work. Her private life, regardless of how reprehensible it might be, did not provide lawful acquiescence to unwanted sexual advances at her work place by her employer."

69. *Price Waterhouse* v. *Hopkins,* 490 U.S. 228 (1989); *Andrews* v. *City of Philadelphia,* 895 F.2d 1469 (3rd Cir. 1990).

70. See *Robinson* v. *Jacksonville Shipyards,* 760 F.2d 1486 (11th Cir. 1991).

71. See S. Burns, "Evidence of Sexually Hostile Workplace," *New York University Law Review,* 21 (1994–95): 357–431.

72. *Burlington Industries* v. *Ellerth,* 524 U.S. 742 (1998). *Clark County School District* v. *Breeden,* 532 U.S. 268 (2001).

73. *Henson* v. *City of Dundee,* 682 F.2d 897 (11th Cir. 1982).

74. *Staton* v. *Maries County,* 868 F.2d 996 (8th Cir. 1989); *Moylan* v. *Maries County,* 792 F.2d 746 (8th Cir. 1989).

75. *Ellison* v. *Brady,* 924 F.2d 872 (9th Cir. 1991; *Andrews* v *City of Philadelphia,* 895 F.2d 1469, 1482 (3rd Cir. 1990); *Spencer* v. *General Electric Co.,* 894 F.2d 651 (4th Cir. 1990). Other cases in the 6th, 8th, and 11th circuits.

76. For discussion of hostile environment, see C. M. Keon, "Sexual harassment: Criteria for defining hostile environment," *Employee Responsibilities and Rights Journal*

(December 1989); see also L. Reinders, "Comment: A reasonable woman approach to hostile environment sexual harassment," *Washington University Journal of Urban and Contemporary Law,* 41 (1992): 227; Arthur Silbergeld, "Reasonable victim test for judging hostile environment—Sexual harassment cases," *Employment Relations Today* (Summer 1991); William L. Woerner and Sharon Oswald, "Sexual harassment in the workplace: A view through the eyes of the courts," *Labor Law Journal,* 41, no. 11 (November 1990): 86.

77. 29 CFR 16.011 (A).

78. *Rabidue* v. *Osceola Refining Co.,* 107 S.Ct. (1983).

79. *Radtke* v. *Everett,* 471 N.W.2d 666 (Mich. 1991).

80. See Ronald Turner, "Title VII and hostile environment, sexual harassment: Setting the standard of employer liability," *University of Detroit Marcy Law Review,* 71 (1994): 817.

81. CFR § 1604.11(d).

82. The *Meritor* court was unanimous on all other issues but split 5-4 on this issue.

83. A good analysis of the respondent-superior and negligence standard and imputed knowledge is in *Hirschfeld* v. *New Mexico Corrections Dept.,* 916 F.2d 572 (10th Cir. 1990).

84. *Saxton* v. *American Telephone & Telegraph Co.,* 10 F.3d 526 (7th Cir. 1993).

85. 29 U.S.C. § 623(a).

86. 29 U.S.C. §§ 623(d), (e) and (f)2. Public employees were included in ADEA coverage by an amendment to the Fair Labor Standards Act. See *Davidson* v. *Board of Governors of State Colleges and Universities for Western Illinois,* 920 F.2d 441 (7th Cir 1990).

87. J. Podgers, "Age shouldn't matter" *ABA Journal,* 93, (10) (October 2007): 63. See also *EEOC* v. *Liggett & Myers, Inc.,* 29 FEP 1161 (E.D.N.C. 1982).

88. *Stillman's* v. *State of Iowa,* 843 F.2d 276 (8th Cir. 1988). Also see *Hoy* v. *Boy Coirco,* F.2d (7th Cir. 1993).

89. Some courts' view poor work performance as a pretext where poor performance was tolerated for a period of time:

Hagelthorn v. *Kennecott Corp.,* 716 F.2d 76 (2nd Cir. 1983).

90. Under CRA91 certain conditions must be met before jury trial is permitted.

91. In *Bay* v. *Times Mirror Magazines,* 936 F.2d 112 (2nd Cir. 1991), it is not a violation to replace an older worker with a younger if the reasons are economic. However, there still is an exposure.

92. *O'Conner* v. *Consolidated Coin Caterers Corp.,* 517 U.S. 308 (1996).

93. Lieber, L. D. "As the average age of the U.S. workforce increases, age-discrimination verdicts rise," *Employment Relations Today,* 25, no. 1 (April 2007): 105–110.

94. Most state laws prohibit age discrimination. State employees are covered under federal law if not under state law: *Davidson* v. *Board of Governors of State Colleges and Universities for Western Ill.,* 920 F.2d 441 (7th Cir. 1990).

95. *Kristoffel* v. *Hangman Ford Service Co.,* 985 F.2d 364 (7th Cir. 1993); *Visser* v. *Packer Engineering Assoc., Inc.,* 924 F.2d 655 (7th Cir. 1991).

96. *Flynn* v. *Shoneys, Inc.,* 850 S.W.2d 488 (Tenn. App. 1992) affirmed (6th Cir. 1993).

97. *Blair* v. *Filters,* 505 F.3d 517 (2008).

98. *Smith* v. *City of Jackson, Mississippi,* 544 U.S. 228 (2005).

99. *Hazen Paper* v. *Biggins,* 507 U.S. 604 (1993).

100. See also *Gross* v. *FBL Financial Services,* 129 S. Ct. 2343 (2009).

101. See *Shell* v. *Metropolitan Life Insurance,* 391 S.E. 174 (1993).

102. *Hazen Paper Co.* v. *Biggins,* 507 U.S. 604 (1993)

103. *Fowle* v. *C & C Cola,* 868 F.2d 59 (3rd. Cir. 1989).

104. *Frieze* v. *Boatmen's Bank of Beiton,* 950 F.2d 538 (8th Cir. 1991); *Goetz* v. *Farm Credit Services,* 927 F.2d 398 (8th Cir. 1991). Circuit courts are split on this issue.

105. See *O'Connor Consolidated Coin Caterers Group,* 116 Sup.Ct. 1307 (1996) where court held that older person doesn't have to be replaced by a person outside the protected class.

106. The courts are more reluctant to consider overqualification as a factor as opposed to age: *Taggert* v. *Time, Inc.,* 924 F.2d 43 (2nd Cir. 1991).

107. 29 CFR § 1625.9(f).

108. See C. A. Cerami, "Special incentives may appeal to valued employees—A supplement to their retirement plan," *HR Focus,* 68 (November 1991): 17.

109. For a discussion of waivers before CRA91, see Ronald Turner, "Release and waiver of age discrimination in Employment Act rights and claims," *The Labor Lawyer,* 5, no. 4 (Fall 1989): 739; also see B. D. Alsher, "Validity of waiver in discrimination cases," *Labor Law Journal,* 42 (February 1991): 81–92.

110. *Oshea* v. *Commerce Credit Corp.,* 930 F.2d 358 (4th Cir. 1991).

111. For increased use of waivers, see "Use of waivers by large companies offering exit Incentives to employees," U.S. General Accounting Office Study (1989).

112. *Lockheed Corp.* v. *Spink,* 116 S.Ct. 1783 (1996).

113. *Oubre* v. *Entergy Operations Inc.,* 522 U.S. 422 (1998). For a good article on waivers, see Bennet Alsher, "Validity of waivers in discrimination cases," *Labor Law Journal,* 42, no. 2 (February 1991): 81.

114. *Wamsley* v. *Chamlin Refining & Chemicals,* 514 U.S. 1037 (1995).

115. *Harvey Karlener* v. *College of Chicago,* 837 F.2d 314 (7th Cir. 1986).

116. See: A. Silbergeld and P. Cosgrove, "Supreme Court settles conflicting opinions on enforceability of releases of claims under the ADEA," *Employment Relations Today* (Spring 1998): 97–101.

117. For additional reading, see R. S. Stith and W. A. Kohlburn, "Early retirement incentive plans after the passage of Older Workers Protection Act," *St. Louis University Public Law Review,* 11 (1992).

118. The RIF could also be a result of a merger when there are two persons for the same job.

119. If as a result of RIF there is a disparate impact, it is very difficult to defend: *Uffelman* v. *Lonestar Steel Co.,* 863 F.2d 404 (5th Cir. 1989). Also see *Barnes* v. *Gen Corp. Inc.,* 896 F.2d (6th Cir. 1990) and *Rose* v. *Wells Fargo & Co.,* 902 F.2d 841 (9th Cir. 1991).

120. *Hillebrand* v. *M-Tron Industries, Inc.,* 827 F.2d 363 (8th Cir. 1987), cert. denied 488 U.S. 1004 (1989).

121. *King* v. *General Electric,* 906 F.2d 107 (7th Cir. 1992). Also see *Bozemore* v. *Friday,* 106 S.Ct. 3000 (1986).

122. Wage levels should not be used as a basis for a RIF: *Tolan* v. *Levi Strauss & Co.,* 867 F.2d 467 (8th Cir. 1989).

123. The use of the term *overqualified* creates an exposure to a lawsuit: *Taggart* v. *Time, Inc.,* 924 F.2d 43 (2nd Cir. 1991). However, an employer can refuse to place an overqualified person on the grounds it may have a negative effect on performance: *Bay* v. *Times Mirror Magazines,* 936 F.2d 112 (2nd Cir. 1991).

124. If there is a labor union, the employer is not required to bargain over RIF but generally is required to bargain over the effects of the RIF decision: *NLRB* v. *Emsing's Supermarket, Inc.,* 872 F.2d 1279 (7th Cir. 1989).

125. See *Gaworski* v. *ITT Commercial Finance Corp.,* 17 F.3d 1104 (8th Cir. 1994).

126. *Alexander* v. *Gardner-Denver,* 415 U.S. 36 (1974).

127. *Circuit City Stores* v. *Adams,* 532 U.S. 105 (2001). For a further discussion, see H. N. Wheeler, "Unions and the arbitration of statutory rights," *Perspectives on Work.* 14, nos. 1–2 (Summer 2010/Winter 2011): 26–28.

128. See *McLaughlin* v. *Richland Shoe Co.,* 108 S.Ct. 1677 (1988); also see *Biggins* v. *Hazen Paper Co.,* 953 F.2d. 1405 (1st Cir. 1992).

129. M. Schwartz and T. Moayed, "Minimizing the likelihood of employment litigation," *Labor-management relations* (Dubuque, IA: McGraw-Hill/ Dushkin, 2006), pp. 151–514.

130. *Employment arbitration* is the term used to distinguish arbitration agreements that apply generally to all employees, from the term *labor arbitration,* which applies to unionized employees covered by collective bargaining agreements.

131. *Gilmer* v. *Interstate Johnson/ Lane Corporation,* 500 U.S. 20 (1991); *Mitsubishi Motors* v. *Soler Chrysler-Plymouth,* 473 U.S. 614 (1985). However, the Supreme Court held that an employment arbitration agreement was not a bar to an EEOC claim in *EEOC* v. *Waffle House,* 534 U.S. 279 (2002).

132. It is common to give educational financial assistance to employees only for those subjects directly related to their job. If other subjects are desired, the employee often does not receive aid for tuition. This should be changed to include broader subjects in the job area.

133. In *City of Riverside* v. *Rivera*, 106 S.Ct. 2686 (1986), the court upheld attorney fees of $245,000 whereas the plaintiff received $33,350. See also *Malarkey* v. *Texaco, Inc.*, 794 F.Supp. 1248 (S.D. N.Y. 1992).

134. See *Miller* v. *Staats*, (D.C. Cir. 1983).

CHAPTER 3

Fair Employment Practices

CHAPTER OUTLINE

The Law in Selection and Placement

The Selection Process

Testing

Background Investigations

The Selection Audit

Legal Issues after Hiring

The acquisition and effective utilization of personnel is crucial to any organization. People add the energy that the organization needs to reach its desired ends. Both public and private institutions use full-time, part-time, temporary workers, and those who are not employees as staffing to achieve their purpose.[1]

Public and private organizations share common elements in acquiring and assigning personnel, including (1) the study of the work to be done **(job analysis)** and determining the qualifications necessary for acceptable performance; (2) applying standard procedures in order to set a stage of equal treatment of applicants ("a level playing field"); (3) almost identical parameters of law in the performance of these activities; (4) common goals of effective personnel selection and conformance to community **diversity** patterns; and frequently, (5) processes:[2]

- Application forms that provide a similar information base
- Tests to measure likely behaviors and competencies
- Interviews to generate greater detail about background and competencies
- Background investigations to verify impressions
- **Probationary periods** to evaluate performance adequacy

THE LAW IN SELECTION AND PLACEMENT

Hiring and assignment practices are totally circumscribed by laws. Early federal requirements were limited and contained in executive orders applicable primarily to federal employees. Title VII of the Civil Rights Act has since become a significant influence on social justice in the workplace. However, other sources of regulations and employer exposure do exist.

Employers must be aware that states, municipalities and other public entities promulgate fair employment regulations. Management must be knowledgeable of these protective statutes administered by governmental agencies such as a Human Rights Division, Civil Rights Commission, or Fair Employment Practices Department that are peculiar to their locale. These statutes include regulations concerning:

- Marital status (Montana)
- Political affiliation (District of Columbia)
- Sexual orientation (Connecticut)
- Sickle cell anemia (Louisiana)
- Smoking habits off site (Minnesota)
- Genetic information (Arkansas)
- Public Assistance status (North Dakota)
- Height and weight (Michigan)
- Physical appearance (District of Columbia)

The Uniform Guidelines on Employee Selection Procedures (UGESP) under Title VII provide standards for selection procedures (29 CFR Part 1607, 1978). These standards enjoin employers to keep records of selection methods and activity, set forth an "80 percent rule" (described in Chapter 2), and set forth rigid but generally accepted professional validation methodology for use in discrimination cases. Complying with selection guidelines minimizes exposure and slows the process, but it needn't impede effective selection of the best-qualified applicant. The guidelines do not force the employer to select a low-level performer.[3]

Exceptions to the Rule (or Bona Fide Occupational Qualifications)

There are several situations in which employers may legally discriminate in selection. These involve situations in which "religion, sex or national origin is a bona fide occupational qualification reasonably necessary to the normal operation of that...business" (Title VII). Examples include restroom attendants, French chefs, and some positions in religious institutions and the organizations that they operate. Differences in benefits because of the higher cost of older workers, where seniority provisions in labor contracts result in apparent disparity and a mandatory retirement age for airline pilots are also examples. These **BFOQs** do not apply to race or national origin.

Fair Selection Devices

Government enforcement agencies have established principles and guidelines that address personnel selection tools designed to achieve equal opportunity. The focus is on evaluating people against the requirements of the situation—most often this means job demands that are determined through job studies—and not peripheral (illegal) considerations. Each technique used is to be demonstrably effective in predicting success in the assignment. An objective in the Federal **Civil Service** Reform Act pronounces a desire "to achieve a work force from all segments of society."[4] Since the advent of equal opportunity and fair employment practices, employment tests, interviews, application forms, and physical examination practices have all undergone criticism, examination, and improvement to achieve an acceptable level of objectivity. Upon legal challenge, the **construct validity** (worthiness) of any device contributing to a selection decision is subject to statistical validation.

Affirmation Employment Action

Affirmative Action (AA) Programs emphasize aggressive recruiting of minorities and veterans to encourage their improved representation at all levels of the workforce. The programs were initiated through executive order, first by Franklin Roosevelt in 1941 and later expanded by executive order

11246 (Lyndon Johnson) in 1965. This order declared that aggressive selection efforts were required by employers that desired to contract with the federal government. In the interest of social equity, a number of private-sector firms have also initiated these plans. Because of record keeping, some firms simply choose to avoid government contracts.

The objective of **affirmative action** programs is accomplished if there is improvement in hiring, training, and promoting minorities or females in those job categories that show underutilization of the protected class and progress toward community diversity patterns. Executive order 11246 and other positive action statutes do not require the employer to hire an applicant who is not the best qualified. Rather, the courts require the employer to make a good faith effort to find and hire qualified applicants who are members of the protected classes. Affirmative action does not demand that underrepresentation of a group be corrected immediately. Rather, the contractor/employer must establish placement goals and demonstrate a good faith effort to improve the number of the protected class that is underrepresented in a particular job category. Due to their acceptance of federal funding, virtually all public employment entities have adopted affirmative action plans.

Affirmative Action for Veterans

As is appropriate, veterans of the Armed Forces of the United States are granted affirmative employment consideration by federal and state governments. Special benefits have been added for veterans of particular conflicts. The military obligation or service of an applicant or employee in federal and state governments is an important consideration. This obligation typically involves veterans' preference action by adding points to entrance test scores and other **accommodations,** especially for disabled veterans.

Federal obligations for veterans are primarily found in 41 CFR 60-250.44. The accommodations are limited in terms of the hierarchical level, the jobs to which credit apply, the military rank of the veteran, and the exclusion of Military Reserve personnel. The reemployment rights of veterans and the benefit plan implications are addressed in a later chapter.

Private-Sector Affirmative Action

The automatic affirmative action requirements of government represent a clear distinction between public and private personnel priorities and procedures. In the private sector, employers must be sure to disregard any Reserve or National Guard military obligations in selection because of the civil rights prohibition against discrimination because of past, current, or future military obligations. Disabled veterans also receive accommodation in the private sector under the Disability Act.

The primary motivation for affirmative action in the private sector is the attraction of government contracts.[5] To be eligible, the employer must adopt an affirmative action program to employ and promote members of the protected class.[6] Although it can be difficult to explain to the sales manager why a government contract was lost due to failure to adopt an affirmative action program, such programs are neither a significant cost consideration nor difficult to institute.

Basic Elements of an Affirmative Action Plan

An affirmative action plan has six basic elements:

1. An Equal Employment Opportunity Policy Statement [41 CFR §§ 60-2.13(b) and 60-2.20]. This is usually a statement from the CEO.
2. Procedures for internal and external dissemination of the policy [41CFR § 60-2.13(b) and 60-2.21]. This element includes large customers and employee groups as well as all employees.

3. Specific allocation of responsibilities for implementation of the plan. See 41 CFR § 60-2.13© for details. It is advisable to include a job description of the person assigned.
4. A workforce analysis of all job titles [41 CFR § 60-2.11(a)].
5. Plan of action [41 CFR § 60-2.13(f) and 60-2.24]. Action steps are specified to overcome any identified problem areas or to show improvement.
6. Internal audit and reporting system [42 CFR § 60-2.13(g) and 60-2.25]. This records what has been accomplished.

It has been judicially determined that the labor market for goal setting is defined as an area where the employer has recruited in the past.[7] However, new recruiting areas should be considered if the old method is not obtaining results. The implementation of an affirmative action program to increase minority job opportunities meets the requirements of Title VII in the recruitment and selection process. A good affirmative action program is part of the employer's defense if a charge is filed for discrimination in hiring. A review of Supreme Court decisions suggests that, in the private sector, affirmative action programs must be remedial and cannot increase the employment participation of one group at the expense of others.[8]

Supreme Court decisions applicable to the public sector appear to allow affirmative action plans to increase participation without proof of past discrimination. However, the action cannot contravene the expectation of competing persons.[9] A compelling interest must be shown.

Reverse Discrimination

Exposure to reverse discrimination charges is often created when the employer wishes to reduce the workforce, make temporary layoffs, or promote, and still comply with an existing affirmative action plan. Over the years, the Supreme Court justices have had difficulty in agreeing how this should be done. In most of the decisions relating to the problem of reverse discrimination and correcting past discrimination by affirmative action, the Court has been widely split.[10]

Affirmative Action in Selection

Where college admissions favored blacks over whites in *Regents of the University of California* v. *Bakke*, 438 U.S. 265 (1978), the Court, by a 5-4 vote, held that this program violated Title VII and the equal protection clause of the Fourteenth Amendment because it favored one class over another. The court considered the students to be in the private sector and struck down the affirmative action plan. However, in *Grutter* v. *Bollinger*, 539 U.S. 306 (2003), the Court upheld a University of Michigan Law School admissions program that considered race as a factor in admissions. This decision suggests that race may be used as a factor to include an underrepresented minority group but not as a factor to exclude that group.

Curiously, again by a 5-4 majority, the same Court that decided *Bakke* in 1978 approved a program that reserved 50 percent of all openings in a maintenance department for black applicants in 1979. The minority applicants had less seniority but were selected over the white applicants. The court in *Kaiser Aluminum and Chemical Corporation* v. *Weber* said this affirmative action program did not violate Title VII.[11] The court reasoned that since it was agreed on by the employees' union, the program was only temporary until racial balance was achieved. The whites were given the same opportunity as the blacks to compete for 50 percent of the job openings. Therefore, the program was not in violation. The courts in subsequent cases allowed past discrimination to be corrected by affirmative action if the conditions in *Weber* were present; otherwise they would revert and find reverse discrimination.[12] See

Chapter 10 for a discussion of affirmative action problems in staff reductions.

Case law, in summary, holds that unless there was a judicial determination that past discrimination existed and the court ordered a remedy, an affirmative action plan could not favor one class over another. Courts strike down affirmative action plans that favor one class over another in hiring, layoff, and promotion as being a violation of the Fourteenth Amendment and Title VII unless a federal government program is involved. An exception would be if the conditions existed as found in *Weber*.[13]

The Compliance Review

Compliance reviews are likely to be required if an employer is a government contractor receiving $10,000 or more annually in federal funds. The compliance review will determine adequacy and implementation of an affirmative action policy. If, in the opinion of the compliance officer, the program is not effective, then recommendations are made to change it. The employer can refuse the changes, and the compliance review officer can recommend cancellation of an existing contract or bar future contracts. The final decision is made by the Office of Federal Contract Compliance (OFCC), subject to judicial review.

To avoid a dispute over the affirmative action program, the employer, after receiving notice from the review agency, should make preparation for the compliance review. Proper preparation will enable the review officer to obtain all the pertinent facts about the program in the shortest time.[14] It will also demonstrate an attitude of cooperation. Records such as applicant flow data, hiring records, and EEO report and number of vacancies, promotions, and demotions should be readily available.[15] Employees are often interviewed, so it is advisable to have representative candidates available if requested by the compliance officer. The employer should be prepared to give a business reason for underutilized categories and other implications of discrimination or lack of good faith effort. Cooperation with the compliance officer is advisable, but it should not extend to those areas where the employer feels the compliance officer is on a fishing expedition. It may be an unreasonable burden to keep or supply irrelevant records.

THE SELECTION PROCESS

Selection decisions apply to all personnel (discernment) transactions, but most of the discussion about legal compliance arises in hiring decisions. Contemporary management education should include the understanding that regulations apply to training, pay, and other decisions beyond selection. Another key point is that any tool used in discriminating among employees for opportunities must be clearly job related and objectively applied. Furthermore, the end result of the selection processes should be expected to evidence a diverse result in terms of age, gender, religion, and so on. If not, the employer should determine the cause rather than leaving it to the determination of a government compliance officer. Failure to be proactive in this area can result in litigation and substantial legal defense fees.

Public-Sector Practices

In federal and many other public organizations, selection is based on the principle of *merit*, referring to fair selection procedures, objectively applied. For example, job studies that determine job content and necessary personnel qualifications are routinely well documented in the public sector. By comparison, in the private sector, where the majority of employers have fewer than 100 people (and no human resources specialist), job analysis is usually informal and exists only in the minds of individual managers. This will invariably result in exposure.

Multiple Public Systems

The federal government has scores of agencies, some of which use centralized recruiting and evaluation of applicants through the Office of Personnel Management. This central system is applied to make use of selection expertise, to develop a bank (registry) of qualified applicants, and to avoid the possibility of political bias.[16] Some units—such as Homeland Security, the Foreign Service, and the Department of Defense—have internal personnel service units. Many states have patterned their personnel selection practices after those of the federal government. Other states have adopted some private-sector characteristics with more responsibility given to the department head.[17] Many municipalities, because of the influence of local business, have patterned their operating style after the private sector. If one considers the collection of differences among federal government agencies, our 50 states, more than 3,000 counties (some larger than a few states), 13,000 school districts, and over 19,000 municipalities (defined by the Census Bureau as "political subdivisions...to provide general local government"), the mix of policies and proceedings in the public sector is overwhelming. An educated speculation is that among the total of public organizations, one-third continue to control the employment choice through a central personnel office, one-third resemble the private sector, and another third have elements of both styles.[18]

Anticipating Personnel Needs

Large public employers and some private-sector firms with seasonal labor demands commonly plan and pre-screen to create a pool of available human resources. The **applicant pool** is a technique by which the employment manager attempts to identify available qualified candidates to fill future vacancies. It is developed by predicting job vacancies in the next employment period by job categories. After determining the need or size of the pool, the employment manager recruits and selects the best-qualified applicants for that job category. When all the candidates have been selected for the anticipated vacancies, recruiting and selection stops until placements are made from those in the applicant pool. In selecting candidates for the applicant pool, those selected are told that when a vacancy occurs, they will be hired; if they are not available when a vacancy occurs, other candidates in the pool will be selected according to their qualifications and the order in which they were accepted into the pool or by other, nondiscriminatory standards.

The courts may require hiring to correct discriminatory practices. A job offer that is refused is the same as a hire in terms of satisfying the judicial requirements.[19] This concept was reinforced by the Supreme Court, where it held that a job offer after refusal to hire stops liability, even though retroactive seniority of six years was not included in the job offer.[20] In view of this rule, one criticism of the applicant pool is eliminated—that is, once someone is placed in the pool, the best qualified may not be available when the vacancy occurs and the underutilized category is not filled. Whether the vacancy is filled or not, so long as the offer is made, a good faith effort has been made to correct the underutilization.

The applicant pool can reduce exposure to affirmative action vulnerability and still allow the employer to hire the best-qualified applicant. When an employer established an applicant pool that had a height requirement, the court found that the pool was not representative because if failed to include qualified persons from all classes.[21]

Groundwork for Hiring

Title VII requires that the evaluation of the applicant must be objective. The practice of selecting candidates by the instincts of supervisor prejudices—often based on a single experience—or other subjective **criteria** will not withstand judicial scrutiny. Indeed, it is doubtful whether subjective methods were ever effective in selecting the best-qualified person. For example, one of the authors knew a supervisor who would not accept applicants who were too rotund because he believed that they were all lazy! The day of the supervisor who believes that he or she can determine the physical strength of an applicant by simple observation is over. As one court said, an "eyeball test" is not valid for determining the strength of an applicant.[22]

To hire qualified applicants within the laws, it is necessary to establish appropriate job and personnel qualifications. Prior to antidiscrimination laws, employers were not required to establish written qualifications, and rarely did.

A *job analysis* is the study of the content of a position. It constitutes the basis for selection and inquiries regarding applicant knowledge and skill. A variety of inputs are normally used to maximize accuracy and completeness. An incumbent of the job might complete a questionnaire, supervisors are interviewed, and the job is observed. Other sources may be used in the pursuit of task identification, responsibility, and demands. The study also helps determine if the position should be subject to overtime (premium) pay. There are no laws requiring job analysis studies or job descriptions. However, knowing job content and conditions is the foundation for objective selection decisions. The discernment of peripheral matters from the **essential job functions** is required by the Americans with Disabilities Act along with identified qualifications for the job as evidence of job-related selection decisions.

The EEOC has indicated that employers *should* "identify the work behavior which…the [selection] procedure is intended to sample or measure." Public-sector employers typically distinguish themselves by being very thorough in this work and drafting the resulting job descriptions.

Job Descriptions

Descriptions are derived from the job analysis and record the duties and expectations for a particular position. They present a picture of why the job exists, under what conditions, and the work it involves. Job descriptions can range from a comprehensive identification of job responsibilities and tasks to a simple job advertisement. In the interest of preventive action, job descriptions should note essential functions (specified in the ADA) and necessary qualifications.Job descriptions may become subject to judicial review. They can be valuable exhibits in EEOC hearings or disputes under the Fair Labor Standards Act.[23] However, they can be damaging to the employer when they have been "massaged" to justify pay or promotion decisions.

An audit of the current job analysis and job descriptions may disclose that any resemblance between what the employee is actually doing and what the job analysis or job description states is purely coincidental. Actual observance of job content for purposes of job analysis and job descriptions is necessary if they are to be used as a basis for employment decisions. Considerations in writing should address the following questions:

Are any listed physical requirements valid?

Do the employees currently doing the job demonstrate the skills and education stipulated?

Is the job description written in simple and understandable language?

An understanding of actual, factual job content provides a firm foundation for employment action.

Recruiting Applicants

The purpose of advertising and recruiting is to generate responses from qualified job applicants. A narrow broadcast of job opportunities can be problematic; therefore, opportunities should be broadcast widely.[24] Although Internet advertising is cheap, media other than the Internet must be used because the Internet audience may exclude older and economically disadvantaged individuals.[25] To ensure that government contractors are providing equal opportunity to qualified individuals, the OFCC monitors and reviews online application systems.[26] The language used may also be perceived as limiting opportunity. Ads seeking "students" (age) and "bus boys" (gender) are ill designed. Restrictive language also limits the response that advertisements are intended to generate.[27]

Another common advertising method is word-of-mouth (sometimes called an *informal contact* or *employee referral*). Many employment managers rightfully believe this to be the best source of qualified applicants for many situations. Courts closely examine this procedure because experience indicates the one worker will rarely refer another of a different race, nationality, religion, and so on. As a result, a "built-in headwind" limits the hiring of minorities if this is the sole source of applicants.[28] If the employee referral approach to recruiting is accompanied by an affirmative action program to encourage minorities and females to apply, the recruiting package might be acceptable to the courts.[29]

An affirmative action program to encourage minorities and females to apply *actively seeks* applicants from such sources as the state employment service, Urban League, minority-oriented media, local Hispanic organizations, women's organizations, and schools with large minority populations. Internal job postings serve to broadcast vacancies among present employees, as shown in Exhibit 3.1.

Position Opportunities Announcement

SUPERVISOR   PAY CLASSIFICATION

DATE OF ANNOUNCEMENT   REMOVAL DATE

REQUIREMENTS

DUTIES

IF YOU WISH TO BE CONSIDERED FOR THIS POSITION, PLEASE CONTACT

JOB TITLE   DIVISION

EXHIBIT 3.1 Sample Internal Job Notice

If the employer chooses single-source recruitment, the procedure will probably not be questioned unless the workforce has a statistical imbalance.[30] The traditional methods of recruiting should not be eliminated because of antidiscrimination laws; the same resources should be used for broadcasting to protected classes as used for other applicants. However, the employer should be alert to limited advertising leading to **disparate impact**. If several sources are used, a disparate impact is less likely.

Private employers often accept résumés in selection. Any undesirable information, such as "religious association" must be redacted immediately. Before any interview, a standard application form should be used in keeping with uniform and consistent practices.

The Issue of Inquiries

Many state statutes, Title VII, and the Age Discrimination in Employment Act prohibit the use of certain questions on the application form and prior to a conditional job offer. The practice of postponing certain questions is reasonable. Why should the employer care about anything else if the applicant does not have the skills to perform the job? This procedure avoids exposure to a challenge by the regulatory agencies. Information useful before a job offer is to be made will not be challenged. An example of this information is shown in Exhibit 3.2.

Possible questions following a conditional offer appear in Exhibit 3.3. The questions to be included would depend on the

---

1. Name, address, telephone number.
2. Are you eligible to be employed in the United States? (Proof of immigration status will be required upon employment.)
3. Are you at least 18 years of age?[31]
4. Previous employment. (Previous 10 years is long enough.)
5. Highest wages on previous job.
6. Previous training or experience related to present known job vacancies.
7. How many days of absence from work the previous year for reasons other than medical?
8. Availability to work: full time, shifts, reasonable overtime, part time, or temporary.
9. Methods of contacting previous employer as to skills or knowledge used in former jobs.
10. If laid off from previous job, is recall a possibility?

EXHIBIT 3.2   Standard Application Form Information

---

1. How long have you lived at present address?[32]
2. Have you had any major illness (treated or untreated) in the last 10 years?
3. Do you have an automobile?
4. Who can we call in case of emergency?
5. Do you have any military obligations?
6. Have you ever been injured on the job?

EXHIBIT 3.3   Appropriate Questions Following a Conditional Offer of Employment

---

DISCLAIMER/UNDERSTANDING NOTICE

I agree that my employment can be terminated, with or without cause, and with or without notice, at any time, at the option of either the organization or myself. This is not a contract of employment. Any oral or written statements to the contrary are disavowed and not to be relied on.

Signature ———————————————   Date ———————————————

WE ARE AN EQUAL OPPORTUNITY EMPLOYER

EXHIBIT 3.4   Sample Employment-at-Will Disclaimer

vacancies under consideration and whether the information is necessary to determine that the applicant is suitable for the vacancies available. To help protect the employer from exposure to lawsuits, the application form should desirably have a *prominent* closing section signed by the employer and applicant that may include certain qualifying questions and should include **disclaimers**[33] (see Exhibit 3.4).

The following disclaimers might also be added:

1. A statement by the employer that the information requested is necessary to determine the best-qualified candidates and will not in any way be used for discriminatory purposes
2. An authorization by the applicant that background can be investigated to reach any employment decision
3. A statement that the applicant understands and agrees, if employed, to abide by all reasonable rules and policies of the employer
4. A statement that if the applicant is employed, this employment relationship is at will and may be terminated at any time by either party with or without cause. (This clause is optional, but enforceable)[34]
5. The applicant's agreement that, in the event of employment, and at all times thereafter, any false or misleading statements, written or oral, are cause for discipline up to and including discharge.

Belated Discoveries

Learning unacceptable things about an employee too late (after the hire) can occur when reference information is delayed. In *McKennon* v. *Nashville Banner*, 66 FEP 1192 (1995), a unanimous Supreme Court held that after-acquired evidence that would have justified a termination nonetheless will not act as a bar to bringing a discrimination claim. The court noted that the purpose of discrimination law is to force employers to examine the motives for their actions and to penalize them if they acted illegally. The court also held that after-acquired evidence of wrongdoing could not simply be ignored, thus not allowing reinstatement because of plaintiff's now-revealed misconduct.

At least four circuit courts have held that after-acquired evidence of prior employee misdeeds, such as false statement on résumés, automatically bars employment discrimination claims. The misdeeds are often uncovered during the discovery phase of job bias litigation. Two other circuit courts have ruled that after-acquired evidence does not shield an employer from liability for discrimination but may limit the relief available. In an Age Discrimination in Employment Act case, one court ruled that employees cannot be denied all relief under the antidiscrimination laws just because the employer discovers prior wrongdoing by the employee that would justify termination. Of some solace to employers, however, the court limited the remedies available in such instances.

Some circuit courts have ruled that if the defendant employer could establish that the plaintiff would not have been hired if the false information was known, dismissal is appropriate. In those cases, established recovery was barred. This is consistent with the Supreme Court expectation that the defendant must establish that the after-acquired evidence standing alone would not result in an adverse decision.[35]

The Supreme Court in the *McKennon* case (66 FEP 1192 (1995)) adopted the tenth circuit position that held in *Summers* v. *State Farm Mutual Automobile Insurance*, 864 F.2d 700 (CA 10, 1988), that after-acquired evidence would not bar a wrongful discharge suit, but would preclude any relief or remedy. The sixth and seventh circuits followed this rule, whereas other courts have held that it does not bar the lawsuit and after-acquired evidence should be taken into consideration when crafting a remedy. The *Summers* court and other circuits held there is no remedy. The Supreme Court adopted the *Summers* rule, which is now the rule in all courts. The *McKennon* case was brought under ADEA, but the court has also ruled that this rule also applies in Title VII and **Equal Pay Act** cases.[36]

The court will almost always support a discharge for falsifying information when applying for work. In *Johnson* v. *Honeywell Systems*, 955 F.2d 409 (6th Cir. 1992), the court upheld a discharge where the misrepresentation was unknown at the time of discharge. The misrepresentation was found during discovery in preparing for a wrongful discharge suit.

The Weighted Application Form

One of the problems that employers have with regulatory agencies is that the application form has questions that are not always job related. When asked why a question is on the form, employers cannot give a business-related answer. One way to be sure the application form is not discriminatory is to use a technique called the **Weighted Application Blank (WAB)** to establish the validity of the information requested. This is a technique that for many years was used to control turnover in the selection of job applicants by analyzing personal history factors that were found predictive. The WAB is more accurately defined as a structured method for determining which characteristics and other variables found in a job applicant are important for success in certain specified jobs.[37]

The concept on which this method was developed is that certain quantitative and objective information is found about each applicant that can predict behavior for a particular job category. For many years, employment managers and supervisors have subjectively determined that a certain type of person will or will not succeed in a certain job. For example, a supervisor believed that all persons from Wisconsin are lazy. Such judgments were usually based on unfounded beliefs that employees who lived far away, had high wages on previous jobs, did not have a car, were divorced, or either quit or were discharged from their previous job were all likely to be short-term employees. The WAB can establish a profile by the use of statistical techniques and analysis that with some degree of accuracy predicts whether certain factors have any influence on job tenure.[38]

Exhibit 3.5 shows some of these factors. The data are taken from a sample of employees on the payroll for a period of three months or less and from another group of employees with one or more years of service. The purpose of this study was to control turnover in the unskilled and semiskilled job categories.[39]

The original list of factors was based on the opinions of the employment manager and over 30 supervisors on what characteristics determine the ideal employee. Of 16 original factors, only 9 were found to differentiate between active groups and rejected groups. This outcome is illustrative of what regulatory agencies are referring to when they insist that a question on the application form have

---

The following factors were utilized in a weighted application blank survey:

1. Commit at time of hire (Y or N)
2. Age hired
3. Weight
4. Height
5. Marital status
6. Number of children
7. Friends or relatives employed here (Y or N)
8. Point of recruiting contact
9. Prior job injury
10. Ten Years of military service
11. Education
12. Duration of last job
13. Number of jobs in last three years
14. Reasons for leaving last job
15. Wage level before hire
16. Type of work on last job

The factors numbered 2, 4, 6, 9, 10, 14, and 16 were discarded because they did not differentiate between the active group and the rejected group.

EXHIBIT 3.5   Factors Utilized in a WAB Survey

The ideal employee had the following characteristics:

1. Is from labor market area within about 20 miles
2. Weighs between 151 and 170 pounds
3. Is married
4. Has friends or relatives who work here
5. Was a walk-in
6. Has education of eight years or more or is a high school graduate
7. Last job was 12 to 23 months in duration
8. Had one to two jobs in the last three years
9. Wages before hire were less than or equal to employer's starting rate.

EXHIBIT 3.6   Ideal Employee Characteristics

a business purpose rather than reflect subjective thinking of the employer. Exhibit 3.6 shows the characteristics of an ideal employee for the department under study.

The Weighted Application Blank as Defense to Questions Asked

The WAB replaces the possible subjective interviewer's biases, which are often barriers in the selection and promotion of the protected classes. It is certainly more defensible in showing nondiscriminatory reasons than the less objective measures used by many interviewers. Like any other selection device, it should first be determined whether the WAB has any adverse impact in the selection of protected classes; if so, then the method used to develop it should be changed or modified for validation purposes. The experience of those who use WAB has been that there is no disparate impact provided that the characteristics used and sample come from all classes of employees.

If the present workforce that is used as a sample has a statistical imbalance, then the WAB would probably be challenged as perpetuating discrimination. The WAB also serves to establish reasons for asking certain questions in the interview that have been found to be predictive of tenure and success on the job. Affirmative action compliance offices and EEOC have consistently stated that there must be a legitimate purpose for asking questions in the interview. Questions to determine characteristics used to score the WAB would have a legitimate nondiscriminatory purpose.

The WAB should be used in the initial screening interview; if the applicant fails at this step of the process, further interviews would not be necessary. This would eliminate the opportunity for supervisor and manager bias at the second level of the hiring process. Selection decision makers should be monitored to ensure their conduct reflects no bias. Each step of the processes should demonstrably contribute to desirable results. The diversity of the workforce, applicants, and new hours should evidence a valid system. If there is no disparate impact in the selection process, auditing can be very brief. It is only when there is a disparate impact that a step-by-step analysis is necessary. An analysis would start with the recruiting efforts to find qualified candidates, followed by the various stages of the selection process. Then a determination should be made of whether the entire procedure results in a disparate impact on members of the protected class.

Interviewing

Personal discussions with applicants help to fill in information gaps, determine personal and communication attributes, and answer questions. The impression each party makes on the other can quell or stimulate subsequent

legal action. A receptionist, or whoever greets people, should be trained on how to treat the disabled, acquire an application form from someone who has sent a résumé, and provide a friendly reception. Anyone who interviews job candidates should be trained to use a pattern of questions to achieve standard consideration and to avoid wayward "off the cuff" remarks about "overly qualified" or questions about an accent or name derivation.

An interviewer may use any job-related questions, but there are some questions that are ill advised and others that are foolish. For example, questions about family, finances, and health are out of bounds. Public organizations normally have a preplanned interview and will apply it in a suitably consistent and uniform manner. In many cases, the interview questions are considered to be a verbal test of the applicant. Private-sector interviews with a greater degree of risk are often less disciplined.

An interviewer can get answers by asking questions in different ways. For example, in most states and under the Americans with Disabilities Act, it is illegal to ask whether a person ever made a workers' compensation claim. There would be no problem in asking, after the job offer is made, whether the applicant is physically *capable of performing the job-related functions of the vacancy.* If in doubt, the employer can require a physical. The job offer would be conditional on passing the physical.

TESTING

Tests in a variety of forms are principal tools in selection decisions. This is particularly true in the public sector where early Civil Service procedure tests were relied on to achieve "merit" rather than patronage in appointments.[40] Some intelligence, aptitude, clerical, numerical, and performance tests can often be of value if the employee's background doesn't provide that input. However, personality or social style tests that normally have only a tangential relationship to success or failure on the job must be tested for some degree of validity before they are administered. In *Karraker* v. *Rent-a-Center, Inc.*, the popular Minnesota Multiphasic Personnel Inventory test (MMPI), originally intended as a clinical tool, was determined to be a *medical examination.*[41]

Polygraph Tests

A major cause of property loss/theft may be related to the use of drugs. The use of polygraph tests and other forms of honesty detectors is therefore considered to be one way to reduce these losses.[42] This may or may not be an effective loss control tool but it does involve a certain degree of exposure. Applicants who seek jobs for the opportunity to embezzle, steal, sell company secrets to competitors, or commit other dishonest acts are difficult to detect. When dishonest acts by employees are not discovered and punished, dishonesty becomes more widespread.

For many years, the use of a lie detector test has been an available—but controversial—method of detecting dishonesty. Polygraph testing and its limitations under the Employee Polygraph Protection Act of 1988 are discussed later in Chapter 12. Most employers have determined that polygraph tests create more problems than they potentially resolve.

Recommended Practices

When it becomes necessary to obtain evidence about the suspected dishonesty of an employee, the first consideration must be what techniques are allowed by federal and state laws. Some states restrict the use of electronic devices in varying degrees, whereas others have no restrictions. Both the polygraph test and search are means of obtaining evidence to determine guilt or innocence. If it is permitted by state and federal law, there is no reason why the polygraph test cannot be used. Not only is it a

method of obtaining evidence, but also exposure of employees to the test may have a chilling effect on employee dishonesty. The human resources practitioner can always consider the possible effects of the use of the polygraph on employee relations. An atmosphere of unwarranted suspicion may cause more harm than the test results can cure; refusal is not an admission of guilt.

In some federal agencies, central testing of applicants refers to the top three scorers ("the rule of three") for a selection by agency management. A "rule of four" (or five) referral is still common in states, counties, and municipalities.

Job-Related Testing

Antidiscrimination laws do not prohibit the use of all tests[43] in the selection process, but they do limit their use.[44] Some private employers feel that the requirement of validation and the risk of being in violation are too great compared to the predictability provided by a test. For this reason, many small employers choose not to use the test as a selection tool, or, if they do, the scores are a very small part of the decision-making process.

Judicial requirements for valid testing can be found in the leading and most-quoted case in antidiscrimination law, *Griggs* v. *Duke Power Co.*, 401 U.S. 424, decided by the Supreme Court in 1971. The selection test used by Duke Power Company to qualify for a training opportunity was the Purdue Vocational Test Form B for initial testing, and Form A for retesting purposes. The time limits were disregarded. It was considered a work test. Applicants protected by Title VII were affected adversely, as shown in Exhibit 3.7.

Notice that 52 of the Caucasians tested were enrolled in a training program, but only 13 African Americans and 5 Hispanic Americans were enrolled. The *Griggs* case contributed to the following principles in pre-employment testing:

Number Tested	Mean Score	Race	Enrolled in Training
108	38.75	Caucasian	52
41	24.92	Negro[45]	13
1	-	Oriental	1
1	-	American Indian	0
14	29.53	Spanish American	5

EXHIBIT 3.7   Troubled Selection Test results

Source: Court records, *Griggs* v. *Duke Power,* 401 U.S. 424 (1971).

1. A test must be job related. If verbal ability is not required to perform functions of the job, one should not test for it.
2. An employer's intent not to discriminate is irrelevant. This is applicable only to Title VII and CRA91; other statutes require intent.
3. If a practice (e.g., training school in the *Griggs* case) is fair in form but discriminatory in participation, it is in violation.
4. The defense for any existing program that has adverse impact is *business necessity.* Business necessity was not defined by the court.
5. Title VII does not forbid testing. Only tests that do not measure job performance are prohibited.
6. The test must measure the person for the job and not the person in the abstract.
7. Less-qualified applicants should not be hired over those better qualified because of minority origins. There is no requirement to hire unqualified persons.

A test that has an identifiable pass/fail score may deny an employment opportunity to a disproportionately large number of the protected class. This prevents an individual from proceeding to the next step in the selection process. It would be in violation of Title VII.[46] In determining whether the procedure has an adverse impact, statistical evidence should be considered; however, a statistically unbalanced workforce (disproportionate number of nonminorities or

females) does not necessarily mean that the selection procedure is in violation. The reason for the condition may not be the selection procedure but a characteristic of the labor market.

Validation of Tests

If a test has an adverse impact on the selection process, as was the case in *Griggs*, it must be validated as to whether it is (1) job related, (2) predictive of performance, or (3) necessary because no less-discriminatory methods are available; then business necessity is required.[47]

Good faith effort or neutrality in placing applicants is irrelevant if an adverse impact results. The court in *Griggs* did not say how the test should be validated, but at the time of the *Griggs* decision, *Albemarle Paper Co.* v. *Moody,* 422 U.S. 405, was working its way through the lower courts. In June 1975, the Supreme Court put to rest the question of what constituted the proper validation of a pre-employment test as well as the back pay issue. In 1963, Albemarle Paper Company adopted the Wonderlic Test A and B series as a screening program for selection of employees. General population norms were used to set cutoff scores until the *Griggs* decision. Thereafter, Albermarle hired an expert in industrial psychology to validate the test. The expert used ratings of job performance from three different supervisors, which were then correlated with test scores. After the validation, 96 percent of the white applicants and 64 percent of the African Americans passed the test. The test scores were used primarily to select and place employees in 11 separate departments where 17 training lines of progression were established.

Exhibit 3.8 shows the placement of employers in the wood yard, which is an unskilled job category. The skilled lines of progression were in the paper mill. To be placed in this line of progression, it was necessary to have a certain score on the Wonderlic test. In Exhibit 3.8, there were a large number of African Americans in unskilled jobs, while in Exhibit 3.9, there were very few. To defend this disparate impact, it was necessary to validate the tests. The validation of the tests by Albemarle was improper to show business necessity because:

1. The validation process used was not related to the job sought. Subjective supervisors' ratings were compared to test scores. The study focused on experienced employees in upper-level jobs; high scores of that group are not predictive of qualifications for new workers to perform lower-level jobs.
2. The supervisors rated older whites and experienced workers, whereas tests were given to job applicants who were younger, inexperienced, and nonwhite.

Wood Yard Department	Negro	White
Yard Crew		
Crane Operator (Large)	0	9
Long Log Operator	0	4
Log Stacker Operator	0	4
Small Equipment Operator	0	4
Bulldozer Operator	0	1
Oiler	0	4
Chip Unloader	1	3
Chain Operator	0	4
Chipper Operator No. 2		
Chipper Operator No. 1	4	0
Tractor Operator	5	0.
Chip Bin Operator	4	0
Laborers	12	0
Service Crew		
Dempster-Dumpster	1	0
Winch Truck Operator	3	0
Winch Truck Operator Helper	1	0
Laborer	6	0

EXHIBIT 3.8   Job Placement with invalid Testing

Source: The appendix to the appellant's brief in *Albemarle Paper* v. *Moody*, No. 74-389.

Paper Mill Department	Negro	White
Paper Machine Line of Progression		
Machine Tender #1	0	4
Machine Tender #2	0	4
Back Tender #1	0	4
Third Hand #1	0	4
Third Hand #2	0	4
Fourth Hand #1	0	4
Fourth Hand #2	0	4
Front Plugger #1	0	4
Back Plugger #1	1	4
Back Plugger #2	0	4
Beaterman	0	4
First Helper	0	4
Brokerman	4	0
Stock Puller	0	0
Laborer	1	0

EXHIBIT 3.9   Assignments for Preferred Personnel

Source: The appendix to the appellant's brief in *Albemarle Paper* v. *Moody*, No. 74-389.

Particular attention has been paid to *Griggs* and *Albemarle Paper* because a substantial part of the EEOC Employee Selection Procedures Guidelines of 1978, as related to testing, had their origin in the *Griggs* and *Albemarle* cases. Legal principles in the guidelines have had little change in subsequent years.

Disparate Impact Threshold

The EEOC Uniform Guidelines use a "four/fifths" or "80 percent" test to determine whether a disparate impact exists. The disparate impact threshold for females is therefore 0.8 times (x) the selection rate for males. For minority applicants, the disparate impact threshold is 0.8 times (x) the selection rate for nonminority applicants. This formula could be safely used for any protected class. However, it would not work if the job class contained only a small number of employees.

Types of Test Validation

There are three types of **test validation** that are stated in the EEOC Uniform Guidelines and have been judicially accepted.

1. *Criterion-related validity* is a collection of data that measure job performance and establish statistical relationships between measure of job performance and test scores. This is the traditional method of validation of pre-employment tests, which has been used for more than 30 years. Supervisor ratings must be objective or will fail to meet the criteria in the *Albemarle* case (the most popular case).

2. **Content validity** correlates certain aspects of the job performance with test scores to measure job performance. This differs from the criterion validation in that the job performance is measured in

the specific job for which the applicant is being tested. This method of validation relies heavily on job analysis methods alluded to by the appellate court in the *Albemarle* case.[48]

3. **Construct validation** is a psychological method of validation based on research that identifies a psychological trait as essential to the successful performance of the job and develops a selection procedure to measure the presence and degree of that trait. Examples of a trait would be leadership ability and ability to work under pressure (not used very often).

An important requirement of the EEOC Uniform Guidelines that has been judicially accepted is found in Section 5(I), where it is stated that procedures to select for a higher-skilled job would not be appropriate if three conditions existed:

1. The majority of the applicants selected do not progress to a higher-level job within a short time after being placed on lower-level job.[49]
2. There is no real distinction between the higher- and lower-level jobs, or selection procedures measure skills not necessary to perform the higher-level job.
3. Knowledge could be acquired on the higher-level job without the employee's being trained on the lower-level job.

The validation process is expensive and time consuming and even when completed may not be accepted by the courts. In view of this lack of certainty in judicial acceptance, the employer should seriously consider whether testing is necessary to predict job performance. Testing is especially subject to exposure if it has an adverse impact; however, a test is permitted if it is given to all applicants, is job-related, is not medical in nature, and is consistent with business needs.

Pre-Employment Physicals

Questions about a candidate's physical ability to perform a job can lead to questions about medical history and pre-employment physical examinations. A job-related pre-employment physical should not be given until a conditional job offer is made.[50] This federal procedure eliminates any exposure from state handicap laws. Tests for illegal drug use are not considered medical examinations. An important step in making a pre-employment physical job related is to be assured that the doctor has knowledge of the physical requirements of the job. Often this is difficult because either the doctor does not want to take the time to study the job or the job content changes so rapidly that it makes the study obsolete in a short time. It is best for the doctor to observe the various jobs. If this observation is not possible, a good job description may be sufficient.

In the job description, the essential physical requirement of the job should be noted; when the job is changed, the job description should be updated and communicated to the doctor. Inquiries as to the applicant's physical condition can be justified in determining job placement after the job offer has been made. If the applicant is handicapped, it may be necessary for the employer to know his or her physical condition in order to accommodate him or her under the ADA. This need justifies a pre-employment physical after the job offer has been made.[51]

Although questions about medical history and physical or mental disabilities are not specifically prohibited by the law after a job offer has been made, they are hazardous unless a specific business purpose can be shown. Instead of asking whether an applicant has any disabilities, one should ask whether any disabilities would interfere with the ability to perform the job for which application is being made. If an applicant does not know, further inquiry as to the physical condition is justified. However, to protect the applicant's right to privacy, disclosure of medical information should be only to persons who have a need to know.

The foregoing discussion on pre-employment inquiries has been directed to those involved in screening applicants; however, as a practical matter, interviews are conducted on all levels of management. To avoid exposure to discrimination and to eliminate prejudice by management personnel, those who interview should be given written guidelines to standardize pre-employment inquiries. All pre-employment inquiries should have the specific purpose of determining the qualifications of the individual applicant as required by the job and not what the interviewer subjectively believes will make a good employee.

Drug and Alcohol Testing

The Department of Transportation requires specific drug and alcohol testing protocol and a program for constant monitoring of vehicle operators, airline, railroad, and maritime personnel, including fire truck drivers.[52] Drug and alcohol testing procedures are discussed more fully in Chapter 4.

BACKGROUND INVESTIGATIONS

In employment, collecting information from sources other than the employee is extremely important. Employers can be guilty of negligence by not investigating people to be placed in positions of public trust, such as child-care workers. Employers are required to obtain an applicant's drug and alcohol test results from the previous employers for the last two years. Due to potential exposure, employers have become increasingly reluctant to release specific information about former employees. As the practice by employers of not supplying information becomes universal, a different exposure is created.[53] The court will protect employers under the qualified privilege doctrine but not for **negligent hiring.** The policy of not disclosing information may eliminate

a small exposure in one area but create a larger exposure in another area. Failure to disclose information on applicants to prospective employers is problematic. If an employer is not liable for negligent hiring, that employer may be liable for negligent retention.

Negligent hiring or *retention* is defined as situation in which an employer is liable to third persons for injury and the employer knew, or should have known, of the threat an employee represented. The employer's negligence must be the proximate cause of the injury to those whom the employer could reasonably expect to come in contact with the employee. The injury does not have to be personal or physical.

Thoroughness of the Investigation

Although there are no hard-and-fast rules on the adequacy of an investigation, there appears to be a greater duty imposed when jobs have a public relationship or expose the employee to opportunities to injure others. There is a greater duty to investigate for a security guard position or taxicab driver than for a bartender.[54] In certain jobs the risk is foreseeable, as in the case of guards or a maintenance worker in an apartment complex. The legal principle is that unless there is a strong reason not to do so, there exists a duty to investigate. As more criminal records become available, courts are requiring a duty to check with increasing frequency.[55] In one case the employer was held liable for hiring a person who committed forgery and fraud. To be liable, the employer must have known or exercised ordinary care to know of the dangerous tendencies. Under tort law there is no liability unless the employer's negligence caused foreseeable injury.[56] Where the applicant had a clear record and nothing to indicate a bad history, there was no duty to check. However, where the employee had a free access to customers' homes, the court held there was a duty to inquire into the applicant's background.[57]

The degree of an employer's liability will depend on the soundness of the pre-employment investigation conducted.[58] Important factors in the investigation are the job responsibilities for which the applicant is being hired and the applicant's record that indicated risk of harm to co-workers or injury to third parties. In *Stephanie Ponticas et al.* v. *K. M. S. Investments,* 331 N. W. 2nd 907 (Minn. 1983), the employer hired a caretaker for an apartment building. The employee had been convicted of armed robbery, burglary, and auto theft. Using his passkey to enter an apartment, he raped one of the tenants. The court held that an employer has a duty to exercise reasonable care in hiring individuals who, because of the nature of their employment, may pose a threat to members of the public.

Another case, *Slaton* v. *B&B Gulf Services,* 344 SE.2d 512 (Ga. App. 1986), involved a truck driver with a criminal record of violent sex crimes and aggravated sodomy while driving a truck for another employer. The new employer gave him instruction not to pick up hitchhikers but the driver did. He raped and threatened to kill the plaintiff in the sleeping compartment of the truck. The court found that it was the duty of the employer to hire reliable drivers. The employer knew, or should have known, that entrusting a truck to a person with history of sex crimes was negligent hiring—a history that the employer had failed to check.

Some courts will hold that if the act was employment related, the employer is liable. In *Tobert* v. *Martin Marietta Corp.,* 621 F. Supp. 1099 (Colo. 1985), the employee was sexually assaulted on the way to lunch, and the court held that it was employment related. The employer failed to make the premises safe for employees.

A negligent retention claim involved a situation where there was evidence that the employee had a drinking problem, and while drinking he assaulted a guest. The court had little difficulty in finding negligent retention.[59] Because there is an exposure to negligent retention complaints, the employer who has knowledge of dangerous tendencies has a duty to other employees to do something about it. It is not uncommon for an employee in the heat of an argument to threaten a supervisor or another employee, and if the employer does nothing about it and later the threat is carried out, there is a strong possibility that the employer will be liable for any resulting injuries under negligent retention decisions.

THE SELECTION AUDIT

Management must provide oversight of selection procedures for job-posting practices, promotion, training, and other opportunities. Undisciplined procedures, especially the recruitment and hiring procedures, can result in numerous legal claims. In order to avoid exposure to lawsuits or a lengthy administrative hearing before a regulatory agency, it is advisable to conduct an internal yearly analysis of the total selection process. To achieve fair employment practices, the established screening procedure should be well conceived and consistently and uniformly applied. The essential functions of jobs should be the basis of applicant evaluation. The application form and offer letters in use should be defensive and certainly without risky content. The conduct of all personnel who are candidates must be examined.

Equal Pay

A well-managed selection process can still suffer legal exposure from the failure to provide equal pay for those chosen for employment. The issue carries over from the previous century. The first involvement by the federal government in the payment of wages occurred in 1938 with the passage of the Fair Labor Standards Act. This Act mandated the payment of government-established minimum wages and overtime premiums. By 1962, the percentage of women in the workforce had increased to approximately 35 percent, but the earnings of women continued to average only 60 to 70 percent of men's earnings for year-round full-time work.[60] Congress considered this a societal problem that the market had been unable to resolve. Accordingly, it amended Section 6 of the Fair Labor Standards Act in 1963, and called the amendment the Equal Pay Act (EPA).[61] The Act states simply that no employer shall discriminate in the payment of wages within a facility on the basis of sex for equal work. Jobs that require equal skill, equal effort, and equal responsibility and that are performed under similar working conditions should have equal pay. If the differential is based on seniority,[62] a merit system, an incentive pay system, or any factor other than sex, then there is no violation.

The EPA statute is easily understood but can cause problems in wage and salary systems. Many employers have depended on loopholes and other defensive provisions for the survival of their wage and salary systems. Sections 201-108 of Title II, CRA91 (the Glass Ceiling Act of 1991),[63] established a study commission to solve the national problem of underrepresentation and artificial barriers to women and minorities in management and in decision-making positions. One of the barriers, according to the Department of Labor, is lack of management perception in determining compensation. The report of the commission helped, but didn't break the so-called glass ceiling.[64] The EPA applies to state and local governments and most of the private sector. Exceptions to coverage are few. Union bargaining must also accommodate equal pay regulations.

Definition of Equal Work

There is a difference in skills, responsibility, and effort in jobs, and that is the primary reason for the difference in wages. The identification of difference in jobs is the purpose of job evaluation and pay equity studies. The first opportunity that the courts had to address these questions was in *Shultz v. Wheaton Glass Co.*, where male selector packers were receiving $.21 per hour more than female selector packers.[65] They performed substantially the same work, which was inspection work, except that approximately 18 percent of the time the male selectors did materials handling tasks.[66] Females were not permitted to perform these tasks because they were restricted from lifting anything over 35 pounds. The court, in a landmark opinion on the interpretation of EPA, established a legal principle in finding a violation of EPA; it has been followed by other courts in many decisions. In view of the refusal of the Supreme Court to review this decision, the principle can be considered as controlling. This principle is sometimes called the "equal work standard," which is explained here:

1. The equal work standard requires only that the jobs be substantially equal and not identical. Small differences will not make them unequal.[67]
2. When a wage differential exists between men and women doing substantially equal work, the burden is on the employer to show that the differential is for some reason other than sex.
3. When some but not all members of one sex performs extra duties in their jobs, these extra duties do not justify giving all members of that sex extra pay.
4. That men can perform extra duties does not justify extra pay unless women are also offered the opportunity to perform these duties.
5. Job titles and job descriptions are not material in showing that work is unequal unless they accurately reflect actual job content.

What is a substantially different job is decided on a case-by-case basis.[68] Where there is a substantial difference in effort, skill, or responsibility, the courts permit a pay differential between the sexes. The principle that job content, not job titles or job descriptions, is what determines whether jobs are equal is followed in the Eighth Circuit.[69]

Another justification for a wage differential between men and women on which the employer relied was shift work. When all men worked the night shift and women the day shift, it was argued by employers that the differential was justified because they were not similar working conditions.

Corning Glass Works v. *Brennan*, 417 U.S. 188 (1974), one of the few EPA cases to reach the Supreme Court, held that working conditions as used in EPA do not refer to the time of day when work is performed and different shifts do not justify a pay differential. This case also established the rule that equal pay violations could be remedied only by raising the women's wages, *not by reducing* the men's, but left open the question of whether changes in job content could remedy the violation. Often employers attempted to justify pay differentials between men and women by arguing that working conditions were not similar, or that the jobs performed by males were more hazardous tasks than ones performed by females. There are situations where this might be a valid defense. However, such a defense should be used with extreme caution. Statistics show that 70 to 85 percent of all industrial accidents are not caused by physical conditions but rather by unsafe acts of the employee. Based on these statistics, hazardous working conditions would not justify the differential if accidents are caused by the employee and not the hazardous conditions.

Measurement of Equality

When considering skills, such factors as experience, training, education, and ability are taken into account. Any one of these factors can justify a differential.[70] Possessing a skill is not enough; the person must also use that skill on the job.[71] Calling one employee a cleaner and another a custodian does not justify a wage differential. It is job content, not job title, that the courts follow.[72] A common "equal skill" situation that courts have struck down is where the employer trains men for promotional purposes but does not offer to train women, who for some reason are not considered in the promotion plans; when the jobs are compared, the trained men have more skills than women.

When male tellers were paid more than female tellers, the employer argued that the males were being trained in all aspects of banking to replace senior officers because they were in a bona fide training program. Subjective evaluation of potential for promotion standing alone cannot justify pay differentials under EPA.[73] In order to justify pay differentials under EPA through a bona fide training program (1) the training program must be open to both sexes, (2) the employees must be notified of the training opportunities, (3) there must be a defined beginning and end to the training program, and (4) there must be a definite course of study and advancement opportunities upon completion exist. It is advisable to describe the elements and requirements of this program in writing.

Responsibility Rationale

The defense of a difference in responsibility to justify unequal pay occurs mostly in administrative, professional, and executive jobs, where before the 1972 amendment these employees were excluded from coverage under EPA. One of the first cases under the responsibility defense was when an employer claimed that men had to make decisions that women did not have to make. The court found that although men did make decisions that women did not, such decisions were subject to review by supervisors. Therefore, the differential was not justified under the responsibility defense.[74]

Often an employer justifies a pay differential between sexes in the same job categories by claiming that one type of work is more difficult than another. When an employer claimed that management of soft-line departments such as clothing, usually managed by women, had less responsibility than hard-line departments such as sporting goods, usually managed by men, the court held that there is no substantial difference to justify less pay for women than for men.[75] In *EEOC* v. *Madison Community Unit School District No. 12*, 816 F.2d 577 (7th Cir. 1987), the court held that paying female coaches of girls' track and tennis teams less than male coaches of male track and tennis teams is a violation of the EPA.

Semantic Issues

One of the factors that will justify differentials is where a properly communicated bona fide merit system is applied without regard to sex. All too often the term *merit pay* is used to include cost-of-living increases, longevity increases, and, general across-the-board increases that have no relationship to meritorious performance.[76] Merit increases that will survive judicial review under EPA are individual increases in pay related to the job performance of that individual. A bona fide merit policy is a pat on the back with dollar bills in the palm of the hand.

Determining a wage level on some factor other than performance is the major fault with merit pay plans and explains why they do not stand judicial scrutiny. In an inflationary period the employer wants to keep earnings in line with the labor market conditions, yet does not want to set a precedent by implying that pay increases are automatic or based on labor market conditions. Rationalizations set in and any believable reason is given. For example, in *Brock* v. *Georgia S.W. College*, 765 F.2d 1026 (11th Cir. 1985), the employer argued that the wage difference was due to a merit system. The court found that the ratings were based on subjective personal judgment, that they were

ad hoc, and that in many cases the raters were ill informed. In order for compensation to be truly based on merit, it should be given at a time when some significant performance has been completed. For administrative purposes, that could be done in future periods, provided that the waiting period is not so long that it chills motivation. In production incentive plans for factory workers, the previous three-month period should be the maximum waiting period, and merit awards should be given separately within two weeks after the end of the merit rating period.

A Bona Fide Merit Plan

In order for a merit pay plan to be bona fide under the various statutes, it must be in writing and contain all or most of the following elements:

1. The employee must believe that good performance will result in additional compensation.
2. There should be a direct correlation between the amount of pay and the exceptional performance, without any upper limits. Upper limits tend to dampen the motivation of certain workers.
3. The employee should understand the merit plan before it is adopted so that there are no surprises at evaluation time. (One of the authors worked with a highly motivated incentive worker. She was asked at 10:30 a.m. how much incentive pay she had earned so far that day and she knew. This employee understood the incentive plan.)
4. The performance should be accurately measured either by objective performance appraisals or by standards of performance with which the employee agrees. If agreement cannot be accomplished, the employer should be sure that it is right and adopt it. Sometimes employees have to work with the plan

before they are convinced they can earn additional money.

5. Base pay should not be less because an employee is on a merit system. Merit pay should be given when performance is above the average worker's base pay.
6. The merit system must be updated periodically. Job content affects the performance; if the system is not current, either the company or the employee is unfairly affected.
7. Managers must believe in the system and be trained to properly administer it.
8. Follow-up procedures are necessary to prevent bias and leniency. Nothing will defeat a merit plan faster than leniency or bias.[77]

Differential Factors

Wage and salary plans based on seniority are not in violation of the EPA if there is a direct correlation between seniority and pay levels and it is otherwise a bona fide seniority plan.

Another concern is the area of employee benefits.[78] In order to justify a pay differential under the EPA, the reason for the difference in benefits must be based on a factor other than sex. One employer argued that requiring a greater pension contribution for females than for males because women live longer was a factor other than sex. The Supreme Court adopted the lower court's position that actuarial distinctions based entirely on sex could not qualify as an exception.[79] In another case, women received lower benefits than men for the same contributions because of sex-segregated actuarial tables. The insured deferred compensation plan was optional as to contributions and methods of receiving benefits. The Court ruled that longevity could not justify a differential under the EPA.[80]

Examples of valid factors other than sex include (1) the "motherhood penalty" (time out of the workforce); (2) temporary or permanent assignments made to a lower-rated job where the incumbent retains the old rate of pay ("red circle rates"); (3) a bona fide training program as discussed in this chapter; and (4) part-time work. The courts take the position that part-time employment (under 20 hours per week) is a factor other than sex to justify a pay differential—not logical, but codified.

Regulation Interpretations

The meaning of the term *establishment* has been expanded to include two or more distinct physical portions of the business as one establishment, so long as they are located in the same physical place of business. Employers must make the *same benefits* available to females as they do to males without regard to cost or actuarial studies. The EEOC has adopted the position that it is a violation of the EPA for employers to pay *a higher rate* to a new male employee than they do to a former or a present female employee.[81]

Pay Differentials Remain

The EPA is not viewed as correcting the differences that existed before the Act.[82] Employers take the position that existing wage and salary systems do give equal pay for equal work; that there is no need to change the policy of determining wages by job evaluation, market conditions, profitability, or competitive practices. Others believe that determining wages by market conditions and job evaluation is subject to built-in sex bias.[83]

A Government General Accounting (GOA) Office study in 2003 concluded that most of the difference between men's and women's compensation during the period of from 1983 to 2000 was because of differences in patterns of work (experience, time out of the labor force, hours worked, and tenure with an employer). However, a third of the difference was attributable to different pay for similar work.[84]

Audit of EPA Compliance

Most employers are in violation of the EPA, and when an employer is challenged, a lengthy and expensive lawsuit results. The factors mentioned previously, although valid, offer very little defense. For this reason, it is good insurance to audit your compensation plan to determine the extent of noncompliance. If it is found that there are serious compliance problems, the corrections can be made gradually and often without anyone knowing a violation ever existed. This is much better than an equal pay complaint by the EEOC where the employer is being accused of taking compensation from the employees in violation of the law. Necessary procedures for EPA audit are as follows:

1. Determine the distribution of pay percentages within each job category and whether they correspond with performance.
2. Examine the average pay level within each job category by race and sex.
3. Study the average pay increase given by each supervisor within each job category.
4. Examine pay differentials among all jobs involving equal skill, effort, responsibility, and working conditions. If you find an instance where a pay differential may be based on sex, eliminate the inequity by bringing the pay of the lower-paid employee to the level of the higher paid.
5. Be consistent in the application of hiring, promotion, and pay increase practices and criteria, to avoid any inference of sex discrimination.
6. Document reasons for pay actions that may later be questioned, and be certain your reasons are legally defensible.

This is not an exhaustive checklist; the basic premise—equal pay for equal work (not necessarily *identical* work)—must be kept in mind to avoid creating inequities and to rectify inequities created in the past. If there is logic to the compensation system, it is much easier to defend when an equal pay charge is made by the EEOC. In summary, management should do three things: (1) have a rational reason for its compensation levels; (2) explain to the employees how their wages are determined, and (3) as much as possible, correct wage differentials between sexes, rather than trying to justify them. Programs and procedures that show good faith efforts to eliminate differences between sexes will provide defense and minimize exposure to litigation.

Comparable Pay for Comparable Worth

Comparable worth is a theory of determining wages by requiring equal pay for employees whose work is of **comparable worth** even if the job content is totally different. The proponents of the theory state that the EPA, Title VII, and Executive Order 11246 require its application. As the percentage of women in the workforce continues to increase, the pressure to remedy the difference in earnings will also increase. Because the EPA failed in other respects, there was hope that the revival of the theory would be legally supported by new interpretation of the EPA or Title VII. The concept became a very controversial equal employment issue.[85] The issue went before the Supreme Court in *County of Washington* v. *Gunther,* 101 S.Ct. 2242 (1981). The Court ruled that the four defenses under the EPA applied when there was an issue of whether Title VII or EPA could be used. The Bennett Amendment required the EPA defenses to be used when there was conflict between EPA and Title VII. Accordingly, the plaintiffs could not apply the "equal work" standard under Title VII. However, the Court stated that this didn't preclude the plaintiffs from starting an action under Title VII, alleging disparate treatment and sex discrimination.

The Birth of Pay Equity Law

Although several circuits had previously held that it is not up to the courts to determine the worth of an employee, the issue was settled in *State of Washington* v. *Am. Federal, State and County and Municipal Employees,* 770 F.2d 1401 (9th Cir. 1985). The court held that Congress did not intend Title VII to interfere with the law of supply and demand or prevent employees from competing in the labor market. A number of states (Michigan, Massachusetts, Colorado, New Mexico, and others) have active groups that pursue political action to achieve greater wage equality. Minnesota has created comprehensive legislation applicable only to the public sector. Most Canadian provinces have also legislated in pursuit of improved equity.[86]

The basis of Minnesota law is a foundation of valid ranking of job content that establishes *comparability among jobs* based on their content and difficulty. Most large private-sector firms apply job evaluation and sometimes market studies to achieve fair pay opportunity across gender lines. Public-sector organizations use Civil Service Classification systems or job-matching tools among jurisdictions. Those advocating additional legislation charge that many job evaluation plans and certainly market (valued) ranking systems are inherently biased.[87] Nevertheless, pay can be compared only to positions that should be comparable in pay. Job equity, however, doesn't necessarily equate with *pay equity*. Pay equity is devoted to pay analysis for gender differentials. Pay disparity can still result from consciously biased decisions (disparate treatment) or unconscious (flawed) decisions about performance or job value perceptions (disparate impact).

Recruiting Practices

One important element in a recruiting audit is to make sure that more than one source is used. There are a variety of methods used to inform the market that a vacancy exists. A second element is that advertisements should be examined to determine whether the wording would exclude members of the protected class. The source contact and the referrals must include recruitment in the labor market that the protected classes normally use. The use of different advertising channels for different job classifications is good evidence that a sincere effort is being made to notify the entire labor market of the job openings. The factor in determining whether recruiting methods are effective is the applicant flow, which should correspond with labor market population statistics on minorities, sex, age, and disabilities.

Application Review

The next step in the selection audit is to analyze the standard application form. The most important element is to determine for what purpose each question is being asked and how the information will be used. If there is a discriminatory purpose for any question, then business necessity must be shown.

Summarizing Selection Audits

In summary, there is a social and legal expectation of equal opportunity in the workplace. It requires compliance with law and preventive measures to avoid legal claims. In order to avoid exposure to distractions and costs, it is advisable to conduct an annual analysis of the full range of selection systems. Management must provide designated oversight of selection procedures for job-posting practices, promotion, training, and other opportunities. Undisciplined procedures, especially in recruitment and assignment practices, can result in numerous allegations, some of which may have some credibility.

To achieve fair employment practices, well-established evaluation and decision-making procedures should be consistently and uniformly applied. The essential functions of jobs should be the basis of applicant evaluation. Several appropriate recruiting options should be employed. There are a variety of methods used to inform the market that an opportunity exists. Advertisements should be examined to determine whether the wording would exclude members of the protected class. The source contact and the referrals must include recruitment in the labor market that the protected classes normally use.

Examine the *standard* application form. Verify the purpose and value of each question. If there is a discriminatory purpose for any question, then business necessity must be shown. Offer letters should be free of any commitments. Provide a letter pattern.

Two items to audit in the interview process are whether there is a standard form of questions asked by each interviewer and whether the criteria established for the job are being uniformly and fairly applied. Interview inquiries practices may be clear but not followed, especially at the second and third interview levels. Inquiries should be made to determine if there are any automatic "disqualifiers" being applied such as arrest records, tests, or being handicapped. As we saw in *Connecticut* v. *Teal*,[88] the law requires an equal opportunity to be employed. If there are any automatic disqualifiers being applied, business necessity must be shown.

Resulting hires should reveal if members of every protected class apply for vacancies. Sometimes an element exists in the employer's practice that has a chilling effect on certain applicants. If this is the case an investigation should determine the cause. The audit must be sufficient to determine whether a disparate impact exists; if diversity is suffering, a step-by-step investigation

is necessary to correct it. Employment selection practices, after 40 years of Title VII and case law, should leave little exposure for lawsuits. One error the employer can make is to select applicants who are not qualified because of a false belief that "we must" under the law.[89]

As a defensive measure, written audit records or notes should be destroyed. Notes of improper actions or negligent conditions can be viewed in court as proof of wrongdoing.

LEGAL ISSUES AFTER HIRING

Probationary Periods

A stark general difference between public and private management models is the role of the probationary period. The public sector normally stipulates that this period is an essential part of the selection process.[90] It can continue for up to one year, not uncommon with law enforcement and fire fighters. Private employers generally avoid lengthy probationary periods because such action suggests a lack of confidence in the employee or, as sometimes happens, an employee doesn't recognize the employment conditions, and infers a property right. A probationary period and under at-will employment condition is largely meaningless because dismissal can occur after one month or one year.

Employee Agreements

There are specific reasons why employers contract with employees. Sometimes it is to prohibit future competition or conflict of interest, sometimes to protect trade secrets or ensure confidentiality, and frequently to clarify the employment relationship (independent contractor, employee agreement, and so on). As previously noted, some states require written agreements with new public employees. In municipal government, a city administrator is often subject to the political winds. It's common practice for a city government to at least contract a severance package with administrators lest political change results in their displacement. Independent contractors often move in and out of several organizations and many employers are concerned with what valuable information is leaving with the independent contractor. Management must consider if there is any need for protection through restrictive covenants. There may be security matters that suffice, such as restrictions of access to sensitive areas, computer passwords, and copy control. In fact, depending on state law, the degree to which an employer acts to protect the assets and demonstrates the critical nature or value of the information can have a considerable impact in subsequent litigation. If employee agreements are deemed necessary, the elements of contract law—an offer, acceptance, and consideration—must be present to bind the agreement, whether in writing or spoken words.[91]

This section on employee agreements is located at this point in the text because agreements are best consummated at, or before, the time of hire, so the act of *employment* serves as the consideration of value. Attempts to use "continued employment" as consideration for signing an agreement have not fared well in courts. Restrictive covenants can be lengthy and include provisions about damages, due cause for discharge, successor companies, and an acknowledgment that the terms are reasonable.

Asset Protection

A number of forms of contract address the protection of an organization's "intellectual property." There have always been "trade secrets" such as product formulas applied in soft drinks and chicken recipes. More common today are patents, device designs, computer developments, and investor lists.

Knowledge of such matters can constitute the essence of an organization's success, and can be extremely valuable. *Conflict of interest* situations are created when commercial or monetary opportunities become associated. A contract seeks to assure employees loyalty in judgment and prohibit benefiting from associated situations of sources. One professional basketball team declared it "prohibit[s] outside work by employees if such work conflicts with the employees' ability to perform their job."[92] *Non-disclosure agreements* (confidentiality) are primarily useful for the protection of information after an employee leaves because common law requires employees to exercise some "duty of loyalty to an employer."[93]

Trade secret law is more common among states because of the Uniform Trade Secrets Act (1985) to which most states have subscribed. Texas, Massachusetts, New York, and New Jersey use common law or have a different statute. These agreements address the wrongful acquisition or disclosure of information and the remedies available. A trade secret is information that is valuable and not readily attainable. *Assignment of patents and inventions* is a protective agreement wherein the employer, as a condition of employment, requires an employee to assign specific rights of inventions or patents. Normally the assignment excludes any inventions that didn't involve any employer resources or apply to that enterprise.

No Compete or Solicitation

A "no compete or solicitation" agreement may be the most common and is intended to prevent an employee from working for a competitor or soliciting business from the employer's customer while as an employee and after separation. Such agreements are normally executed on the first day of employment to avoid additional consideration. Agreements are customized to achieve a reasonable prohibition of competition in terms of geography and the period of time (usually several years for sales people). They may voided or modified if a court feels the employee is being denied a livelihood or restricted unreasonably. Often, restrictions in regard to trade secrets or confidentiality are included in the document.

Employee Agreement

A normal employment agreement specifies the duties or title, pay, and caveats regarding at-will. It should specify that there is no other agreement and perhaps include special severance pay considerations.

CASE 3.1

Selection Compliance

The county HR director learned in a Monday morning meeting that a crew leader from the night shift had been sent to a maintenance shop/garage in a remote corner of the county to establish a new work site. The crew leader was to initiate hiring of an operating crew of three people, all of whom must be commercially licensed truck drivers who would be performing the bulk of the work. These new employees were to service county roads and resources located in that area. This was an unusually expedient action resulting from the election of a county commissioner from that area. Office equipment, trucks, and additional equipment and supplies were en route. With winter weather approaching, the crew leader was to initiate hiring and work projects as soon as possible. A permanent supervisor would be appointed and be on site within three weeks.

The HR director was surprised, but immediately recognized the risks of legal exposure in the situation. He announced in the meeting he would send someone to "help" with the hiring for a few days. The only possible person he could send was a personnel assistant who was scheduled for vacation the next week, and so there were only several days to attend to matters at the site. He instructed the assistant to take the necessary actions to ensure compliance with the law. Other matters could wait several weeks, but the employment and other critical compliance actions must be addressed immediately.

Nearing the maintenance shop, Betty, the personnel assistant, observed signage for an Indian Reservation. When greeting the crew leader, she observed him handing out an "off the shelf" application form to someone already inquiring about a job. Her first action was to use a black marker to obliterate the inquiries on the remaining application forms about military background and social security number. The state didn't prohibit these questions, but the questions could be suggestive of illegal discrimination.

Considering the legal mandates, what might be done in the next few days to provide for regulatory compliance in the employment process? ▄

CASE 3.2

Preventive Measures in Selection

Kathy was selected to be the unit manager of a county maintenance facility three hours away from the county offices. She had worked on county road crews and performed some related administrative duties for several years while taking courses in pre-engineering at a vocational school. She had shown some leadership in her years with the county, but had never had supervisory responsibilities. As part of her new duties, her unit was expected to function in accord with county policies, practices, and employment laws. The county agreed to pay for a course in Human Resource Management and another in Supervisory Techniques offered as evening adult education through a nearby community college. It was also arranged that on those occasions when Kathy came to the county offices on business, she would at least for a month arrange to spend two hours with the human resources director for coaching on personnel management matters. A priority would be employment matters because of legal vulnerabilities and Kathy's inexperience.

Understanding that vital regulatory matters have been previously established, what selection practices, procedures, and suggestions might be addressed in the coaching sessions that will serve to prevent any legal issues at this unit? ▄

CASE 3.3

Non-Compete Agreement

Jim Monson had begun his last trimester of Chiropractic School working as an intern at a private chiropractic firm in his hometown. The company was owned by Larry Lewis, who had been in business for himself for over 15 years and ran the only chiropractic business in a rural Wisconsin town of 2,000 people. Lewis Chiropractic, LLC, was a small firm and, after Jim's internship was finished, he was to become the first associate and third employee of the firm. When initially discussing a potential contract for employment, Larry insisted that a "no compete" clause was unnecessary in this case and asked Jim to submit a sample contract to use as a guide. Jim purposely removed the "no compete" clause in the sample he submitted because Larry had said it wasn't an issue. When Larry offered him the position, Jim turned down the offers he had received from firms in other cities because he had found his ideal situation. He saw himself putting in a few years, learning the business with Larry and then starting his own chiropractic firm somewhere in town. However, when he was presented with an annual contract from Larry, Jim found that it contained a section called Covenant Not to Compete. This covenant mandated that, for a period of three years from the date of termination of the contract, Jim was not to "directly or indirectly maintain an office or otherwise render chiropractic services within a 10-mile radius of the premises of Lewis Chiropractic, LLC." Because he had previously turned down offers from other firms, had a home, and had bills to pay, Jim accepted the contract and went to work for Lewis. The situation was still appealing to him.

The compensation clause of Jim's contract stipulated that he was to receive a base salary of $2,000 per month to be paid bimonthly on the 15th and last day of the month. In addition, he was to be given a commission of one-half of all the revenue he brought in to the company that exceeded a stated amount, which was to be paid on the 15th as well. The remaining half of this extra revenue was kept by the firm. This clause essentially meant that the more esoteric or comprehensive cases Jim worked on, the more money he stood to make. The Responsibilities section of the contract outlined the way the business would be run. Jim would have use of his own working and office space along with any equipment, supplies, and administrative staff resources he required. The office administrator was to schedule new patients according to their preference for either Jim or Larry unless a patient was specifically referred to Jim or Larry by an outside source. Once a new patient was seen by either of the doctors, they were put into his pool of patients and each of the men was then responsible for the patients in their pool.

Jim soon accumulated a large patient pool that rivaled and eventually surpassed Larry's. He became so popular that new patients who asked to see Jim often were told they had to see Larry first just so they could be diagnosed. Over the course of his four years at the firm, Jim began to realize that he was only being assigned the mundane, lower-paying cases and the more complex cases were going to Larry, even though those patients had requested Jim specifically. The patients were being told that Jim was booked and that they'd have to see Larry initially, which made them part of Larry's pool of patients and, hence, his responsibility going forward. In addition, Jim was not being paid regularly, twice a month as his contract had stipulated. After further investigation Jim found that he was not being given credit for the correct number of cases that he had handled for the last couple of years. In total, he calculated that he had been denied almost $6,000 worth of work in the two years he had looked into. When he brought his information forward to Larry, he "investigated" Jim's claims and eventually told him that an error in the scheduling software was pushing Jim's clients to Larry.

Jim had seen enough. He submitted his two-week notice and left the firm for a larger firm in a nearby city. During his 7 months of working at his new firm, Jim hired a lawyer and had her look into his old contract and his claims of breach. He was hoping that the non-payment of wages and fees were enough to invalidate the Covenant to Not Compete.

Might Larry's alleged breach of the compensation clauses of the contract invalidate the non-compete clause?

Is the non-compete clause enforceable if Jim opens his own practice in the same town as Lewis Chiropractic?

How is this matter likely to be resolved? ■

Summary

For over 50 years equal employment opportunity has been the law of the land. It remains the principal subject of employment law activity and is well monitored by the EEOC and the OFCC as well as state and local agencies. This chapter describes how employers must select, interview, evaluate, and otherwise qualify individuals for employment in compliance with these laws. The matters of affirmative action and possible reverse discrimination are also considered. The intended result is to include a diversity of personnel throughout the organization to reflect the diversity of the host community.

This is accomplished through an analysis of the job to be filled followed by utilization of consistent and valid tests, interviews, and background investigations to explore candidate competencies. Particularly in the public sector, there are regulations requiring the preferential consideration of veterans and minorities who have been historically disadvantaged. The chapter concludes with a consideration of selection audits and certain post-hiring issues.

Key Terms

job analysis 59
diversity 59
probationary period 59
BFOQ (bona fide occupational qualification) 60
Civil Service 60
construct validity 60
affirmative action 61

accommodations 61
applicant pool 64
criteria 65
essential job functions 65
disparate impact 67
disclaimer 68
Equal Pay Act 69

Weighted Application Blank (WAB) 69
test validation 75
content validity 75
construct validation 76
negligent hiring 77
comparable worth 83

Questions for Discussion

1. What is job analysis and how does it relate to job descriptions?
2. Discuss the importance of validity and the various types of validity for selection instruments.
3. What are the basic elements of an Affirmative Action Plan?
4. Why might an employer make a "conditional offer" of employment?
5. How can applicant interview training be useful in compliance with the law?
6. Explain why a question might be innocent and legal but viewed as inappropriate to others?
7. How could refusing to hire a convicted felon be unlawful?
8. Why should an applicant be required to sign an application form?

9. Why do some situations justify a pre-employment physical exam and others do not?
10. What is the purpose of a Weighted Application Blank?
11. What defense does the employer have when its selection process appears to have an adverse impact on a protected class of employees?
12. Explain the four-fifths rule to determine the existence of a disparate impact.
13. What is negligent retention?
14. What are the characteristics of a bona fide merit pay plan?
15. Consider your own employment application process experiences. Can you relate any procedures or requirements that might have created an exposure for the employer?

Notes to Chapter 3

1. For a discussion of employee liabilities, see "The expanding workplace: Telecommuting and legal liability under OSHA, ADA and W. W. Wade," *Labor Law Journal*, 50, no. 4 (Winter 1999): 242–263.

2. D. Patton, *Human resource management in the public sector* (Boston: Houghton Mifflin, 2002), p. 216.

3. *Texas Department of Community Affairs* v. *Burdine*, 450 U.S. 248 (1981).

4. PL 29-454 section 2301.

5. M. D. Esposito, "Update your affirmative action plan," *The Human Resources Yearbook* (Englewood Cliffs, NJ: Prentice Hall, 1992/1993): p. 9.5. Also see L. Mead and J. Kleiner, "What new rights law means to organizations," *Labor Law Journal* (October 1995): 627.l.

6. This is the basis for set-aside programs in the public sector. *Metro Broadcasting, Inc.* v. *Federal Communications Commission*, 110 S.Ct. 2297 (1990).

7. *Hazelwood School District* v. *United States*, 433 U.S. 299 (1977).

8. *City of* Richmond v. *J. A. Croson Co.*, 109 S.Ct. 706 (1989).

9. *Metro Broadcasting, Inc.* v. *Federal Communication Commission*, 110 S.Ct. 2997 (1990).

10. *Astroline Communications Co.* v. *Sherberg Broadcasting* (consolidated opinion), 110 S.Ct. 997 (1990). Set aside programs are no longer legal, unless there is a compelling interest to do so.

11. *Kaiser Aluminum and Chemical Corporation* v. *Weber*, 443 U.S. 193 (1979).

12. *Regents of the University of California* v. *Bakke*, 438 U.S. 265 (1978).

13. Congress by statute can constitutionally favor one race over another: *Fullilove* v. *Klutznick*, 444 U.S. 448 (1980). Otherwise a compelling interest has to be shown.

14. A good policy is to obtain a copy of the EEOC compliance manual and have it visible at the time of the review. Also the combined poster "EEOC Is the Law" should be posted.

15. The Standard Compliance Review Report requires the company to complete an adverse-impact analysis of all promotions and terminations. A compelling interest has to be shown.

16. This historic (civil service) system exercises varying degrees of control and provides a predetermined number of previously approved job candidates, often from 3 to 6, from which the department can choose.

17. Sally Selden, *Human Resource Practices in State Government*, 61, no. 5 (Sept./Oct. 2001): 599.

18. D. Patton, *Human resource management: The public service perspective* (Boston: Houghton Mifflin, 2002), p. 46.

19. A remedy for a statistical imbalance caused by discriminatory practices is a court order to require the employer to hire a certain percentage of the protected class discriminated against. The employer therefore must take the best qualified within those classes to comply with the court order.

20. *Ford Motor Co.* v. *EEOC*, 102 S.Ct. 3057 (1982).

21. *Shutt* v. *Sandoz Crop Protection Cor.*, 944 F.2d 1431 (9th Cir. 1991). A 21-member labor pool was used although 106 members of all the sales representatives were available; the court found it was not a representative labor pool. For further information on the applicant pool concept, see Justice Powell's opinion in *Regents of University of California* v. *Bakke*, 438 U.S. 265 (1978). In *Johnson* v. *Transportation Agency*, 107 S.Ct. 1442 (1987), the court in approving the applicant pool concept stated that an affirmative action plan that requires all applicants in the pool to compete with all other applicants is acceptable.

22. *EEOC* v. *Spokane Concrete Products*, 534 F. Supp. 581 (E.D. Wash. 1982).

23. *Henchey* v. *Town of North Greenbush*, 831 F. Supp. 960 (ND NY 1993).

24. See *Stacks* v. *Southwestern Bell Yellow Pages*, 17 F.3d 316 (8th Cir. 1994).

25. Study, Online Recruiting Should Diversify, not Replace, traditional hiring. *Nation's Restaurant News*, 42, no. 45 (November 17, 2008): 8–12.

26. *Human Resource Magazine*, 53, no. 11 (November 2008): 12.

27. D. Arthur, *Recruiting, interviewing, selecting, and orienting new employees,* 2nd ed. (New York: American Management Association, 1991), p. 52; R. Gatewood and H. Field, *Human resource selection* (Chicago: Dryden Press, 1990), Chapter 10, p. 421.

28. In *EEOC* v. *Detroit Edison Co.,* 512 F.2d 301 (6th Cir. 1975), the court concluded that employee referrals would perpetuate the imbalance in the workforce in favor of white males that already existed at the facility.

29. *Diggs* v. *Western Electric,* 587 F.2d 1070 (10th Cir. 1978), *United States* v. *Georgia Power Co.,* 474 F.2d 906 (5th Cir. 1973).

30. *EEOC* v. *Chicago Miniature Lamp Works,* 947 F.2d 292 (7th Cir. 1991), some courts will hold that it is the most efficient and economical method, word-of-mouth recruiting is legal notwithstanding statistical imbalance: *EEOC* v. *Consolidated Service Systems, Inc.,* No. 91-3530 and 92-1879, unpublished opinion (7th Cir. 1993).

31. Under the Fair Labor Standards, young people are prohibited from performing hazardous work and certain hours, State laws must also be consulted.

32. Courts have upheld continuing residency requirements in the public sector. See *McCarthy* v. *Philadelphia Court Service Commision,* 424 US 96 S.Ct. 1154, 47 L.'Ed' 2nd.

33. To be deemed suitable, disclaimers should be bold, conspicuous large letters. *Silchia* v. *MCA Telecommunications Corp.,* 942 F.Supp. 1369 (D. Colo. 1996).

34. Public organizations granting job property rights would exclude this statement.

35. *Welch* v. *Liberty Machine Works, Inc.,* 23 F.2d 1403 (8th Cir. 199), *Frey* v. *Ramsey County Community Human Services,* 517 N.W.2d 591 (Minn. Ct. App. 1994).

36. *Wallace* v. *Dunn Construction Company, Inc.,* 62 F.2d 374 (11th Cir. 1995).

37. "Development and Use of Weighted Application Blanks," rev. ed., no. 55 (Minneapolis: University of Minnesota, Industrial Relations Center, 1971).

38. Although there is not an absolute correlation between tenure and success on the job, for the purpose of WAB analysis, tenure of one or more years on the job is predictive of some degree of success based on the assumption that if an employee lasts one year or longer, performance has been rated as acceptable.

39. The WAB technique assumes that there is an opportunity to select from the labor market.

40. *Karraker* v. *Rent-a-Center, Inc.,* Alan Goldstein & Soshanna Epstein, "Personality testing in employment," *Labor Lawyer Journal* (July 1995): 243–252.

41. Ibid. p. 252.

42. Elliot Lasson, "How good are integrity tests?" *Personnel Journal,* 71 (April 1992): 35; also see Office of Technology Assessment, "The use of integrity tests for reemployment screening" (1990): 8.

43. See C. Allen, "Black and white controversy," *Insight,* 8, no. 2 (January 13, 1992): 4.

44. See Uniform Guidelines of Employee Selection Procedures, 29 CFR Section.

45. Term used in court records is "negro." The term is now considered improper in antidiscrimination documents.

46. *Connecticut* v. *Teal,* 102 S.Ct. 2525 (1982).

47. CRA91 permits the employee to show that a less-discriminatory practice can be used.

48. Job analysis as used by the court is a statement that provides basic information about job requirements and characteristics of persons who can successfully perform the job.

49. A short period is a matter of judgment of the enforcement agency and the courts. The length of time would be somewhat related to the degree of the skill required.

50. ADA allows employers to require if certain conditions

51. Treatment of handicapped workers is found in Chapter 4.

52. *Department of Transportation,* FMCSA 49 CFR, parts 653 and 654.

53. "Negligent referral: A potential theory for employer liability," *Southern California Law Review,* 64 (1991): 1645; see also A. Ryan and M. Lasek, "Negligent hiring and defamation," *Personnel Psychology,* 44 (Summer 1991): 293–391.

54. In *Welch Mfg. Co.* v. *Pinkerton's,* 747 A.2d 436 (R.I. 1984), the court held that a police record and contacting two former employers was not enough. In *Burch* v. *A&G Associates,* 333

N.W.2d 140 (1983), the court said that a taxi-cab company has a higher duty to investigate than other employers. However, in *Evans* v. *Morsell*, 95 A.2d 480 (Md. 1978), the court said there was very little duty to check on a bartender. See also *Kassman* v. *Busfield Enterprise, In.*, 639 P.2d 353 (1981).

55. For further reading, see R. Jacobs, "Defamation and negligence in the workplace," *Labor Law Review* (September 1989): 52.

56. *Harvey Freeman & Sons* v. *Stanley*, 384 SE.2d 682 (Ga. App. 1989).

57. *Abbott* v. *Payne*, 457 So.2d 1156 (Fla. 1984).

58. *Tallahassee Furniture Co.* v. *Harrison*, 582 So.2d 744 (Fla. App. 1st Dist. 1991).

59. *Pittard* v. *Four Seasons Motor Inn*, 688 P.2d 333 (N.M. App. 1984).

60. The percentage of women in the workforce in 1993 was over 45 percent, and their wages were 68 percent of men's wages: U.S. Department of Labor, *Monthly Labor Review* (January 1993).

61. *Katz* v. *School Dist. of Clayton, Missouri*, 557 F.2d 153 (8th Cir. 1977).

62. Interpretive regulations were issued by EEOC. They give the EEOC position on all of these factors (29 CFR Part 1620). Case law is in accord.

63. See U.S. Glass Ceiling Comm. (Robert B. Reich, Chair), *A solid investment: Making use of the nation's human capital* (Washington, DC: USDOL), approved November 21, 1995.

64. Ibid.

65. 21 F.2d 259 (3rd Cir. 1970), cert. denied, 398 U.S. 90 (1970).

66. Right after the enactment of EPA, the first loophole that employers attempted to exploit was to change the job content to include tasks that women did not normally perform.

67. Meryl Gordon, "Discrimination at the top," *Working Women* (September 1992): 8.

68. In *Glenn* v. *General Motors*, 841 F.2d 1567 (11th Cir. 1988), the court said that the difference in skills and duties must be substantial to justify a pay differential.

69. *Katz* v. *School Dist. of Clayton, Missouri*, 557 F.2d 153 (8th Cir. 1977).

70. In *EEOC* v. *McCarthy*, 768 F.2d 1 (1st Cir. 1985), the court held ability to be more important.

71. *Fowler* v. *Land Management Group, Inc.*, 978 F.2d 158 (4th Cir. 1992).

72. *Aldrich* v. *Randolph Central School District*, 963 F.2d 520 (2nd Cir. 1991).

73. *Marshall* v. *Security Band & Trust Co.*, 572 F.2d 276 (10th Cir. 1978).

74. *Hodgson* v. *Fairmont Supply Co.*, 454 F.2d 490 (4th Cir. 1972).

75. *Brennan* v. *T. M. Fields, Inc.*, 488 F.2d 443 (5th Cir. 1973).

76. J. Kanin-Lovers and R. Bevan, "Don't evaluate performance—Manage it," *Compensation Benefits*, 1 (March–April 1992): 51–53; D. Guns II, "Merit Pay—An Unbalanced Approach to Pay for Performance," *Personnel Journal*, 71 (April 1992): 16.

77. R. Selwitz, "Blueprint for performance pay," *ABA Bank Journal*, 82 (May 1990): 18; J. A. Parmele, "Five reasons why pay must be based on performance," *Supervision*, 52 (Fall 1991): 6–8; J. Feldman, "Another day, another dollar, needs another look," *Personnel*, 68 (January 1991): 9–11.

78. *Braatz* v. *Labor Industry Review Comm.*, 496 N.W.2d 597 (U.S. Sup.Ct. 1993).

79. *City of Los Angeles* v. *Manhart*, 435 U.S. 702 (U.S. S.Ct. 1978).

80. *Arizona Governing Committee for Tax Deferred Annuity and Deferred Compensation Plans, Etc., et al.* v. *Nathalie Norris, Etc.*, 103 S.Ct. 3492 (1983).

81. Must include all major factors to compare differential. *Smith* v. *Virginia Commonwealth University*, 68 FEP cases (8th Cir. 1993).

82. E. M. Bowen, "Closing the female pay gap: Redefining the Equal Pay Act's affirmative defense," *Columbia Journal of Social Problems*, 17 (1994): 225.

83. J. Quinn, "Visibility and value: The rule of job evaluation in assuring equal pay for women," *Journal of International Business*, 25 (1994): 1403.

84. U.S. General Accounting Office, *Women's earnings: Work patterns partially explain differences between men's and women's earnings*. Washington, DC: Author, 2003), pp. 43–44.

85. J. Hersch, "The impact of nonmarket work on market wages," *American Economic Review*, 81 (May 1991): 157; P. F. Orazem, "Comparable worth and factor point pay in state government," *Industrial Relations*, 31 (Winter 1992): 135–215.

86. Although attempts to amend the EPA and apply it to pay equity have been introduced in Congress, none have been successful.

87. J. Quinn, "Visibility and Value: The rule of job evaluation in assuring equal pay for women," *Journal of International Business,* 25 (1994): 1403.

88. *Connecticut* v. *Teal,* 102 S.Ct. 2525 (1982).

89. For a review of the effectiveness of selection procedures, see K. Buckner, H. Field, and H. W. Holley, Jr., "The relationship of legal case characteristics with the outcomes of personnel selection court cases," *Labor Law Journal,* 41, no.11 (January 1990).

90. Personnel Practices, Columbus County, OR.

91. *Jostens Inc.* v. *National Computer systems, Inc.,* 318 N.W.2d 691 703-04 (Minn. 1982).

92. Included in a handbook prepared by one of the authors.

93. *Anderson Chemical Co.* v. *Green,* 66 S.W.3d 434-442 (Tex. Ct. App. 2001).

CHAPTER 4

Disability, Medical Leave, Religious Accommodation, and Substance Abuse Issues

CHAPTER OUTLINE

Definition of a Disabled Person

Disability under the Law

Accommodation for Physical Handicaps

Americans with Disabilities Act

Family and Medical Leave Act

Accommodation for Religious Beliefs

Drug and Alcohol Issues

AIDS in the Workplace

Antidiscrimination statutes require the employer not to take race, sex, national origin, color, age, or **disability** into account when making an employment decision. The intent is to achieve a workplace where discrimination based on these factors is not present. Title VII of the Civil Rights Act requires that all individuals in a protected class are to be treated alike. The law requires equal employment opportunity in addition to providing special protections for employees with a disability or limiting religious belief by requiring accommodation.

DEFINITION OF A DISABLED PERSON

Disability in the workplace is defined by the courts. Based on recent case law it is apparent that the Equal Employment Opportunity Commission has adopted a definition of *disability* similar to that found in the Rehabilitation Act of 1973. The EEOC Compliance Manual Section 903 provides guidance in determining whether or not an individual has a "disability" as defined in Title I of the Americans with Disabilities Act of 1990 (**ADA**), as amended in 2008 (**ADAAA**).[1]

The definition of *disability* under the ADA reflects congressional intent to prohibit specific forms of discrimination that people with disabilities face. Because this definition is designed to eliminate discrimination prohibited by the ADA, it may differ from the definition of disability under other statutes. A definition of whether a complaining employee has a disability turns on whether he or she meets the ADA definition of that term. An employee has a disability for purposes of the ADA if she or he

1. has a physical or mental **impairment**, including episodic impairment, that substantially limits a **major life activity** or major bodily function;
2. has a medical history or record of a physical or mental impairment; or
3. is regarded as having such impairment.

In court, an employee must satisfy at least one of these requirements to be considered an individual with a disability. Following the passage of the ADA, various jurisdictions and the Supreme Court acted to narrow the scope of impairment and somewhat limit the protections provided in Title I. The ADA Amendments Act (ADAAA) was designed to overturn these limitations and broaden the scope of the term *disability*, both under the ADA and the Rehabilitation Act.[2]

The law recognizes that the existence of these conditions may sometimes interfere with performance. State legislatures, Congress, and the courts have also recognized that there are limits to the measures that employers have to take if such conditions unduly interfere with performance. This is known as **undue hardship** and will not require the employer to make adjustments. It is because of the conflict between disability or religious belief and the legitimate requirements of employers that the courts have developed the concept of **reasonable accommodation**.

The discussion in this chapter differs from chapters where other antidiscrimination laws are discussed. In this chapter it is recognized that the disabled, religious, and/or handicapped employee may be treated differently; the issue is to what extent reasonable accommodation is required and the degree or duty to accommodate. With respect to religious beliefs, the employee can subjectively choose whether or not his or her beliefs should take precedence over conflicting employment requirements. The disabled employee does not have this choice.[3]

ACCOMMODATION FOR PHYSICAL HANDICAPS

The two federal statutes that prohibit discrimination because of handicap are the Americans with Disabilities Act and the Rehabilitation Act of 1973. The Americans with Disabilities Act of 1990, amended (42 U.S.C. 12101-12213), prohibits discrimination against a qualified person in all employment practices. Titles I through IV deal with discrimination against disabled persons in the private and public sectors. Title V prohibits retaliation or coercion in response to enforcement. Enforcement of ADA provisions is through the EEOC. Claims of retaliation under ADA may be redressed only by equitable relief; retaliation plaintiffs are not entitled to compensatory or punitive damages.[4] The act provides a clear and comprehensive mandate to eliminate discrimination based on disability.[5]

Guidelines by the EEOC make it clear that an employer may ask certain questions about reasonable accommodation at the pre-offer stage if it is reasonable to believe that the applicant will need accommodation because of an obvious or voluntarily disclosed disability, or when the applicant has disclosed a need for accommodation. The employer may also ask certain questions about an applicant's ability to perform specific job functions at pre-offer and inquire about nonmedical qualifications such as education and work history. The employer may also ask an applicant to describe how he or she would perform job-related tasks. Employers that utilize psychological pre-employment testing must be careful not to include disability-related questions in these tests. Failure to eliminate such questions may result in a violation of the Act.[6] For employers, the heart of the ADA is the requirement that they make reasonable accommodation, without undue hardship, for any qualified individual who can perform the essential functions of a job.[7]

Undue Hardship

Undue hardship is a defense available to employers but the hardship must be greater than *de minimis*. Based on the EEOC Compliance Manual and case law under the ADA, undue hardship exists when it

1. imposes an undue financial burden on the employer;
2. is unduly extensive, substantial, and disruptive to the workplace;
3. poses a direct threat to the health and safety of the employee or co-workers;
4. unduly disrupts the nature and operation of the business; and
5. can be shown that the proposed accommodation is unreasonable due to the size and financial capability of the employer.

AMERICANS WITH DISABILITIES ACT

The Americans with Disabilities Act defines a *disabled individual* as a person with a physical or mental handicap that "substantially limits one or more life activities," such as caring for oneself, walking, hearing, seeing, speaking and, of course, working. The 2008 amendment added "major bodily function" as a substantially limiting factor. The Act further requires that the employer not discriminate in hiring, promotion, or assignment on account of disability. The employer is most likely to violate the ADA when requiring an applicant to take a pre-employment physical or inquiring about the nature

or severity of an applicant's apparent or stated disability. Specifically prohibited by the 2008 amendment is any test, standard, or other selection criteria based on uncorrected vision standards. However, the employer may inquire about the applicant's ability to perform job-related functions after a job offer has been made.[8] The most important requirement for the employer is to ask disabled applicants or present employees what jobs they think they can perform after a conditional job offer has been made. Jobs that these individuals indicate that they cannot perform can then be eliminated. Normally an individual will not claim or attempt to perform a job that the disability prevents him or her from doing.

Jobs that people think they can do but that the employer or supervisor believes they cannot perform are the ones that may create a problem. The employer is entitled to take facility requirements into consideration in making a determination as to whether or not a particular employee can satisfactorily perform a job (see Exhibit 4.1).

Reasonable Accommodation under the ADA

The ADA requires that an employer make "reasonable accommodations" for qualified disabled workers so that they can perform the "essential functions" of a job. Fundamentally, a reasonable accommodation is anything that does not create an undue hardship for the employer. *Reasonable accommodations* include modifications or adjustments to the job application process; modifications or adjustments to the work environment or to the manner and/or circumstances under which a job is typically performed; and modifications or adjustments that enable a qualified employee to enjoy equal benefits and privileges with those enjoyed by other employees. This definition may even include the assignment of an employee to a different supervisor.[9] However, the employer is not

1. Make facilities more accessible, particularly if these facilities are open to the public.
2. Review job descriptions to make certain that all the essential functions of the job are included. This should be done by an outside consultant or an industrial engineer.
3. Eliminate all pre-offer medical examinations. As discussed in other chapters, all job offers should be contingent on meeting certain specified criteria.
4. Always attempt to accommodate a disabled person. Utilize the interactive process. Undue hardship will be decided on a case-by-case basis, but not before an attempt has been made. It is the failure to attempt to accommodate that will cause exposure to litigation.
5. Appoint an ADA coordinator to become knowledgeable in compliance with the ADA, and have that person report to the CEO or other top management official.

EXHIBIT 4.1   Guidelines for Minimizing Exposure to ADA Claims

required to eliminate or reassign the essential function of a job, lower production standards, or provide personal use items such as eyeglasses or hearing aids to handicapped individuals. Neither can the employer be required to violate the rights of other employees covered by a collective bargaining agreement. The employer is obligated to make a good faith effort to accommodate employees through an informal interactive process during which the employer and the employee attempt to determine a reasonable accommodation together.[10] However, under the 2008 amendment, the employer is not required to accommodate an individual who satisfies only the "regarded as" prong of the definition of disability. Failure to reasonably accommodate qualified employees and/or failure to utilize this interactive process to arrive at a reasonable accommodation is a violation of the ADA.[11]

The essential function of a job generally means the fundamental job duties of the job or position that the individual with the disability holds or desires. It does not include the marginal functions of a position. A job function may be considered essential for any of several reasons. For example, a function may be essential because the reason the job or position exists is to perform the function. It may also be essential because of the limited number of employees available to perform it,

or the function may be highly specialized so that individuals hired to fill the position are selected for specific expertise or ability to perform the function. In establishing "essential functionality," the employer is entitled to utilize its judgment, written job descriptions, time studies, an explanation of the consequences of not requiring a disabled employee to perform the function, work experiences of past incumbents, and work experiences of those employees in similar jobs. However, it must be noted that in the event of a lawsuit it is likely that a jury may ultimately determine what the essential functions of a job are at a particular facility.[12]

Rehabilitation Act of 1973 and the ADA

The Rehabilitation Act of 1973 became more important with the passage of the ADA because the definition of a handicapped worker under the Rehabilitation Act of 1973 is adopted by the ADA. Case law under the 1973 act is also given great weight by the EEOC when interpreting the ADA. The strict requirement for accommodation, as well as other requirements under the ADA, were continued by the courts and are now required under the Rehabilitation Act.[13] The Rehabilitation Act of 1973 (87 Stat. 355, 29 USC Sect. 701–94) requires federal contractors to take affirmative action to hire or promote qualified handicapped individuals.[14] The affirmative action required of government contractors and employers' receiving federal assistance is similar to that required under Executive Order 11246 (discussed later) with one exception. By definition, a handicapped worker is not as qualified as a nonhandicapped worker for all job assignments. Therefore, there is a duty placed on the employer to accommodate the handicapped worker by making an effort to place the applicant or employee in a job that the person is qualified to perform with the same competency as a nonhandicapped worker. The Rehabilitation Act of 1973, Section 503, requires any business that has a contract of $2,500 or more under the Act and provides services or personal property to any agency of the federal government to take affirmative action to employ handicapped workers. This requirement also applies to subcontractors. This means that virtually every employer that sells or provides services directly or indirectly to the federal government is covered under the Rehabilitation Act. If the employer has government contracts that exceed $50,000, a written affirmative action program must be developed.[15]

Definition of a Handicapped Person

The Rehabilitation Act defines a *handicapped person* as "any person who has a physical or mental impairment which substantially limits one or more of such person's major life activities and has a record of such impairment, or is regarded as having such impairment." The court has held that under Section 504 if any injury makes a person not able to perform the job that person is not qualified.[16]

Many of the issues that courts have to decide under the Act concern the definition of a handicapped person. The statute provides that "no otherwise qualified handicapped individual shall, solely by reason of his [or her] handicap, be discriminated against." Any allegation of discrimination immediately raises the issue of whether the person is in fact handicapped.[17]

Judicial Definition of a Handicapped Employee

The definition of a handicapped employee is found in *Southeastern Community College v. Davis*, 442 U.S. 397 (1979). The plaintiff in *Davis* was a deaf applicant to a nursing school. She could not understand speech without lip reading. The school refused to admit her on the grounds that her hearing disability would make it unsafe for her to be a nurse. The court said that under Section 504 of the Rehabilitation Act of 1973, an "otherwise qualified person means one who is able to meet all of the program's requirements in spite of the handicap."[18]

The courts have stated that although certain physical conditions such as height, weight, and strength may render the employee incapable of performing the duties of the job, they are not impairments that substantially limit one or more major life activities. An applicant who was denied employment because of morbid obesity may be able to prove discrimination under Section 504 of the Rehabilitation Act.[19] The key question is whether she can perform the job in spite of morbid obesity.[20] Many states do not consider a medical condition a handicap; others, such as New York and California, do. Most state courts are following the federal courts in interpreting their handicapped laws by deciding on a case-by-case basis. It is worth repeating that the best policy is to determine treatment on a case-by-case basis and wait for ADA interpretation of each factual situation. We do know that the handicapped individual has more rights since the passage of ADA.

Accommodation for Handicapped Persons

The extent to which a covered employer must accommodate a handicapped worker depends on the applicable section of the law.

Section 504 deals with recipients of federal financial assistance. The employer is obligated to treat handicapped and nonhandicapped individuals equally. Under Sections 501 and 503, federal employers and contractors may be obligated to take affirmative action to employ and promote in employment qualified handicapped individuals. Regardless of whether an employer is covered by Section 501 or 504 or by a state law, there still is a duty to make reasonable accommodation.[21] Clearly, the courts have struggled with the requirement of reasonable accommodation for many years and employers have been held to differing degrees of obligation depending on what section of law they are under or whether there is an applicable state law. The ADA also has an influence on these obligations. In order for a court to find an issue of reasonable accommodation, there must be a job available. The Rehabilitation Act of 1973 is not a "make work" public employment statute but is an attempt to prohibit discriminatory placement for existing positions.

The court guideline for reasonable accommodation is found in *Southeastern Community College* v. *Davis,* mentioned earlier. The plaintiff, being deaf, could not meet all of the requirements of the program unless the standards were substantially lowered, and Section 504 does not impose this obligation on an educational institution. In *Stutts* v. *Freeman,* 694 F.2d 666 (11th Cir. 1983), the applicant could perform all the duties of the job but could not pass the aptitude test. It was not necessary to pass the test to perform the essential functions of the job. The court held that refusal to try the plaintiff on the job was a failure to accommodate. Some courts have liberally interpreted the *Stutts* decision in favor of the handicapped person and required the employer to make some modifications.[22] Other courts consider the *Davis* decision as not requiring any modifications. This is the majority rule in the circuit courts under the Rehabilitation Act, but not ADA.

BFOQ as Applied to Accommodation

One factual situation that often arises is when the employer feels that although the handicapped person can perform the essential functions of the job, he or she would not be able to perform it safely. This would be a bona fide occupational qualification (BFOQ) exception. The standard for BFOQ was established in *Weeks* v. *Southern Bell Telephone and Telegraph Co.,* 408 F.2d 228 (5th Cir. 1959), and followed in most state and federal jurisdictions. The court in *Weeks* said that in order to establish a **BFOQ** for sex discrimination, the employer "must show that all or substantially all members of the class would not be able to perform safely and efficiently the duties of the job." This is often difficult to show.

Although cases concerning the question of reasonable accommodation are decided on a case-by-case basis, one common thread running through all the decisions is that the employer must make a bona fide attempt to accommodate.[23] The problem that the human resource practitioner or manager often has is that supervision has a subjective notion that the handicapped worker cannot perform the job and refuses to give him or her an opportunity to perform. The reason often given is the risk of future injury. Unless there are objective facts to substantiate the reason, it will not stand judicial scrutiny.

Bona Fide Effort to Accommodate

To avoid liability for discrimination against a handicapped person, the employer must make a good faith effort to accommodate. Often supervisors will give a subjective reason for not making an attempt. The courts in any area of discrimination will no longer tolerate apparently arbitrary action on the part of management. The statutory duty to accommodate does not require the employer to prejudice the safety of the individual or co-worker. The law does not interfere with business objectives, changing methods of doing business, or in any way intentionally increasing costs.[24] What the courts and Congress are telling the employer is that he or she must make a bona fide attempt to accommodate. When making this attempt, failure to accommodate is not the issue as long as the effort was made in good faith without intent to discriminate. The court will seldom find that the reason accommodation cannot be done is not a good business practice or that it is uncommon in business. They leave the determination of good business reasons up to management as long as the reasons are nondiscriminatory. Most reasonable offers of accommodation satisfy the statute. The Supreme Court has made it clear that the employee does not have the unilateral right to select the accommodation.[25] From case law it is safe to say that it is better to be wrong than not to attempt to accommodate and make no offer at all.

Other Issues

Seniority and arbitration are normally topics of concern in a unionized environment. There are, however, many employers who have unilaterally established seniority systems and grievance and arbitration procedures independent of a collective bargaining process or a union presence. Accordingly, case law regarding the conflict between reasonable accommodation requests and seniority, and between arbitration agreements and legal action pursuant to the ADA, are of relevance to employers that have adopted either or both of these policies. When seniority systems are well established, either through collective bargaining or company policy, the Supreme Court has held that seniority will prevail and that an accommodation that violates the rights of other employees is not reasonable.[26]

Employers have also attempted to immunize themselves from employee lawsuits by adopting arbitration agreements as a condition of employment, which requires employees to submit all disputes that may arise in the course of their employ-

ment to final and binding arbitration. Baker, an epileptic, was employed by the Waffle House restaurant group and signed such a mandatory arbitration agreement. He subsequently suffered a seizure and was discharged. He ignored the arbitration procedure and filed a complaint with the EEOC under the ADA. The EEOC subsequently brought an enforcement action against the employer that was challenged because Baker had not exhausted his remedy under the arbitration provision. The Supreme Court held that the EEOC had the right to pursue the matter, the arbitration clause notwithstanding. Although Baker may have been bound by the arbitration clause, the EEOC is not.[27]

FAMILY MEDICAL LEAVE ACT

The **Family Medical Leave Act (FMLA)** of 1993 was amended in 2008 by Section 585 of the National Defense Authorization Act.[28] This amendment became effective in January 2009 as a result of the Labor Department's adoption of a Final Rule, which updates the FMLA regulations to implement new military family leave entitlements. These entitlements permit a spouse, son, daughter, parent, or next of kin to take up to 26 weeks of leave to care for a member of the Armed Forces (including National Guard or Reserves) who is undergoing medical treatment, recuperation, or therapy, is otherwise in outpatient status, or is on the temporary disability retirement list because of a serious injury or illness.

Following the 2008 amendment, there are now three types of leave available to employees for personal or family illness or injury situations:

1. Leave for the birth or adoption of a child
2. Leave because of a "serious health condition" of an employee or his or her spouse, child, or parent
3. Leave to serve as a military caregiver

"Serious health condition" means a condition that renders an employee incapable of performing the essential functions of the job.

FMLA Benefits

The FMLA provides for unpaid leave of up to 12 weeks for specified purposes (26 weeks for **military caregivers**); continuation of health benefits while on leave; reinstatement to the same or equivalent job upon return from leave; and a prohibition against disciplining an employee for taking leave. The statute covers all public employers and private employers who employ at least 50 employees during at least 20 workweeks in the current or previous calendar year. To be a covered employee, an individual must have worked for the employer for 12 months (52 weeks) and have worked at least 1,250 hours in the 12 months before the leave is taken. The employee must also be employed at a worksite where the employer employs 50 or more workers within a 75-mile radius.

Calculating Leave and Leave Years

The 12 workweeks of leave are based on the employee's usual workweek. For example, a full-time employee would be entitled to 40 hours of work for 12 weeks, or 480 hours of leave per year. Part-time employees have their leave entitlement calculated based on their work schedule. For example, the employer could use a weekly average of the hours worked over a 12-week period prior to the requested leave to calculate a normal workweek for a part-time employee. Holidays or plant shutdowns are excluded from this calculation.

The employer may use a calendar year or any fixed 12-month period such as a fiscal year or a year beginning on the employee's anniversary date in calculating leave eligibility and entitlement. This fixed 12-month period can be a year rolling forward measured from the employee's first use of FMLA leave or a 12-month period rolling backward from the first date of use.

Requesting Leave

The employee is required only to indicate to the employer that leave is needed for health care. He or she does not need to specifically mention FMLA or leave qualified under the Act. The employer is expected to obtain additional information through informal means.[29] Oral notice by the employee is sufficient to trigger the requirements of the Act. "Foreseeable" leave requires the employee to provide 30 days' advance notice of leave taking. When leave is unforeseeable, notice should be given as soon as practical, typically within two days. These notice provisions may be modified by a collective bargaining agreement.

Notice need only be given one time for recurring, intermittent, or reduced schedule leave. The employee should give the employer sufficient information to let the employer know that leave is for an FMLA reason. The employer should inquire if the employee wants to substitute paid leave for FMLA leave or advise the employee that she or he is required to exhaust available paid leave before utilizing unpaid leave.

Employer Notice in Response

The employer is required to advise the employee if leave will be counted against his or her FMLA entitlement; of any medical certification requirements and the consequences of failing to meet these employer requirements; and regarding whether or not a fitness-for-duty examination will be required when returning to work. The employer must also notify the employee of the circumstances under which the employer will require substitution of paid leave, any requirements for the employee to make premium payments to maintain health benefits and the consequences of failing to meet those requirements, the employee's potential liability for health insurance premiums if he or she fails to return from FMLA leave, and the employee's right to be restored to the same or equivalent position when returning to work.

Qualifying Exigency Leave (Military Caregiver Only)

Exigency leave is designed to enable families of members of National Guard and Reserve units to manage the affairs of the service member while he or she is on active duty. Twelve weeks of job-protected leave are available for any qualifying exigency, including short-notice deployment, military events and related activities, childcare and school activities, financial and legal arrangements, counseling, up to 5 days of rest and recuperation, and up to 90 days of post-deployment activities.

Family Members with Serious Health Conditions

As noted, FMLA leave is limited to provide care for the serious health conditions of spouses, children, and parents. No other family members qualify. "Caring for" includes both the physical and psychological care of family members. The Act covers in-patient care as well as out-patient care. In-patient care includes overnight hospital, hospice, or residential medical care facility stays. It includes follow-up treatments and recovery, mental health treatment, substance abuse treatment, cosmetic surgery, and other elective procedures requiring in-patient care.

Out-patient care covers incapacity of more than three days requiring continuing medical care so long as the condition renders the patient unable to work, attend school, or perform regular daily tasks. It includes two visits to a health-care provider or one visit to such a provider resulting in a regimen of continuing treatment, such as prescription medication, or physical therapy using special

equipment. It also includes pregnancy and prenatal care so long as the patient is under continuing medical supervision, even if medical care is not required in connection with each period of incapacity. Leave for this purpose may be taken in increments as small as one hour or less.

Leave under FMLA is also allowable for chronic serious health conditions such as asthma, diabetes, epilepsy, and other long-term, recurring medical conditions that cause episodes of incapacity. The patient must receive periodic medical treatment, but need not receive medical treatment in connection with each period of incapacity. Long-term or permanent incapacity is also covered for conditions such as Alzheimer's disease, strokes, or terminal cancer so long as the patient is under continuing medical supervision. Finally, leave is available in order to receive and/or recover from restorative surgery following an accident or injury, or for multiple medical treatments for conditions such as cancer, severe arthritis, or kidney disease. The condition must be likely to result in incapacity of more than three days if left untreated. Under these circumstances leave may be taken as needed in small increments.

Regulations

The 2008 regulation changes adopted by the U.S. Department of Labor eliminated certain employer requirements. Under the new regulations, employers are no long subject to a categorical penalty when an employee suffers individualized harm. The regulations also invalidated the court-ordered requirement that the employer can be required to provide additional FMLA leave time for failure to properly designate FMLA leave.[30] The regulations also specify that "light duty" does not count as FMLA leave time and cannot be deducted from an employee's entitlement. Employees may voluntarily settle or release their FMLA rights without court or Department of

Labor approval either prospectively or retroactively. For example, an employee who asserts that "I can't afford to take unpaid leave" may be deemed a waiver of FMLA rights.

ACCOMMODATION FOR RELIGIOUS BELIEFS

It is the employer's duty to accommodate an employee's religious beliefs, based on the Title VII prohibition against discrimination and the U.S. Supreme Court's holding that an employer has the duty to accommodate its employees' exercise of religious activities in the workplace so long as the accommodation does not create more than a *de minimis* cost to the employer.[31] The statute does not require complete religious freedom in an employment situation since in many instances this would interfere with the normal conduct of the business.[32] A nonprofit religious organization can legally discriminate on the basis of religion when making an employment decision. What Title VII does require of other employers or labor unions is to make reasonable efforts to accommodate the religious beliefs of the employees or applicants.[33] The duty to accommodate includes religious observance as well as religious beliefs—for example, teaching a Bible class at night, serving as a lay preacher, or going to summer Bible camp. However, the religious observance is not unlimited. The Civil Rights Act of 1991 specifically permits religious organizations to require job applicants and employees to conform to their beliefs. When the employee has a belief that conflicts with the church, the employee's belief is the controlling factor.

Although the requirement that employers accommodate religious beliefs has been generally accepted for at least 30 years, it is significant to note that in the past 10 years there has been a 60 percent increase in the total number of charges filed with the EEOC based on claims of religious discrimination or harassment in the workplace. In 2006 alone there were 2,541 such charges filed. This may well be attributable to the growing demand by evangelicals and others to pronounce and practice their faith in the workplace.[34]

The Concept of Accommodation

The concept of accommodation is rooted in the case law on religious discrimination as a violation of Title VII and the U.S. Constitution. Title VII allows the employer to discriminate on the basis of religious beliefs if "it is unable to reasonably accommodate to an employee's religious observance or practice without undue hardship on the conduct of the employer's business."[35] The extent to which the employer must disrupt the business to accommodate for religious observance was decided in *TWA v. Hardison,* cited earlier. The court required the employer to show reasonable efforts to accommodate. If rescheduling work assignments causes seniority to be violated, co-worker rights to be infringed upon, or other changes in normal operations that would have resulted in increased costs in order to accommodate, it would not be religious discrimination to refuse to do so. Under *Hardison,* the court found that the employer only had to assume minimal costs to accommodate; otherwise it would be discriminating against other employees for whom no similar expenses were made. Alternatively, if the employer failed to show, for example, that rescheduling Saturday work was no additional cost and further evidence revealed that other employees volunteered to work, accommodation would not be deemed an undue hardship. More recently, the U.S. Court of Appeals has held, in the case of a Jehovah's Witness, that an employee could be required to work on Sundays after religious services if the employer had already accommodated her by allowing her to attend the Sunday services, Thursday services, and to swap shifts to attend church conventions.[36]

As a general rule, employers should consider reasonable requests for accommodation so long as no legitimate undue hardship is created. If accommodation will largely preserve the employee's job (compensation, terms and conditions of employment, without adverse consequences to the employer), then the employer should accommodate the employee.[37] Although only *de minimis* accommodation is required, a good faith effort is still the rule. In *Proctor v. Consolidated Freightways Corp. of Delaware*, 795 F.2d 1472 (9th Cir. 1986), the employee was told at the time of hiring that she would be required to work on Saturdays, but this did not relieve the employer of the duty to make a reasonable effort elsewhere to accommodate.

Alternative Accommodations

Although in almost every situation the employer has a duty to make a good faith effort to accommodate, once this effort has been made the requirements of the statute are satisfied.[38] In *Ansonia Board of Education v. Philbrook*, the employee, after six years of being employed as a schoolteacher, joined a church that prohibited members from working on certain holy days—a practice that caused him to miss six school days a year. The board policy was to grant three days for sick leave and three days for personal business leave. The employee wanted to take these six days for religious observance. The school board offered leave without pay and several other alternatives to accommodate him, but it rejected the employee's request that he be permitted to use personal business leave for religious purposes. The Court held that when there are several possible alternatives, the employer need not grant the one the employee prefers. Further, the employer

does not have to show that each of the employee's alternative accommodations would result in undue hardship. All the employer has to do is offer a reasonable accommodation, and an unpaid leave is reasonable unless a personal business leave is allowed for other employees. If other employees are allowed paid leave for any purpose, this could be discrimination.

Accommodation for Union Dues

A common situation involving religious discrimination occurs when, under a collective bargaining agreement, all employees must pay dues to the labor union, and an employee, because of religious beliefs, refuses to do so. The union then demands termination under a union security clause, but the employer refuses. Courts that have considered this question have held that if the employee tenders the amount of the dues to charity, this is a reasonable accommodation of the employee's religious beliefs by both the union and the employer.[39]

Employees' or applicants' religious observance and beliefs should not be a problem to the employer in view of the *Hardison* case. When an applicant is hired and there is some indication that religious beliefs will interfere with the employment situation, the employer should not refuse to hire the applicant, since that would constitute discrimination because of religion. The applicant, however, should be informed that an attempt will be made to accommodate; if that is not always possible, the applicant must decide whether to accept the job and from time to time not be able to observe religious beliefs, or decline the job offer. Legally it is extremely important for the employer to attempt to accommodate when requested to do so because of religious beliefs. Failure to make a reasonable attempt will invariably result in violation even though it can be shown in retrospect that accommodation was not possible.

DRUG AND ALCOHOL ISSUES

Nearly 75 percent of adult illicit drug users in the United States are employed on a full- or part-time basis, as are approximately 80 percent of adult heavy drinkers and binge drinkers, according to a survey conducted by the U.S. Substance Abuse and Mental Health Services Administration.[40] Indeed, drug and alcohol abuse is a serious problem for most employers. The problem is so serious because of the high cost of workers' compensation, absenteeism, and health care, not to mention the loss of productivity and resulting poor quality work.

Most companies have responded to the widespread use of drugs and alcohol by mandating the testing of applicants and existing employees. According to recent survey by the Society for Human Resource Management (SHRM), 84 percent of employers conduct pre-employment drug testing, nearly 75 percent conduct **reasonable suspicion drug testing**, and 39 percent conduct random drug testing of at least some personnel.[41] These numbers may be somewhat inflated since many small employers are not affiliated with SHRM and have no HR specialists. Although testing is expensive, particularly for small firms that test only employees who hold sensitive positions, it is likely to be cost effective in the long run. Many states have statutes that specifically permit drug testing. The Drug Free Workplace Act of 1988 (P.L. 100-690, Sect. 5151 et seq., 102 Stat. 403) applies to all federal employees and private employers doing business with the government.[42] Unfortunately, there is no effective pre-employment test for alcohol abuse although employees reasonably suspected of alcohol use at work can be tested to reveal impairment. Employers typically equate a positive drug test with impairment as part of their drug testing policy.

Need for a Drug-Testing Policy

No matter how large or how small the company, a drug-testing policy should be written and the policy should be in place before drug abuse problems appear. Indeed, the existence of a policy with the proper communication may prevent a substance abuse condition from developing in the workplace. Another reason for having a policy is that some states by statute require a written policy before any testing can be performed, and then a great deal of freedom is given for testing.[43] The existence of a drug policy will likely prevent exposure to a claim of invasion of privacy. The employee is forewarned that the policy will be enforced. A violation will result in severe disciplinary action up to and including discharge. If the employee objects to the policy, he or she will have an opportunity to seek employment elsewhere. For this reason all policies should have a time period before they become effective. Some courts will hold that continued employment after the policy has been announced is implied consent to its terms, and therefore the policy does not constitute an invasion of privacy.[44]

Essential Elements of a Policy

The purpose of the drug-testing policy should be clearly stated in order to discourage the use of drugs and discharge should be the last resort for violation of the policy. The policy should not be one that some other company has adopted but rather should fit the needs and environment of the company where it will be enforced. Drug policy in the public sector needs to be different from the policy for private-sector employees because public-sector employees have the protection of the Fourth Amendment of the Constitution. A public-sector drug policy usually applies to present employees and to pre-employment procedures. In the private sector, the type of industry may also warrant different procedures. There is more latitude for enforcement in jobs involving significant risks of injury to co-workers, the public, or those who have security responsibility.

The policy should define a substance abuser, a definition that may not always agree with that of the state or federal statute. The definition may be different, but it cannot violate a statute. The Rehabilitation Act of 1973 [Sect. 706(7) (b)] states that drug abuse is covered by the Act if the substance use threatens the safety of others or interferes with job performance. The Act is silent on whether a person in treatment is a handicapped person. A drug abuser is not considered a disabled person, but a person who has participated in a drug treatment program is protected under ADA.[45] Although there may be some question under a state or federal statute as to whether a particular condition constitutes a handicap,[46] there should be no question under the policy if the term is properly defined. Using its own definition, the employer can always make a policy more specific or clearer than a statute. It would be enforced as a policy rather than relying on a statute.

Surveillance for Presence of Drugs

In any surveillance issue, the law considers the balance between the employee's privacy rights and the employer's need to protect property and the safety of others. The most reliable surveillance for drug abuse is observation on the job. The policy could be written to require any person who observes the use or possession of drugs in the workplace to report it to management or be subject to discipline for failure to do so. There are many warnings of drug abuse in the workplace that management can detect with unobtrusive observation. Chronic or unexplained absenteeism, difficulty in concentration, spasmodic work patterns, generally lower job efficiency, strained relationships with co-workers, deterioration of personal appearance, and excessive use of breath purifiers are all indications to management of possible drug or alcohol abuse. Observation of any of these conditions should be further investigated to determine the cause.

Frequently, observance on the job comes in the advanced stages of drug use and most employers will likely desire to correct the problem sooner. For this reason, testing has become the most popular method of surveillance.[47] A surveillance method should not be used unless there is some reason to believe that the employee may be using drugs. The reason can be somewhat subjective, but it should be objective enough to show that it is not random. The Supreme Court has held that random testing or investigative testing is permissible only when public safety is involved or it is job critical.[48] Most state statutes also permit random drug testing where safety considerations or certain other conditions are present.

Testing Procedure for Drug Abuse

The following procedures in Exhibit 4.2 are examples of steps that can be taken in the adoption and implementation of a drug testing program or as a management proposal to the union in negotiations.

Surveillance methods to control drug abuse that could be used, depending on state law, include television surveillance, electronic eavesdropping devices (approximately one-half of the states prohibit these), and undercover investigation. Any surveillance method used should be stated in the policy together with a statement of when and how it might be used. If a polygraph test is used, considerable care should be taken in its administration, since this could be found to be an invasion of privacy or a violation of federal and state statutes. Polygraph tests should be administered by a professional, and the employee should sign a statement before seeing the results that the questions asked were job related and reasonable. If the employee refuses to answer questions, she or he should be asked the reason.[49]

1. Prior to testing, the employee should be given a chance to list any drugs taken in the last month and under what circumstances.
2. When requested to take a test, the employee will be informed why the test is necessary, and if there is any other way to get the facts the company will use it first.
3. If the first test is positive, the employee will be suspended. Further testing by a licensed laboratory will be required before any further action is taken or the results released.
4. Test results will be disclosed only to those persons who have a need to know for job-related decisions. Any further disclosure must be with the employee's consent.
5. Upon receipt of final test results, if positive, the employer will give the employee an opportunity to explain or challenge the results before taking disciplinary action.

EXHIBIT 4.2   Drug Testing Procedures

Regulation of Off-Duty Drug Abuse Activity

A positive drug test may be the result of off-duty use. To take action on the use of drugs away from the workplace, the employer must show that off-duty conduct affects the job or the employer's business. If an employee is arrested or convicted on a drug charge, the arrest or conviction must render the employee unable to perform his or her job satisfactorily or affect the employer's business before he or she is disciplined. It is best to suspend the employee pending further investigation in such cases. When the policy defines a positive drug test as evidence of impairment, the employer's ability to discipline for off-duty drug use is enhanced.

Correction of Drug Abuse by Employer

When the employer is positive that the employee is a drug abuser, the matter can be handled internally without the help of law-enforcement authorities. The policy should make it clear that discipline will be delayed or reduced if the employee voluntarily enters treatment. If the employee has undergone treatment and reverts to drug use, then termination may be the only alternative. The termination should be for violation of

the policy for the use of drugs that affects performance or the safety of others, and no mention should be made of any illegal activity.[50] The employee should always be given the option to enter treatment or resign. Treatment becomes a condition of employment. To avoid an unemployment compensation claim it should be made clear that the employee can remain as an employee only if treatment is successfully completed.

Policy on Alcohol Abuse

Although there is some similarity between drug and alcohol abuse, such as treatment, high costs to employer in health care, loss of production, and causes of death and disability from auto accidents, the incidents should be treated differently. The problem of alcohol is often more an employee relations problem than a legal one. Many states consider it an illness, whereas others consider it a handicap. The techniques used for detection in alcoholism are not as legally restrictive as in the case of drugs. The use of alcohol is a legal activity and the danger of defamation is not as great. Not infrequently a person using drugs is illegally selling drugs as well. An alcoholic can legally buy all the liquor she or he wants and doesn't inflict the habit on others. For this reason there is more tolerance in treatment of an alcoholic than of a drug abuser. Other reasons for treating the two differently depend on job category or type of industry.

Surveillance for Alcohol Abuse

The method selected for surveillance for alcohol abuse is practically unrestricted. Observation and undercover methods are the most effective and should be designed to encourage the employee to seek help. Undercover methods often involve the use of treated alcoholics to detect abuse among fellow workers and then an attempt to get the problem drinker to seek help. Another effective method is the use of **assessment centers** located in most large cities. The assessment center will determine whether the problem is caused by alcohol and if so whether the person is addicted to it and needs treatment. Often the problem might be alcohol, but the person is not an alcoholic. Rather, he or she uses poor judgment in drinking too much at a particular time. This is common in driving while intoxicated (DWI) situations.

The policy on alcoholism should not have as its objective abstinence from the use of alcohol unless the individual cannot control its use. In this respect alcohol abuse differs from drug abuse. The employee must recognize that she or he has a problem and needs help. If the employee doesn't realize this and fails to seek help and the problem continues, an intervention pursuant to the policy may be necessary. The policy should therefore include a step-by-step procedure to correct the problem insofar as uncontrolled use of alcohol affects the work of the employee. See Exhibit 4.3 for how a policy on alcoholism should be stated.

It must be remembered that, unlike drug abuse, alcoholism does not usually affect the co-workers' performance. The alcohol abuser can be tolerated longer than the drug abuser. The objective of a policy on alcohol is to eliminate the job-related problem, and the policy for drug abuse is to eliminate the use or possession of drugs.

Policy Needed to Avoid Legal Exposure

The problem of substance abuse by workers is not likely to disappear. Accordingly, the employer must continually educate management personnel to cope with it. A policy that is legally sound and considers employee relations consequences in its enforcement must be communicated to management personnel and all employees. The purpose of the policy is to discourage, and hopefully

---

1. After the employee admits that he or she needs help, the employee should be referred to an assessment center. If the employee refuses and alcohol is suspected to be the cause of the work-related problem, then terminate. The policy should clearly state that the options are to take treatment and continue as an employee or quit.
2. Once the employee agrees to seek help, treatment should be offered and medical leave without pay granted. Most companies cover this under their health-care and sick leave policy. (A few states require it.)
3. While in treatment the employee should maintain his or her employee status. The employer's policy should determine what benefits he or she should have; however, they should be the same as for other illnesses or handicapped persons.
4. Only after the employee refuses treatment or treatment fails should the employee be terminated, not for alcoholism but for the work-related problems caused by the use of alcohol. Termination should always be for the result, not for the cause. If it is for the cause, it is often difficult to correct.

EXHIBIT 4.3   Elements of an Alcohol Policy

eliminate, substance abuse in a particular workplace. The employee must therefore be put on notice concerning the existence of a policy and what action the employer will take if the policy is violated. The policy must be sensitive to the employee's expectations of privacy, the rights of co-workers, and the employer's desire to have a safe and efficient operation. It must also advise an alternative of treatment once it is determined that the applicant is an abuser. Reasonable means to determine facts, including testing, are judicially acceptable.[51]

The courts have been extremely reluctant to interfere with an employer to correct a problem that affects the business and safety of others. In this respect the rights of the employer are greater than privacy rights of the employee. Substance abuse is no exception. There is no interference from the law, provided the employer has as its objective the correction of substance abuse in the workplace and not correction for the good of society.

Employer Third-Party Liability for Inebriated Employees

Most courts have been reluctant to hold the employer liable when employees become inebriated at company-sponsored events or when employees are sent home after drinking at work, and later injure or cause damages to others. In some states, even where negligence is shown, the courts have held that the state "Dram Shop" laws do not apply. In *Meany* v. *Newett*, 367 N.W.2d 472 (Minn. 1985), the court refused to apply the "Dram Shop" statute to the employer. It was shown that the employer was negligent in serving the inebriated employee at a company-sponsored event. The employee later injured another person in an accident when driving while drunk. Decisions from the highest courts of New York, Maine, Kansas, and Minnesota have held that employers should not generally be held liable to third parties for the actions of the employees who

become intoxicated at company-sponsored events (outside scope of employment).

In *Meyers* v. *Grubaugh*, 750 P.2d 1031 (Kansas S.Ct. 1988), the employee drank beer before going off duty. While going home he was involved in an accident that caused injury to the plaintiff. The court held that the employer is not liable for off-duty conduct of the employees, although the condition was caused while on duty. This is the majority rule, but courts in some states (for example, Texas and New Jersey) have held otherwise. Because the employer has the protection of the law does not mean that the employer should be indifferent to the potential problem of drinking at company-sponsored events. There is always an exposure to lawsuit, and to some extent there is a moral obligation to control employees at a company-sponsored event such as a Christmas party. The employer can avoid a possible lawsuit either by having a cash bar or by controlling the period of time that a free bar is open. One way to do this is to start serving the food after a short refreshment period. If an employee comes to the event intoxicated, she or he should be sent home.

AIDS IN THE WORKPLACE

To properly address the problem of AIDS in the workplace, the employer must have a basic understanding of the nature of the disease, modes of transmission, testing and disclosure of results, and the nature of the disability that results from the disease.[52] A suggested strategy for the employer is to have a planned program on the "back burner" to be used when needed. In addition, employees should be currently educated on all aspects of the disease. The purpose of this section on AIDS, as distinguished from the section on drugs and alcohol, is to prepare the employer to cope with the problem when it exists. AIDS is reliably diagnosed as a disease that causes the human immune system to be incapable of fending off certain fatal illnesses. An HIV-positive test result means that the person has the virus that could cause AIDS; however, not all HIV-positives end up with AIDS. There is a difference between being HIV-positive and having AIDS. Managing AIDS in the workplace has become a business problem.

Some 20 years ago anyone testing positive for HIV was likely facing a death sentence. The HIV virus almost always led to AIDS and then to cancer or one of the other fatal conditions that a weakened immune system could not fight off. Although there is still no cure for AIDS or HIV, new highly effective drugs permit most workers with the HIV virus to continue their employment. AIDS may not have been a workplace issue in the past, but it is today.[53]

The HIV virus infects persons in various stages and is contagious in all stages. During the first stage of the virus a person is exposed to HIV but has no physical symptoms. There is no certainty that a person in this category will ultimately develop AIDS. During the second stage infected persons develop mild symptoms, including weight loss, abnormal fatigue, and swollen lymph nodes. At this stage the victim may have moderate illness that affects the job but for the most part is able to work. Approximately 25 percent of this group will develop AIDS. In the next stage the person develops AIDS from the previous stage. He or she may contract such rare diseases as Kaposi's sarcoma and certain types of rare pneumonia. This individual often will be able to work but will be absent due to illnesses more than normal. In the final stage of AIDS a person is in the advanced stage of the illness. She or he requires extended hospitalization and is most likely unable to work. It is at this stage that the disease is usually fatal.

Transmission of the Disease

The chance of transmission of the disease for employees who work alongside each other is rare unless there is a direct exchange of blood or other body fluids such as saliva. Many employees are reluctant to accept this and fear possible infection and/or are reluctant to work with infected employees because of the social stigma attached to HIV/AIDS. However, medical data are in agreement that AIDS can be transmitted only through intimate sexual contact, intermingling of blood or blood products, and perinatal transmission from infected mothers to their offspring. All epidemiological evidence indicates that only blood and semen are the proven media of transmission. Employees who claim that they can contract AIDS by sharing a restroom or a drinking fountain, washing in the same sink, sharing a desk or a chair, using the same telephone, eating at the same table, wearing the same protective clothing, or talking at a meeting need more education on transmission of the disease.

Statutory Protection of AIDS

Most employers are prohibited under federal, state, and local laws from discriminating against a handicapped person. For the employer to take any position other than that the HIV/AIDS victim is disabled or handicapped would result in exposure. AIDS/HIV-positive individuals may be considered disabled within the meaning of the ADA. The Supreme Court held in *Bragdon* v. *Abbott*, 524 U.S. 624 (1998), that an individual with asymptomatic HIV can be disabled because the disease interferes with the major life activity of reproduction. Gay men who have attempted to rely on the *Abbott* decision have had mixed results.[54] Further, the Fifth Circuit Court of Appeals subsequently found that an HIV-positive employee who had decided not to have children and had taken steps to prevent a pregnancy was not disabled within the meaning of the ADA, thereby depriving him of protection under the statute and the ability to request reasonable accommodation.[55] The Rehabilitation Act protects only otherwise qualified employees. Some courts will hold that in certain jobs the infected person is not "otherwise qualified."[56]

Another defense available to employers is to contend that infected employees will pose a direct threat to themselves or others around them in the workplace. This defense has been particularly successful when the courts have held that the plaintiff (HIV-positive employee) has the burden of establishing that he or she is not a direct threat to himself or herself or other individuals.[57] In a related case, an applicant foreign service officer, Lorenzo Taylor, brought suit against then Secretary of State Condoleeza Rice when he was denied a position in the U.S. Department of State which had a rigid rule against hiring HIV-positive individuals.[58] The State Department contended that although otherwise qualified, Taylor was rejected because he was a direct threat to himself given the likelihood of assignment to a foreign country with multiple health risks.[59] When the court found that there was more than enough evidence for the matter to go to a jury, the State Department settled with Taylor in 2008. At the same time it announced that it was changing medical clearance rules that disqualified HIV-positive applicants. Taylor subsequently accepted a position with the U.S. Department of Health and Human Services.[60]

Accommodation under the Rehabilitation Act Relating to AIDS

Normally a person with AIDS is "otherwise qualified" under the ADA as amended. Until the employee is in the advanced stages of disease caused by the HIV virus, he or she can still perform the duties of the job. It is therefore very difficult to remove an employee under the Rehabilitation Act.[61] Under the ADA a person with AIDS is disabled. When such a person is discharged for AIDS, the Americans with Disabilities Act would be violated, unless the condition was such that the person could not perform all the duties of the job or if the termination is because of documented excessive absenteeism.

Tests for AIDS

The courts generally will not permit testing for HIV in the absence of a state statute.[62] In view of the available medical information, the employer has no demonstrable interest that would justify testing applicants or employees for HIV, although a person with AIDS could affect production. The reliability of the tests is questionable. If the test is positive, the information is of little value to the employer, since the mere presence of HIV does not affect the job. Since a test has no job-related purpose, there is no justification for testing either applicants or present employees. In the case of applicants, they likely would create more job risk as to turnover, absenteeism, and medical care costs than an applicant without AIDS, but under most state laws AIDS is not a reason for rejecting an applicant who is considered handicapped.[63]

Knowledge of the presence of HIV should be received only from the employee or when his or her physical condition interferes with the job relationship. AIDS may be the cause of absenteeism or poor performance, but the employment decision should be made on the job-related result and not on the cause. When considering testing, one question should be asked: Why do I want to know? If you do know, what use is the information, other than to expose confidentiality to those who do not have a need to know? An AIDS employee's cost in health care can be lessened by reducing the insurance coverage according to case law.[64]

Problems with Co-Workers of Workers with AIDS

Whereas a reluctant co-worker can be disciplined for refusing to work with or accommodate an person with HIV/AIDS, voluntary compliance supported by education is the preferred approach. The employer's greatest exposure results from supervisors who attempt to avoid the problem by discharging or transferring the individual infected by HIV, or by refusing to discipline employees who refuse to work with HIV/AIDS-infected individuals. Educating employees and anticipating problems is the best course of action. Research has shown that both gender and fear of AIDS are predictors of the likelihood to discipline co-workers of an infected employee. Men are more likely than women to be fearful of the disease, and men are less tolerant than women in terms of their attitudes toward AIDS, and are more likely to be disapproving of homosexuals who have contracted the disease than are women.[65] If the employer wants to do something with the person who has AIDS, there are several good business reasons to take action. However, few of them will stand judicial review.[66] Such defenses as the assertion that AIDS can be transmitted by casual contact, that the cost of health insurance premiums for HIV/AIDS-infected employees is excessive, that the disease is fatal so it is useless to train because training costs will be too high, and that any employee with AIDS is more accident prone may sound logical to the employer, but the court will seldom agree. The defense of customer or co-worker rejection has also been rejected in other areas, such as sex and race discrimination.[67]

The only answer to the co-worker who objects to working with a person with AIDS is education at all levels of the organization. It is advisable to have a doctor as well as a supervisor present the information. This policy of education is easily stated, but often it is not the solution to an all-too-frequent employee relations problem. Suppose an employee suspected of being a "gay" has recently had an extended period of absences and while at work looks flushed and weak. A group of employees approaches the supervisor and state that they represent the concerns of all the employees in the department. They

think that the "gay" employee is infected with HIV. They demand that the employer test the employee and put him or her on an extended leave of absence until the test results are known. They express fear for their own health and that of their families. The employees threaten that the whole department will refuse to work unless their demands are met or the employer can prove that the suspected employee does not have AIDS.

Situations like this put the employer "between a rock and a hard place." Employees covered by the National Labor Relations Act (NLRA) do have the right to withhold their services because of unsafe working conditions. An employee who believes that a fellow employee endangers his or her health has, under both the NLRA and Occupational Safety and Health Act (OSHA), the right to refuse to work. The employee who is suspected also has certain rights under ADA and most state statutes. Furthermore, there is a potential invasion of privacy issue. If a union is involved, the matter is more complicated and could end up in a grievance proceeding or an unfair labor practice, depending on the employer's response. Transferring the employee to another department would only move the problem to another work group. Suppose the employee admits she or he is HIV-positive or already has AIDS. This doesn't mean other employees can be infected except as discussed earlier. Legally the employer may have a difficult time avoiding exposure to a lawsuit or an unfair labor practice charge.

The solution to such a problem is not found in the literature nor can it likely be obtained from legal counsel. The employer must probe for the solution.[68] Education programs must be changed; more emphasis must be put on transmittal of accurate information. Try to convince the employees that their reservations are without medical authority; talk to the suspected employee and get his or her reaction and ask for help.

If several alternatives are explored and none of them offers a solution, then the employer must decide what is best for the organization. Either tell the complaining employees "to walk" or quit and get replacements or deal with the suspected employee in the best possible way to prevent a lawsuit. The next time the problem comes up the solution may be entirely different, depending on the employees involved. See Exhibit 4.4 for further recommendations for dealing with AIDS in the workplace.

Arbitrator's Position on Disabled Employees

If a dispute involving a disabled employee end up in a grievance/arbitration procedure, litigation will be avoided and the final decision will be by an arbitrator. A well-established principle in arbitration is that an employer may discharge an employee who cannot perform the duties of the job because of a physical impairment.[69] Some arbitrators will hold that under a labor agreement the disabled person must be placed in a job that the employee can perform, even if it means displacing a junior worker.[70]

Policy on Life-Threatening Diseases

The policy should address HIV/AIDS alone but include all life-threatening diseases. To single out one disease that may be currently a problem is a shortsighted policy that could cause exposure to litigation. It is difficult to make a policy that is flexible, but at least the company's position is communicated to the employees. That is the reason for, and objective of, the policy. The following elements should be included in the policy:

1. The contagious nature of an employee's illness will be determined by medical examination.
2. As long as an employee has acceptable performance, he or she can continue to work unless by medical determination the condition is a threat to others.
3. If an employee's condition creates a problem to co-workers, reasonable accommodation will be made wherever possible.
4. An employee's health condition is personal and confidential.
5. When a life-threatening disease causes a problem, the legal rights of co-workers, management, and the person with the

---

1. AIDS should be treated like any other disability that is covered by state or federal laws against discrimination (more than three quarters of the states have such laws).
2. Educate co-workers about AIDS before an actual case presents itself. How it is transmitted and why it is not a work-related condition should be stressed.
3. Maintain confidentiality of all medical records.
4. Do not in any way discriminate against a person with AIDS. Be able to document any discipline as nondiscriminatory.
5. Do not exclude AIDS victims from training or consideration for promotion. (Hard to sell, so find another reason.)
6. Accommodate or make a good effort to accommodate the AIDS victim by offering a transfer to a similar job or by any other reasonable action.
7. Don't test for AIDS, whether it be an applicant or a current employee.
8. Six to nine percent of HIV-positive persons get AIDS .
9. Have a policy that communicates the company's position.

EXHIBIT 4.4   Recommendations for Dealing with AIDS in the Workplace

illness must be balanced on a case-by-case basis. Considerable weight will be given to science and medical knowledge; myths, speculation, and hysteria will not be considered.

The main point to remember when dealing with employees with AIDS is that they fall into a protected class that must be reasonably accommodated. What this means is a question that the courts have not yet decided. Exactly what kinds of accommodations are required are ultimately up to the courts, but when in doubt the employer should engage the affected employee in an interactive process and attempt to reach a mutually agreeable accommodation.

When the employer discovers that an employee has AIDS (not just the HIV virus), sick leave can be offered as a partial solution to the problem. The employee may also be entitled to disability benefits. This approach doesn't necessarily prevent a lawsuit, however, because the benefits are usually lower than full salary. Further, forcing sick leave may increase the exposure, particularly where HIV is involved. Whatever else works, *do it*, as long as the employee does it voluntarily and it decreases exposure to a lawsuit.

CASE 4.1

Bring the Work to the Employee?

Judy Johnson worked as a technician in a lab. Her employer was aware that she had some back problems from a prior injury. She complained to her supervisor that she had aggravated this injury at work. Johnson applied and was approved for what was then called by the company "Sickness & Accident" (S&A). This provided the employee with full pay and benefits for up to 52 weeks. Johnson left work in August 2009 and did not have a planned date of return. During her absence she tried remedies that included treatments from a chiropractor and a surgery. According to the employee, neither of these helped her pain. She remained out under S&A for the entire 52-week period.

Near the end of the 52-week S&A period, Johnson informed the company that her back was not any better and that she wanted to apply for long-term disability (LTD). The company's medical department requested an evaluation by another doctor to assess whether the employee should be granted LTD. It was determined by the company doctor that the employee could return to work with employer accommodations. Subsequently the LTD request was denied.

When asked when she would return to work (with accommodations), Johnson responded that under the direction of her primary caregiver (a chiropractor) she could not travel more than 25 miles in a car to work. Johnson lived 35 miles from the lab. She proposed that the employer accommodate her by allowing her to work from home. The company rejected this request and demanded that she return to work or be dismissed. Johnson then hired an attorney who threatened to sue the company for discrimination under the Americans with Disability Act.

Is the company required to accommodate Johnson's request? Is her proposed accommodation reasonable? What exposure does the company have if it terminates Johnson? ■

CASE 4.2

FMLA, ADA, or Workers' Comp?

Jerry was a forklift operator at a distribution warehouse that processed material in and out for 18 hours a day. The full-time staff usually numbered about 75. Frank, a warehouse supervisor, received a report on Tuesday morning that Jerry, one of the regular fork lift drivers who had been employed for five years, had sprained (or otherwise injured) his arm while lifting some material on the job the previous day. Jerry's wife called later that morning and told Frank that Jerry was at an urgent care center. Later in the day Jerry called to say that he was to see his own doctor on Thursday and would probably be "re-slinged" following his visit to the doctor.

Based solely on these representations, the supervisor didn't think that Jerry would miss more than one week's work, and next week he could assign Jerry to operate an electric hand cart while others would be loading and unloading. However, Frank didn't know how to classify Jerry's status and brought the problem to the HR office. The HR manager checked Jerry's record and noted that Jerry had eight days (64 hours) of accrued sick leave.

What course of action would you recommend as an HR practitioner? Which law applies? Can several legal obligations be accommodated? To which status should the employee be assigned for this week? Next week? ▣

Summary

As you read in Chapter 2, antidiscrimination statutes require the employer not to take race, sex, national origin, color, age, or disability into account when making an employment decision. Title VII of the Civil Rights Act requires that all individuals in a protected class are to be treated alike. The law requires equal employment opportunity in addition to providing special protections for employees with a disability or limiting religious belief by requiring accommodation. Laws such as the ADA as amended, FMLA, and the Rehabilitation Act have required employers to make reasonable accommodations to otherwise qualified employees. Topics such as drugs and alcohol are discussed, along with HIV and AIDS in the workplace.

Key Terms

disability   94
ADA (Americans with
    Disabilities Act   94
ADAA (ADA Amendments
    Act)   94
impairment   95
major life activity   95

undue hardship   95
reasonable
    accommodation   95
BFOQ (bona fide occupational
    qualification)   99
FMLA (Family Medical
    Leave Act)   100

military caregivers   101
reasonable suspicion drug
    testing   105
assessment centers   108

Questions for Discussion

1. How have the courts redefined major life activity? Do you agree with the changes?
2. As an employer, what would you do to minimize exposure to ADA claims?
3. What are the responsibilities of the employee and the employer under the FMLA?
4. What recourse does an employee have if he or she does not like the accommodation made by the employer?
5. Suppose you are an HR manager tasked with drafting a drug policy. What would you include in the policy and what guidelines would you follow?
6. What FMLA benefits are available to "military caregivers"?
7. Under what circumstances may employers intervene or take disciplinary action against an employee who is abusing drugs while off duty?
8. What liability do employers have for employees who become inebriated at company-sponsored events when the alcohol is provided by the company?

Notes to Chapter 4

1. Public Law 110-35. For a discussion of disability as defined prior to ADAAA, see C. Anderson, "What is 'Because of the disability' under ADA? Reasonable accommodation, causation and the windfall doctrine," *Berkley Journal of Employment and Labor Law*, 27, no. 2 (2006): 323–282.
2. For example, see *Toyota Motor Mfg., Kentucky* v. *Williams* 534 U.S. 184 (2002); *Chevron* v. *Echazabel*, 536 U.S. (2002).
3. A. Mayerson, "The Americans with Disabilities Act of 1990—An historic overview," *The Labor Lawyer* (Winter 1991).
4. *Alvarado* v. *Cajun Operating Company, dba AFC Enterprises*, 588 F.3d 1261 (9th Cir. 2009).
5. This includes constructive discharge situations where intent can be shown. *Johnson* v. *Shalala*, 998 F.2d (4th Cir. 1993).
6. *Karraker* v. *Rent-A-Center, Inc.*, 411 F.3d 831 (7th Cir. 2005).
7. A qualified individual is a person who can perform all the essential functions of the job with or without reasonable accommodation. The employer makes the assessment of which job functions are essential.
8. See S. 933, Sect. 102(b) [1-7] of Title I for the full text of prohibitions.
9. J. McDonald, "I want a nicer boss," *Employee Relations Law Journal*, 31, no.1 (Autumn 2005): 79–88.
10. E. J. Felsberg, "Providing reasonable accommodations under the Americans with Disabilities Act," *Employment Relations Today*, 32, no. 3 (Fall 2005): 105–110. See also J. Hafen, "Making reasonable accommodations for employees with mental illness under ADA," *Employee Benefit Plan Review*, 61, no. 3 (September 2006).
11. *EEOC* v. *Sears Roebuck & Co.*, 417 F.3d 789 (7th Cir. 2005), 2005 U.S. App. LEXIS 16707. For a discussion of the costs and benefits of accommodation, see H. Schartz, D. Hendrikcs, and P. Blanck, "Workplace accommodations: Evidence based outcomes," *Work*, 27, no. 4 (2006): 345–354.
12. *Barber* v. *Nabors Drilling U.S.A., Inc.*, 130 f.3d 702 (5th Cir. 1997).
13. Undue hardship is also a defense under the Rehabilitation Act.
14. A qualified individual under the Rehabilitation Act is a person who can perform all essential functions of the job with or without reasonable accommodation.
15. Employers not covered by the Rehabilitation Act are covered by the ADA if they have more than three employees.
16. *Chiari* v. *City of League City*, 920 F.2d 311 (5th Cir. 1991).
17. ADA uses the term *perceived to be handicapped*. Individuals who are not known to be disabled cannot claim discrimination under the ADA. Basically the ADA definition and the Rehabilitation Act of 1973 definition of a disabled person are the same.
18. This would appear to be discrimination because the individual can meet the requirement but the employer doesn't think that she or he can.
19. *Morbid obesity* is defined a 100 pounds overweight for the height.
20. K. Kramer and A. Mayerson, "Obesity discrimination in the workplace: Protection through a perceived disability claim under the Rehabilitation Act and the Americans with Disabilities Act," *California Western Law Review*, 31 (1994): 41.
21. W. E. Barlow, "Act to accommodate the disabled," *Personnel Journal*, 70, no. 11 (November 1991): 119.
22. *Arneson* v. *Heckler*, 946 F.2d 90 (8th Cir. 1991).
23. "Discrimination of religious harassment under Title VII," *Labor Law Journal* (December 1995): 732.
24. Unpaid leave is not a reasonable effort to accommodate under ADA, *Meyer* v. *U.S.* 50 F.2d (3rd Cir. Cal. 1995).
25. *Ansonia Board of Education* v. *Philbrook*, 107 S.Ct. 376 (1986).
26. *U.S. Airways Inc.* v. *Barnet*, 535 U.S. 391 (2002). Seniority rights also trump accommodations under the Rehabilitation Act of 1973.
27. *EEOC* v. *Waffle House, Inc.*, 534 U.S. 279 (2002).
28. Public Law 110-181, Enacted January 28, 2008.
29. 29 C.F.R 825.303 (b).

30. *Ragsdale* v. *WolverineWorld Wide*, 535 U.S. 81 (2002) where the court imposed a penalty of additional FMLA leave when the employer made an improper designation of leave as FMLA leave.

31. *TWA* v. *Hardison*, 32 U.S. 63 (1977).

32. *Corp. of Presiding Bishops* v. *Amos*, 107 S.Ct. 2862 (1987). Applies to all religious beliefs, even though the religious order approves: *Frazee* v. *Illinois Dept. of Employment and Security*, 109 S.Ct. 1514 (1989).

33. All religious beliefs must be accommodated if one belief is accommodated. *EEOC* v. *Universal Mfg.Corp.*, 914 F.2d 71 (5th Cir. 1990).

34. M. Downey, "Keeping the faith," *HR Magazine* (January 2008): 85–88.

35. For a good background on accommodation, see T. Brierton, "Religious discrimination in the workplace: Who's accommodating who," *Labor Law Journal* (May 1988): 299. See also D. Massengill and D. J. Peterson, "Job requirements and religious practices: Conflict and accommodation," *Labor Law Journal* (July 1988): 402.

36. *Bush* v. *Regis Corp.*, WL42306693 (11th Cir. 2007).

37. *American Postal Workers Union* v. *Postmaster General*, 781 F.2d 772 (9th Cir. 1986).

38. *Wilson* v. *US West Communications*, 58 f.3d 1337 (8th Cir. 1995).

39. *Tooley* v. *Martin Marietta Corp.*, 648 f.2d 1239 (9th Cir. 1981); *Nottleson* v. *Smith Steel Workers*, 643 F.2d 445 (7th Cir. 1981). However, in *Wilson* v. *NLRB*, 920 F.2d 1282 (6th Cir. 1990), the court took an opposite view, ruling unconstitutional an accommodation to force payment to charity when contrary to religious beliefs. The employee must belong to a religious order and not have an individual belief (minority rule).

40. K. Durso, "Alcohol and other substance abuse: Prevalence, cost and impact on productivity," *Employee Benefit News*, 18, no. 11 (September 2004): 37.

41. N. Delogu, "Essential elements of a drug-free workplace program," *Professional Safety*, 52, no. 11 (November 2007): 48–51; K. Klein, "Establishing a drug free workplace," *Business Week Online* (August 2, 2007): 14.

42. "The legal side of workplace drug-free policies," *Safety Compliance Letter*, 7, no. 2487 (March 2008): 7–13. The act does not require testing, but it would be difficult to comply without required testing.

43. For example, see Minnesota Statutes, 181.94–181.97.

44. J. Olsen, "Legal and practical considerations in developing a substance program," *Hofstra Labor Law Journal*, 8, no. 1 (1990): 24.

45. D. Hatch, J. Hall, M. Kobata, and M. Denis, "Alcoholism and the ADA," *Workforce Management*, 85, no. 19 (October 2006): 9.

46. How the use of drugs affects the work must be considered. *Teahan* v. *Metro North Commuter R.R. Co.*, 951 F.2d 511 (2nd Cir. 1991).

47. Drug and alcohol testing have been held by the NLRB to be mandatory subjects of bargaining. Clearly this limits the employer's discretion in a unionized workplace.

48. *Chandler* v. *Miller*, 117 S.Ct. 1295 (1997); *Skinner* v. *Railway Labor Executives Association*, 109 S.Ct. 1402 (1989), and *National Treasury Employees Union* v. *Von Raab*, 109 S.Ct. 1384 (1989).

49. In *O'Brien* v. *Papa Gino's of America*, 780 F.2d 1067 (1st Cir.1986), the court held that the discharge was not wrongful when the polygraph test revealed that the employee was using drugs, but upheld a jury award of $400,000 for invasion of privacy because the administrator went beyond permissible bounds in questioning.

50. Treatment is not required by the ADA, but other federal statutes require it.

51. *Despear* v. *Milwaukee County*, F.3d 635 (7th Cir. 1995).

52. N. Ever, "Trends for managing AIDS in the workplace," *Personnel Journal*,(June 1995): 125.

53. Anat Arkin, "Out of the shadows," *People Management*, 11, no. 23 (November 2005): 24–28.

54. S. Seidenberg, "The HIV conundrum," *ABA Journal*, 92, no. 8 (August 2006): 40–45.

55. *Blanks* v. *Southwestern Bell*, 2002 WL31355003 (5th Cir. 2002).

56. *Leckelt* v. *Board of Commissionsers of Hospital District No. 1*, 909, F.2d 820 (5th Cir. 1990).

57. S. Christie, "AIDS, employment, and the direct threat offense: The burden of proof,"

Fordham Law Review 76, no. 235 (October 2007): 235–282.

58. S. Seidenberg, "The HIV conundrum," *ABA Journal*, 92, no. 8 (August 2006): 40.

59. *Taylor* v. *Rice*, 371 US App. DC 383 (2006).

60. S. Barr, "Refusing to give up on the foreign service," *The Washington Post* (February 25, 2008).

61. *Severino* v. *North Fort Myers Fire Control*, 935 F.2d 1179 (11th Cir. 1991); *Leckelt* v. *Board of Commissioners of Hospital District No. 1*, 909 F.2d 820 (5th Cir. 1990).

62. *Glover* v. *Eastern Nebraska Community of Retardation*, 867 F.2d 461 (8th Cir. 1989) cert. denied; *Leckelt* v. *Board of Commissioners of Hospital District No. 1*, 900F.2d 820 (5th Cir. 1990).

63. States such as California, Massachusetts, Iowa, and Texas prohibit testing for AIDS or HIV.

64. *Greenberg* v. *HHH Music*, 946 F.2d 506 (5th Cir. 1992), cert. denied 1992.

65. M. Vest, K. Tarnoff, C. Carr, J. Vest, and F. O'Brien, "Factors influencing a manager's decision to discipline employees for refusal to work with an HIV/AIDS infected co-worker," *Employee Responsibilities and Rights Journal*, 15, no. 1 (March 2003): 31–43.

66. *Petri* v. *Bank of New York*, 582 N.Y.S. 2nd 68 (N.Y.S. Ct. 1992).

67. *Sprogis* v. *United Airlines, Inc.*, 44 F.2d 1194, 1199 (7th Cir.1971) cert. denied; *Diaz* v. *Pan American Airways, Inc.*, 442 F.2d 389 (5th Cir. 1970), cert. denied; *Wigginess* v. *Fruchtman*, 482 F.Supp. 681 (S.D. N.Y. 1979), cert. denied.

68. For a judicial and arbitral forum on employees infected with HIV, see R. Burger and G. Lewis, "AIDS and employment: Judicial and arbitral responses," *Labor Law Journal*, 43, no. 5 (May 1992): 259.

69. *Bucklers, Inc.* 90 LA 937 (Braufman, Arb.); *Nursing Home* 88 LA 681 (Sedwick, Arb.).

70. *International Paper Co.* 94 LA 1990 (Mathews, Arb.)

CHAPTER 5

Compensation Directives

CHAPTER OUTLINE

Fair Labor Standards Act

Compensable Time

Working at Home

Overtime Cost Control

Independent Contractors

Equal Pay Act

Unemployment Compensation

Workers' Compensation

Federal statutes administered by the Department of Labor (DOL) play a primary role in public and private-sector compensation. As a general theme, the statutes are intended for the welfare of the worker. The National Labor Relations Act (NLRA) balanced economic power and mandated collective bargaining, whereas the Fair Labor Standards Act (FLSA) is intended to reduce the number of worker hours and to protect against child labor abuses. Workers' compensation and unemployment compensation are programs that apply to both public and private management schemes. Health insurance mandates apply to both sectors as well, but the public-sector retirement plans are normally legislated and are exempt from the *Employment Retirement and Security Act.*

FAIR LABOR STANDARDS ACT

Direct Pay Regulations

The Fair Labor Standards Act is an original cornerstone of human resource management. Until its enactment in 1938, the employer and employee negotiated the wage and hourly pay one-on-one.[1] After the Fair Labor Standards Act, Congress passed several other statutes to improve wages: Walsh-Healey Public Contracts Act,[2] Davis-Bacon Act,[3] Service Contract Act,[4] and Equal Pay Act,[5] to name a few.[6]

This section is concerned with the situations that frequently arise under the FLSA and the problems involved in compliance. Minimum wage requirements under the act involve a relatively small percentage of the gainfully employed, and have fewer compliance problems than other sections of the act. Therefore, they are not discussed in this chapter.[7]

Legal compliance and cost control under FLSA focus on determining compensable hours, determining eligibility for overtime pay, a worker's status as an **independent contractor,** and pay for **meal periods** [8] Managers accept these long-standing provisions as a necessary cost of doing business. The FLSA does restrict the freedom of the employer in the payment of wages, but it does not prevent the establishment of policies and procedures to control costs.[9]

Historically, violations under the FLSA can exist for a long time before anything happens. Often an employee does not protest an incidental violation because the violation is not known to be one. Or it may be more convenient for the employee to ignore the requirements of the act.[10] When "the honeymoon is over," the employer usually regrets the casual practice.

An investigation for compliance by the **Wage and Hour Division** of the Department of Labor can be caused by complaints from the employee, unions, or competitors. Most investigations are initiated through employee or union complaints. Seldom does the agency make spot-checks, unless it finds a flagrant violation in one company and wants to determine if it is a common practice throughout the industry. Compliance with most provisions of the act is not difficult if the employer knows the regulations, but sometimes it can be an employee relations problem. Often when a condition is questionable, such as an exempt or nonexempt classification (overtime premium pay or not), the employer takes the risk.

Coverage

The FLSA covers most employers, including:

- U.S. federal government
- State and local governments
- Private employers who have annual gross sales of at least $500,000
- Private employers engaged in interstate commerce[11]

Because this definition excludes small enterprises, most states have enacted "small" fair labor standards acts that cover employees not included in the federal act. For this reason, whenever an employer–employee relationship exists, it is rare that employees are not covered. Section 203 exempts enterprises such as religious organizations and mom-and-pop businesses where only the family is employed. Nonprofit organizations do not have a primary business purpose, and seasonal recreational establishments are also exempted under the act. State and local governments are not exempt because of the Supreme Court decision in *Garcia* v. *San Antonio Metropolitan Transit Authority,* 105 S.Ct. 1005 (1985).

Exemptions are numerous under FLSA. The determination of when an employee comes under these exemptions is discussed in subsequent sections. There are special overtime rules for firefighters, law-enforcement personnel, and hospital and facility care people in residence. If a state law is stricter than the federal law, it will supersede the federal law; otherwise, the federal law controls. Any agreement between an employer and employee to waive coverage is illegal, void, and unenforceable, except under conditions that will be treated later in this chapter.

Penalties for Violation

The Fair Labor Standards Act is enforced by the Wage and Hour Division of the Department of Labor (DOL) and includes criminal and civil penalties for willful violations. In *Williams* v. *Tri County*

Growers, Inc., 747 F.2d 121 (3rd Cir. 1984), the court said that the lack of filed complaints does not mean that the employer did not intend to violate the law. Other courts were more liberal, and stated that if the employer merely knew that the FLSA was a consideration during the time the act was being violated, it was willful.

The Supreme Court in *Trans World Airlines* v. *Thurston,* 105 S.Ct. 613 (1985), rejected this concept and defined *willful* as where the "employer either knew or showed reckless disregard for the matter of whether its conduct was prohibited by the ADEA." If the employer didn't have knowledge, there was no reckless disregard. The Thurston thinking was adopted in *McLaughlin* v. *Richland Shoe Co.,* 108 S.Ct. 1677 (1988). The court stated that the employer acted willfully if it "knew or showed reckless disregard for the matter or whether its conduct was prohibited by the Fair Labor Standards Act."[12]

The employer would not be charged with a willful violation unless it knew or should have known that the action was violating a statute and made no attempt to comply.[13] This would make it very difficult to sustain a willful violation unless the employer intentionally violated the statute or totally disregarded it. Certainly, advice of counsel or serious consideration as to whether a statute was being violated would be sufficient to make any violation "nonwillful."

Where no willful violation is found, the penalty is restitution in the form of back pay. The amount of back pay and liquidated damages awarded is discretionary with the court. In 2008, a "willful" determination cost *Wal-Mart* a settlement of $54 million. The company was charged with willfully compelling employees to work "off-the-clock" and depriving personnel of meal and **rest periods.**[14]

Often, it is difficult to determine damages incurred by an employee because of an employer's failure to pay overtime. The courts have stated that, in the absence of employer records, the employee's reasonable recollections of the hours worked is sufficient.[15] In all situations under the act, the plaintiff has a right of jury trial; the successful plaintiff may obtain attorney fees and costs from the defendant.

COMPENSABLE TIME

The FLSA does not limit the hours that an employee can work, but does require that the employee be compensated for all the time worked. The act governs the procedural aspects of paying employees and establishes minimum standards. An employer was held to violate the FLSA when it paid wages to employees 14 to 15 days after payday.[16]

In *Biggs,* the State of California paid state workers two weeks late because the state legislature had not approved funding and the governor had not signed the state budget. When the established payday was missed, William Biggs filed a class action lawsuit for highway maintenance workers. The state argued that the FLSA requires employers to pay a minimum wage, but it does not require that the wage be paid promptly. The court rejected this argument, stating that "shall pay" plainly connotes "shall make a payment." If a payday is missed, the employer has not met its obligation to pay.

The Fair Labor Standards Act also provides that the employee must be compensated at time-and-one-half for all hours over 40 in one work week. The act contains no definition of *work* and only a partial definition of *hours worked.*[17] A study of the countless court cases on the subject of **compensable time** discloses that if the employee is serving the interests of the employer, then it is considered time worked, according to the act. It is immaterial whether the work was requested by the employer or authorized, so long as it was performed or the employer had reason to believe that the work was being performed. If the work is performed, it is difficult for the employer to plead no knowledge. The work product is something the employer knows, or should know about, with reasonable effort. Whenever the employee worked and the employer failed to pay for the work done, there is an exposure to overtime back pay.

Sleep Time

Under the statute, an employee must receive at least five hours of sleep in a 24-hour period. It need not be contiguous,[18] but **sleep time** cannot be frequently interrupted or the entire period is compensable[19] [29 CFR 553.223(c)].

Meal Periods

The FLSA does not require payment for meal periods when employees are serving their own interests [29 CFR 553.223(c)]. Mail carriers must remain in uniform during lunch hour, and are often subjected to job-related questions by patrons. These occasional questions do not substantially interfere with their personal time, warranting compensation for lunch hour.[20]

However, in many work situations employees are working on behalf of the employer.[21] A shipping clerk is not required to, but chooses to remain at the desk during meal periods, eating a brown bag lunch while directing the unloading of a truck and chewing on a sandwich. An administrative assistant works on crossword puzzles at her or his desk during lunch break; the supervisor asks for a file. A maintenance mechanic is called to repair a machine during lunch hour. In all these situations, the employer often does not pay for meal periods. But if these employees are acting on behalf of the employer during a substantial part of the meal period, the meal period is considered time worked.[22]

Volunteering for Tasks

When the duties performed during lunch hour are related to the work normally assigned, the work is compensable. If work during meal periods is voluntary, it is not compensable; but often there is a fine line between what is voluntary and what is not. Many assignments appear to be voluntary; but if they are refused, seriously adverse consequences result. This makes them not truly voluntary.

These examples are common situations where the employer unknowingly has considerable exposure. An agreement to exclude sleep and meal time from compensable hours is not enforceable when the agreement is extracted by the threat of termination.[23] If the employee is never relieved from serving the employer's interest, all inactive hours and active hours are compensable.

Often an employer is not aware of tasks performed. If the actions taken are a matter of personal convenience or to please the employer, the time should not be counted as compensable work time. The agencies and the courts state that it must be shown that the work performed is not benefiting the employer to be held noncompensable.

The leading cases on meal periods are *Mumbower* v. *Callicott* and *Marshall* v *Valhalla*, 590 F.2d 306 (9th Cir. 1979). The general rule is that the employee does not have to be completely relieved from duty. But the personal time must be long enough to enable the employee to use the time for his or her own purpose.[24] This often comes up when waiting time is involved. If the waiting time is part of the job, it is compensable; if the employee is free to use the time for his or her own purpose, it is not considered waiting time.[25]

A distinction must be made between waiting to go to work and being engaged to wait to go to work. If it is the latter, then it is compensable. An employer required the workers to wait for customer flow before they were paid for working. The court held that this waiting time was compensable. The employees were ready, willing, and able to work when they arrived at the worksite. This is an example of being engaged to wait for work.[26]

Another problem arises when the employee is required to be on call. The usual rule is that if the employee is not required to remain on the premises, but is required to remain available for contact by the company officials, it is not considered work time while on call. However, if the employee is required to remain on the employer's premises or in such close proximity that he or she cannot use the time effectively for his or her own purposes, it is work time on call. The controlling factor is whether employees can use the time for their own purposes.

Early to Work

Another common employer exposure occurs when an employee comes to work well before the regular starting time. For example, when a spouse drops an employee off, or with car pooling, the employee arrives at the worksite early. Being a good employee, he or she performs duties before being clocked in. This is compensable work time that the employer neither stops nor approves but tolerates. The work performed before starting time must be an integral part of the employee's duties. Pre-shift work is almost always held to be compensable. When a butcher sharpened his knives outside shift hours, the Supreme Court held it compensable.[27]

A leading case involves employees who were required to fill out daily time and requisition sheets, assemble material to be used on the job, fuel the trucks, and pick up a daily work plan before starting work at 8:00 a.m. The court stated that the test in these cases is whether the activities are an "integral and indispensable" part of the performance of the regular work and is in the ordinary course of the business.[28] Time spent is compensable if it is necessary in the performance of the job. For example, an electrician putting gas in a truck is not doing electrical work, but it is necessary to

the business and it benefits the employer. This definition has been supported in other jurisdictions.[29]

Rest Periods

Rest or snack periods are usually paid, as a policy matter. Under the Department of Labor interpretations (29 CFR Sect. 785.18), breaks less than 20 minutes are compensable. However, this interpretation can be successfully challenged.

Some courts, because employees are serving their own interests, do not support the Wage and Hour Division's position. In *Cole* v. *Farm Fresh Poultry, Inc.*, 824 F.2d 923 (11th Cir. 1987), the court stated that reliance on a Labor Department interpretive bulletin that is vague with broad concepts will not relieve the employer from paying for overtime. The statement in the bulletin making breaks of more than one-half hour noncompensable was not a defense when the employees could not use the time for their own purposes. In all these situations, a bulletin or a guideline is only a position of the department and can be challenged, and often the courts will not validate what the bulletin says. Unchallenged, these bulletins or guidelines are often treated as the law.

Other courts enforce the regulation on the presumption that rest periods promote efficiency, which is in the employer's interests. A safer approach, if the employer does not want to pay for rest periods or snack periods, would be to offset rest periods against other working time, so total hours worked do not exceed 40. This offset has been approved by at least two courts.[30] However, this is not always possible; and the employee relations situation could become problematic. See the case study *The 10-Minute Meal Period* later in this chapter.

Early Chores

If a nonexempt person is instructed to pick up mail or make coffee before clocking in, the time is compensable. The test is whether it is an integral part of the job. This is certainly an exposure to a complaint if the employee calls the Wage and Hour division. The employer, to avoid exposure, should either require an exempt employee to make the coffee or have it done after the start of the shift. Making it strictly voluntary on the part of the employee would greatly reduce the exposure.

There would be a serious exposure if the employee was required to be at the worksite 20 minutes before the start of the day to make coffee. If exempt and nonexempt personnel drank the coffee, the exposure would be even greater. Most offices make coffee. When they do it, and who drinks it, would probably influence the degree of exposure.[31]

Travel Time

Travel time and walking time are not compensable under the Portal to Portal Act[32] unless there is a custom or practice that makes it compensable. In the building trades, most labor agreements have a clause that pays for portal-to-portal time. If travel time is integrated with work and does not involve merely getting to work, it is compensable. An example would be travel on company business by nonexempt field workers or repair personnel. If it is a routine assignment, the pay doesn't start until reaching the worksite. Under the Portal to Portal Act, this would be going to and from work and not compensable. The change in the worksite is a regular part of the job. If the same nonexempt employee had an occasional assignment in a distant city, travel time would be compensable.[33] This is not going to and from work as a regular part of the job.[34]

Travel time also must be considered on a weekly basis; the employer can avoid excessive overtime due to travel by giving **compensatory time** off in the same work week in which the overtime was earned. Often, travel time is spent for meetings and training programs. The usual rule is that if time spent in the training program is not compensable, neither is the travel time.

Training and Overtime[35]

The criterion to determine if a nonexempt employee is to be paid for participating in a training program is whether or not the employee is performing any significant amount of work that benefits the employer.[36] Another important factor in this connection is whether or not the training is compulsory. (Related training in apprenticeship programs is an exception.) Being necessary for advancement or to prevent obsolescence doesn't imply that it is compulsory unless the employer tells the employee that she or he must take the training or be terminated. Another problem with formal training is whether or not a trainee must take a course to get a job. If so, overtime would be due for an employee if the training puts the employee over 40 hours for the week. IRS withholding and state workers' compensation and unemployment insurance coverage would have to be paid if the trainee were an employee.

The Wage and Hour Division criteria for determining whether or not a trainee is an employee have been accepted by most state and federal courts. These guidelines state that a trainee is not an employee if:

1. The training program is similar to that which would be offered at a vocational school although the employer facilities are being used.
2. The training is only for the benefit of the trainee.
3. The trainee does not displace regular employees.
4. There is no immediate benefit to the employer who provides the training, although the training or lack of it causes a disruption in the operations.
5. The trainees are not guaranteed a job at the end of their training period.

6. The trainees are informed that they will not be paid for the time spent in training.[37]

In the airline industry, the question has been raised if flight attendants and reservation agents must take training before hiring. Most of these programs met the preceding criteria; and the trainees were not considered employees.[38]

As for training programs for current employees,[39] the criteria are similar. The time is not compensable under Wage and Hour Division rules if:

1. The session is held outside of working hours.
2. Attendance is, in fact, strictly voluntary.
3. The training session is not directly related to the employee's job.
4. The employee does not perform any productive work while attending the meeting or training session.

Change Time

The issue of **change time** often comes up when the employer requires the shift going off to instruct the shift coming on about what has happened during the preceding shift. By rule, the instructions are for the benefit of the employer; therefore the work should be compensable. However, the courts have only rarely found such work to be compensable. A New York court so held in *Arcadi* v. *Nestle Food Corp.,* 38 F.3d 672 (2nd Cir. 1994). But it must be noted that, in this case, the union attempted to obtain an overtime payment provision for time spent changing into work uniforms through collective bargaining but subsequently dropped this request at the bargaining table.

The company denied a grievance over the issue and the employees filed suit in U.S. District Court alleging violation of the FLSA. On appeal, the Second Circuit Court held that the FLSA excluded changing time from coverage unless it was expressly included in the collective bargaining agreement or acknowledged by custom or past practice.

Preparation Time

Related to clothes changing time is the issue of "donning and doffing" at shift start and end.[40] This is often an issue in the fresh meat businesses, and also among police who must "don" equipment. The *Dager* decision found that "donning" was not compensable but that change time during the shift would be. Other cases on this issue arising in San Leandro(CA), San Diego (CA), and Richmond (VA) resulted in conflicting decisions. In *Powell* v. *Carey International, Inc.,* limousine drivers were to be paid for customer waiting time and driving from one assignment to another, but not for donning and doffing uniforms.[41] In food processing, the most recent case favored management's view that the practice is not compensable under FLSA.[42]

Working at Home

Some employers treat individuals who perform work at home as independent contractors, not subject to the minimum wage and overtime provisions of FLSA. However, in almost every reported wage/hour case turning on their status, such "home workers" have been found to be employees covered by the FLSA. In deciding whether an individual is an "employee," the courts follow the directive of the U.S. Supreme Court that the "economic realities of the relationship govern,"[43] and the focal point is whether the individual is economically dependent on the business to which he or she renders service.

Employers are required to keep certain records for home workers, in addition to those required for all nonexempt employees. These required records are described in 28 CFR Sect. 516.31. With respect to each lot of work, the employer must record (1) the date on which work is given out to, or begun by the worker, and the amount of such work given out or begun; and (2) the date on which work is turned in by worker, and the amount of the work turned in.

Normally, travel to and from the employer's place of business is commuting time, and not compensable (see 29 CFR Sect. 785.35). However, the Department of Labor's enforcement policy, in the case of home workers, is that time spent traveling to and from the employer's premises to obtain materials or equipment and/or to deliver finished work is primarily for the employer's benefit and therefore is compensable work time.

Overtime Eligibility

In most companies, the control of overtime costs hinges on the classification of employees into exempt and nonexempt (from overtime pay) classifications. Often, some employees may appear to be wrongly classified. An employer may classify an employee as exempt by job title.[44] One manager, when challenged about a job title, remarked, "It's cheaper to give a job title than pay more money." Changing a classification downward may create an employee relations problem because of loss of prestige or the employee perception that he or she is being exploited. Other employees sometimes prefer to be classified as hourly to be eligible for the overtime pay premium.

Overtime Directives

The FLSA establishes a standard of 40 hours in a consecutive seven-day period beyond which employers are to pay an additional 50 percent of normal pay for hours worked. The number of hours is not limited, under FLSA. The extra cost serves as a deterrent to excessive hours. Public safety positions often have different work weeks; for example, police may be subject to 43 hours at "straight time" and firefighters are subject to 54 hours.

Almost all states have supplemented the FLSA. Employers not involved in Interstate Commerce and not subject to the federal law sometimes "march to their own tune." For instance, Kansas and Minnesota have higher hours (46 and 48, respectively) for a threshold before premium overtime pay is required. Alabama, California, Alaska, Nevada, and Wyoming require overtime premium pay after eight hours of work each day. Michigan has opened the option of compensatory time off in lieu of pay, and South Carolina also permits this policy for public employees.

Department of Labor guidelines and some case law provide guidance in dealing with such issues. Each case is decided on its own merits. Each company must decide to what degree it is in compliance with the FLSA. Is the exposure to a possible violation great enough to justify the employee relations problems that may be caused by making unpopular decisions? When dealing with questionable areas, management will sometimes take the position that the employee relations problem has more benefits than the potential cost of the exposure. Management will wait for the Wage and Hour Division or the courts to tell them that they are wrong.[45]

The Salary Test

The Wage and Hour Division uses an annual **salary test** amount to determine generally whether a position is included in any of the exemptions from overtime premium pay. If an employee is paid less than a certain salary (in 2010, $23,660 annually), that employee must be paid one-half the overtime premium. This is known as the "short test." An important provision of the salary test is that an exempt employee cannot be docked when working less than 40 hours per week.[46] In *Abshire v. County of Kern*, 908 F.2d 483 (9th Cir. 1990), the court held that docking for absences of less than a day is "completely antithetical to the concept of salaried employees."[47]

The salary test alone doesn't render a particular position exempt. In *Donovan* v. *United Video, Inc.*, 725 F.2d 577 (10th Cir. 1984), the court found that although salary level was very important, it alone does not make the position exempt.[48] The duties of the job must also be considered. The position is not compensated for the time spent on the job, but for the value of services performed. A salary or a job title will not make an employee exempt. The key to whether an executive, professional, administrative, or outside sales position is exempt is the type of work that is being performed.[49]

Outside Salespersons

Another exempt classification is **outside salespersons.** Under Section 213(a)(1) of the FLSA, outside salespersons are exempted if they sell regularly, or obtain orders for goods or services, while off the employer's premises. Comparatively speaking, this classification is less troublesome than administrative, professional, or executive classifications because the activities can be more readily defined.[50]

Other exempt employees typically include professionals who have been hired because of their advanced training, creative abilities, or specialized technical skills; administrators who hold positions in which they apply independent judgment in support of management, such as purchasing agents and HR managers; computer specialists involved in systems analysis, programming, and software engineering who earn at least $27.63 or more per hour. Nonadministrative police officers, firefighters, and reserve public safety positions are normally not exempt.

Other Considerations

Most employees tend to stress the importance of their jobs. Often, when interviewed by a compliance officer, they rate their jobs at a level higher than their actual positions justify, thereby implying **exempt status.**[51] In fact, their positions are often nonexempt. There are many gray areas where exempt and nonexempt classifications are interpreted for reasons other than payment of overtime, such as simple convenience. As a result, the employer is continually exposed to violations. A business decision is often necessary about whether to risk the exposure for personnel relations or to comply with the FLSA and avoid potential back pay.

Case Law Exemptions

Several potential problems may determine nonexempt status. Some of the more common are:

1. Attempts to exempt "white-collar" employees based on the quantity, not the quality of their work performance
2. Compensation systems for exempt employees that do not focus on the work achievement of the position
3. Incentive compensation not based on factors that reward achievement of job-related goals
4. Any compensation system that uses hourly pay rates for every position (this will put the exempt status of all positions in jeopardy)

Applied Administration

A necessary step in exemption determination is to assign one position the responsibility for judging exemptions. This position should be given the authority to determine whether a position is exempt or nonexempt. Supervisors and managers often have a self-interest in making an employee exempt or nonexempt without a serious consideration of job content, so this can be a thankless assignment. It is necessary to educate supervisors regarding the basis for exempt and nonexempt classification decisions.[52]

When determining exempt or nonexempt classifications, there is no exposure to violations if an employee is wrongly classified as nonexempt and paid overtime. It is only when the employer has liability for overtime pay. An employee can be misclassified as exempt for a considerable period of time but nothing will happen until there is a complaint. In anticipation of a Wage and Hour investigation, it is advisable to keep a record of hours worked by questionably exempt employees, although it is not necessary under the rules. Compliance with any statute starts with knowing the requirements of that statute. The employee relations consequences must be integrated with any policy of compliance. The decision then becomes a business decision, with consideration given to the legal exposure.

Subjectivity in Determinations

One reason why exempt classifications are troublesome is that in the final analysis, a part of the determination is subjective. One example was a fast-food chain that had all the assistant managers classified as exempt supervisors. Wage and Hour determined that they were nonexempt employees. The court gave the following rules to determine whether assistant managers were supervisors (executives).[53]

1. They must recommend hiring and firing.
2. They must direct the work of two or more persons.
3. They must have management duties.
4. They must regularly and customarily exercise discretion.

In any given situation, subjective determination must be made whether management duties existed and if discretion was customarily and regularly exercised.

Three elements are necessary for an employee's position to have an exempt status:

1. Weight must be placed on job duties that are usually considered exempt, with less weight placed on job title. In *Blackmon* v. *Brookshire Grocery Co.*, 835 F.2d 1135 (5th Cir. 1988), the court held that meat department managers were

not supervisors when they spent two-thirds of their time cutting meat.[54]
2. The exempt duties must actually be performed, not just assigned or expected.
3. The level of compensation should be above the minimum required for the exempt classification.

When in doubt about an employee's status, it may be advisable to check with the local Wage and Hour office. The caller does not have to provide identification; but even if he or she does, the Wage and Hour Department is not likely to follow up with an investigation. It normally requires an employee complaint to trigger an investigation.

OVERTIME COST CONTROL

Often the employee's desire for overtime pay is stronger than the desire of the employer to limit overtime. This makes the cost of overtime difficult, but not impossible, to control. A waste control clerk or sales service expeditor can always find a reason to work overtime when money is needed.[55] Overtime can be largely controlled by requiring authorization before overtime can be worked. However, the promulgation of a rule is not enough. The rule must be consistently enforced and if the employee works the overtime, then the overtime earnings must be paid.[56] Wage and Hour takes the position that unauthorized overtime still must be paid if known or tolerated, and the courts have sustained this position.[57]

Compensatory Time Off

The federal law requires that overtime be paid only after 40 hours are worked in one work week, but compensatory time off can be exchanged any time during the scheduled work week in order to avoid overtime. In the private sector, overtime hours worked in one week *cannot* be offset by granting compensatory time off in *another* week. However, in the public sector, the Wage and Hour Division grants exceptions. For public employees, compensatory time off may be approved in lieu of overtime pay for irregular or occasional overtime work by both exempt and nonexempt employees. Federal, state, and local governments can pay overtime hours in $1\frac{1}{2}$ times pay, or hours of "comp" time.

Stabilizing Overtime Pay

A "Belo" contract is a guaranteed wage contract made with the nonexempt employee, where hours vary widely from week to week. It provides a fixed weekly pay. This is an effective method to control overtime, while the employee controls hours of work. It is widely used for field repair service, customer service jobs, and other situations where the job requires work off the premises by nonexempt employees.

The conditions necessary to qualify for a Belo contract were stated by the Supreme Court in *Walling* v. *Belo Corp.,* 317 U.S. 706 (1941). The court listed five requirements:

1. The duties of the job covered by the Belo contract must require working hours that fluctuate above and below 40 hours per week.[58] This is the key requirement. The fluctuation must not be caused by economic conditions or employer control, but by job duties of the employee.
2. The contract must pay the employee a regular hourly rate above the statutory minimum wage requirements.
3. The weekly guarantees must pay at least one and one-half times the regular rate for all hours over 40.
4. The contract cannot cover more than 60 hours a week.
5. The total hours to be worked and paid for weekly must be agreed on in writing with an individual or union.
6. Records of actual hours must be maintained.

Exhibit 5.1 shows a Belo contract that complies with these requirements.

Applied Administration

The total hours inserted in the last line of the Belo contract must bear a "reasonable relationship to the hours an employee actually works." This is usually determined in the first contract by past overtime records. However, the actual hours worked before a Belo contract are usually greater than those worked after the Belo contract. When the incentive to work overtime is removed by the

---

_____(Company Name)_____ hereby agrees to employ _____(Name of Employee)_____ as _____ at a regular hourly rate of pay of $_____ per hour for the first forty (40) hours in any work week and at the rate of at least time and one-half or $_____ per hour for all hours in excess of forty (40 in any work week, with the guarantee that _____(Name of Employee)_____ will receive in any work week in which he or she performs any work for the company the sum of $_____ as total compensation for all hours performed up to and including (insert the total hours agreed upon; however, hours agreed upon cannot exceed 60 hours per week) hours.

COMPANY NAME

By _____

Accepted:
____Employee's Signature_____

EXHIBIT 5.1   A *Belo* Contract

Belo contract, the overtime hours usually decrease with no effect on job performance. To anticipate a decrease in hours by entering less than the previous average would not be in violation of the Belo requirements, but may result in the employee not signing it. A better plan would be to review the contract in six months or a year, basing the average hours on the experience under the Belo contract.

In the second contract term, the hours could be reduced if the average justifies it. If the hours are reduced to the average, the employee is not being rewarded for efforts in doing the work in fewer hours.

Compliance and Overtime Control

Supervisors should be made aware that if the employee is required or permitted to work overtime for the employer's benefit, the employee must be paid. Management must authorize it, and the rule must be enforced. For the employer to control overtime, two strong positions must be taken. First, remove the control of hours from the employee. Second, if control of the overtime hours cannot be removed from the employee, and exempt status cannot be justified, the Belo contract or some other pay plan should be considered. If a Belo plan is not possible and there is an uncontrollable fluctuation in the hours worked, another plan should be submitted to the Wage and Hour Division for approval.

INDEPENDENT CONTRACTORS

Independent contractors are workers who are not employees. Typically, they are temporary consultants. Employers are sometimes tempted to avoid the costs and responsibilities associated with hiring an additional employee by claiming that those who perform certain services are independent contractors. Where the independent contractor relationship has been established, both parties enjoy certain advantages:

Employer Advantages

1. The requirements of the Fair Labor Standards Act do not apply. Overtime premiums need not be paid.
2. Unemployment compensation payroll taxes do not have to be paid.
3. Social Security taxes do not have to be paid.
4. City, state, and federal income taxes do not have to be withheld.
5. Compulsory workers' compensation coverage does not apply.

Worker Advantages

1. The worker has much greater flexibility with respect to the time, place, and manner of performance of services.
2. The independent contractor has enhanced flexibility with respect to the deduction of business-related expenses. For example, employees may deduct only those business and miscellaneous expenses that exceed 2 percent of their adjusted gross income, but independent contractors may deduct 100 percent of their expenses related to self-employment.
3. Independent contractors may establish individual pension and profit-sharing plans that may be more desirable than those offered by employers. Obviously, there is considerable economic advantage in avoiding the statutory requirements.

There is strong incentive for establishing an independent contractor relationship wherever possible, but there are also certain risks in doing so.[59]

Risks in the Relationship

Although there are advantages, so are there risks if the Wage and Hour court finds that an independent contractor is, in fact, an employee.[60] No statute defines the exact meaning of an independent contractor. The interpretation is left entirely to the courts, using agency principles. The principal liabilities, if it is determined that an independent contractor is an employee, are:

1. The amount of the employee's state and federal income tax, plus interest, due to the failure to withhold under IRS regulations
2. Unpaid overtime or minimum wages under the FLSA
3. Liability to the state for unemployment compensation insurance tax
4. Expenses incurred under the common law for a work-related injury, due to the failure to carry workers' compensation insurance
5. The employer's amount owed on the employee's Social Security taxes, plus what is owed by the employee, in addition to the interest on the entire amount, due to the failure to withhold

To determine whether an independent contractor relationship exists, one must look to the common law,[61] the IRS code, National Labor Relations Board (NLRB) cases, decisions under the FLSA, state agencies' positions on workers' compensation coverage, and liability for unemployment insurance. Most of these agencies use either all or part of the common law definition, but some put more stress on certain factors than others. For example, the NLRB looks only at the control factor, whereas the IRS looks to see whether or not it was a businesslike operation.

Guidelines

The courts have said on numerous occasions that no one element establishes an independent contractor relationship.[62] The historic base for determining if such a relationship exists comes from the law of agency. An attempt to define the distinction between an employee and an independent contractor was made by the *Restatement of the Law of Agency* (2nd, Sect. 220), which stated:

While an employee acts under the direction and control of the employer, an independent contractor contracts to produce a certain result and has full control over the means and methods that shall be used in producing the result. He is usually said to carry on an independent business.

In *Nationwide Mutual Ins. Co.* v. *Darden*, 12 S.Ct. 1344 (1992), the Court held that an individual is an employee under the Employment Retirement Income Security Act (ERISA) unless Congress says otherwise. The Court used the common law person agency principle in determining whether there was an independent contractor. Under ERISA, the Court in *Darden* listed the factors to be considered when determining whether there is an independent contractor or employee relationship. The Court pointed out (at 1349) that no one factor is decisive.

The Fifth Circuit, in *Reich* v. *Circle C. Investments, Inc.*, 498 F.2d 824 (5th Circ. 1993), found one factor that would indicate topless dancers were independent contractors. But on balance, four other factors made them employees. In this situation, the dancers received no compensation from the club; they received only tips from customers. And, at the end of each night, the club received $20 from each dancer, regardless of how much the dancer made in tips from dancing on the tables. The club claimed this was rental. However, the club controlled the number of customers and tables.

The court focused on control, investments of the worker (costumes and a padlock), opportunity for profit (the club controlled the customer flow, where money could be made if the dancer was popular), skill and initiative required to perform the job (no training was needed), and permanency of the relationship (this was very short). This would indicate a nonemployee status, but the court decided other factors outweighed the short employment relationship, and found the dancers to be employees. The main factor was control.

The Supreme Court has identified two main conditions for finding that an independent contractor condition exists. First, there must be independent performance of the assigned job. Second, the initiative and decision-making authority must involve the performance of the work by the independent contractor.[63] The major factor in the determination of independent contractor status is the degree of employer control. With a greater degree of employer control, it is more likely the worker will be found to be an employee. A person who is required to comply with instructions about when, where, and how to work is ordinarily an employee. Some employees who are experienced or proficient in their work need little instruction; however, this does not put them in an independent contractor status. The control element is present if the employer retains the right to instruct.

For the purpose of determining an employer–employee relationship under the National Labor Relations Act, the board applies only the right of control test. If the person for whom services are performed retains the right of control of the end result, in addition to the manner and reasoning to be used in reaching that result, the board will find that an employer–employee relationship exists.

The right to instruct a person who works for the employer eight hours a day in one job and cleans the office at night, or mows the lawn on Saturday, often makes a worker an employee. If an employer–employee relationship exists, overtime compensation is due for all hours worked over 40 per week, unless a flat fee is greater than time-and-a-half for hours worked. There is an implied right to instruct a person who works for the employer eight hours a day on one job and does additional work in off hours. If there is an employee–employer relationship, overtime compensation is due. If the flat fee exceeds the overtime rate for the hours worked, then there is compliance. If an employer assumes that an independent contractor relationship exists and in fact it does not, the exposure in other areas is far greater than the payment of overtime. Because of this exposure, the employer should be cautious when treating the relationship as an independent contractor status. Serious consideration should be given to requesting a determination from the appropriate regulatory agency. Most agencies will furnish a list of guidelines on request. Such a request may not trigger an investigation.

Examples of Relationships

To prevent exposure to liability, when an employer assumes an independent contractor relationship exists but an employer–employee relationship legally exists, some examples may be helpful.

When a gasoline distributor leased stations to operators, the court found that not only was the lessee an employee but those persons whom the lessee hired were also employees of the distributor. The evidence showed that the distributor controlled the hours of operation, the prices of major items, and the daily management of money, and took the risk of profits and loss. The court reasoned that the employees of the lessee were an integral part of the operation; therefore, they were also employees of the distributors and the lessee.[64] Other cases where the court found an employee–employer relationship were where an agent who operated a retail cleaning outlet under a contract was held to be an employee of the owner[65] and where crew leaders for a builder were registered under a state law as labor contractors but were, in practice, employees.[66] In the Fifth Circuit, a contract laborer who was a mechanic and supervisor was held to be an employee; however, the contract laborer who was a subcontractor of this employee was held to be an independent contractor.[67] The test in these cases is whether the party for whom the service is being performed retains control over the outcome.[68]

Essential Elements

Because of the risks involved and the possibility of litigation, employers should have very strong reasons for attempting to establish an independent contractor relationship. If such a reason does exist, then it is advisable to state specifically in the agreement that:

1. The only supervision will be related to result and not to method.[69]
2. As much as possible, the individual will make the investment in equipment.
3. The independent contractor will be responsible for the profit or loss of the operation.
4. In all other respects, the independent contractor will be performing as a separate business.
5. The employer does not provide benefits, such as holiday or vacation pay.
6. The person is to be employed for a specified length of time.
7. The method of pay is different than for employees.
8. The materials and equipment will be supplied by the contractor.[70]
9. The parties enter into the relationship with a specific intent: to create an independent contractor relationship.
10. The work is either a distinct occupation or a business.

Use of Contracts

The economic reality of the relationship is the strongest element in establishing an independent contractor relationship that will stand the scrutiny of the courts and the regulatory bodies. If such a relationship is intended, it must be objectively established by a written agreement. The contract should be written with a careful eye toward common law and agency interpretation. The contract must emphasize the preceding 10 elements. Creating an independent contractor status is one way to control overtime. Extreme care should be taken to make certain that, although an independent contractor status was intended, an actual employee–employer relationship does not exist. Liability for uninsured workers' compensation and payment of unemployment, Social Security, and withholding taxes often offsets the advantages of establishing a questionable independent contractor status. Administrative agencies and the courts will give great weight to the agreement. However, they will also look to other factors that reflect the tasks of the individual, the terms and conditions of employment, and whether the parties are following the agreement. In questionable situations, professional advice should be considered. This demonstrates a good faith effort to comply with the law.

The Fair Labor Standards Act, as well worn as it is, still provides the media with frequent opportunities to publicly expose employers caught in noncompliance. To prevent any such negative situations:

1. Avoid hiring young people for the wrong hours and types of work.
2. Don't permit overtime-eligible employees to "come early," "stay late," or "take work home."
3. Demand accurate work time records, including work occurring during lunch time.
4. Be sure any designated independent contractor positions qualify as such.
5. In the private sector, don't apply compensatory time off that carries beyond the designated work week.
6. Pay overtime-eligible personnel for all work beyond the 40-hour work week.

EQUAL PAY ACT

The first direct involvement by the federal government in the payment of wages was in the original 1938 Fair Labor Standards Act. For the next 25 years, there was no further interference with the employers' right to determine wages of their employees.

Congress reacted to the perceived problem of gender pay inequity in 1963, when it amended Section 6 of the Fair Labor Standards Act, and created the Equal Pay Act (EPA).[71] The EPA simply states that no employer shall discriminate in the payment of wages at a property, on the basis of sex, for equal work. Jobs that require comparable competencies and are performed under similar working conditions must have equal pay. If the differential is based on seniority,[72] a merit system, an incentive pay system, experience,[73] or any factor other than gender, there is no violation.[74] Although the standards are clear, mistakes are common.[75]

Sections 201 to 208 of Title II, CRA91 (the Glass Ceiling Act of 1991),[76] established a study commission to address the national problem of underrepresentation and artificial barriers to women and minorities in management and in decision-making positions. One of the barriers, according to the Department of Labor, is the lack of management perception in determining compensation. The report of the commission improved conditions but didn't break the glass ceiling.[77]

The EPA applies to state and local governments under a 1974 amendment to FLSA, most of the private sector and unions. Exceptions to coverage are few. As a Title VII issue, the pursuit of equal pay has the potential of extending to any worker who feels mistreated, let alone unequally compensated.

Definition of Equal Work

There is a wide variety of skills, responsibility, and effort in different jobs. That is the primary reason for the difference in wages; but the "going rate" is also a large determinant. The identification of differences in jobs is the purpose of job evaluation and **pay equity** studies.

The first opportunity that the courts had to address these questions was in *Shultz* v. *Wheaton Glass Co.*, where male selector packers were receiving $.21 per hour more than female selector packers.[78] Women performed substantially the same inspection work as men, except that approximately 18 percent of the time the male selectors performed materials handling tasks.[79] Females were not permitted to perform these tasks because they were restricted from lifting anything over 35 pounds. The court, in a landmark opinion on the interpretation of EPA, established a legal principle in finding a violation. In view of the refusal of the Supreme Court to review this decision, these principles can be considered as controlling. These principles are sometimes called the *equal work standard* (see Exhibit 5.2).

1. The equal work standard requires only that the jobs be substantially equal and not identical. Small differences will not make them unequal.[80]
2. When a wage differential exists between men and women doing substantially equal work, the burden is on the employer to show that the differential is for some reason other than sex.
3. Where some, but not all, members of one sex performed extra duties in their jobs, these extra duties do not justify giving all members of that sex extra pay.
4. That men can perform extra duties does not justify extra pay unless women are also offered the opportunity to perform these duties.
5. Job titles and job descriptions are not material in showing that work is unequal unless they accurately reflect actual job content.

EXHIBIT 5.2   The Equal Work Standard

What is a substantially different job is decided on a case-by-case basis.[81] If there is a substantial difference in effort, skill, or responsibility, the courts permit a pay differential between the sexes. The principle followed in the Eighth Circuit is that job content, not job titles or job descriptions, determines whether jobs are equal.[82] Calling one employee a cleaner and another a custodian does not justify a wage differential.[83]

Another justification for an employer's wage differential between men and women is shift work. When all men worked the night shift and women the day shift, it was argued by employers that the differential was justified because of dissimilar working conditions. In this case, one of the few EPA cases to reach the Supreme Court, it was held that working conditions did not refer to the time of day when work is performed. Thus, different shifts do not justify a pay differential.[84]

This case also established the rule that equal pay violations could be remedied only by raising the women's wages, not by reducing the men's wages. But it left open the question of whether changes in job content could remedy the violation. Often, employers attempted to justify pay differentials between men and women by arguing that working conditions were not similar, or that the jobs performed by males were more hazardous tasks than the ones performed by females. There are situations where this might be a defense. However, such a defense should be used with extreme caution. Statistics show that 70 to 85 percent of all industrial accidents are not caused by physical conditions but by unsafe acts of the employee. Under these statistics, hazardous working conditions would not justify the differential, if accidents are caused by the employee, not the conditions.

Measuring Equality

When considering skills, such factors as experience, training, education, and ability are taken into account. Any one of these factors can justify a differential.[85] Possessing a skill is not enough; the person must necessarily apply that skill on the job.[86] A common "equal skill" situation that courts have struck down is when the employer trains men for promotional purposes but does not offer to train women. When the jobs are compared, the trained men have more skills than the untrained women.

Where male bank tellers were paid more than female bank tellers, the employer argued that the males were in a bona fide training program, being trained in all aspects of banking to replace senior officers. Such subjective evaluation of potential for promotion, standing alone, cannot justify pay differentials under EPA.[87] All such training programs should be put in writing and offered to all employees who qualify regardless of gender or race.

The following criteria must be met in order to justify pay differentials under EPA through a bona fide training program:

1. It must be open to all.
2. All employees must be notified of the training opportunities.
3. There must be a defined beginning and ending of the training program.
4. A definite course of study must be documented, and advancement opportunities, upon completion, must be available.

The Responsibility Rationale

The defense of a difference in responsibility to justify unequal pay occurs mostly in administrative, professional, and executive jobs. In one of the first cases under the responsibility defense, the employer claimed that men had to make decisions that women did not have to make. The court found that although men did make decisions that women did not, these decisions were subject to review by supervisors. Therefore, the differential was not justified under the responsibility defense.[88]

Often, the employer may justify a pay differential based on gender in the same job categories by claiming that one type of work is more difficult than another. For example, an employer claimed that management of soft-line departments such as clothing, historically managed by women, had less responsibility than hard-line departments such as sporting goods, usually managed by men. The court held that there is no substantial difference to justify less pay for women than for men.[89] In *EEOC* v. *Madison Community Unit School District No. 12*, 816 F.2d 577 (7th Cir. 1987), the court held that paying female coaches of girls' track and tennis teams less than male coaches of male track and tennis teams is a violation of the Equal Pay Act. More recently, in *Weber* v. *Infinity Broadcasting*, 2006 WL 891138 (E.D. Mich. 2006) a Michigan court found a female disk jockey was paid significantly less than two male disk jockeys in violation of the EPA.

Semantic Issues

A properly communicated, bona fide merit system that is applied without regard to sex is one of the factors that will justify differentials. All too often the term *merit pay* is used to include labor market increases, longevity increases, and general across-the-board increases that have no relationship to meritorious performance.[90] Merit increases that will survive judicial review under EPA are individual increases in pay related to the demonstrable job performance of that individual.

Determining a wage level on some factor other than performance is a major fault with merit pay plans and a primary reason for being unable to withstand judicial scrutiny. In an inflationary period, the employer wants to keep earnings in line with the labor market conditions without setting a precedent by implying that pay increases are automatic, or based on labor market conditions. Rationalizations set in and any believable reason is given. In *Brock* v. *Georgia S.W.*

College, 765 F.2d 1026 (11th Cir. 1985), although the employer argued that the wage difference was due to a merit system, the court found that the merit ratings were based on subjective personal judgment, ad hoc; that the wage difference was due to the merit system; and that, in many cases, the evaluators were ill informed.

For compensation to be based truly on merit, it should be delivered when some significant performance has been accomplished. A delay in reacting to special achievement can chill motivation. For production incentives, the previous two-week period should be the maximum waiting period. White-collar merit awards should also be awarded within two weeks of the period of accomplishment.

A Bona Fide Merit Plan

In order for a merit pay plan to be bona fide under the various statutes, it must be in writing and contain all or most of the following elements:[91]

1. The employee must believe that good performance will result in additional compensation.
2. There should be a direct correlation between the amount of pay and the exceptional performance, without onerous caps. Upper limits tend to dampen the motivation of many workers.
3. The employee should understand the merit plan before it is adopted so that there are no surprises at evaluation time.
4. Performance should be accurately measured either by objective appraisals or by standards that the employee accepts. If agreement cannot be reached, the employer should be sure about what is fair and adopt it. Sometimes employees have to work with a plan before they are convinced they can earn additional money.

5. Base pay should not be less because an employee is on a merit system. Merit pay should be given when performance is above the norm.
6. The merit system must be updated periodically. Job content affects the performance; if not current, either the company or the employee can be unfairly affected.
7. Managers must believe in the system and be trained to properly administer it.
8. Follow-up procedures are necessary to prevent bias and leniency. Nothing will defeat a merit plan faster than leniency or bias.[92]

Audit Compliance

It should not be surprising, in light of the preceding discussion, that many employers are in violation of the Equal Pay Act. When challenged, they face a lengthy and expensive lawsuit. The factors mentioned previously, although valid, offer very little defense. For this reason, it is good practice to audit compensation plans to determine the extent of exposure. Where serious compliance problems are found, the corrections can be made. This is better than an equal pay complaint by the EEOC. An EPA auditor should:

1. Examine pay differentials among all jobs involving similar or equal skill, effort, responsibility, and working conditions. Finding any instance where a pay differential may be based on sex, eliminate the inequity by bringing the pay of the lower-paid employee to the level of the higher-paid individual.
2. Determine the distribution of pay percentages within each job category and whether they correspond with performance.
3. Analyze the average pay level within each job category by race and sex.
4. Study the average pay increase given by each supervisor within each job category.

5. Look for consistency in the application of hiring, promotion, and pay increase practices to avoid any inference of sex discrimination.

This is not an exhaustive checklist; the basic premise, equal pay for equal work (not necessarily identical work), must be kept in mind to avoid creating inequities and to rectify past inequities. If there is logic to the compensation system, it is much easier to defend when an equal pay charge is made by the EEOC. Programs and procedures that demonstrate good faith efforts to maintain fair pay among workers will minimize exposure to litigation.

In summary, management should do four things:

1. Have a rational reason for its compensation levels.
2. Explain to the employees how their wages are determined and changes to be instituted.
3. Document the sound reasons on which pay actions are based.
4. Correct unjustifiable wage differentials between sexes, rather than trying to rationalize them.

Comparable Pay for Comparable Worth

Despite EPA, there continues to be a substantial disparity in earnings between men and women. Although the Equal Pay Act didn't overcome gender wage disparity, the proponents of equal pay believe that combining the Equal Pay Act with Title VII and Executive Order 11246 goes far in achieving that goal. The concept is a very controversial equal employment issue.[93]

The Birth of Pay Equity Law (Comparable Worth)

Edicts and statutory requirements by states have attempted to create pay equity based on the "**comparable worth**" of the job. Many cities now use a job evaluation system to determine the comparable work value of the work performed by each class of its employees. Evaluation system options include:

1. Use the state job match.
2. Use or modify systems used by other public employers.
3. Design your own system.
4. Purchase a privately owned (consultant's) system.[94]

Several circuit courts have held that it is not up to the courts to determine the worth of an employee. The issue was apparently settled in *State of Washington* v. *Am. Federal, State and County and Municipal Employees*, 770 F.2d 1401 (9th Cir.1985). The court overturned a lower court decision supporting the "comparable worth" concept and held that Congress did not intend Title VII to interfere with the law of supply and demand, or prevent employees from competing in the labor market. Subsequently, a number of states have experienced active groups (Michigan, Massachusetts, Colorado, New Mexico, and others) pursuing political action to achieve greater equality.[95] Minnesota has created legislation applicable only to the public sector.[96] In pursuit of improved equity, most Canadian provinces have also legislated for stricter equity laws.

Most large private-sector firms apply job evaluation and market studies to achieve fair pay opportunity across gender lines. Public-sector organizations use Civil Service Classification systems or job matching tools as a basis to determine comparable pay. Those advocating additional legislation charge that many job evaluation plans and market (valued) ranking systems are inherently (historically) biased.[97] Nevertheless, positions can be compared only to other positions that should be similar in pay (i.e., similarly classified).

Job equity, however, doesn't necessarily equate with pay equity. Job equity deals with setting the pay guidelines for different positions. Pay equity is devoted to pay analysis for gender differentials. Pay disparity can still result from consciously biased decisions (disparate treatment) or unconscious (flawed) decisions about performance or job value perceptions (disparate impact) despite job value comparability. This is currently a developing issue in human resource law.[98]

For almost 100 years, the federal government has pursued pay equity through the application of job classification (job ranking). Early landmark legislation in human resource law was directed at "standardizing the classification and grading of civil service positions according to duties in ascending order of responsibilities" (the Classification Act of 1923).[99] In time, the ranking of jobs cascaded through states to many counties and municipalities. Over time, the application of job-ranking techniques progressed to large firms in the private sector, also. In order to arrive at a fair basis for pay, there must be a standard tool for measuring multitudes of jobs; job evaluation results in job classification.

Pay Replacement Obligations

Government bodies have sponsored financial support for employees who are injured at the workplace (workers' compensation), become unemployed (unemployment insurance), or who become unable to work because they are of retirement age or have suffered a total disability (Social Security). This legislation, along with the Fair Labor Standards Act, is the foundation for the financial sustenance of our workers.

UNEMPLOYMENT COMPENSATION

The stated purpose of unemployment compensation (UC) laws is to provide benefits for persons unemployed through no fault of their own. For more than 50 years, unemployment compensation insurance has been considered one of the most successful social insurance programs. Unemployment compensation insurance had a welfare origin. The early drafters of this legislation wanted the benefits to partially replace wages during periods of limited unemployment. Because wages were being replaced, workers would not have to meet the "needs test" of traditional welfare programs. The U.S. Congress usually extends the benefit period during an economic downturn. Congress generally supports the proposition that getting money into the economy at a time when it is most needed speeds up recovery.

Historical Basis for Unemployment Compensation

Unemployment compensation insurance is not a new idea. By 1800, trade unions were providing economic aid for members forced into temporary idleness. After 1850, supplemental UC benefits were provided in such European countries as Germany, Austria, Belgium, and most of Scandinavia. The first public UC insurance law was passed in 1898, when the city of Ghent in Belgium, passed a local ordinance that supplemented trade union benefits. In 1911, England established the first compulsory UC system.

In the United States, as in European countries, the beginnings of unemployment compensation are found in trade union benefit plans. The first plan was established by a New York printers' local in 1831. From this period to 1932, UC was provided either by trade unions or by joint plans produced by agreement between employers and unions. Private voluntary plans established by individual employers existed, but were not as common as trade unions' plans.

During the Progressive Era described in Chapter 1, there was a movement to establish a public compulsory unemployment compensation plan. In 1916, limited UC was passed by

the Massachusetts legislature. More than 20 other states followed. Some states hesitated to pass unemployment compensation legislation, perceiving it would put them at a competitive disadvantage.

This competitive concern of the various states caused pressure for legislation on the federal level. The debate over which governmental body should be responsible for the legislation delayed action by both federal and state legislative bodies. By 1935, the federal concept had won the battle. Unemployment compensation was included in the Social Security Act.

Taxation by Federal Government

Federal legislation is an example of the federal government's ability to use its taxing power to encourage states to adopt certain policies. The Social Security Act of 1935 provided that all employers who were not exempted had to pay a federal tax on wages, in part to fund the unemployment compensation program. The federal government would return over 90 percent of the tax if the state adopted an approved program. The UC section of the act provided that the federal government would set certain minimum standards. The states were to decide what type of plan best suited their needs. If a state had no plan, or if the state law was not in compliance with the federal law, the employers would still be taxed, but the tax would not be returned to the states. As anticipated, all 50 states passed laws.

It is not the purpose of this chapter to present the law in any particular jurisdiction. The chapter will provide only an overview. The administrative procedures are common to most jurisdictions. However, the law differs from state to state in the payment of benefits and level of state taxes. knowledge of both the federal and state law is essential for effective cost control.

Excluded Workers

Excluded workers under the federal law include:

1. Employees who are paid less than $1,500 in wages in a three-month period
2. Domestic workers
3. Farm workers
4. State, county, and city workers, with some exceptions
5. Employees of the federal government, if covered by another program
6. Employees of certain nonprofit organizations (religious, charitable, or educational organizations)

Financing Benefits

The unemployment compensation system is financed by two taxes. The state tax finances the benefits, and the federal tax finances state and federal administrative costs. The federal government taxes 6.2 percent of the first $7,000 in wages paid to each employee. A credit of 5.4 percent is returned. This leaves 0.8 percent to be used to finance state and federal administrative costs. The tax is also used to maintain a loan fund from which the states may borrow if they exhaust their funds available to pay benefits.

All states have adopted an experience rating system to encourage employers to maintain stable employment. These systems excuse employers with stable employment from paying all or part of the state unemployment tax, and grant a credit against the federal tax. State taxes are usually based on a "flexible" taxable wage base; increases in the wage base automatically follow increases in statewide wage levels. The taxable wage base ranges from $15,000 to $29,700. In all states, only the employer is taxed for unemployment compensation benefits.[100]

Although each state is free to develop its own plan, most states follow the model plan recommended by the federal government. Through funding regulations, the federal government retains a degree of control and forces some standardization among the various states.

Constitutional Restrictions

State unemployment compensation statutes are limited by the U.S. Constitution. One state denied benefits when an employee voluntarily quit for religious reasons. The Supreme Court held that this was a violation of the First Amendment.[101] The Supreme Court also struck down a Utah statute that denied benefits to pregnant women without regard to physical capacity to continue working. The court found this a violation of the Fourteenth Amendment.[102] However, the employee could continue to work after the baby was born. The court allowed the State of Missouri to deny benefits if the employee left the job due to pregnancy and there were no openings when she was able to return. The court in *Wimberly* v. *Labor and Industrial Relations Commission*, 107 S.Ct. 821 (1987), stated that pregnancy is not a job-related illness; and as long as pregnancy leaves are not treated differently from other illnesses, it is legal to deny benefits.

Courts generally hold that a state cannot deny benefits when the employee is protected by an antidiscrimination law. In one case, an employee joined a church 2 1/2 years after being employed. Her new religion prohibited working on Saturdays. She was discharged when she refused to work on Friday nights and Saturdays. The court held that denial of benefits would violate the First Amendment, although she had worked Saturdays until Saturday became her Sabbath. Whether or not she could be discharged was not an issue.[103]

States can deny benefits when an employee is discharged for religious use of drugs. The drug used in question was a violation of a state statute, although it was off duty conduct. The denial of benefits was not considered to be a First Amendment violation.[104] A state can deny benefits to claimants who are attending school. Night school students cannot be denied benefits because they would be available for work.[105]

When New York gave unemployment compensation benefits to strikers, the court held that it was not a violation of any clause in the Constitution and it was within the authority of the state to do so.[106] In *Brown v. A. J. Gerard Mfg. Co.*, 695 F.2d 1290 (11th Cir. 1983), the circuit court held that unemployment compensation could not be deducted from a Title VII back pay award.[107] The NLRB reached a similar conclusion in *NLRB* v. *Illinois Department of Employment and Security* 988 F.2d 735 (7th Cir. 1993).

Provisions of State Laws

The federal government requires certain conformity provisions before the employer as taxpayer is granted tax credits. However, the states have considerable flexibility to design their own program. To ensure that the UC payments are in keeping with the intent of the federal law, it is necessary for the states to establish eligibility requirements. The state must also establish benefit amounts and reasons why an unemployed individual should be denied benefits or be disqualified from receiving further benefits.

In developing rules to determine the right to receive benefits, states have generally followed the principle that UC is intended to provide temporary financial assistance to persons who are out of work through no fault of their own.[108] In order to carry out the intent of the act, state laws require eligible claimants to remain available for work and to be seeking work actively, or face the loss of benefits. This requirement is loosely administered in many states.

Variation of Benefit Levels

One way to instill an incentive to seek work is to establish benefit levels that pay only a portion of the wages that an employee would have received if fully employed. On the other hand, the states want the benefit level high enough to cover the claimant's non-deferrable expenses. Usually, this is a weekly benefit equal to about 50 percent of the claimant's normal weekly wage. Some states use the claimant's average weekly wage as a guideline for determining benefits.[109]

Most states set the absolute minimum and maximum benefit amount based on the employee's weekly earnings. Others determine the minimum and maximum on the average statewide annual wage. The minimum benefit requires a certain level of earnings; if an employee earns below that level, no benefits are paid. The amount of benefits is usually a fixed sum, but in a few states it depends on the number of dependents.

More than 14 states provide for the payment of dependents' allowances. Although there is some variation, generally a dependent must be wholly or mainly supported by the claimant to qualify. In almost all states, the waiting period to receive benefits is one week, although a few states pay benefits on the first day of unemployment. All states have a maximum period for benefits. This varies from 26 to 36 weeks.[110] Congress usually extends the period during an economic downturn.

Disqualifications for Benefits

The laws of various states follow the intent of the federal statute by establishing disqualification provisions. Each state has certain procedures to be followed for obtaining facts involved in a disputed claim. The state agency responsible for payment of compensation claims makes a determination whether the claimant is disqualified.[111] The employer or claimant may appeal and request a hearing. The decision of the hearing referee as to disqualification may be appealed to a higher reviewing authority. Subsequent appeals then may be carried to the state courts. If a constitutional question is involved, the U.S. Supreme Court has jurisdiction. Some states merely disqualify the claimant for a period of time. Other states deny the benefits for the entire period of unemployment if certain facts exist.

Reporting Termination Information

Before information is reported to the agency, the reason for separation should be well established. The reason given by the employee for an involuntary quit is often quite different from that stated by the employer in response to a claim. When an employee is discharged, a documented statement should be given to the employee, stating the reason for the discharge. Nothing weakens a case more than a showing that one party changed the statement of the reason for the discharge after the claim was filed. The reason given to the employee should be the same as what will later be reported to the state agency.

When a claim is filed, the agency will request separation information. The person responding to this request should first make sure that the facts stated coincide with the material available in the personnel records. When reporting separation information, give facts, do not give conclusions. Avoid subjective terms such as *not cooperative, unsatisfactory,* and *poor worker.* They mean nothing to the person making the determination. It is also advisable to expand the reason given. For example, when reporting a voluntary quit, the reason for the quit might be:

1. To return to home duty
2. To seek other employment
3. To get married
4. Dissatisfaction with the job
5. Failed to report after ___ days contrary to policy

These are all reasons to disqualify the claimant. If the facts exist, it is wise to give a definitive reason that the agency has previously held to be disqualifying.

In discharge cases, the separation information should establish that the action was willful or detrimental to the employer's interest. If the employee had been previously warned, give the date and a report of what was said. Stay away from vague or undocumented recollections when reporting the information. If you do not have good documentation, do not make the statement. Rely instead on credible supervisor testimony in the event that you have to go to a hearing.

Claiming the employee was unable to perform the job is always damaging.[112] It is better to say that employment rules were violated and then specify the rules that were violated, introducing evidence that the employee was aware of the violation when committing the act. Say when or how it was communicated, explaining that the employee had been previously warned, if such was the case. Claiming that the employee was "rude to customers" has very little meaning unless specific incidents are cited. If the employee was guilty of excessive absenteeism, give the dates of warnings and state the number of times absent. Show that the number is excessive in comparison with the records of other employees.

When answering an agency request for information, remember that separation information aids in getting the proper determination from the agency. This will reduce the number of appeals. Often, the person supplying the information limits the statement of information to the space provided in the form. Usually, this space is not enough. When it is not, attach another sheet and use all the space necessary. The information provided in response to the initial request guides the agency in making a determination whether the claimant is qualified. It also is the basic information that is used in the event of an appeal.

The appeal process seeks to obtain facts that verify the original position of the employer. For this reason, more time should be spent in providing complete information in the first step than in all the others. Time spent in supplying the original information will reduce the number of appeals.[113]

If the person supplying the information has some doubts about what should be included in the initial response, he or she should get expert help. Often, so much damaging information has been reported in the first response that the employer is unable to rehabilitate its case.

Qualifications of Benefits

Whenever the claimant is receiving any type of income, the employer should question it. Such income is often disqualifying. Income such as holiday, vacation, and back pay may be disqualifying in some states. Even though the statute may not be specific as to kinds of income, any income should be considered.

The state laws typically require the claimant be unemployed and available for work. The receipt of any income from a physical disability would raise a question as to whether the claimant is available for work. Pension payments indicate retirement from the labor market; therefore the claimant is not available for work. The federal law requires the state to reduce the weekly benefit payments by the amount received per week from any source. States may reduce the benefits on less than a dollar-for-dollar basis in order to take into account any contributions that the worker must make to an employer-deferred compensation or retirement plan.

Voluntary Quit without Good Cause

Benefits are paid to persons who are out of work through no fault of their own. It would therefore follow that a voluntary quit would automatically disqualify. Every state will disqualify individuals who bring about or perpetuate their own unemployment. If they quit their job without good cause, commit work-related misconduct, or refuse suitable work, they have caused their own unemployment. Most states disqualify until the claimant meets earning requirements for a new base period.[114] However, some states just reduce benefits.

The issue of whether the voluntary quit is without a cause attributable to the employer is important. If it is found that the quit was no fault of the employer, benefits may be still paid to the claimant, but in some states the employer's experience rating will not be charged. Most employers do not recognize this. They attempt to justify the discharge by misconduct, which is often difficult to prove. If they argue that it wasn't a cause attributable to the employer, they would have better employee relations. The employee would get the benefits, but the employer's account would not be charged. Accordingly, the employer's experience rating would not be affected. The benefits come out of the general fund in some states. The referee takes a dim view of an employer who is trying to deny benefits solely to avoid a charge to its experience rating.

Quitting must be work related; otherwise good cause cannot be established. Sometimes a quit can be deemed a constructive discharge. To establish constructive discharge, the claimant must show that a prudent person would have quit under similar working conditions. Sexual harassment is a good example. Whether the claimant attempted to remedy the situation prior to quitting is highly relevant.

Some reasons for quitting that disqualify a claimant's request for benefits are:

1. To accept other work
2. To join or accompany a spouse or companion (some states will not disqualify)
3. To go to day school
4. To retire
5. To become self-employed

Often, there is a fine line between a voluntary quit and a discharge. In most states *a quit* is defined when the employee exercises, directly or indirectly, a free-will choice to terminate the employment relationship.[115] Whenever possible, the employer should call a separation a voluntary quit, such as when the employee fails to report for work after a certain number of days. A *discharge* is usually defined as an employer action that indicates to the employee that his or her services are no longer wanted.

A supervisor had a heated argument with an employee; the employee walked away toward the door, and the supervisor said, "Keep on walking!" This was a discharge. If the supervisor had let him walk through the door, however, it would probably have been a voluntary quit.[116] Resigning in order to avoid discharge is usually held to be a quit. Also, a good personal reason is not usually considered enough of a justification to leave a job; the claimant will be disqualified unless discrimination is involved.

Disqualification for Misconduct

Misconduct is the most common issue in disqualification proceedings. *Misconduct* that results in disqualification is defined as "conduct resulting in willful or wanton substantial disregard of the employer's interests." Misconduct was first defined in *Boynton Cab Co. v. Newbeck*, 296 N.W.2d 636 (Wis. 1941). It is one those rare decisions that has been adopted by all the states. Often the employer confuses willful misconduct with inability or negligence.[117] If a school bus driver has three accidents in 30 days, this may not be misconduct; rather, it might be merely negligence. It is not disqualifying. If an employee throws paper, swears, and insults the boss, this may be misconduct, but it would have to be shown that the incident constituted a substantial disregard for the employer's interests.

Misconduct Schemes

In misconduct cases, the employer must have acted reasonably to control or prevent the employee's behavior. there must be no question that the employee was aware of the work rule violated. In determining what constitutes misconduct, the employer's condoning of similar behavior is relevant. This question often comes up where alleged discrimination has not been properly investigated. Misconduct usually means something different to the employer from what it means to the agency or appeal referee.

An employer should never let the possibility of unemployment compensation benefits interfere with the decision to discharge. Once that decision has been made, the method used in the discharge will sometimes determine whether the employee will receive benefits. It would be a mistake to argue that the employee should be denied benefits because of misconduct. It could be argued that it was a cause not attributable to the employer.

In misconduct cases, the employer must show that:

1. An existing rule was violated.
2. The rule was communicated to the employee prior to the violation.
3. A direct causal relationship existed between the offenses committed and the discharge.[118]

It is important to remember that the longer the interval between the offense and the discharge, the less chance there is for sustaining the termination before an appeal referee. Normally, an act is considered misconduct when:

1. It is not an isolated incident (unless gross misconduct, such as a felony, is involved).
2. It is detrimental to the employer's best interests (usually a monetary consideration).
3. It takes place during working hours on the employer's premises.
4. The employee's act disregards job duties that were previously defined and communicated by the employer.

If the action meets this definition and is well documented, it will usually be considered misconduct.

Gross Misconduct

Some states identify two levels of misconduct—gross misconduct and simple misconduct. In gross misconduct, the employer has no duty to warn or to show that the employee was aware of the work rule violated. Stealing from the employer, willful destruction of property, sabotage and unprovoked insubordination, for example, would be in this category.

Drug Testing

Employee drug testing has opened up a whole new set of problems in unemployment compensation law.[119] The issue in most of these cases is whether the refusal to take a drug test is misconduct. Different states have decided this issue differently.[120] The employer can avoid this exposure by adopting a policy that an employee's refusal to take a drug test is a voluntary quit. The employee has a choice of quitting or taking the test. Refusal to take a drug test can hardly be a willful or wanton substantial disregard for the employer's interest (misconduct definition). The employee's claim that drug testing is an invasion of off-duty privacy is not given credence in most state courts.[121] If the employer's records show that the employee refuses to take the test, contrary to a communicated policy, a quit is much better than using misconduct as the reason. However, it must be made clear that the employee has an option to continue working if the test is taken.

If misconduct evidence is not strong, the employer should argue that the cause of the separation was not attributable to the employer. The burden is then on the claimant to show that he or she did not cause the separation. In controlling UC insurance costs, there is no substitute for a clearly communicated policy. The communication should be done in such a manner that there is no doubt that, if a violator is caught, disciplinary action will be taken.

The Use of Appeal Proceedings

If the claimant or the employer objects to a determination made by the agency, either party has the right to appeal. The most common type of appeal concerns rights to benefits. Issues such as ability to work, unavailability for work, or failure to accept suitable work may arise after benefits have been received, and the question of whether the employee is eligible for benefits must be considered periodically during the benefit period.

The appeal must be filed within a specified time, which varies from state to state. In all states, the time limit allows no exceptions. The agency loses jurisdiction if the appeal is not made within the time limits, and the right to appeal is lost forever. Failure to file an appeal within the specified time limits is one of the most common reasons that employers lose appeals. Often, the determination notice from the agency goes to the employer's tax or finance department. It may be put aside, or the person responsible may be away on vacation or sick. As a result, the opportunity to appeal is lost. When the person regularly responsible for appeals is not available, provision should be made for a trained substitute.

No Waiver or Agreement

The employer and claimant may decide to make an agreement or draft a waiver. The employer may agree to pay the benefits if the claimant agrees not to do certain things; or the employer may decide to pay benefits. This type of agreement is not valid. Only the agency decides when benefits will be paid.

Hearsay evidence is inadmissible in judicial proceedings. In an unemployment hearing, however, the referee may admit hearsay evidence but cannot use it as the sole basis for a decision. As a practical matter, the referee may treat hearsay evidence any way he or she wishes.

Preparations for an Appeal

To prepare for the presentation before the appeals referee, the first step is to examine the statement that the claimant made to the agency, comparing it with the one the employer made. If an inconsistency is apparent, as is usually the case, the employer must seek facts to support the validity of its statement.

Witnesses are often required. If so, they should be prepared before the hearing. Some referees question the claimant before the employer has a chance to do so. The proceeding is mostly fact-finding and is designed for laypersons. Formal rules of evidence usually are not observed. Seldom is any evidence excluded. When in doubt, put it in. Either party may object to the remarks or evidence admitted, but it is advisable to do so in a nonlegal way, since objections are commonly overruled. There is no substitute for the credible, direct testimony of a witness.

When it is difficult to get operating people to document their actions, the best way to ensure documentation in the future is to have the supervisor testify. Frequently, the testimony will induce the claimant to deny previous statements. The importance of the document becomes obvious. The employer will have fewer problems obtaining documentation when the claimant denies the supervisor's statements under oath.

If there are some legal arguments, it is best to present them in writing. It is a good idea to seek help in preparing the memorandum. if the argument is unusual, providing a short memorandum citing similar case law is advisable. One should also take advantage of the opportunity to make a summary—called a *closing statement* in legal proceedings. It is not necessary to quote a lot of authority, but it is useful to the referee for both parties to summarize their positions. The state agency personnel, other than a referee on the case, will usually give help in this area. After the hearing, the referee will take the case under advisement and render a decision. The proceedings are recorded on tape or by court reporters. In most states, however, a transcript is seldom made unless the case is appealed.

Employers should always consider an appeal when they receive an adverse decision that they believe is not sound. Sometimes certain witnesses were not available at the time of the hearing or certain evidence was overlooked. At the appeal level, it may be proper to ask for a remand in order for other evidence to be considered.

If a key person is not available for an extended period of time, and it is not possible to get the hearing postponed, the employer may have to go forward with the best effort possible. If the employer receives an adverse decision, the testimony of the unavailable key person might have changed the position of the referee. A request for a remand is in order, and will probably be granted.

The hearing at the appeal level follows the same nonlegal format as the first hearing. It is advisable to prepare a memorandum before the hearing. At this time, the employeer will state its position and the reasons for the appeal. This statement should not introduce any new evidence, but simply point out that based on the evidence presented, the determination of the referee was in error. If new evidence not previously available is to be introduced, the memorandum should request a remand. It is important to give a summary, in writing, at the close of the hearing.

Use of Attorneys in the Appeal Process

Unemployment compensation hearings and appeals are a quasi-judicial process, yet many employers feel more secure if an attorney represents them. The increased complexity of the appeals process has encouraged employers to seek legal representation. However, getting too legal in a process that is basically nonjudicial is often fatal.[122] Many states—for instance, Michigan and New Jersey—do not permit attorneys to appear before the Employment Security Commission's referee hearing as representatives of employers. Even the courts recognize that non-attorneys can represent both parties before referees.

There are situations where parties, if made aware of the opposition's representation, would have chosen to also be represented by counsel. Usually, the referee does not know of attorney representation status until the hearing, thus making it even more difficult to determine whether representation is needed. A better procedure would be to call the opposing party to ask if he or she is going to be represented. Both parties may then decide what to do about representation.

The best role of an attorney in UC hearings is to help the client prepare the case, not to be present at the hearing. Representation at a fact-finding hearing often makes the proceeding too legal, which may be disadvantageous.

Reasons for Unsuccessful Appeals

Many cases are lost, not on the merits, but by the quality of the presentation. Often, the people directly involved in the case do not testify. Frequently, witnesses are not properly instructed on what the case is about, or they don't take the task seriously.[123] The employer must present only the objective facts, eliminating all subjectivity. Most appeals proceedings are lost for the following reasons:

1. Witnesses do not have actual knowledge of the facts.
2. Proper documentation of facts is not available at the hearing.
3. The employer fails to give a clear reason for termination.

Policies and Practices to Reduce Costs

All unemployment compensation disputes start with the termination process. Although many states have laws that disqualify the claimants from receiving benefits if they quit voluntarily, many types of terminations can result in benefits being paid. Employers often invite this result by giving an ambiguous or incorrect reason for the termination. An employee is disqualified from benefits if the termination results from one of the following:

1. General job dissatisfaction because of lack of advancement
2. Low wages
3. Too much travel
4. Failure to request or return from a leave of absence
5. Failure to attempt to remedy a negative work situation with the employer (this is particularly damaging to the claim for benefits)
6. Marital or domestic situations

The following reasons for quits are considered a good basis for benefits, a cause not attributed to the employer, and may not be charged to the employer's experience rating in some states:

1. Health reasons
2. The employer moves outside the commuting area
3. Forced or requested resignation (opportunity to quit before being discharged)
4. Quitting because of smoking ban at the workplace

One of the most difficult and important problems is being sure that the proper procedure is followed in the discharge. Supervisors often do not think about the unemployment compensation consequences when they decide to discharge. This oversight can be damaging.

The Audit of Charges

One of the areas most often overlooked in the control of unemployment compensation insurance costs is the audit of the quarterly statement, where all the charges to the employer's account are listed. Even with advanced technology, many errors can creep into this statement. Because state tax rates are experience rated, finding these errors can be an important step in cost control.

Since the finance department usually pays the taxes, some employers leave the responsibility of the audit to the finance group. This is often a mistake; the finance department usually does not have the facts necessary to make the audit. Some errors to look for in an audit are the following:

1. In the extreme case, a charge may be made for an individual who was not even employed by the organization.
2. If an employee has not earned enough wages during the base period, no charge should be made, even though he or she may otherwise be qualified to receive the benefits.
3. Sometimes a charge to the employer's account is made when the employee has already been disqualified.
4. The appeal may be pending, in which case the account should not be charged, according to the law in most states.
5. In some situations, the employee may be suspended for a period of time, such as after being arrested and awaiting trial. Benefits should not be paid for this period until a determination has been made.
6. Some states have a disqualification waiting period. An audit may show that benefits were charged for this period.

The appeal procedure for incorrect charges is very simple. Usually, all the employer must do is to point out the mistake, and the agency immediately makes the correction. A hearing is rarely held over incorrect charges. The law and regulations are clear on the conditions under which charges should be made. If an undercharge is found in an audit, the employer has a moral duty to call it to the attention of the agency. In some states there is a statutory duty to report undercharges.[124]

So many mistakes occur in the charges that outside consultants can make a good income by auditing reports for various organizations. They usually charge a percentage of the amount saved. Organizations that have a high experience rating that puts them at or near the maximum tax sometimes do not bother to audit the report. Wrong charges will not materially affect the tax rate, but this practice is shortsighted. If the tax rate does come down for the next rating period and the practice of auditing the charges has not been established, a great deal of money may be lost. Auditing the quarterly reports should be done as routinely and automatically as auditing the accounts receivable or checking material received at the shipping dock.

Claim Control Programs

It becomes extremely advantageous to keep benefits charged to the account at the lowest possible amount. This will not happen without some affirmative action through claim control programs and personnel policies. Some suggested policies and programs are as follows:

1. Plan manpower needs to avoid layoffs. Often, overtime is cheaper than hiring additional employees, when one considers the cost of hiring and training a new employee plus fringe benefit costs as well as unemployment compensation costs.
2. Where possible, cross-train or hire employees who have several skills.

This allows lateral or upward transfers that not only save unemployment costs but also provide flexibility in work assignments.

3. Have one person that is knowledgeable of unemployment compensation rules and appeal procedures responsible for the entire program.

4. Have the person responsible for the program audit all charges to the account, such as quarterly reports. Often, wrong charges to the account are found. They can be corrected by a mere protest by the employer representative who is familiar with the employees.

5. When in doubt about a determination as to whether the claimant is entitled to benefits—*appeal it*. Over half of all initial benefit determinations appealed by the employer are reversed on appeal. It is particularly important to appeal determinations where a wrongful discharge claim is possible. Failure to appeal may imply that the wrongful discharge claim has merit.

6. Hold exit interviews for all terminations where possible. Attempt to reach a mutual agreement on the reason for termination. In unemployment compensation matters, employees may have a short memory.

It is in both parties' best interests to provide information concerning separations, to protest adverse claims, to document files, to attend appeal hearings with appropriate witnesses, and to have a basic understanding of the appeal process.[125]

Becoming familiar with the unemployment compensation procedure requires little training, but the potential financial rewards are great. This is one area where the human resources department or other staff departments can show big savings with a little effort.[126] After one has experience with a few cases, and is exposed to various situations, the process becomes easier. In rare cases, the practitioner should seek help. More attention to this area is long overdue in most organizations.

WORKERS' COMPENSATION

Workers' compensation (WC) is an old concept. The purpose and intent can be traced as far back as the time of Henry I of England. Workers, compensation laws provided that if a person is on a mission for another and death occurs in the course of the mission, the sender or creator of the mission is responsible for the death. Likewise, an early German law held masters liable for the death of their servants. A money payment had to be made for an injury or death.

The present WC system had its origin in German law. In 1838, the German state of Prussia passed a law making the railroads liable for injuries to their employees and passengers, unless caused by acts of God or negligence on the part of the injured employee. The first modern workers' compensation law was adopted in Germany in 1884. This law required compulsory insurance for industrial accidents. The reason for pressure to pass such a law was a socialist movement supporting it. The Iron Chancellor, Otto von Bismarck, wanted to head off the socialist movement and pushed the law through the Reichstag. The German approach to WC was a compulsory system. The common law defenses of assumption of risk, contributory negligence, and fellow-servant doctrine were too harsh for the social thinking of the late nineteenth century. The impetus was to treat workers' compensation as a part of a broad social insurance system.[127]

The movement to require employer responsibility for their injured workers was part of the Progressive Era reforms discussed earlier. It was based on the belief that misfortunes, disability, and accidents of individuals are a social matter—that the state has a duty to take care of the injured, regardless of any other facts. In 1902, Maryland passed an act providing for a cooperative accident insurance fund. This was the first legislation embodying any degree of the compensation principle. This and later laws in Massachusetts and Montana were declared unconstitutional as a denial of due process. The first real workers' compensation law was passed in New York in 1910, but like the others it was declared unconstitutional.[128] This decision was met with an explosion of opposition; President Theodore Roosevelt was so angry that he openly advocated changing the judicial system. Following this decision, states began to develop more liberal policies toward the injured worker. In 1911, Wisconsin passed the first WC law that stood a constitutional test.[129] By 1925, 24 states had passed laws. The last state to do so (Mississippi) passed its law in 1948.

Space prevents this chapter from describing the current law of each jurisdiction. The law differs in each state with respect to benefits levels, administration, eligibility, and premium costs. This chapter provides only an overview workers' compensation law. Knowledge of the law in the state where the employee works is essential for effective cost control.

Basic Concepts

All workers are covered with the exception of railroad and maritime workers, other than seamen, who have never been covered by state laws.[130] All the state laws have six basic concepts:

1. To provide benefits regardless of fault or financial condition of the employer[131]
2. To reduce delays caused by litigation and controversy over responsibility for the injury, thereby reducing attorney's fees[132]
3. To relieve public charities of the financial drain caused by occupational injuries or diseases. The legislative bodies reason that the employer is in a better position

to pay for the social ills caused by occupational injury by passing the cost to the consumer than the government is through taxation (an astute political decision)
4. To encourage employer interest in reducing accidents by making the employer liable for all costs[133]
5. To generate maximum employer interest in safety and rehabilitation through an appropriate experience-rating mechanism
6. To promote frank study of causes of accidents (rather than concealment of fault)—reducing preventable accidents and human suffering

There is a wide difference of opinion on whether these objectives have been achieved. However, the National Commission on State Workers, Compensation Laws concedes that reform is needed, but that the workers' compensation system is fundamentally sound. Both the National Commission on State Workers, Compensation Laws and a task force in the Department of Labor have rejected proposals to replace the various state systems with one federal program.

State Administration

The administrator of a workers' compensation system considers that the most important element in administration is to make the employer financially responsible for benefits. The second-most important element is to supply the employer with all the necessary data to control the cost. However, the biggest problem the state administrator of WC has is the lack of data for effective cost control. Employers must rely on a relationship with the employee and outside sources that have a substantial influence on the employer's costs. Once the employer learns how to establish the proper relationship with other related sources, policies or practices can be instituted that will reduce the costs. These policies and practices will be recommended in the last section of this chapter after many of the problems related to the system have been discussed.[134]

Serious Injury

The employer should endeavor to assure that the best possible medical care is being provided to an injured employee.[135] If financial assistance is necessary, it should be obtained. The employee should be assured that if he or she is not able to return to the old job, the employer will try to accommodate by finding other jobs or provide rehabilitation training for other vocations. This is the law.[136]

For the seriously injured employee, suggested employer practices include:

1. Visit the hospital immediately and assess how or through whom the employee can best be relieved of any worry.
2. Contact the family; if the injured wants to be left alone, offer help indirectly through someone else if such help is needed.
3. Keep in touch with the employee, to show interest in the recovery progress and to assure the employee of returning to the job. Accommodation, rehabilitation, possible job vacancies, and so on, should be discussed.
4. Avoid any implication that it will be necessary to obtain legal counsel at the early stage of recovery. Explain the workers' compensation law and company employee benefits. If a lawyer becomes involved, establish a relationship with the employee's lawyer. Inform the attorney that the company is aware of the law and will keep the matter as nonlegal as possible.[137]

A Doctor's Relationship

To reduce costs successfully, the employer must have the cooperation of the doctor or doctors involved. This is sometimes difficult due to the conflict of interest with the patient–doctor relationship. The doctor often aids the employee in continuing to be paid for not working when physically able to do so. Instances of no-work slips without seeing the doctor, diagnosis of a condition over the telephone, or light-work slips that do not define light work are not uncommon. These problems can be eliminated by an employer–doctor relationship. To establish an effective employer–doctor relationship, the following suggestions should be considered:

1. The employer should inform the doctor of the physical requirements of certain job categories. This can be done with a doctor's visit to the plant site. If this is not possible, send an accurate job description listing the physical requirements of the job. Often, bad medical opinions are caused by the doctor not being informed.
2. If a medical opinion is suspect, the employer should challenge it by sending the employee to another doctor. If the employee refuses, inform the employee that you are stopping the benefits unless she or he returns to work.
3. The employer should establish sound back-to-work procedures that are based on the physical condition of the employee.

A double standard for occupational and for nonoccupational injuries confuses the doctor. The return-to-work policy must not exclude any "make-work"—that is, a job that is created simply to give a worker something to do. The result is that there is no work time lost to an accident and the company's safety record appears to be unblemished. The job the employee returns to must exist, and if the injured worker doesn't perform the work, some other worker must. The employer should inform the doctor about the employee's activities off the job after the injury. If the employer cannot get an accurate medical opinion, the employer should consider finding the right doctor. Without an accurate medical opinion about the employee's physical condition, back-to-work programs are useless.

Insurance Carrier Relationship

The proper relationship with the insurance carrier is extremely important, especially for small companies who do not have large legal staffs, human resources practitioners, and a security department to investigate doubtful claims.[138] If the insurance carrier does the proper job, it can make a real contribution in controlling costs. Many times the insurance carrier, when trying to obtain a new account, will stress the effectiveness of its cost control department. An employer, in considering the selection of an insurance carrier, should attempt to evaluate how effective the carrier's claim control department is.

To develop an effective relationship with the insurance carrier for claim control it is suggested that when injuries are first reported to a state commission and insurance company, the employer should "flag" all doubtful claims and demand that they be thoroughly investigated. In almost yearly surveys by the National Institute for Occupational Safety and Health, it is reported that nationally less than 10 percent of workers' compensation claims are contested. When investigating a doubtful claim, the employer's representative should take an active part in the investigation. All pertinent facts must be given to the insurance carrier. The carrier must then make a thorough investigation. Contested claims should not be settled by the insurance carrier unless the employer approves. Settlements often have employee relations consequences. Sometimes it may be advisable to litigate, even though from at economic perspective the case should be settled. Many lawsuits are tried on other than an economic basis. It should be noted that many insurance carriers

have no real interest in premium cost control. Experience-rated premiums usually have a percentage of add-on costs for administration. As premium costs increase, so do profits through administration charges.

Defining an Injury

For an injured worker to receive compensation benefits, there must be a showing that he or she was an employee of a covered employer—that an accidental injury occurred in the course of employment. In addition, the employee must give timely notice to the employer or provide some legitimate excuse for not doing so. The wage basis on which his or her compensation is paid must be agreed on, the duration of the disability must be determined, and if it is a permanent disability the degree of disability must be medically established.

Mental Condition

Early interpretations of an injury were limited to a traumatic physical injury. The courts, in keeping with the social welfare intent of the law, have expanded this definition to include various nontraumatic events. Some courts take the position that in order for a disabling mental condition or a nervous disorder to be compensable there has to be a traumatic incident. Other courts require only a mental stimulus, such as shock, to make a condition compensable.[139]

Accidental Injury

All but six states require that an injury be accidental before it can be compensable. The basic element of an accident is that some part of the incident must be unexpected. Most states require that the injury be traceable to a reasonably definite time, place, and occasion or cause. This comes up often in heart, back, or other conditions that could happen off the job. Most courts require that the exertion has to be in some way unusual for the injured worker, although it may not be for other workers.

The accident requirement is also important for infectious diseases that result from unusual or unexpected events or exposure. If the disease follows the accident, it is usually considered an accident and there is little litigation over this. Some states make a disease compensable by statute without the requirement of an accident. Without a statute, the courts in other states have held that an unexpected contraction of an infectious disease is an injury by accident. Some courts reason that the invasion of the body by microbes is in itself the injury.[140]

Injury Must Arise Out of Employment

The question of whether an injury must arise out of employment is the leading cause of litigation. Generally speaking, the injury must be work related and in the course of employment.[141] One consideration is whether the job involves a risk. If the risk is personal, then it is not compensable. For example, it was considered a risk associated with the job when an employee was mugged while dropping off the mail on the way home from work.[142]

Some courts will hold that if the risk is increased by the job assignment, it is compensable. If the employee was injured by an "act of God" (e.g., lightning or an earthquake), the large majority of the courts would hold that such an injury arose out of employment. Working conditions increased the probability of injury.

Sometimes the injury is related to the personal condition of the worker. The general rule is that this is compensable if the employment in any way contributed to the final disability. If the injury was caused by *placing the person* in a position where the condition was aggravated or was weakened by strain or trauma, it is compensable. Thus, if a person had a heart attack or an epileptic seizure and fell to the floor, this would probably be held to be

personal. However, if, while in a high place, a worker fell due to an epileptic seizure, the employment would have contributed to the final injury.

The majority of the courts also hold that where the original injury was in the course of employment, every natural consequence that results from the injury is also compensable. However, there may be an intervening cause attributable to the employee's own intentional conduct. For example, if a driver runs over a child while driving in the course of employment and subsequently gets a divorce and has a nervous breakdown, it would be a question of fact. Did the incident of employment cause the condition? Was the divorce caused by the incident? Did either one cause the mental disorder? This is a situation where it would be difficult to avoid litigation unless employer wants to settle.

Definition of Course of Employment

The course of employment requirement is concerned primarily with the time and place of the injury, as well as the activity of the employee when the injury occurred. The hard-and-fast rule would be that only an injury received during working hours would be compensable. However, in line with the welfare concepts of WC, this has not been followed in all cases. Much has to do with the type of work being performed and whether there is a causal relationship between the work and the injury. Traveling between assignments has been found compensable.

When a salesperson was returning home from a call after normal hours, the court held that this was not compensable because there is nothing unusual about a salesperson returning home after normal hours. However, if this had been a person who normally quits at 4:30 p.m. and for some reason had to work overtime, the result might have been different.

Work Site Results in Differences

It also makes a difference if the person is an outside worker, an inside worker, or living on the premises. If the person is an inside worker, the course of employment starts the minute she or he steps on the premises. For an outside worker (such as a salesperson), the usual interpretation of course of employment is that when he or she leaves home, the work period starts and is covered until returning. If the employee is living on the premises, most state courts will call everything "course of employment" except eating, bathing, sleeping, and dressing.

Because a worker is injured on the premises doesn't always mean the injury is compensable. If the injury is caused by an activity that substantially departs from the usual employment duties, some courts will consider this outside the scope of employment.[143] Other courts will hold that this is still the scope of employment.[144] If an employee disobeys orders and is injured, it can be argued that this is outside the scope of employment and not compensable. Employers must also integrate workers' compensation coverage with the Americans with Disabilities Act (ADA). In the hiring procedures, they cannot ask about WC claims until a conditional job offer has been made.[145] They must know the essential functions of the job to prevent injuries and provide for reasonable accommodation to the disabled. There is a serious exposure to a discrimination charge if the entire situation is not properly handled. The advice of an attorney may be needed.

Another problem is retaliation when the employee files a WC claim. The ADA and state statutes have resulted in an increase the frequency of retaliation charges. An employer will claim it is a disability, an employee will say it was because a WC claim was filed.

Drug-related accidents are often compensable when the injury occurs during the course of employment. If the employer enforces a strong policy of no use, possession, or sale of drugs, it appears that a good argument could be made for a discharge if the policy is violated. However, it is doubtful whether the employer would be relieved of paying WC benefits. Off-duty use of drugs should not be permitted if the employee comes to work under the influence (thus a testing policy is needed). The employer could make a strong case that there is too much danger of injury to self or co-workers and that such injury would be compensable.

An Injured Employee

An employee who is discharged and has a work-related injury often alleges that the discharge is wrongful. The employee seeks damages beyond the state workers' compensation statute through a wrongful discharge claim. In such a case, the lawsuit typically alleges that the discharge is in retaliation for filing a workers' compensation claim. Such a discharge would be contrary to public policy because the employee was exercising a statutory right in claiming compensation for an injury. When back injuries leading to frequent absences result in termination, the employer may defend its decision to discharge by alleging excessive absenteeism on the part of the employee. Since it is contrary to public policy in most states to discharge for exercising a right under a statute, a court must often determine whether the discharge was for excessive absenteeism or for filing a claim under the statute. The employer should make sure that the discharge was for a valid reason, and not for filing a workers' compensation claim.

A nurse technician injured her back while helping a patient into bed. She was ordered by her doctor not to work for three months. She returned to work after a month and her condition recurred seven months later. She was off for another long period. The next year she was absent 128 days, 29 days the following year, and 34 days the first five months of the third year. She was then discharged. The reason for discharge was excessive absenteeism. After her discharge, she filed a workers' compensation claim and sued. The statute prohibits discharge for filing a complaint under WC. The court held that her discharge was for excessive absenteeism that was caused in part by the work-related injury. The court noted that the statute protects the employee if the reason for discharge was for exercising a right under the statute. The real reason in this case was excessive absenteeism.[146]

Another plaintiff sustained a series of work-related back injuries. After the second injury, he was asked to return to light duty for a short period and to delay filing a workers' compensation claim, since in 10 days the company would receive a six-month award for no lost time because of an accident.[147] After a week of light duty, he returned to his old job of forklift operator. About a month later the plaintiff became ill at work and slipped and fell while descending stairs (a common case when the injury is not work related and the employee claims it is). Six months later the employee had back surgery, after which the doctor advised him to return to work. He was restricted to lifting less than 75 pounds. The personnel manager disputed the validity of the last injury as being work related. Rather than letting him return to work, he sent him to the company doctor. The company doctor sent the employee back to work, but restricted him to lifting to 50 to 60 pounds. After working for a short time, the employee was discharged because "he was physically unable to perform his job without causing a safety hazard to himself and fellow employees." The employee alleged the discharge was in retaliation for filing a WC claim. The jury awarded $50,000 in actual damages and $75,000 in punitive damages. The court held that the jury could reasonably find malice and intentional infliction of emotional distress. The verdict was especially damaging to the employer. The plant manager became angry when the employee reported the condition for the second time. He questioned the validity of the injury as being work related. *The court was displeased with the employer's action in disputing the claim* for disability payments.

The difference in the outcome of these cases is that in the one case the company didn't question the validity of the claim. The employee may have been using the back as a pretext to be off work, but the employer just waited until there was enough absenteeism to discharge. In the other case, the company first wanted to protect its safety record and asked the employee to cooperate. The company was creating a job and not making a back-to-work decision based on medical opinion. Some employers use a technique that says to the employee, "You and I know that you are not going back to work for some reason other than your back." This may be acceptable for a doctor, but not for an employer.

It often becomes a question of how far the employer has to go in accommodating the handicapped employee to avoid violation under ADA or a state law. Whether or not the injury is job related doesn't affect the duty to accommodate; however, as a practical matter the court may be more sympathetic to a job-related injury. In *Carr v. General Motors Corp.*, 389 N.W.2d 686 (Mich. 1986), the employee was operated on for a ruptured disk. After the operation, he was medically restricted from lifting 50 or more pounds. He requested a promotion to a job that required lifting more than 50 pounds. He was refused the promotion because of the lifting restrictions. He contended that the job required lifting only a small percentage of the time. Other workers in the department could lift for him. He argued that the employer could accommodate without undue hardship. The court held that in the majority of the states, the employee must perform all the essential functions of the job. *The duty to accommodate is relevant only when the employee can perform the job.* A claim for discrimination under ADA is not valid unless the person is qualified to perform all functions of the job.

Identifying Pretext

When an employer receives notice of a back condition, it must be treated like any other physical condition. It must be assumed that the employee is willing to return to work as soon as it is medically possible. A bona fide effort on the part of the employer and the employee will be beneficial to both. If the effort is unsuccessful in returning the employee to work, the employer's posture may change. The employer should investigate whether the employee is developing a nonmedical reason not to return to the job. The employer must always be aware that there are a few employees who are not motivated to return to work. They use their physical condition as a pretext to collect benefits for not working. This type of employee should be handled differently from an employee with a bona fide injury.

The employer must be certain that the employee is falsely using the disability as a reason not to return to work. To treat a situation as a pretext when in fact it is a bona fide condition can be disastrous, especially if the condition is caused by a work-related accident.[148] The employer should *treat all physical conditions as legitimate*. If substantial facts indicate that the physical condition alleged by the employee is not work related, the employer should treat the employee accordingly.

There is a certain pattern of events that may indicate pretext on the part of the employee:

1. The injury alleged is in the back or is a condition that is equally difficult to determine medically.
2. The exact date of the injury is not certain, but usually it occurs on Monday morning.
3. There were no employees present when the injury occurred. The incident is usually a fall or slipping in a remote place—the steps to the locker room, the parking lot, and so on. If a back injury, it could be from lifting as a regular part of the job. It is seldom the usual work-related incident that can be identified.
4. It was reported to the supervisor several days or even weeks after it happened. The employee usually states that at first the injury didn't seem to be severe enough to report.
5. The supervisor to whom it was reported is one known not to record incidents.
6. The employee never commits a major rule violation but does just enough to harass the supervisor (not wearing safety glasses, filing many grievances, taking long coffee breaks, going to the restroom often, and so on).
7. The employee's statements are not logically true but could be true, so that an investigation is required before action can be taken.

When the incident has these elements, there is at least a suspicion that it is not work related. When there is suspicion, several steps can be taken to validate your suspicion:

1. Investigate the employee's record. Determine whether there is a previous pattern either with other employers or in different jobs with the same employer.
2. When in doubt, get more than one medical opinion.
3. Make every effort to accommodate even where you believe that the condition is a pretext. Avoid adversity and give the employee the benefit of the doubt. If a good faith job offer is refused, the employer should immediately take steps to stop the benefits. Sometimes the insurance carrier will resist this but it is the only way the employer can determine whether the condition is a pretext for not returning to work.
4. Give medical leave or terminate where the employee has a recurring condi-

tion (on or off the job) after a bona fide attempt to return the employee to work. Under ADA and most state statutes, the employer would have to make an attempt to accommodate before termination. The courts have consistently held that under WC there is no obligation to treat the employee any differently from other employees. If the employee is excessively absent due to a work-related injury, he or she can be terminated like any other employee.

Some states have statutes that prohibit discharge while the employee is on WC. In this case, medical leave would be an answer. The courts hold that the employer is not expected to show different treatment because of a work-related injury. If the employee is not physically able to work, the remedy is benefits under WC and not special treatment at the work place.

5. Investigate all doubtful claims of disability. Often, the employee is at home doing physical work that medically he couldn't do when on the job. If another medical examination allows the employee to return to work, he or she should be terminated if he or she fails to do so. The termination record should state it is a voluntary quit for failure to report to work. In these doubtful situations, termination should be the last resort.

Physical therapy should be attempted. If accommodation is not possible or physical therapy fails, then a medical leave without pay is the best solution. A policy or labor agreement may permit termination because of the length of the absence or failure to return to work when medically authorized.

Return-to-Work Procedures

An important element in any back-to-work procedure is development of the proper atmosphere. The employer must be interested in the welfare of the injured employee and his or her family. The employer must immediately show some concern about the employee's condition.[149] One of several ways to do this is to explain the benefits the injured is entitled to under WC and how to start receiving those benefits. There is nothing that will impede a back-to-work program more than creating an adverse situation. One of the most important aspects of recovery from any physical condition is the attitude of the worker. Nothing can happen until she or he wants to return to work.

Make sure the doctor understands the physical requirements of the job the employee was performing before the injury or the job you want him or her to return to. No back-to-work procedure should be considered without a valid medical opinion. Often, more than one opinion is needed to be assured it is medically sound and not influenced by the employee.[150] To bring an employee back to work to protect a safety record is a short-term way of creating more costs. This creates an exposure to legal proceedings when up to that point the whole matter was nonlegal. On the other hand, some state laws tend to prefer some employment accommodation or transitional effort.

The next step is a good faith job offer, but the employer should be certain it is a job the employee can do. The job offer should be made even though the compensation is not the same or there is a belief that the employee will not accept. In most states, there is mitigation of damages if a suitable job offer is made. It doesn't have to be accepted. For purposes of mitigation of damages, most states define a suitable job as one that the employee can perform according to the employer's standards. It must also be within the employee's medical restrictions. It must restore the employee as close as possible to the economic status he or she had before the injury. Successful back-to-work procedures restore morale in an injured employee. They reduce WC or health-care costs and exposure to invalid claims.

Organize to Control Costs

Often, the employer gets so discouraged with the legal interpretation of the law that he or she gives up trying to do something about it.[151] It is only when the employer decides to do something about it that costs can be controlled. The first step is to make someone responsible for being knowledgeable about workers' compensation and to carry out a program of action, including individual case management. Second, do what is possible to prevent injuries and illness.

Limit Workers

Limiting workers who are eligible is a technique applied in some states. Colorado, Montana, and North Carolina are among a few states where aliens can enjoy benefits if they are legally eligible to work. Others permit non-residents the benefits; others prohibit benefits and most are silent on the issue. In *Financial Executive*, Stephanie Sorenson noted increasing compensation, medical cost patterns and mentioned drug and hospital costs, chiropractic fees and government imposed treatment guidelines as contributing factors. She suggests, reviewing all bills, managing absenteeism, employer involvement in cost control and choice of providers.[152]

The Delayed Recovery Syndrome

Delayed recovery is the situation where the employer becomes the most discouraged. The employee has a work-related injury and has been off work for three months. His doctor says he can come back to work. The employee says he has a terrible pain and insists that he cannot work. It is difficult to get someone back to work unless there is a desire to do so. The employee is getting some kind of gain from the injury that outweighs the benefits of getting well and going back to work. Researchers call this a delayed recovery syndrome, not malingering.[153] They note that many serious accidents are caused by internal conflicts of a personal nature, such as divorce or separation, drug or alcohol abuse, sex problems, or pending litigation. These factors may delay recovery. The most important thing to remember, according to research, is that delayed recovery is an emotional problem. Although it is unconscious, it is real. For example, the golfer honestly believes that he cannot return to work but *can* play golf.[154]

Stopping Malingering

There are employees who deceitfully manage to convince their doctors, employers, and insurance carrier that they are unable to function on the job. These people—often called *malingerers*—appear to prefer to stay at home and collect a modest income rather than return to work. Some even attempt to collect unemployment benefits at the same time as workers' compensation.[155] Unlike the delayed recovery syndrome, true malingering is conscious avoidance of responsibility. Malingering is difficult to prove. A number of alternatives should be considered before resorting to termination:

1. Offer a suitable job that the person can medically perform. This is required by ADA and most state statutes. Work closely with the doctor, since the employee will often resist. Even work with a rehabilitation consultant if a good one is available.
2. Get the person active to help regain strength and psychological well-being. Most back injuries medically require only a few days of bed rest. If the employee resists, get a medical directive.
3. Offer relaxation training; stress and other psychological factors can aggravate back and neck conditions. Deep breathing and other techniques can relieve this. Get the doctor involved

to encourage the employee to do something to help in recovery.

Steps to Reduce Costs

As an employer, let the employee know that you need her or him back on the job. Call or visit the employee during recovery. Strongly encourage treatment programs. If nothing works, then terminate her or him for being absent from work or not following medical directives. Some type of litigation will likely follow, so be prepared for it. Other steps to consider include:

1. Monitor early, especially in the case of a serious injury. Give the employee information before he or she seeks outside help. It is too late if the employee has to see a lawyer for necessary information. Keep in touch after the first contact.
2. Get a medical assessment as soon as possible. One way to do this without being defensive is to make a sympathetic inquiry about the employee's financial condition.
3. Make a job offer as soon as medically possible. This should not be a make-up job but one that is contributing and useful. Consider light-duty work, but only where there is not an exposure to doing other work that the employee is not physically capable of. In sports medicine, when an athlete is injured he or she must keep up with normal practice that is within the person's capacity, even though he or she is unable to play.
4. Get a rehabilitation assessment where necessary. It is possible that the injured may not be able to return to the old job but can do something else. It should be done within 30 days after the injury to be successful. This is an effective technique for the delayed recovery syndrome and complies with ADA.
5. Monitor the medical aspects; this is extremely important. Medical opinion and directives are given great weight in hearings and by the courts.

If the foregoing steps do not work and you cannot think of anything else, then terminate. Studies in all states have disclosed that litigation is second only to permanent and temporary disability costs in workers' compensation cases. Many researchers believe that the biggest contributing factor to WC costs is employer complacency.

The total cost of workers' compensation coverage (medical and disability benefits) was $57.6 billion in 2008. Some $29 billion was expended for medical expenses and $28.6 billion for cash (income replacement) benefits. Employers incurred costs of $89 billion. This information was reported by the National Academy of Social Insurance (NASI, 2010). As one employer put it, "This is worth going after."

CASE 5.1

The 10-Minute Meal Period

The employees made a deal with their manager that if they took a 10-minute lunch period they would be able to quit 20 minutes early and still work eight hours per day. (They also had two rest periods.) After a 3-year period, one employee evidently got indigestion or a nervous stomach and complained to the Wage and Hour Division.

The division took the position that under its regulations, CFR Sect. 785.18, this must be a paid period because it was less than 20 minutes. Investigation revealed that employees left their machines and went to the lunchroom for 10 minutes (one even stated that he went home for lunch). When the bell rang, they all returned to their machines. The Wage and Hour Division demanded two years' back pay (the maximum amount allowable under state statute) because employees worked 40 hours and 50 minutes per week under their interpretation. This amounted to over $12,000 for about 60 employees. The employer took the position that employees were serving

their own interest for the 10-minute meal period, thus the break was not work time and therefore not compensable, refusing to pay. Wage and Hour threatened litigation.

Is the meal period compensable?
How might this problem have been avoided? ■

CASE 5.2

Employee or Contractor?

Lisa, the owner of a small company, decided that marketing the products of her machining company would benefit if the company had a product quality certification. She undertook the process to win a certification, which required the critical analysis and documentation of each task used in the processes. Her Uncle Jake had been an industrial engineer prior to his retirement 10 years ago and was capable of undertaking that aspect of the certifying procedure. She would have able and reliable help and Jake would enjoy a measure of independence if he worked as an independent contractor. Lisa agreed to pay Jake a daily rate for each work day. They signed an agreement stipulating the independent contractor status, pay rate and a monthly pay date. Jake agreed that he would pay any taxes. Family members were a little concerned about Jake's physical ability to undertake this project that was expected to require at least a full year, and possibly two, to complete the work. As a result Lisa had Jake enrolled in the company health plan. Lest he get injured

on the job, she also added him to the workers' compensation insurance plan as a supervisor.

Jake and Lisa examined the methodology required by the certification system, agreed to what it required, and Jake set to work. Lisa assigned a data input clerical person to convert Jake's notes because Jake wasn't accomplished with a keyboard. The analytical work and documentation proceeded well. Jake did exercise some flexible scheduling to accommodate an occasional "sleep in." Other employees referred to him as "Uncle Jake." The only interruption in progress was a two-week period when Lisa had Jake oversee a night shift crew while the supervisor was on vacation.

Are there any reasons why the IRS would question Jake's independent contractor status? What supports that status? Do any conditions compromise that status?
What are "swing" factors that could establish Jake's status one way or another? ■

CASE 5.3

Exempt or Nonexempt

Fred Ball was an accountant in the finance department of the Little Italy Pasta Company and had been employed in that capacity for three years. Fred held a B.S.B. from Midwest State University and was enrolled in a Master of Accountancy program in a "weekend college" program at City University. Fred was paid $25 an hour for a 40-hour week. All company accountants were paid on an hourly basis, although the chief accountant was paid a monthly salary. Fred was also paid a premium of $50 a week for any new account that

he was assigned. This premium was only paid for the first three months that he handled the new account because of the additional work required to set up and regularize these accounts.

Fred had no set hours and worked his own schedule. He was allowed to work flexible hours, Monday through Saturday and was not required to submit a time card. No one was allowed to work on Sundays without the express permission of the plant owner and manager. Fred was classified as an exempt employee for overtime purposes.

Is Fred properly classified as an exempt employee?

What potential exposure does the company have under the Fair Labor Standards Act?

How might this exposure be reduced? ■

CASE 5.4

Forced Vacation

Jack Franklin is an exempt employee working as a systems analyst for the McGuffey Company, a human resources services firm. Jack continually works more than 80 hours in a two-week period. However, due to some graduate classes he is taking, Jack works only 4 hours during the day every other Friday. Because Jack has worked less than 8 hours in a given day, the employer forces him to take 4 hours of vacation for each of the days that he worked less than 8 hours during a single day.

The issue from the employee's perspective is that he should not have to use vacation when taking a couple of hours off during the day. This is particularly true when the time off is to further his education. The employee is clearly an exempt employee in a professional role and puts in more than enough time working. Jack believes he should be paid for a full day's work for working less than 8 hours in a day.

The employer's argument is that there is a department policy stating that every employee must work a minimum of 8 hours during the day. This is an informal policy that is normally adhered to only when needed to please the controller of the company. Additionally, the company handbook states an employee will not be docked pay as long as he or she works a minimum of 4 hours in a day.

Can the company force Jack to use his vacation for the time that he attends classes on Fridays?

Can they reduce his pay if he runs out of vacation time? ■

CASE 5.5

Work-Related Injury?

The company safety director reads in the local paper that a softball team that Terry, one of the company's employees, plays for won the city championship on Saturday afternoon. The story also notes that there were three injuries during the game, but the names of those injured were not reported. Terry reports a back injury at work on Monday morning. The investigator tells the safety director that the injury probably happened while playing ball. However, the insurer is unlikely to dispute the claim.

What course of action should the employer follow?

Should the employer contest if the insurer denies the claim? ■

CASE 5.6

Mary Hogan's Back Injury

Paul Smith, department superintendent of Acme Bag Company, noticed that the conveyor belt was jammed with paper bags. He told Mary Hogan, a polypropylene (PE) inserter on the machine, to get a pallet and remove the bags from the belt. Mary replied, "I am not able to because my back is bothering me." Paul replied, "Get one that you are able to handle."

Mary replied, "I will not do it." Paul said, "I think you can do it." Mary said, "No." Paul said, "You are terminated; clock out and leave the plant." Mary Hogan did just that.

Mary Hogan was initially employed by Acme as an unskilled worker; she worked in various unskilled positions throughout the plant during the 10 years of her employment. Eighteen months after her initial employment, Mary filed a charge with the Mill City Civil Rights Commission under the city ordinance alleging that the company discriminated because of her gender. She had been given a two-day suspension for refusing to mop the floor. She alleged that males and minorities were not required to do so. Mary did not file a grievance under the labor agreement over the suspension. A similar charge was filed with the EEOC under Title VII. The charge was investigated by the city. Before the investigation under the EEOC charge, Mary amended the charge, alleging that Acme had refused to allow her to return to light duty of lifting 10 pounds or less. She alleged that this was a violation of Title VII and state law. Acme had not received any medical report of Ms. Hogan's condition for 11 months. This amended complaint was based on the fact that Ms. Hogan was not given the opportunity to work for the 11-month period. The state civil rights specialist discovered that Ms. Hogan had not worked for 11 months and inquired about the absence. The specialist was told by Acme that Ms. Hogan was on a medical leave. Acme stated they would be glad to have her return to work if the company doctor approved it. Acme further stated, when questioned, that the reason Ms. Hogan had not returned to work was that she had not contacted Acme stating that she was physically able to perform the job in the plant that she had previously selected or that she could perform any other job.

Acme received a medical report from the company doctor stating that Ms. Hogan was able to lift only 5 to 20 pounds. Eleven months before her stated condition, Ms. Hogan had signed a statement that she would perform only the job as bottom feeder and table loader, jobs that required lifting 20 to 35 pounds and 60 to 75 pounds respectively. This is the reason Acme gave her medical leave.

Ms. Hogan had applied for unemployment insurance, which Acme originally contested on the grounds that the claimant was on medical leave. It was ruled that Hogan was available for work, and she received unemployment compensation. The notice to allow unemployment benefits was not received by the Acme plant. It was sent to the parent company's office, which failed to forward it and did not appeal. No medical leave was applied for by Ms. Hogan under the terms of the labor agreement. However, Ms. Hogan's status was considered a voluntary medical leave during the period she was off work. Premiums for her health insurance were paid by Acme rather than terminating her as permitted by the labor agreement. During the 11-month period Ms. Hogan was considered by Acme as not available for work but was never contacted to determine her status.

When Hogan was called to return to work after being contacted by the civil rights specialist, she stated that she was still under a doctor's care. After two weeks she inquired when she could see a company doctor. On advice of corporate counsel, the personnel coordinator arranged an appointment. The company doctor stated that she could return to light work, but lifting 40 to 50 pounds repetitively would cause back symptoms. Ms. Hogan was notified of her physical condition, which permitted her to return to work a week later. She agreed to return to her old job of bottom feeder (requiring lifting of 25 to 40 pounds).

The next day she alleged that she hurt her back. A meeting was called to determine what job Hogan could do. With the union present, she was asked what she wanted to do. She selected the table loader job and was returned to that job for the remainder of the day. (This required the lifting of 40 to 50 pounds, which was contrary to the doctor's advice.) On the following day, her husband called and stated that she hurt her back on the previous day and wanted an appointment to see another doctor. Hogan assumed that this other doctor would be somebody other than the company doctor. She was told she could see any doctor whom she wanted. She requested the company doctor. An appointment was made with the company doctor the following day.

Nothing was heard from Hogan after her physical examination until her husband called five days later. He wanted to know what the doctor had found, stating that the doctor never told her the results of the recent examination. When told that nothing was wrong with her, she stated that she wanted to see another doctor. She went to see another doctor. Ten days after her most recent physical examination she was ordered to return to work in the next three days. Rather than return to work, she saw another doctor who authorized her to return to work. However, rather than return to work, she saw another doctor who authorized her to return the next day but no heavy lifting. She reported to work the next day. She told her supervisor that she could not load tables.

As a result of her statement, a meeting was held on the same day with the union and management. Hogan requested that she be taken off the table loader job and be assigned to PE inserting. It was explained to her that this job requires lifting 50 to 70 pounds. Hogan performed the job of PE inserting until she was discharged for refusing to get a pallet. Her complaint to the state civil rights commission was again amended, stating that her discharge was due to retaliation for filing the original complaint. As a result of the discharge, a grievance was filed under the labor agreement and the dispute was submitted to arbitration. The arbitrator upheld the discharge for insubordination.

The state civil rights commission, after an investigation, determined that there was no basis for the gender discrimination charges regarding the suspension for refusing to mop the floor. However, the commission had reasonable cause to believe that Hogan was discriminated against for not returning to work for 11 months and that the discharge was in retaliation for filing a complaint. The civil rights commission in its conciliation proposal demanded $9,000 in back pay and reinstatement. A conciliation meeting is the next step. If this failed, the matter would go before the state civil rights commission hearing examiner; an appeal from that decision would be to the district court.

Management has to make a decision to settle or fight. What would you recommend? What are the bases for your recommendation?

What mistakes were made by the company in handling this matter? ▪

Summary

Every aspect of employee compensation is affected by legislation in both the public and private sectors. This chapter addresses basic federal legislation concerning compensation. The Fair Labor Standards Act, adopted in 1938, defines employee activity that is compensable and eligible for overtime pay. An amendment to FLSA provides for equal pay for women. During the 1930s, the federal government in effect mandated workers' compensation and unemployment compensation, worker welfare initiatives that are administered by the states and that require cost control measures by employers. The chapter provides the legal foundation and describes some of the difficulties created for employers by these latter enactments.

Key Terms

independent contractor 120	compensable time 121	salary test 126
meal periods 120	sleep time 122	outside salesperson 127
Wage and Hour	travel time 124	exempt status 127
Division 120	compensatory time 124	pay equity 134
rest periods 121	change time 125	comparable worth 138

Questions for Discussion

1. What is considered compensable time under the Fair Labor Standards Act?
2. Describe the overtime requirements and stipulations under FLSA.
3. Is the FLSA applicable to working for an employer at home?
4. List five factors that distinguish an independent contractor and five factors indicating that an individual is an employee.
5. What is the "salary test"?
6. To what extent can workers work during breaks and lunch time without being paid?
7. Under what circumstances can compensatory time off be used?
8. Identify four reasons why an employer might appeal an unemployment compensation charge.
9. What is the meaning of the "course of employment" requirement in workers' compensation?
10. Under what circumstances might drug-related accidents be compensable?

Notes to Chapter 5

1. Stephen E. Condrey (Ed.), *Handbook of human resources management in government* (New York: John Wiley and Sons, 2005), p. 598.
2. 41 U.S.C. Sects. 35–45.
3. 40 U.S.C. Sect. 276.
4. 41 U.S.C. Sects. 351–358.
5. 29 U.S.C. Sect. 206 et seq.
6. See Stephen Light, "Interpreting the Fair Labor Standards Act," *Golden Gate Law Review*, 2, no. 1 (1991): 147.
7. The 1989 amendment deals mostly with minimum wage and certain tips on training.
8. See "Handy reference guide to the Fair Labor Standards Act," U.S. Dept. of Labor, WH Publication 1282, April 1990.
9. See *Labor Law Journal*, 46, no. 18 (August 1995): 469, 486.
10. The basic statutory *limitation* for liability is two years (three years for willful violations). As one manager told the author, "I have been doing it unintentionally for five years. I am already three years ahead if found wrong."
11. *Employee* has been interpreted to mean any individual who is "dependent upon the business to which they render service"; *Bartels* v. *Birmingham*, 332 U.S. 126 (1947); *Weisel* v. *Singapore Joint Venture, Inc.*, 602 F.2d 1185 (5th Cir. 1979).
12. The court in *Richland* virtually put to rest all appellate court conflicts over the definition of *willful* in all statutes relevant to FLSA, Equal Pay, Walsh-Healy, and so on.
13. *McLaughlin* v. *Richland Shoe Co.*, 108 S.Ct. 1677.
14. *Braun* v. *Wal-Mart, Inc.* Case No. 19 CO-01-9790 Mn. Dakota County, June 30, 2008.
15. *Mumbower* v. *Callicott*, 526 F.2d 1183 at 1186 (8th Cir. 1975).
16. *Biggs* v. *Wilson*, 1 F.3d 1537 (9th Cir. 1993), *cert. denied*.
17. R. Doyle, Management: A process for building the work productivity and profitability throughout your organization (New York: American Management Association, 1992).
18. Where employees were required to remain on the premises, the employer had to pay for sleep time: *Agilar* v. *Association for Retarded Citizens*, 285 Cal. Reptr. 515 (Cal. App. 4th Dist. 1991).
19. Sleep time is compensable if interrupted by patient care: *Hillgren* v. *County of Lancaster*, 913 F.2nd 498 (8th Cir. 1990).
20. An occasional emergency interruption would not cause an employer to pay for meal time.
21. *Taylor-Callahan-Coleman Counties District Adult Probation Department* v. *Dole*, 948 F.2d 953 (5th Cir. 1991). See also *Henson* v. *Pulaski County Sheriff Dept.*, 6 F.3d 531 (1993).
22. A special arrangement could be made to allow a 45-minute lunch period, deducting 30 minutes per day for the meal period and paying for 15 minutes at an overtime rate.
23. *Johnson* v. *Columbia, S.C.*, 949 F.2d 127 (4th Cir. 1991).
24. *Owens* v. *Local 169, Association of Western Pulp and Paper Workers*, 971 F.2d 347 (9th Cir. 1992).
25. *Martin* v. *Ohio Turnpike Commission*, 968 F.2d 606 (6th Cir. 1992), *cert. denied* 1993.
26. In *Bright* v. *Houston Northwest Medical Center Survivors, Inc.*, 934 F.2d 671 (5th Cir. 1991), the employee had to wear a "beeper," stay sober, and be at the worksite 20 minutes after being called. The court said the employee still could use the time for own benefit, so call time was not compensable. Also *Smith* v. *City of Jackson, Miss.*, 954 F.2d 296 (5th Cir. 1992).
27. *Mitchell* v. *King Packing Co.*, 350 U.W. 260 (1956).
28. *Dunlop* v. *City Electric*, 527 F.2d.
29. *Marshall* v. *Gervill, Inc.*, 1195 F. Supp. 744 (D.C. Md. 1980).
30. *Mitchell* v. *Greinetz*, 235 F.2d 621 (10th Cir. 1956); *Ballard* v. *Consolidated Steel Corp.*, 61 F.Supp. 996 (S.D. Cal 1945).
31. A client once asked a woman in a law office to get him a cup of coffee. When she returned she asked him what she could do for him. Realizing he had mistaken his attorney for a secretary, he apologized. She said she didn't mind taking her time at $200 an hour. The cup of coffee cost him $50.

32. 29 U.S.C. Sects. 251-62, an amendment to the Fair Labor Standards Act.

33. Usually hours worked begin when the employee is required to be on the premises and perform work that is an integral part of the employee's assignment.

34. A management employee once asked the author if he could leave early to get ahead of the traffic. The author told him to leave when the author did at 6:00 p.m.; there was no traffic then.

35. The leading case is *Walling* v. *Portland Terminal Co.,* 330 U.S. 148 (1947).

36. There must be a benefit to the employer to be counted as overtime: *Martin* v. *Parker Protection District,* 774 F.Suppl. (D. Colo. 1991).

37. On time spent on meeting, see William L. Richmond and Daniel L. Reynolds, "The Fair Labor Standards Act: A Potential Legal Constraint upon Quality Circles and Other Employee Participation Programs," *Labor Law Journal,* 37, no. 4 (April 1986): 244.

38. See *Donovan* v. *American Airlines,* 686 F.2d 267 (5th Cir. 1982).

39. Under 29 CFR part 516 and 778, 56 Fed. Reg. 61100 (1991), employees who lack a high school or an eighth-grade education level are exempted from 10 hours per week overtime for training. The training time must be paid for at the regular rate and taken during working hours. This is called *a remedial education exemption.*

40. *Dager et al.* v. *City of Phoenix,* Case No. 2:06 cv-P1412 PHX - JWS (2009).

41. *Powell* v. *Corey Int'l Inc.* No. 05-21395-CIV, 2007 WL 49442 (S.D. Fla Feb 1, 2007).

42. *DeAsencio* v. *Tyson Foods, Inc.* 06-3502 3d Cir. Sept 6, 2007.

43. *Dole* v. *Snell,* 875 F.2d 802 (6th Cir. 1989). Also see *Brock* v. *M. W. Fireworks, Inc.* 871 F.2d 307 (8th Cir. 1989).

44. The state of Utah.

45. For further research on exempt classifications, see James A. Prozzi, "Overtime payment in the managerial employee—Still a twilight zone of uncertainty," *Labor Law Journal* (March 1991): 18.

46. See James A. Prozzi, "Docking pay of managerial employees: The Wage and Hour Law's trap for the employer," *Labor Law Journal,* 42, no. 7 (July 1991): 444.

47. Split in circuit courts.

48. *McDonnel* v. *City of Omaha.* 999 F.2d 1293 (8th Cir. 1993), *cert. denied,* 1994.

49. See K. Paco, "What it doesn't take to be a salaried employee: The future of docking," 215 LEXIS 49 (1993).

50. *Rorch* v. *Newspapers of New England Daily,* Labor Rev. No. 210 (NH 1993).

51. Some states issue a bulletin on how to determine exempt status. See Minn. Rules Chapter 5224-0010 and 5224-0340 (1989).

52. For a questionable exempt employee, it is advisable to have the employee make his or her own job description. The WH is more likely to accept it.

53. *Donovan* v. *Burger King,* 672 F.2d 221 (1st Cir. 1982).

54. In *Brock* v. *Norman's Country Market, Inc.,* 825 F.2d 823 (11th Cir. 1988), the court said time is not the only factor in determining executive duties; whether they are discretionary supervisory functions must be considered.

55. One author once made a study of overtime for nonexempt group leaders and found that their overtime increased before they went on vacation and before Christmas.

56. 29 CFR Sects. 778.316 and 785.11 and 785.13. Also see *Lindow* v. *United States,* 738 F.2d 1057 (9th Cir. 1984).

57. The author once discharged an employee on Christmas Day. One author knew that an employee was working overtime to keep up in his work without recording it but could never catch him. The employee never suspected somebody would be around on Christmas Day to find him working.

58. This is enforceable, although an agreement to waive the provisions of the FLSA is not.

59. The IRS estimates that more than 3 million workers are misclassified as independent contractors and that $1.5 billion in taxes are lost each year.

60. The IRS has information on how to identify an independent contractor. Most other agencies issue similar guidelines.

61. M. Hulen et al., "Independent contractors, classification issues," *American Journal of Tax Policy,* 11 (1994): 13.

62. For discussion on totality of circumstances, see *Oestman* v. *National Farmers Union*

Insurance, 958 F.2d 363 (10th Cir. 1992); also IRS Rule 87–41.

63. For a complete analysis of factors used by the Supreme Court in determining an independent contractor, see E. Delaney and R. Hollrah, "Independent contractor vs. employee," *Employer's Handbook* (Washington, DC: Thompson Publishing Group, 1992).

64. *Marshall v. Truman Arnold Distribution Co.,* 640 F.2d 906 (8th Cir. 1981).

65. *Donovan v. Sureway Cleaners,* 656 F.2d 1368 (9th Cir.).

66. *Marshall v. Presidio Valley Farms, Inc.,* 512 F.Supp. 1195 (W.D. Tex. 1981).

67. *Donovan v. Techo, Inc.* 642 F.2d 141 (5th Cir. 1981).

68. *Reich v. Circle C. Investments, Inc.,* 498 F.2d 824 (5th Cir. 1993).

69. *Fianti v. William Raveis Real Estate, Inc.* (233 Conn. 690, 1995).

70. *Varisco v. Gateway Science and Engineering* 2008 166 Cal. App. 4th 1099.

71. *Katz v. School Dist. of Clayton, Missouri,* 557 F.2d 153 (8th Cir. 1977).

72. Interpretative regulations were issued by EEOC. They give the EEOC position on all of these factors (29 CFR Part 1620). Case law is in accord.

73. *Brinkley v. Harbour Recreation Club,* 180 F.3d 598 (4th Cir. 1999).

74. *Warren v. Solo Cup Co,* 516 f.3d 627 (7th Cir. 2008).

75. Civil Action No. 03-CF-4990, N.Y., 2003, (3-31-2009).

76. See U.S. Glass Ceiling Comm. (Robert B. Reich, Chair), *A solid investment: Making use of the nation's human capital.* Washington, DC. Approved November 21, 1995.

77. Ibid.

78. 21 F.2d 259 (3rd Cir. 1970), cert. denied, 398 U.S. 90 (1970).

79. Right after the enactment of EPA, the first loophole that employers conceived in EPA was to change the job content to include tasks that women did not normally perform.

80. Meryl Gordon, "Discrimination at the top," *Working Women* (September 1992): 8.

81. In *Glenn v. General Motors,* 841 F.2d 1567 (11th Cir. 1988), the court said that the difference in skills and duties must be substantial to justify a pay differential.

82. *Katz v. School Dist. of Clayton, Missouri,* 557 F.2d 153 (8th Cir. 1977).

83. *Aldrich v. Randolph Central School District,* 963 F.2d 520 (2nd Cir. 1991).

84. *Corning Glass Works v. Brennan,* 417 U.S. 188 (1974).

85. In *EEOC v. McCarthy,* 768 F.2d 1 (1st Cir. 1985) the court held ability to be more important.

86. *Fowler v. Land Management Group, Inc.,* 978 F.2d 158 (4th Cir. 1992).

87. *Marshall v. Security Band & Trust Co.,* 572 F.2d 276 (10th Cir. 1978).

88. *Hodgson v. Fairmont Supply Co.,* 454 F.2d 490 (4th Cir. 1972).

89. *Brennan v. T. M. Fields, Inc.,* 488 F.2d 443 (5th Cir. 1973).

90. J. Kanin-Lovers and R. Bevan, "Don't evaluate performance—Manage it," *Compensation Benefits,* 1 (March–April 1992): 51–53; D. Guns II, "Merit pay—An unbalanced approach to pay for performance," *Personnel Journal,* 71 (April 1992): 16.

91. This usually happens when the employer does not want to set a precedent of granting cost-of-living increases or longevity increases, thus calling it merit. The misuse of the term becomes evident in EEO cases where a merit increase is given one month and an employee is discharged the next month for poor performance. Misuse of the term is widespread.

92. R. Selwitz, "Blueprint for performance pay," *ABA Bank Journal,* 82 (May 1990): 18; J. A. Parmele, "Five reasons why pay must be based on performance," *Supervision,* 52 (Fall 1991): 6–8; J. Feldman, "Another day, another dollar, needs another look," *Personnel,* 68 (January 1991): 9–11.

93. J. Hersch, "The impact of nonmarket work on market wages," *American Economic Review,* 81 (May 1991): 157; P. F. Orazem, "Comparable worth and factor point pay in state government," *Industrial Relations,* 31 (Winter 1992): 135–215.

94. *League of Minnesota Cities.*

95. Richard Stillman II, *Public administration* (Boston: Houghton Mifflin, 2000), p. 479.

96. State Government Pay Equity Act of 1982 (M.S. 43A) and Local Government Pay Equity Act of 1982 (M.S. 47.991-471.999).

97. J. Quinn, "Visibility and value: The rule of job evaluation in assuring equal pay for Wwmen," *Journal of International Business*, 25 (1994): 1403.

98. State Government Pay Equity Act of 1982 (M.S. 43A) and Local Government Pay Equity Act of 1982 (M.S. 47.991–471.999).

99. Patton, David, *Human resource management: The public service perspective* (Boston: Houghton Mifflin, 2002), p. 39.

100. See "Highlights of state unemployment compensation laws" (Washington, DC: National Foundation for Unemployment compensation and Workers Compensation, January 1995).

101. *Thomas* v. *Review Board of Indiana Employment Security div.,* 101 S.Ct. 1425 (1981); see also *Frazee* v. *Illinois Dept. of employment and Security,* 109 S.Ct. 1514 (1989).

102. *Turner* v. *Department of Employment and Security of Utah,* 423 U.S. 44 (1975).

103. *Hobbie* v. *Unemployment Appeals Commission of Florida,* 107 S.Ct. 1046 (1987).

104. *Department of Human Resources of Oregon* v. *Alfred L. Smith,* 110 S.Ct. 1595 (1990). Usually drug use must be job related, but here the Supreme Court said that use didn't have to affect performance.

105. In *Idaho Dept. of Employment* v. *Smith,* 434 U.S. 100 (1977).

106. *New York Telephone Co.* v. *New York State Department of Labor,* 440 U.S. 519 (1979).

107. This is well-settled law: *EEOC* v. *Enterprise Assn. Steamfitters Local 638,* 542 F.2d 579 (2nd Cir. 1979).

108. Matheny, K., "Labor dispute disqualification for unemployment compensation benefits," 95 *W. Va. L. Rev.* 791 (1993).

109. Benefit levels continually increase, although in some states tax rate schedules have decreased.

110. Unemployment Compensation Act of 1992 (P. L. 102–318).

111. For further information on disqualification, see "Highlights of state unemployment compensation laws," National Foundation for Unemployment Compensation and worker's Compensation, January 1992, pp. 63–86.

112. Most state case law holds that discharge for incompetence is not misconduct, and benefits are paid: *Larson* v. *Employment Appeal Board,* 474 N.W.2d 570 (Iowa 1991).

113. Malin, Martin H. "Unemployment compensation in a time of increasing work-family conflicts." 29 U.Mich.J.L.Ref. (1996).

114. A common disqualification is not earning sufficient wages during the base period.

115. See *Bongiovanni* v. *Vanlor Investments,* 370 N.W.2d 828 (Minn. App. 1985), for a discussion of a quit.

116. *Brown* v. *Port of Sunnyside Club, Inc.,* 304 N.W.2d 877 (Minn. 1981).

117. *Richers* v. *Iowa Dept. of Job Service,* 479 N.W.2d 308 (Iowa 1991), the court said that inability or incapacity is not intentional; it cannot be misconduct.

118. Some states hold that the loss of a driver's license necessary for performance of job duties is misconduct. In other states it would be exposure to litigation: *Markel* v. *City of Circle Pines,* 479 N.W.2d 382 (Minn. S.Ct. 1992).

119. Some states hold that refusal to take a drug test is misconduct: *Fowler* v. *Unemployment Compensation Appeals* 537 So.2d 162 (Fla. 5th DCA 1989); see also *Schwamb* v. *Administrator, Division of Employment Security,* 577 So.2d 343 (La. 1991).

120. Gary Coffey, "Ruling backs work-related drug testing," *Nashville Business Journal* (October 15–19, 1990): 1–24.

121. A state did not violate the First Amendment when it denied benefits where an employee was discharged for religious drug use on his own time. The drug use was a violation of a state statute.

122. For a complete discussion on the use of counsel in unemployment proceedings, see *The Labor Lawyer,* 4, no. 1 (Winter 1988): 69.

123. In the opinion of one commissioner's representative, the worst witnesses are accountants, the next worst witnesses are personnel directors, and the third worst witnesses are CEOs.

124. An employee's wages were overpaid one week and two weeks later were underpaid. He complained to the paymaster for being

underpaid. The paymaster asked why he didn't complain when overpaid. The reply was that he could tolerate one mistake, but not two.

125. "Employers may reap savings from improved unemployment comp. benefits administration," *Employment Benefit News* (1992): 87.

126. For several years the author had an undisclosed personal goal to save his employer four times his annual salary. Savings in workers' compensation and unemployment compensation were two areas that greatly contributed to achieving this goal. Undisclosed goals of this nature afford job satisfaction when one attains them and do little harm if one fails.

127. For a more complete discussion of workers' compensation in Europe, see Ralph H. Blanchard, *Liability and compensaton insurance* (East Norwalk, CT: Appleton-Century-Crofts, 1917); *Ives v. South Buffalo Railway Co.*, 94 N.E.2d 431 (N.Y. App. 1911).

128. *Ives v. South Buffalo Railway Co.*, 94 N.E.2d 431 (N.Y. App. 1911).

129. By 1920, nearly half the workers were covered by some sort of workers' compensation and the court rejected the employer's arguments of due process: *White v. New York Central Railroad*, 343 U.S. 188 (1917).

130. Railroad workers are covered by the Federal Employer's Liability Act (FELA). FELA is not technically a compensation statute and requires injured workers to sue the employer

131. Also see "An employer's guide to employment law issues," *Small Business Office*, Vol. II, 1994, 65. 432 E. Seventh St.

132. Statutes in most of the states not only fail to reduce litigation but they also make litigation necessary to resolve the issues.

133. The cost must be excessive in relation to other costs before the employer's interest is aroused beyond moral consideration. Minnesota, Massachusetts, and several other states have changed their laws to increase the incentive to return to work. They have cut costs in most areas, but have made some change in the benefit levels. This area is subjected to considerable lobbying pressure in every legislative session.

134. For control of abuses under workers' compensation, see Bruce S. Vanner, "Cut beneath abuse of workers compensation," *Personnel Journal*, 67, no. 4 (April 1988): 30.

135. To reduce costs, the Massachusetts legislature in 1992 established a fraud bureau for WC cases, and set up procedures for managed care. In 1995, Minnesota's objectives were to reduce costs.

136. This concern should not imply a guilt complex on the part of the employer because this would have a chilling effect on anything that the employer does for the benefit of the employee. Avoiding a guilt complex is especially important when informing the next of kin of an occupational death, if emotional and legal consequences are to be avoided.

137. Sometimes a lawyer becomes involved in a probably third-party product liability lawsuit against the manufacturer of the machine that caused the injury. The employer should not aid in such a lawsuit until the workers' compensation case is closed. Often cooperation in the third-party suit can adversely affect the employer's workers' compensation case.

138. If the employer is self-insured, *insurance carrier,* as used herein, should be interpreted to mean the consulting organization or whoever is responsible for claim control.

139. See *Kinney v. State Industrial Commission*, 423 P.2d 186 (Ore. 1967) for a view of not requiring a physical trauma and see *Sibley v. City of Iberia*, 813 P.2d 69 (Ore. 1991) for requiring a physical trauma. See also Derek R. Girdwood, "Can I collect workers compensation benefits if my job drives me crazy?" (comment), *Detroit Civil Law Review* (1992): 591.

140. HIV has been found to be within the definition of *occupational disease* if it is acquired during the course of employment: *Hansen v. Gordon*, 602 A.2d 560 (Conn. S.Ct. 1992).

141. A company picnic can be in the course of employment, *Ludwinski v. National Carrier*, 873 S.W.2d 890 (Mo. App. E.D. 1994).

142. *Wayne Adams Buick, Inc. v. Ference*, 421 N.E.2d 733 (Ind. 1981).

143. For a discussion in which horseplay was considered to be the course of employment, see G. Caruso and M. Alberty, "Worker's

disability compensation," *Wayne Law Review,* 38 (1992): 1292.

144. See *Hoyle* v. *Isenhour Brick & Tile Co.,* 293 S.E.2d 196 (N.C. 1982), where the employee was killed while driving a forklift truck in violation of rules and the court held it was compensable because he was acting in behalf of the employer.

145. Some states deny WC benefits if the applicant lied on an application form about a disability.

146. Majority opinion upholds discharge because of absenteeism due to work-related injury: *Johnson* v. *St. Francis Hospital,* 75 S.W.2d 925 (Tenn. App. 1988).

147. *Malik* v. *Apex Intern. Alloys, Inc.,* 762 F.2d 77 (10th Cir. 1985).

148. See "Hiring the handicapped: Overcoming physical and psychological barriers in the job market," *Journal of American Insurance* (3rd Quarter 1986): 13–14.

149. Most states stress early employer response after an accident and good back-to-work procedures. See "Controlling workers' compensation costs," Minnesota Department of Labor and Industry, Research and Education Unit, July 1991; also J. Gardner, "Return to work incentives," Workers Compensation Research Institute, April 1989, p. 1.

150. R. A. Deyo, A. K. Diehl, and M. Rosenthal, "How many days of bed rest for acute low back pain?" *New England Journal of Medicine,* 315, no. 17 (October 1986): 1064–1070.

151. "Worker's compensation costs can be controlled by managed care," *Employment Alert* (Boston: Warren Gorham Lamon), 9, no. 22 (October 22, 1992): 5.

152. "Controlling workers' compensation medical costs," *Financial Executive,* 22, no. 9 (November 2007): 29–32.

153. E. Yehn, "The myth of malingering: Why individuals withdraw from work in the presence of illness," *Milbank Quarterly,* 64 (1986): 622.

154. A 10-year study reported in 1991 made on 3020 Boeing Company employees reveals that 60 to 65 percent of back problems are due to psychological factors.

155. Workers' Compensation for Illegal Aliens, "National underwriters/property and casualty risk and benefits management," 5/15/08, 112, no. 17, pp. 12–13. See also *Correa* v. *Waymouth Farms et al.,* 2003, Minn LEXIS 394 (Minn. July 3, 2003. Even fraud may not prohibit benefits. In this case, a worker was granted benefits even after it was determined that he used fraudulent documents to the job. *Benjamin Amoah* v. *Mallak Management LLC et al.;* N.Y. Supreme Court, Appellate Division 3rd Judicial Department No. 504220, October 30, 2008.

CHAPTER 6

Occupational Safety and Health Law

CHAPTER OUTLINE

The Smoking Decline

Safety as a Management Function

The General Duty Clause

A Future for Ergonomics

Safety as an Organizational Responsibility

E ach year more than 5,500 people are killed "on the job" with a ratio of about 10 private-sector employees to one public-sector employee.[1] There are almost four million reportable (medically treated) injuries each year, one-third of which are in manufacturing and construction industries and the remainder in the service sector with retail and health-care industries reporting notable percentages.[2] Particularly dangerous occupations are taxi drivers and convenience store clerks who work nights. Besides the personal tragedies, workplaces are disrupted and costs are incurred; therefore employers have a big stake in caring for their human assets.

The development of workplace safety law generally parallels the growth of government influence in the conduct of our commercialism. One of the early legislative efforts addressed mining safety in 1891. In keeping with the power of industrialists of that time, there was no inspection authority.[3] "In 1900 no laws existed for business owners to provide even minimally safe job sites."[4] In 1938, the Fair Labor Standards Act restricted the working hours of youngsters under the age of 16 and prohibited dangerous work (driving, power equipment) for those under age 18. In 2005, Wal-Mart paid a fine of $135,000 because younger workers operated chain saws, paper balers, and fork lifts. State laws commonly have additional limitations.

Today, a number of government agencies and most states administer safety mandates or regulations. These include the Department of Energy, the Department of Labor, the U.S. Coast Guard, and the Federal Aviation Administration. The Occupational Safety and Health Administration (OSHA) (1970) is widely applicable and its impact overshadows other health and safety legislation. It is occasionally intrusive in the jurisdictions of other agencies.[5]

The Federal **Drug-Free Workplace Act** administered by the Department of Labor requires that all businesses that have contracts with the federal government that exceed $25,000 must certify a drug-free workplace. The 1988 law requires that the employer notify employees of its drug-free policy and provide education and rehabilitation programs.

Transportation workers in aviation, trucking, railroads, and mass transit whose work can result in injury to others are subject to drug and alcohol testing under the stipulations of the Omnibus Transportation Employees Testing Act of 1991 (CFR Part 40, the Office of Drug & Alcohol Policy & Compliance [ODAPT]). The DOT administering the law and testing of "safety sensitive employees" is subject to a strict protocol for testing accuracy and confidentiality.

THE SMOKING DECLINE

Presidential **Executive Order 13058** (Clinton) essentially banned smoking in the federal service in 2007. This order established a smoke-free environment for federal employees and members of the public visiting federal facilities. Exceptions to this policy include:

1. Designated smoking areas that are enclosed and exhausted directly to the outside
2. Residential accommodations
3. Rented and leased space in federal buildings leased to nonfederal parties
4. Places of employment in the private sector or in other nonfederal governmental units where federal employees are assigned permanently or intermittently
5. Certain narrow exceptions established by Agency head

States and municipalities have followed with smoking prohibitions in public places and commercial establishments. Public places include public transport equipment, elevators, retail stores, restaurants, and schools.

Twenty-five states have laws prohibiting smoking in private-sector worksites, restaurants, and/or bars. Smoking is a health hazard to workers, and private employers have also acted to protect nonsmokers.[6]

Due to increasing health insurance costs, many employers have adopted a total ban on smoking in the workplace, avoided hiring smokers, and encouraged employees who smoke to participate in smoking cessation programs. Employer initiatives in this area have reduced the number of employees who smoke and discouraged those who are considering becoming smokers.[7]

The terrorist act of September 11, 2001, created an awareness of a new threat to the nation's workplaces from terrorist groups and individuals. The increased need for national safety provisions resulted in concerns for the protection of our imports, food and water, and chemical facilities. Specific steps have been taken in workplaces to improve employee background investigations, establish identification systems, and improve emergency response plans, access control, and surveillance and guard staff.[8] Many establishments, particularly governments with more than 50 employees, have written security programs.[9] It's reasonable to believe that more regulations will be promulgated to address terrorist threats.

State and local regulations also play a vital role in employee safety. Fire and safety provisions for building are promulgated in local building codes across the nation.

SAFETY AS A MANAGEMENT FUNCTION

Attending to the safety of an organization's human resources is a top management responsibility. The implementation of a program or procedure can be accomplished by anyone with the ability to learn regulations and to apply suitable skills. However, the closer leadership is to the center of safety concerns, the better.[10] Back-to-work assignments are easier. A personnel specialist or other staff administrator more remote from working conditions and activity is at a disadvantage.

An assigned safety administrator cannot achieve workplace health and safety alone. It requires the cooperation of the affected workers. The well-being of the workforce might involve a number of people directing health and wellness programs; maintenance management; and medical, security, and fire prevention. Human resources personnel can at least contribute to research, record keeping, and training support.

Stakeholders

Top management has abundant reason to be committed to safety.[11] An injury-free workplace facilitates productivity and contributes to a favorable public image. Once management demonstrates a commitment, everything else seems to fall into place. The supervisor, too, has a stake in an effective safety effort.[12] Safe conditions and practices cannot be separated from productivity. The same techniques a supervisor uses to obtain good production are used to prevent accidents. A worker's stake is self-concern as well as financial. Workers' compensation benefits typically do not pay full wages.[13]

A good safety program is accident-prevention awareness and good work practices. It will contain the following elements:

Organizing Safety Efforts

1. There must be a demonstrated interest of top management. They must make each position in management responsible for safety quality or cost. One of the major mistakes management makes is to depend on a safety director to reduce accidents.[14] As one manager foolishly put it, "We've got a safety director; if accidents aren't reduced, we replace the safety director." Safety is everyone's business. A safety director is a resource person who can keep all members of management involved and establish liaison with the workers. When management focuses all the responsibility to a safety director, results will suffer.

2. Management, supervisors, and workers will participate in identifying and analyzing existing hazards. All work-related hazards and unsafe acts are communicated to affected employees repeatedly. Having a safety program does not guarantee compliance with OSHA, but will improve some situations and help defend a citation.

3. Causes of accidents must be identified. The major cause of accidents is *unsafe acts*. Physical plant *conditions* cause about 15 percent of all accidents and must not be overlooked. A safety work order should be given top priority by maintenance. The exposure will exist until it is corrected. (A prompt response shows concern by management and reminds the employee to work safely.) To correct *unsafe acts* is a training function not without problems. All the domestic problems and frustrations outside the workplace are brought to the worksite and many unsafe acts occur when the employee is thinking about something other than the job.

4. Communicate about safety matters continually. Information from the National Safety Council and other organizations can be helpful. Desired practices and procedures must be instituted. The company develops literature to sell a product. Literature to sell safety and health programs must be developed in the same way. Tailgate meetings at the start of the shift and other safety messages all help condition the employee and to understand expectations. In industrial or "hard hat" conditions, there may be a body of safety rules.

5. Investigate each accident. One author, as safety director, audited programs in subsidiary plants. All he had to look at was the first report of injury forms (required in most states). If the correction to be made said, "Be more careful," he knew that the safety program needed work. If management starts out with the belief that all accidents have a cause, then the investigation and remedy are on the right track.

A safety program that contains these basic elements will cut workers' compensation costs and reduce absenteeism due to work-related injuries. Common basis for measuring effectiveness are workers' compensation claims and the number of injuries requiring medical treatment. An organization should maintain a current file of all federal, state, and local workplace safety regulations.

Discipline for Safety Violations

No employee, whether a union steward, a member of a safety committee, or a member of a protected class, has the right to violate a safety rule. The law is quite clear that the employer can take disciplinary action to enforce well-founded safety rules. The discipline may be challenged because there is a protective clause under the act, but this protection cannot be used by an employee to defend the violation of a safety rule. The act specifically states that it's the employer's obligation to provide employees with a safe place to work, and not allow injury to oneself or co-workers.

One problem with taking disciplinary action for a safety rule is top management's belief that the facility is a safe place and discipline isn't necessary. However, OSHA and most safety codes say otherwise.[15] Safety codes state that it is the employer's responsibility to prevent accidents. It is no defense that it was "an act of God" or that the accident was caused by an unsafe act or a mechanical happenstance that could not be prevented, or that the employee was informed of the rule but didn't follow it.[16] Some believe that the injury itself is enough to get the message across. This is not true.[17] Another reason for reluctance to discipline for a safety violation is employee statutory protections for whistle blowing, workers' compensation claims, and retaliation. However, if the reason for the discipline is the legitimate violation of a safety rule, no statute will prevent it. OSHA and most statutes give employers **enforcement** power; all they have to do is use it. OSHA will cite the employer when a rule is not enforced.

THE OCCUPATIONAL SAFETY AND HEALTH ADMINISTRATION[18]

The stated purpose of the OSHA Act is to provide for the general welfare to assure, as far as possible, every working man and woman in the nation safe and healthful working conditions and to thereby preserve human resources. It applies to all companies in interstate commerce and the federal government. It gives the states an option to adopt their own safety and health legislation provided that state and local public employees are covered. About two dozen states, including approximately 11 million covered workers, have chosen to have their own law and agencies. Such latitude enables states like California to initiate "heat illness" and "language education" standards to fit their particular circumstances.[19] The federal agency monitors state conditions and may intervene if there are problems.[20]

Several states have imposed the development and administration of complete written safety programs for hazardous industries. In Minnesota, this legislation is M.S.-182.653 subd.8 of statute Chapter 182 (1990) and specifically includes:

- Goals and objectives
- Assignment of responsibilities
- Hazard abatement
- Accident investigations
- Safety committees

State plans must adhere to stringent guidelines whereupon the federal unit remits supportive financing.[21] In the end, state and federal programs are very similar and the units cooperate and collaborate.

Purpose of the Law

Congress believed the nation's workers would be safer and safety efforts better evaluated if Congress legislated to:

1. Encourage employers and employees to institute new programs and perfect existing ones.
2. Give employers and employees separate responsibilities and rights to achieve safe working conditions.
3. Authorize the Secretary of Labor to set safety and health standards and grant power for their enforcement.
4. Provide for a number of trained compliance inspectors.
5. Encourage labor–management safety committees to help create a safe place to work.

Statistics show that workplace injuries and deaths have been significantly reduced since OSHA, even though the workforce is larger. Then, too, jobs in manufacturing have declined relative to those in the service sector, which are less dangerous. Additionally, material-handling equipment continues to reduce the necessity of physical labor.

The OSHA Act emphasizes prevention. It requires protective equipment, procedures, and safe practices to abate hazards and to prevent injuries. Employers are expected to adopt those measures. Literature on work-related accidents indicates that years ago management's first concerns were with problems that arose after the accident occurred.[22]

Standards and procedures are most effective when endorsed and adopted by the workers. Demonstrations of a management commitment, training and education, and attention by supervisors must be applied to win a mental and emotional endorsement and consciousness of people. Safe workers are not born—they are made.[23]

Workplace Violence

A workplace hazard that has received considerable attention in recent years, and one that is best detected by workers, is workplace violence. It includes verbal abuse, threats, and physical assaults. The Department of Justice reports that nearly one million violent crimes occur each year at job sites. Many are committed by employees but others are perpetrated by outsiders. No workplace is immune. In the first weeks of 2010, national media reported a murder in a Las Vegas courthouse; three workers were killed and five others wounded by a gunman at a plant in St. Louis; and three employees were wounded by an outsider at an Atlanta worksite.

Employers can be held liable for acts of violence that occur in their workplaces if reasonable care is not exercised. Taking reasonable care includes diligent background investigations of new hires, and providing clear and demonstrable instructions to all employees to report disturbing behavior or threats. Providing adequate lighting on the property, prohibiting workers from working alone in isolated locations, controlling plant access, and promptly involving law enforcement when appropriate also demonstrate reasonable care.

Responsibility

The Occupational Safety and Health Administration fixes the responsibility for accidents on the employer, who *must* comply with its standards. The act has no provision to affect employee conduct. Congress clearly felt that the employer is in a better position to prevent unsafe acts and correct unsafe conditions than for the law to force employees to comply.[24]

The National Labor Relations Board and the courts also hold that safety is the responsibility of management. Employees have no direct right of enforcement. If a union is involved, safety is a mandatory subject of bargaining. However, employees can complain to OSHA about unsafe conditions, and under certain circumstances they can refuse to work.[25] Employees will sometimes use unsafe conditions as a means of harassment or an expression of dissatisfaction with other areas of the employment relationship. When an employee complains of an unsafe condition, OSHA must inspect.[26]

Standards

Hundreds of standards (a prescribed condition) have been promulgated by OSHA agencies. Published standards fall within:

General Industry (29 CFR 1910)

Construction (29 CFR 1926)

Maritime (29 CFR 1915–19)

Agriculture (29 CFR 1928)

Some of the most widely applied are the blood-borne pathogen standards in health care, the hazardous chemical communication (HAZCOM) standards throughout industry, and chemical process safety management. The standard with the greatest applicability is dealing with emergency evacuation, which received a surge of appreciation following the disastrous evacuation of the Twin Towers on 9/11. This regulation requires all employers to have the following action plan. If there are more than 10 employees, the action plan must be in writing:

- A procedure to report an emergency
- An emergency alarm system
- A diagram of exit routes
- Unobstructed exit routes
- Available medical assistance within minutes
- A point of congregating following exiting
- Training of each employee
- A designated person to contact for questions

Compliance with the standards will not prevent all accidents; in fact, it is not uncommon for a company to have a good accident-prevention program and still be cited by OSHA for violations.[27] Although it is demoralizing to everyone involved, OSHA is mandated to ensure that standards are followed. If OSHA is accepted as an injury-prevention partner, its consulting services can be used.[28]

Training Records

Serious advocates of preventing employee injury or illness, and those who anticipate that someday OSHA officials will be on site, will fulfill the expressed training expectations of applicable standards. Any issues with OSHA will surface in an employer's training activity and records. Records of the date, instructor and attendees should be kept for training in the following subjects:

- Hazards of the workplace
- Emergency evacuation procedures
- Blood-borne pathogens protection
- Blood-borne pathogens exposure procedures
- Hearing protection
- Respirator use
- Noise exposure
- Hazardous chemical communication
- Eye protection
- Fire extinguishers
- Industrial trucks
- Radiation exposure
- Power controls (lock-out of machinery)

Compliance

The OSHA Act of 1970[29] does not define safe working conditions, but does establish two types of obligations.[30] The first obligation is a restatement of the common law and requires the employer to provide a place of employment that is free from all recognized hazards. This "general duty clause" in simple terms states that the employer is responsible for any condition that is recognized or foreseeable to be unsafe or injurious to one's health. The obligation further requires the employer to take necessary steps to correct this condition, including the proper training, supervision, and discipline of employees, subject to a citation by inspectors.

The second obligation imposed on the employer is to comply with specific standards promulgated under the authority of the Secretary of Labor.[31] The violation of the standards subjects the employer to citations, civil and criminal penalties,[32] or litigation.[33] Principal among these standards are mandates for personal protective equipment, industrial truck operation, first aid, first aid provisions, and injury and training records and reports. Hazard abatements required by OSHA are ever present in the form of hard hats, masks and gloves in the dental office, and those noisy back-up alarms on trucks. Two popular publications to help small employers are *Small Business OSHA 2209* and *Emergency and Evacuation OSHA 3085.*

THE GENERAL DUTY CLAUSE

Section 5 (a)(1) of OSHA (commonly referred to as the **general duty clause**) states: "Each employer shall furnish to each of his employees employment and a place of employment which are free from recognized hazards that are causing or likely to cause death or serious physical harm to his employees."[34]

The clause is usually used by OSHA where there are no published standards. (It is also used for **ergonomics** citations.) OSHA has to prove several elements to find a violation of the general duty clause.[35] Although some conditions may be recognized hazards, employer knowledge of, and the feasibility of, abatement methods are difficult to prove. An injury is not

required to establish a hazard under the general duty clause, but specific abatement methods must exist.[36] When the general duty clause is used for a violation, the employer should carefully consider contesting it.[37] Many OSHA inspectors believe that whenever there is an injury, the general duty clause has been violated. Case law does not support this view.[38]

Inspections

Regulators routinely inspect the most hazardous workplaces, provide consultative visits, and respond to complaints (Section 8(a)(i)). OSHA is required to give notice to the employer under the law before the inspection is made. Some regional directors will give an early notice, but notice can be given at the time of the inspection.

According to studies, unsafe acts by employees are the major cause of accidents. As with any regulatory agency, good faith efforts will go a long way in reducing citations and penalties. In 2007, OSHA conducted 38,000 inspections and issued 89,000 citations.[39]

Advice for Inspections

Suggestions for good management record keeping in anticipation of an OSHA inspection include:

1. Have good records. Keep the employees informed of the number of injuries by posting the required log at least every six months.
2. "The first report of injury" should reflect the corrective steps taken—not "Be more careful." Give these records to the OSHA inspector before they are requested.
3. Have an active safety committee that keeps good records.
4. Keep good records of all the safety activities and have them available for the inspector.
5. The person assigned to accompany the inspector should be well trained. Make

sure all members of management know the action plan for when an inspector arrives.

6. Try to determine the reason for the inspection. Sometimes inspectors will not tell or will not give the real reason. The law says they have to give some reason.
7. Insist on a closing conference before the inspector leaves the facility.
8. Treat the inspector like a professional; they are experts.
9. Absolutely do not agree to an abatement. This admits the violation of the standard cited.
10. Agree to nothing that is questionable, but avoid an adverse relationship.

Some OSHA inspections are limited due to budget considerations. There are about 2,400 inspectors responsible for millions of workplaces. The company itself should make periodic internal inspections, which can help prepare for the inspector's arrival. The organization never knows when an OSHA inspector is going to appear, so it should be prepared to explain why temporary hazards exist. The inspector will not accept an economic reason for an OSHA violation.

Appeal Procedure

Employees (or the employee representative) who do not agree with a citation received by the employer can appeal the matter to OSHA. A hearing is held before an administrative law judge who makes a recommendation to the Commission. The recommendation is usually accepted and made a final order. The Occupational Safety and Health Review Commission (OSHRC), as an independent agency, can reverse OSHA decisions. The case then goes to the court of appeals and ultimately to the Supreme Court (if *certiorari* is granted). In practice, labor organizations bring most of the cases. Affairs concerning OSHA become

a matter of legal interpretation and the parties usually have a lawyer represent them at hearings before OSHA administrative law judges and other steps in the appeal procedure.

Employee Rights under OSHA

Employees have specified rights under the OSHA Act, which are listed on a required poster. Complaints must have a legitimate basis. Employees can complain about safety conditions and hazards to their union or to the government and can request and participate in an investigation. Employees can also file a complaint or grievance over a safety issue or alleged violation of OSHA standards. Significantly, employees are protected from reprisal such as threats, reduction in pay or hours, or a demotion for complaining or exercising their rights (Section 11c).

Allegations of punishment for submitting safety complaints are processed through the Office of Whistle-blower Protection. Whistle-blower protection also protects such employee actions under the Safe Drinking Water Act, the Toxic Substance Control Act, the Clean Air Act, the Solid Waste Disposal Act, and the Federal Rail Safety Act.

Refusal to Work

The right of an employee to refuse to work in unsafe conditions is protected by two different statues: Sections 7 and 502 of the Labor Management Relations Act of 1956 (LMRA)[40] and Section 11(c)(1) of the OSHA Act.[41]

Refusal under the National Labor Relations Act

In interpreting the National Labor Relations Act (NLRA), the courts have stated that a **refusal to work** is protected by the act. There must be good faith belief based on objective evidence that the working conditions are unusually dangerous. The workers must also be competent to testify as to the physical conditions present.

The protection under Sections 7 and 502 of NLRA is exclusive. A no-strike clause in the labor agreement or an arbitration clause does not affect the employees' rights, although arbitration is permitted if the labor representatives choose to seek that forum under the labor agreement. In order to receive NLRA protection in a dispute over unsafe conditions, there must be concerted activity. That is, the employee must have talked to co-workers or have acted specifically on behalf of himself or herself *and* other workers. Where an employee acted unilaterally in refusing to drive a truck that he or she contended was unsafe, the Supreme Court stated that as long as it was consistent with the labor agreement, the employee's activity was protected.[42]

Refusal under OSHA

The right under OSHA of the employee to refuse to work under unsafe conditions is found in the Secretary of Labor's interpretation of what constitutes discrimination under Section 11(c)(1) of OSHA. The Secretary's directive interpreting this section stated that an employee can refuse to work if (1) the employee's fears were objectively reasonable, (2) the employee attempted to get the employer to correct the condition, and (3) there was not time to use the normal enforcement procedures under OSHA (or any other statute) so the danger could be eliminated.

This interpretation was at issue in *Whirlpool Corp.* v. *Marshall,* 445 U.S. 1 (1980). The Supreme Court held that in order to have a violation of 11(c)(1) of OSHA, two conditions must exist: (1) a reasonable belief that the employees will be placed in jeopardy of injury or death and

(2) a reasonable belief that there was no other alternative but to disobey the employer's order (no opportunity to go to an OSHA office or seek redress from another level of management). The court further held that this may be termed a strike and although the employees would be protected, they would not receive pay for not working. The court also reaffirmed the rule established under Section 502 of NLRA that if a hazardous condition was found not to exist, or if employees were acting in bad faith, they could be discharged for insubordination.

In cases subsequent to *Whirlpool*, the courts have often cited *Whirlpool* as their authority, but do not require the conditions stated in *Whirlpool*. In one case, a foreman refused to work when he believed the condition to be unsafe. The court ordered his reinstatement, citing *Whirlpool* as authority.[43] This is an example of the court following *Whirlpool* although the conditions listed by the court were not present. If an employee has objective evidence of the unsafe condition, it would appear that he or she may refuse to work, regardless of whether the earlier mentioned noted conditions under *Whirlpool* were met.

Administration

Congress created three federal agencies to implement the provisions of the OSHA Act. These agencies are the Occupational Safety and Health Administration (OSHA), the Occupational Safety and Health Review Commission (OSHRC), and the National Institute for Occupational Safety and Health (NIOSH).

OSHA

Located with the U.S. Department of Labor and operating at the direction of the Secretary of Labor, OSHA is the primary administrative agency of the act. It is authorized to create and adopt standards, interpret regulations, conduct the previously mentioned inspections, and enforce the act in cases of noncompliance. Historically, there has been some conflict between the Secretary of Labor and the OSHRC over which agency has primary authority in the interpretation of ambiguous regulations. This conflict was apparently resolved in favor of the Secretary of Labor when the Supreme Court decided *Martin* v. *OSHRC* in 1991.[44]

OSHRC

The Occupational Safety and Health Review Commission is an autonomous agency composed of three members appointed by the president of the United States. It was created to review enforcement actions under OSHA initiated by the Department of Labor. The Department of Labor has primary responsibility in inspection, interpretation of standards, and enforcement, but only OSHRC has the authority to assess penalties for violations. These decisions are appealable in the federal courts. A recent decision involving penalties assessed by OSHRC involved an incident where an employee died, allegedly as the result of violations of the act. OSHRC found the employer culpable and assessed a civil penalty, which the company appealed. The appellate court found that the employer was guilty of a willful violation of the act and upheld the monetary penalty imposed by OSHRC.[45]

NIOSH

The National Institute for Occupational Safety and Health has become the leading workplace safety research organization in the United States. It was created to study workplace safety, health, and ergonomic issues and has been allocated grant funds to support independent research conducted outside the agency. NIOSH also provides technical assistance to OSHA and researches, develops, and recommends standards for adoption. Additionally, NIOSH provides technical information for exposure standards for radiation, noise, air, chemicals, and protective clothing.

Standards

The Secretary of Labor has authority under the act to promulgate standards. These standards may be interim, permanent, or emergency standards. *Interim standards* were initially authorized as temporary standards for a two-year period following adoption of the act. *Permanent standards* can either be newly created or based on a revision of the interim standards. Unfortunately, the adoption of permanent standards has been both a political exercise and an attempt to adopt meritorious and relevant safety standards. When OSHA develops a proposed standard it is subjected to a 30-day public review period. Any interested party may request a public hearing on the proposed standard and its effective date. At this point, the Secretary of Labor has the discretion to delay the effective date of the implementation of the standard indefinitely. The courts have held that even a delay in implementation of up to four years is within the discretion of the Secretary.[46]

Emergency standards are also deemed temporary and are imposed only by the Secretary of Labor when there is sufficient cause to believe that workers are in imminent danger from unsafe working conditions or exposure to toxic substances. Emergency standards become effective when published and can be effective for only six months if they are not subsequently promulgated as permanent standards.

Appeal of Standards

OSHA standards may be appealed by any person, employer, or employee who believes that she or he has been adversely impacted by a standard. Filing of an appeal will not normally delay implementation and enforcement of the standard. Standards will be upheld if the court finds that they are supported by substantial evidence. The lead case in this area is *Industrial Union Department, AFL-CIO* v. *American Petroleum Institute* 448 U.S. 607 (1980), where the Court held that the Secretary of Labor must initially find that the standard is necessary to protect employees against a significant risk of health impairment.

A FUTURE FOR ERGONOMICS

The Occupational Safety and Health Administration has also developed ergonomics guidelines for some industries, but is not yet enforcing rules. Ergonomics (from Greek words *ergon,* "work," and *nomos,* "law") is the science of adopting the mechanics of a job to fit an employee's movement. In short, ergonomics involves the study of the relationship between the workers and their jobs. Defined by OSHA, an *ergonomist* is an individual who holds a recognized degree or professional credentials in ergonomics or a closely allied field, and who has demonstrated the ability to identify and recommend effective means of correction for ergonomic hazards in the workplace.[47]

Repetitive motion injuries from video display terminals, chronic eye fatigue, and carpal tunnel syndrome[48] are examples of conditions that can be corrected by ergonomics.[49] Many employers have concluded that certain repetitive movements are the cause of cumulative trauma disorders. For example, such conditions are prevalent in the meat-packing industry, and guidelines have been promulgated for those activities. Ergonomic guidelines have also been established for nursing homes. Studies have suggested that there is considerable opportunity for safer, ergonomically sound practices in many other industries.[50]

SAFETY AS AN ORGANIZATIONAL RESPONSIBILITY

Accident prevention cannot be legislated. Congress realized that and put sole responsibility on the employer. Under the common law, the employer must provide a safe place to work. The Occupational Safety and Health Administration reinforced the common law with specific physical conditions to be satisfied.

Safe practices require training to be provided by the employer. The employee must want to work safely or be convinced to do so. When employee cooperation fails, enforcement through discipline may be necessary. Although current human resources practice favors voluntary over forced compliance, it does not eliminate the need for the employer to communicate clearly to its employees that discipline will result from repeated failure to follow safety rules or to comply with the written safety plan. Representative William A. Steiger, (R-Wis.) co-author of OSHA, said shortly after the act was passed that both employers and employees would benefit from reduced accidents. If this is to occur, it is essential that there be voluntary compliance through safety committees and self-inspections.[51]

All too often, the employer becomes concerned with compliance with the standards promulgated by OSHA, forgetting that the objective of these standards is to prevent accidents. Compliance, whether voluntary or forced, does not prevent unfortunate incidents or relieve the employer of liability.

CASE 6.1

Repetitive Injury?

Harvey had a machining job at a new workstation. It was similar to his last job in that it involved picking up a casting from a pallet, performing milling operations, and putting it aside to a pallet for finished product. In this job, the incoming pallet was stacked higher because the pieces were only about 25 pounds. This machine was somewhat more complicated than the one he worked on previously and so the job paid a little more.

Orville, the previous worker on the job, had developed a sore back doing the work and so Harvey was provided the opportunity. After a month Orville was still sore and his doctor didn't want him to return to that job. Harvey was healthy and didn't have any trouble—for about a week.

After two weeks on the new job Harvey found that lifting the pieces to and from the machine when the pallet was full (stacking the top layer) was difficult and strained his back. He also found that picking up pieces and putting them aside when the pallets were about empty made his lower back ache. He asked the supervisor if the loads could be positioned better but the supervisor didn't see how, and nothing was done. During a lunch break, Harvey learned that Orville had complained, too. Harvey asked his union steward if anything could be done. The union steward talked to the safety coordinator who replied that the supervisor didn't think anything could be done. Besides the coordinator was confident that every OSHA regulation was satisfied and there was no standard for such a situation. Harvey's back got worse.

One day an OSHA officer showed up and wanted to tour the plant but specifically to observe Harvey's workstation. The safety coordinator was very confident of compliance but was shocked in the closing conference with the inspector when the inspector made reference to a citation for a violation!

What practical matters should have been considered by the company?

What OSHA standard(s) were overlooked? ■

CASE 6.2

Safety Regulations for a New Business

Lyle Zabel, an experienced office manager, was sent by a temp agency to help out an entrepreneur named Al who was just starting a business. Al had started three field crews of six people each in the last 10 days working on irrigation projects in the county. In town, he had a warehouse area, a loading dock, and a small office with some furniture. Al needed a payroll system, a purchasing system, and other things he hadn't thought of. He had ordered several computers, an industrial lift truck for handling irrigation pipe warehousing, and storage racks, which were to be delivered next week. This would be Lyle's physical location, though there was an office for Al when he stopped by.

In the brief meeting between the two, Lyle assured Al that with the help of another person or two, cell phones, and a credit card, Lyle could establish the administrative necessities, collect employee information, find forms, get the crews paid and relieve Al of most of the "paperwork" he so disliked. Lyle set about establishing his relationships with the bank and vendors, checked proper licensing with the State Attorney General, and so on. Lyle also thought to call an OSHA office with his own cell phone to inquire about any safety regulations, a subject that Al hadn't mentioned. In a five-minute conversation, he learned of more than a dozen safety regulations (he finally quit taking notes) with which the business must comply as well as some required training. He also realized that he needed a copy of the General Industry Safety Standards for the details.

What did Lyle find in the safety standards that must be acted on?

What training would be required? What provisions adopted? ■

Summary

The nation's safety regulations tend to have the advantages of greater specificity and clarity than other human resources law regulations. OSHA imposes several obligations on employers through adopted standards and provides for inspections to ensure compliance with those **standards**. The law requires that employers provide readiness for personnel evacuation if it should become necessary and requires the identification and abatement of any hazards. The law also grants employees certain rights, including the right to refuse work under some circumstances, and promotes their involvement in creating and maintaining a safe workplace. Finally, it requires the maintenance of detailed injury and illness records, the provision of safety training, and the posting of reports.

Ergonomic guidelines have also been established under OSHA for some industries but these guidelines are not currently being enforced. Certainly, employee involvement in safety is desirable, but OSHA makes it clear that safety is ultimately the responsibility of the employer.

Key Terms

Drug-Free Workplace Act   171
Executive Order 13058   171
enforcement   173

general duty clause   176
ergonomics   176
refusal to work   177
standards   182

Questions for Discussion

1. What are the requirements of the General Duty Clause?
2. How is OSHA enforced?
3. What public safety law requires the testing of millions of transportation employees?
4. What conditions must be met before an employee may refuse to work under OSHA or the NLRA?
5. What is the role of the Secretary of Labor in implementing the OSHA Act?
6. What OSHA standard applies primarily to medical care activity?
7. What is ergonomics? Identify two common conditions that can be corrected by ergonomic measures.

Notes to Chapter 6

1. U.S. Department of Labor, Bureau of Labor Statistics USDL - 1202 August 9, 2007.
2. U.S. Department of Labor, Bureau of Labor Statistics USDL - 1562 October 16, 2007.
3. U.S. Department of Labor Mine Safety and Health Administration History of Minnesota Safety Abstract.
4. "History of Mine Safety and Health Legislation" in A. Wong, *A cultural history of the U.S.: The 1900s* (San Diego: Lucent, 1998).
5. Fitzpatrick, John J. Jr. "OSHA jurisdiction," *Labor Law Journal*, 30, no. 2 (February 1979: 84–87.
6. J. Douville, *Smoking hazards in the workplace.* New York: Van Nostrand Reinhold, 1990.
7. Center for Disease Control and Prevention, National Health Survey Interviews 2006.
8. G. Seivold (ed.), *2008 security regulations, compliance and liability prevention manual.*

New York: Institute of Management Administration, 2007.

9. *2005 survey of workplace violence*. Bureau of Labor Statistics, Dept. of Labor, October 27, 2006.

10. R.W. Lack, "The safety-HR connection," *Personnel Journal* (July 1992): 18.

11. For a good review of safety programs, see M. Cook, "How to run a safety incentive program," *The human resources yearbook, 1992/93*. Englewood Cliffs, NJ: Prentice Hall), p. 12.1. Also see newsletters of state agencies.

12. In *Leich* v. *Hornsby* 885 S.W. 2D 34 (Tex. Appl. 1994) employer and officers were held liable for failure to provide safety equipment.

13. For state maximum benefits, see Cook, "How to run a safety incentive program," p. 12.19.

14. See "Training program results measured in a unique way," *Supervision*, 53 (1992): 18.

15. The state cannot impose safety rules without the federal government's approval: *Gade* v. *National Solid Waste Management Association*, 1992 LEXIS 3686 (1992).

16. An employee cannot be sanctioned for the employer's criminal violation of OSHA: *Legacy Roofing Inc.* v. *State Department of Labor and Industries* 129 Wash. App. 356, 119 p.3d 366 (2005).

17. Richard Braden, "Can OSHA survive in the new international economic order? New constraints on the promulgation of permanent health standards," *In the Public Interest*, 14 (1994–1995): 121.

18. 29 USC - 651 et seq.; 29 CFR Parts 1900 to 2400.

19. "Grassroots Workplace Protection," 2009 OSHSP A Report, p. 17.

20. J. Deschenaux, "OSHA calls for corrective action in state run programs," *SHRM News* (October 1, 2010).

21. State Planning states bring safety control home.

22. H. Wigmore, "Responsibility for tortious acts: Its history," *Harvard Law Review*, 7, no. 6 (January 1894): 315–337; C. Beard, "The Industrial Revolution," U.S. Department of Labor Bulletin 20 (1927); *OSHA handbook for small business*, U.S. Department of Labor OSHA No. 2209 (Revised).

23. See "Is your safety attitude showing?" *Bureau of Business Practice*, no. 2012 (June 25, 1992).

24. The Secretary of Labor may require workers to wear testing equipment for OSHA inspections: *Martin* v. *Trinity Industries*, 959 F.2d 45 (5th Cir. 1992).

25. *Whirlpool Corp.* v. *Marshall*, 445 U.S. 1 (1980).

26. An employee complaint can establish probable cause for a search warrant: *Martin* v. *International Matex Tank*, 928 F.2d 614 (3rd Cir. 1991) The employer must comply: *Justice* v. *Martin*, F.2d 121 (7th Cir. 1991), cert. denied.

27. See "All about OSHA," U.S. Department of Labor, OSHA 2056 (1991 Revised).

28. *Pedraza* v. *Shell Oil Co.* 942 F.2d 48 (1st Cir. 1991).

29. 29 U.S.C. Sect. 553-651 et seq. It preempts most state safety laws: *Gade* v. *National Solid Waste Management Association*, 1992 LEXIS 3686 (1992).

30. See "Safety law," Minnesota OSHA Dept. of Labor and Industry (Fall 1995).

31. Enforced by OSHA, a division under the Secretary of Labor. Standards are subject to judicial review. See *AFL-CIO* v. *OSHA*, 965 F.2d 962 (11th Cir. 1992).

32. Interest on penalties starts on the date of the penalty rather than the date of final judgment: *Reich* v. *Sea Sprite Boat Co.*, 50 F.3d 418 (7th Cir. 1995).

33. For case law on standards, see M. Berger, "Recent developments in OSHA litigation," *Labor Law Journal*, 4, no. 3:11 (November 1992): 687–694.

34. Sect. 5(a)(1) 29 U.S.C. 654.

35. See E. Faulke, Jr., and T. Beck, "The general duty clause of the Occupational Safety and Health Act of 1970," *Labor Law Journal*, 44 (March 1993):131.

36. For a detailed discussion of the general duty clause, see M. Thothstein, *Occupational safety and health Law*, 3rd Ed. St. Paul, MN: West, 1990 (with updates); S. Bokat and A. Thompson III, *Occupational Safety and Health Law* (Bureau of National Affairs, 1988), p. 114.

37. *Ed Taylor Construction Co.* v. *OSHRC*, 88-2463 (1992).

38. M. Cook, *The human resource yearbook 1992/1993* (Englewood Cliffs, NJ: Prentice Hall): 12.7–12.15.

39. U.S. Department. of Labor, OSHA, December 2008.

40. LMRA Section 502 states: "...nor shall the quitting of labor by an employee or employees in good faith because of abnormally dangerous conditions for work at the place of employment of such employee or employees be deemed a strike under this Act." Section 7 of the Act gives the employees the right to strike.

41. OSHA Section 11©(1) states: "No person shall discharge or in any manner discriminate against any employee because such employee has filed any complaint or instituted or caused to be instituted any proceeding under or relating to this Act or has testified or is about to testify in any such proceeding or because of the exercise by such employee on behalf of himself or others of any right afforded by this Act."

42. *NLRB* v. *City Disposal Systems, Inc.*, 104 S. Ct. 1505 (1984).

43. *Donavan* v. *Hahner, Foreman, Harness, Inc.* 736 F.2d 1421 (10th Cir. 1984).

44. *Martin* v. *OSHRC*, 499 U.S. 144 (1991).

45. *A.E. Staley Manufacturing* v. *Chao*, 295 F.3d 1341 (D.C. Cir. 2002).

46. *Industrial Union Department, AFL-CIO* v. *Hodgson*, 499 F.2d 467 (D.C. Cir. 1974).

47. *Ergonomics program management guidelines for meatpacking plants* (Washington, DC: U.S. Department of Labor, OSHA, 1991): p. 21; also R. Weltmann, "A work-place designed to be efficient can save money-MC," *Workers compensation cost Control* (Boston: Northeast), July 1992, p. 3.

48. *Schulp* v. *Auburn Needleworks, Inc.*, 479 N.W. 2d 440 (Neb. 1992).

49. Data from the Bureau of Labor Statistics state that over 50 percent of all occupational illnesses are due to repetitive motion. Repetitive injuries accounted for 40 percent of all injuries in 1990.

50. See C. Gross, "Reduce musculoskeletal injuries with corporate ergonomics program," *Occupational Health and Safety*, 1 (1992): 28–33. Also *Employee Benefit News*, 14 (April 1992): 15; H. J. Reske, "Repetitive stress suits consolidated," *ABA Journal*, 78 (September 1992): 21.

51. See W. Steiger, "OSHA: Four years later," *Labor Law Journal*, 25 (December 1974): 723; also M. Berger, "Recent developments in OSHA litigation," *Labor Law Journal*, 43, no. 11 (November 1992): 694–698.

CHAPTER 7

Employee Information and Communication Mandates

CHAPTER OUTLINE

T he role of government in personnel information and knowledge management could hardly be more pronounced. Employers are required to communicate with and educate employees on obligatory subjects; record hundreds of bits of specific data; secure files for stipulated retention periods; and create precisely defined reports and documents to be provided employees and other annual reports for government agencies. All this must be done while protecting employee privacy rights, avoiding defamation exposure, and attending to the work of the institution. The potential for management errors in employee privacy protections, which may result in implied contractual obligations or defamation exposure, exists throughout an employee's tenure.

A managed program of information handling and oversight is requisite if exposure is to be avoided. Three primary areas of employer failure often resulting in government intervention involve: overtime pay violations, sexual harassment, and eligibility of immigrant workers. The costs of overlooking Consolidated Omnibus Budget Reconciliation Act (**COBRA**) obligations and creating unintended contracts cannot be ignored. Medical care providers are particularly vulnerable to personal health information privacy violations.

COMMUNICATIONS DIRECTIVES

Readers will be familiar with the first level of communication mandates: notification of employee rights and employer prohibitions pursuant to wage and hour requirements, safety restrictions, the Family Medical Leave Act (**FMLA**), ADA, Polygraph Protection and other federal regulations. Federal law requires notification regarding these employee rights to be posted prominently, in heavily traveled locations, in all facilities. Government contractors have special posting requirements. Many states also require posting of their employment regulations. All federal policies and regulations should also be communicated in written form, either in an employee manual, handbook, or bulletin format, in addition to the posting requirements. Sexual harassment policies should be distributed in written form and discussed with new employees. There may also be corresponding state laws that may be more restrictive than the federal regulations. Federal contractors must notify employees of their drug-free commitment, pursuant to the Drug Free Workplace Act. Employers who drug test under the Department of Transportation (DOT) guidelines must notify all employees who are to be tested. Contractors are also required to post notices of Walsh-Healy and Davis-Bacon statute application.

Safety materials in the form of facility egress diagrams, which are part of a larger obligation of training for emergency evacuation and current annual reports of injuries, should be routinely posted in industrial facilities. Organizations with "hard hat" work are also responsible for notification and training about hazards in their workplace—most commonly toxic chemicals, blood-borne pathogens, personal protective equipment, and industrial vehicle operation.

Communication to employees by mail concerning certain benefits is also necessary. Those individuals eligible for group insurance programs are to receive a notice of the possibility of insurance continuation upon separation (COBRA). Within four months of hire, a Summary (Benefit) Plan Description is to be provided to all participants. Upon the loss of health insurance at termination, and in some states life insurance, a second notice of COBRA eligibility, using certified mail or other suitable method that provides proof of receipt, is required.[1] Savings and retirement programs such as 401(k) and 403(b) plans require quarterly status reports to participants; defined benefit pension plans require an Annual Benefit Summary report to employees.

Aside from the previously mentioned mandated notifications, there are other matters that employers should communicate to avoid exposure. For example, all employees must be aware of the expectations, rules, and standards against which they will be measured, and for which they are held accountable. Employers are well advised to provide warnings before dismissal, under the doctrine of due process. An important unspoken condition that influences potential legal issues is a demonstrated application by the employer of uniform and consistent practices over time.

The Family and Medical Leave Act (FMLA)

The Family and Medical Leave Act was signed by President Clinton in 1993, although the Department of Labor regulations implementing the Act were not promulgated until 1995. The Act provides workers with up to 12 weeks of leave per year for personal illness or the illness of an immediate family member. The regulations define an immediate family member as a spouse, child, or parent. Leave may be utilized to care for an elderly parent, the birth of a child, or the adoption of a child. Workers are entitled to a continuation of all employer-provided benefits while on FMLA leave and to reinstatement to the same or a similar position when they return from leave. Employees may not be disciplined or retaliated against for utilizing or requesting leave.

The employer is required to post a notice of the protections afforded by the Act and the procedures for obtaining leave. If the employer has a handbook, a provision describing FMLA must be included.

The Family and Medical Leave Act covers all public employers and private employers who employ at least 50 employees during at least 20 workweeks in the current or previous calendar year. To be eligible for leave, an employee must have been employed for at least one year and have worked a minimum of 1,250 hours during the previous year. The employer is permitted to use the calendar year, a fiscal year, or a rolling year beginning with the employee's first utilization of leave in determining the minimum hours worked for eligibility.

Worker Adjustment Retraining and Notification Act (WARN)

Notification of the layoff of groups of employees is required under the Worker Adjustment Retraining and Notification Act (WARN). This legislation was created due to large-scale worker dislocations occurring as a result of plant closings. This Act became effective on February 4, 1989, and is enforced by the U.S. Department of Labor. Employers are prohibited from ordering a plant closing or mass layoff until the end of a 60-day waiting period, and after providing written notice to each employee of the closing or layoff. Rather than notify every affected employee, an employer may serve notice to each "employee representative" (union). State-dislocated worker programs created or designated under Title III of the Job Partnership Training Act must also receive notice of the closing or layoff. The chief elected official of the unit of local government where the closing or layoff is to occur must also be notified. If there is more than one unit of local government, an employer must notify the chief elected official representing the local governmental unit to which the employer paid the highest taxes in the preceding year. No WARN notice is required if the shutdown is not foreseeable.

There are several situations under which an employer may provide less than 60 days notice of the proposed plant closing or layoff. An employer may order a shutdown of a single site of employment[2] if, at the time that notice would have been required, the employer is actively seeking capital or business which, if obtained, would allow the employer to avoid or postpone the shutdown.[3] This provision applies only if the employer has a reasonable good faith belief that giving the notice would prevent the employer from obtaining the needed capital or business.

A plant closing or mass layoff may be ordered before the conclusion of the 60-day notice period if it was caused by business reasons not reasonably foreseeable at the time notice should have been given. No notice is required if the closing or layoff is due to any form of natural disaster, such as a flood or earthquake. Considerable litigation has arisen under WARN, since unions have standing to sue under the Act. However, civil actions to enforce WARN are subject to the applicable state statute of limitations.

HARASSMENT AND NEW EMPLOYEE EDUCATION

Laws and regulations require employers to educate new employees early in the employment experience. For example, employers in Illinois, Maine, and Michigan are required to have all new employees understand the prohibition of **harassment** in the workplace.[4] Tennessee and Nevada require training for all new public employees. California and Connecticut require training of all supervisors. The EEOC, in its Enforcement Guidelines (15 or more employees), expresses the expectation of "periodic training" of supervisors and managers. Employers who have violated these regulations have been mandated to provide periodic education. For a sample of this type of legislation, see Cal. Code Regulations Sections 708-1, Rule 80.11 (c) that became effective August 17, 2007.

California and other states require that instruction/training be provided by experienced employment law attorneys or college-level instructors. Instruction is to be provided concerning all protected classes, including those physically or mentally limited and people with uncommon sexual orientations. The subject matter includes the law, its importance and prevention, and corrective techniques using "interactive educational methods." Instruction time is "periodic," and measured in hours, not minutes.[5]

Negligent Training

A problem related to harassment education is the emerging case law that holds an employer liable when training is inadequate, and a third party is harmed. **Negligent training** is most likely to arise in situations where an employer's business is service and employees engage with customers. These are some preventive steps an employer might take:[6]

1. Confirm the claims of skills and experience of new employees.
2. Abate the risks of harm through training of employees who work with equipment and matters that are harmful and hazardous.
3. Include procedures to protect third parties' health and safety (including employees).
4. Evaluate the training activity to determine its effectiveness to reduce negligent risks.

Conduct Control

Although the *Meritor* case discussed in Chapter 2 did not specifically define what is unwelcome, when knowledge is imputed the employer can define these elements with an enforceable policy and training. The employer must recognize that there are some gray areas and may develop a policy that goes further than the law. It is then the policy that is violated, rather than an uncertain area in the law.[7] The law recognizes that the employer may have difficulty in eradicating sexual harassment because it can be difficult to define, but what the court will not recognize is the failure of the employer to act, after it has actual or imputed knowledge.[8]

Complaint Investigation

If the employee complains about being harassed, do not wait for a lawyer's decision; investigate immediately. Prompt investigation followed by a written warning normally will relieve the employer of liability. The employer can take steps to remedy the problem, which should be adequate.[9] If the employee has a bona fide belief that she or he is being harassed, it should be addressed by the employer. Through separate interviews with both the person involved and the complainant, the employer can determine how to relieve the situation and eliminate exposure to a lawsuit. At this point it is an employee relations problem, not a legal problem. The legal issue does not arise until a complaint is filed and an adverse relationship is created. However, doing something about the complaint promptly will usually avoid litigation and the legal costs that follow.[10]

Immediacy

Whether or not an investigation is immediate is determined on a case-by-case basis. Some of the considerations are:

1. What, specifically, is the harassment? Sexual favors for job opportunities demand quicker investigation than an allegation of **hostile environment**.
2. What is the size of the company? In a large company with a hierarchy of management, it would take longer to start an investigation than in a small company without communication hurdles.

3. How well does the company know the employees involved, or how much investigation is needed to get both sides of the facts before the complaint can be evaluated?

4. Is this an isolated incident?[11]

When making a decision as to whether harassment exists, it is essential not to falsely accuse an employee of harassment, because a false charge is just as serious as not dealing with an employee who is guilty of harassment. Get both sides of the situation. Some employers prefer an outside investigator in order to make the investigation appear impartial.

Steps in an Investigation

The steps to be taken in an investigation include:

1. Interview both parties.
2. Interview other workers (potential witnesses).
3. Have more than one person weigh the evidence.
4. Review evidence with the accuser.

Necessary Ingredients for Policy

In the *Meritor* case, the Supreme Court said that, in order to bring an action for sexual harassment, it must be shown that the conduct complained of is unwelcome, the employer has knowledge or there is reason to impute knowledge, there are job opportunities involved, or there is hostile environment. How the courts subsequently define these elements is not important if the employer drafts the proper policy. The policy must be internally enforced, and each of the requirements clearly defined.[12] This is extremely important where, under a collective bargaining agreement, the employee has a right to arbitrate a discharge for harassment and the arbitrator is barred from reinstating the employee when the policy is violated.

Note that government expectations of policy include what most would define as procedures. Hence, when considering the harassment pronouncement, think in terms of both a policy and procedure:

1. The policy should prohibit both quid pro quo and environmental harassment, and it should state that the employer would try to protect confidences.
2. The policy should require the employee to report any unwelcome event or condition. A failure to report suggests a welcome relationship.
3. The hostile environment should be defined as containing sexual advances, innuendos, or vulgar statements that the employee considers hostile or objects to. Although the law may not always consider isolated instances as a hostile environment, the employer can do so for investigation purposes.[13]
4. Provide a list of people to whom incidents should be reported and the steps of an objective investigation.[14]
5. The policy should warn the employee that once it is conclusively established that the policy (not necessarily the law) has been violated, swift and corrective action will be taken.
6. If substantial facts cannot be established, it should be explained to the complaining party that the relationship would be monitored for a period of time.
7. There shall be no retaliation for reporting a complaint. This is an enforceable promise from the CEO. The policy should state than an unwelcome relationship exists as soon as the employee says so. This eliminates any confusion that the parties may have when harassment exists. The policy will further state that any unwelcome advance will be investigated as soon as possible after the employer knows or should have known of the incident.

Reporting Procedure for Policy Violation

An environment is hostile for purposes of investigation and action when the employee says so, or the management, using the "reasonable-man" test, considers it hostile. As in other necessary elements for sexual harassment, the policy puts the responsibility on the employee to define harassment; the law steps in only after the employer does nothing about it. Because the policy stresses reporting, a procedure should be included in the policy, or otherwise communicated to supervisors and employees. The essential elements of a reporting procedure are these:

1. State that a complaint of harassment conduct can be reported to any member of management. The name of the person or persons involved must be disclosed.
2. State the method of investigation and the appropriate time limits. Time limits should be very short.
3. State that the employer will correct any valid sexual harassment complaint that is reported.
4. Give assurance that the information will be confidential and there will be no retaliation whatsoever.
5. Clearly state the company's position on failure to report. In this case, it means the existence of a welcome relationship and the employee does not consider the incident or condition unwelcome. State that a fear of loss of a job is not a reason for not reporting to some member of management.

The existence of a policy does not relieve the employer of liability unless it requires reporting. In *Yates* v. *Avco Corp.*, 819 F.2d 630 (6th Cir. 1987), the court found that although a policy existed, it was not effective in encouraging the employee to report; therefore knowledge was imputed and the employer was held liable.[15]

Enforcement

Sexual harassment conduct is not any different from any other undesirable conduct with which the employer must cope in the workplace. Enforcement of house rules is always a problem; however, prohibition of sexual harassment is a priority legal matter that must be enforced. To expect a policy to eliminate harassment's existence is unrealistic. An effective policy and procedure may only cause the activity to go underground. True, the employer may be relieved of some liability if the policy is effective. The key to control harassment is the employee's complaint, which forces the person involved to define it as unwelcome, so the employer must investigate. Sexual harassment creates a great and continuous exposure for the employer.

POLICY AND ITS COMMUNICATION

Communications Methods

Management uses a variety of media to influence and inform employees. It often begins the communication system with public image activities and a job advertisement. Internal methods include electronic mail, employee handbooks, bulletin boards, messages posted on employee lockers and in rest rooms, and messaging through supervisors. In smaller organizations, more person-to-person methods are used, supplemented with written material. Mandates not only dictate the messages to be delivered but often stipulate the method of delivery as well.

An accommodating communications device is mandated for those who provide telephone services to the general public. TDD telecommunications devices for the deaf are required under ADA legislation. It is part of facility access provisions of the Accessibility Guidelines for Buildings and Facilities (ADAAG) September 2007.

Written Policy

Policies are written position statements declared by executive management that apply throughout the organization. They are usually about fundamental matters and often leave open the options on how the position might be satisfied. They are a formal method of expressing how certain matters are to be handled. They can offer some help as evidence of good faith but can also pose a problem if they convey something not delivered. Sometimes, those who draft policies get specific, as is the case with the Federal Sexual Harassment Policy that proceeds to enumerate mandated procedures, thereby becoming a "position paper," well beyond a normal statement of policy.

Developing Policy

The government dictates some policies. The EEO and OSHA statutes declare national policy that doesn't require mandated prominent statements, as is the case for Sexual Harassment and the Family Medical Leave Act. Two more policies act as preventive action to avoid lawsuits: a policy that addresses employee use of company electronic equipment, and a specific search and seizure procedure. As a practical matter, statements in a policy manual often relate to defensive positions that demand uniform administration to avoid lawsuits. for example, when one department requires employees to sign out when leaving the facility during meal periods and another department in the same organization does not, the immediate consequences may be minimal. However, if one department has a different leave of absence policy from that of another, possibly because the decision has been left up to the supervisors, the exposure to litigation under the discrimination laws is real; a uniform company policy may be desirable.

The real test for deciding whether or not to adopt a policy in a given area depends on whether the employer can affirmatively answer the following questions:

1. Does the policy aid in the solution of important ongoing HR matters?
2. Is the policy mandated by law?
3. What are the potential consequences of not having a policy statement?

The answer to the third question may not be simple. An element of uncertainty always surrounds dealing with law. Certain policies may be necessary for selected job categories, such as antitrust violation restrictions for sales-related jobs and conflict of interest policies. Matters such as overtime pay and safety training must become standard practice. Often, the policy manual becomes the repository for describing benefits programs such as vacations and holiday pay. These may more practically be published in a separate booklet, not in the policy manual or handbook. In determining what principal matters should be communicated to employees, management should keep in mind that once the communication is issued, it can be problematic to change it immediately. Employees have a right to rely on a policy statement. This is not to say that policy cannot be changed, but it should not be changed so quickly that someone suffers a loss because of abrupt change.

Drafting Policy

Management should start with the assumption that the best policy is no policy. Rules limit options and don't always accommodate changing situations. If management wants to function in a certain manner, it can do so with spoken declarations and follow-up. When written communications become necessary, a decision should be made: Should it be a policy or a guideline? A communicated statement can be interpreted as contractual. A guideline for supervisors can be enforced by selected discipline. Statutes and case law may also limit flexibility, contrary to the best interests of the organization.

One person should be designated responsible for the original draft of a proposed policy, but a contributing committee should be appointed to work on revisions. Policy development is a process, not an event. The work required should be carried out as are other projects, with an objective and time frame.

1. Policies should be short, unambiguous and as simple as possible. These criteria are important from both the legal and employee relations standpoints. If you include too much, the policy will not be followed by even the most conscientious managers. It also runs the risk of lawsuits that the policy was intended to avoid. If you have too little detail, you may also invite litigation to interpret the meaning of the statement.

2. Make every policy as flexible as possible. Provide an escape hatch as wide as possible. Stay within the legal limits and organizational objectives. This might sound like double-talk at first, but an example might help clarification. Suppose that a supervisor decides to do something about the poor quality of the output. The supervisor announces a policy of progressive discipline. The first offense will result in a written warning, the second in a lay-off, and the third in discharge. After the warning and discipline, an employee turns in a poor-quality product for the third time. The policy calls for discharge. The supervisor faces a situation where one operator is ill and another is on vacation. If the employee is discharged as the policy requires, no one will be available to run the machine. The supervisor has to meet a deadline for an important customer. The dilemma could have been avoided if the statement had been more flexible for the third offense. It could have called for severe discipline to be applied, up to and including discharge. A faulty, committed practice is not worth upsetting a customer.

3. Keep the language trouble free and nonlegal. Using such terms as "we have the right to" when you already have the right, may raise a question about whether you are giving away or retaining part of the right. Similarly, if you state that "exceptions may be made for," you raise unnecessary questions. In the absence of a statement that "there will be no exceptions," you imply that you could make them. If exceptions may ever be necessary, you won't need a policy to make them. Normally it will not set a precedent. If there are too many exceptions, that particular policy is suspect.

4. Clear, concise, and straightforward wording with few syllables is essential. The intended audience must understand it. Nothing is more damaging to credibility than disagreement on the meaning of a statement.

5. Indicate that the authority is coming from top management and that the policy is firm. When you make commitments, it opens exposure to lawsuits.

Once the few policies are drafted, they should be reviewed by upper management, to be revised on the basis of the comments received. The second draft should be reviewed at the next level of management and again revised. The process should be repeated on a step-by-step basis until everyone from top management to the first-line supervisors has had an opportunity to review and contribute to the policies. Have counsel review the document and give a legal opinion, not a personal belief. This shows that the employer made a good faith effort to draft a policy suitable to the particular needs of the organization. Further, the participation will foster ready acceptance.

A possible issue is the degree of management willingness to enforce the policy. Management must make a decision that it is going to do so. The first step in enforceability is a clear statement from top management. All too often, this statement has a tone that seems to ask for cooperation rather than one of giving direction and indicating an intention of enforcement. Language that merely asks for cooperation is difficult to enforce, because it indicates that compliance is voluntary.[16]

The final step is to field-test the statements for a period of time as guidelines before they are finally adopted as policy. This is not always possible. During the entire review and testing, the substance of the initial statements by top management will probably not be notably altered, although the wording certainly may.

Revision of Present Polices

In many cases, policies already exist in some form. They should be periodically examined to see if they are legal, followed, and remain useful. To comply with new laws and court decisions, revision is occasionally necessary. Perhaps the company has been organized by a union since the last policy was written, or the organizational structure may have changed. A union has a right to challenge the reasonableness of the policy. Whatever the reason, an important point is that a policy change should not become effective for a period of time. Employees should be allowed enough time to look for a new job if they do not like the new conditions imposed by revisions.

Handbooks

It's very probable that some organizations have only a file of some ideas, past practices, or notes. Management and supervisors may express "policies" verbally because nothing is in writing. It's highly recommended that an effort be made to collect, consider, compile, document, and communicate vital policies. Some states require safety policies; every organization should also have a commitment to prevent harassment.

The statement in Exhibit 7.1 from the top executive does not clearly express that management will enforce the policies. Instead, it seems to allow the managers to enforce the policies if they wish to do so. This approach creates the greatest possible exposure to lawsuits. The managers who do enforce the policies expose those who do not. A manual with this type of statement from the top is merely a guideline. It should not be communicated to the employees. Doing so opens the possibility that the manual will be considered a contract.

Preferably, declare that top management will use its authority to support and enforce the provisions of the manual. State strongly what is expected of the employees. Exhibit 7-2 reflects language that not only communicates but also is enforceable. It does not require a written policy to avoid violations of antidiscrimination laws. Any employer can follow a nondiscriminatory course without policy. Policies that cannot, or will not, be enforced should not be included.

THIS MANUAL CONTAINS THE MOST RECENT OPERATING AND STAFF POLICIES FOR ABC COMPANY. I URGE YOU TO REVIEW THEM SO THAT IF YOU HAVE ANY QUESTIONS YOU CAN ADDRESS THEM THROUGH THE PROPER CHANNELS. I HOPE YOU WILL FIND THIS MATERIAL USEFUL IN CARRYING OUT YOUR RESPONSIBILITIES.

EXHIBIT 7.1 Undesirable Handbook Introduction

> The purpose of these rules is to clearly inform you of the terms and conditions of employment to which we are all subject. Compliance with these rules will also promote our desired community and customer image.

EXHIBIT 7.2   Statement of Policy

All manuals or handbooks should have a sign-off statement by the employee whereby it is agreed that the manual or handbook will be followed and that its provisions are understood. Exhibit 7.3 contains some recommended wording.

The Role of the Handbook

Handbooks are one of a number of ways to transmit messages. The remarks that follow apply to handbooks and any written materials used in initial employee communications. For a organization of 25 employees or fewer, it is doubtful whether a bound glossy booklet with color art is necessary. Communications in a small organization are often more effective by dealing with the employees directly. Items that are required to be put in writing can be done by memo or a letter to the employees. The written word does improve the clarity of a message. For new employees, it also provides reference material to review later. A handbook can serve a number of purposes, for example:

1. It can express a welcome from an executive.
2. It can establish the fact that the material applies to a broad range of employees.
3. It can clearly state that a handbook is not a contract, potentially an important element in litigation.
4. It provides uniformity and consistency. When the company's policies are stated in writing, they enhance the credibility of the company's position to outsiders.
5. It is useful as a reference for supervisors in uncertain situations.
6. It can negate or disprove allegations of contrary oral statements or commitments.
7. It can promote positive aspects of the workplace and can communicate policies and advantages of a union-free environment.

Problem Expressions

There is no substitute for a definitive choice of words that accurately reflects intent. If you don't mean it, don't write it or say it. If there is no intention of implying permanency of employment, the use of the term *probationary period* should be avoided, as should the following:

1. We reserve the right to . . .
2. Exceptions may be made for . . .
3. You have permanent employment.
4. There is job security here.

I, _____ have read and understand, and have in my possession, the Company's policies and procedures. I agree to abide by policies in the manual and if there is at any time something that I do not understand, I agree to ask a company representative.
  Signature _____

EXHIBIT 7.3   Employee Sign Off

5. These rules are guidelines . . .
6. We pay fair wages.

These are all terms that can have one meaning to the employees and another to management personnel. They may also be interpreted by the plaintiff's attorney differently than was intended by management. It is obviously problematic when the courts accept arguments by the employees and award large amounts for breach of contract. It is ironic, but true, that the courts take the position that the employee is considered to have no legal knowledge but that the employer is aware of the legal consequences of every statement it makes. Under these circumstances the employer must consider every clause in the employee handbook not only for its communication value but also for its potential legal consequences.

Contents

In writing a handbook, the employer should tell the employee what is expected of him or her, not what the employee should expect from the company. Newcomers will accept clear and definite direction and expectations. If this theme is carried out, it is beneficial for the material to be viewed as a contract. It would be enforceable against the employee if it should ever become necessary. A handbook should be specific about:

1. Conduct that will result in disciplinary action, including dischargeable offenses. These include immediately dischargeable offenses where the employee has been forewarned before committing the act. The listed causes should be as specific as possible as to the conduct, but a clause should be inserted that states that discharge will not be limited only to that offense, but others as well.

2. Rules of unacceptable conduct, including absenteeism, tardiness, leaving the worksite, and abuses of break time, work schedules, overtime, and so on.

3. Certain safety rules and the requirement that are to be followed.

4. A policy on harassment of all types, including but not limited to sexual harassment, should also be stated in a personal communication and periodically in writing.

5. A policy on searches that involves company and employee property. This should also be stated in a separate communication as well as in writing.

6. A policy on drug testing and alcohol abuse.

7. Any complaint procedure to be used.

8. The availability of family medical leave, if the employee qualifies.

Other Considerations

The handbook could well contain a clause that defines misconduct, which will aid in unemployment compensation appeals and legal interpretations, such as COBRA. Exhibit 7.4 is a misconduct and discharge policy that might appear in a handbook.

Whenever the employee willfully, wantonly, and adversely affects the employer's or other employees' interests, it will be considered a gross misconduct that will result in immediate discharge, once the facts are ascertained. The following violations will be considered gross misconduct. [List the violations—no more than 15; 10 is better.]

The employee will be warned either verbally or in writing for violation of all other offenses not listed above [excluding those that have been added to the above list after due notice]. It is considered gross misconduct to repeat a violation after being warned in writing or being disciplined, and where both parties understand that another violation will result in discharge for gross misconduct.

EXHIBIT 7.4   Misconduct Statement

From time to time, it may be necessary to change or add rules and procedures governing employees. Such changes will be posted well in advance of their effective date, after which time they will become a part of this handbook.

EXHIBIT 7.5   Statement Reserving the Right to Modify or Change the Handbook

The handbook should inform the employee that changes may have to be made to the handbook. Exhibit 7.5 is suggested language to cover this contingency.

The employer should be assured that the employee not only has read the handbook but also understands it. Sometimes the employee will state that she or he understood it when it was presented, but actual comprehension was limited. This is particularly problematic with employees who have limited English speaking or literacy skills. To eliminate this problem, the handbook should contain a statement that the employee should ask questions at any time the handbook appears to be unclear. Exhibit 7.6 is a suggested statement that should be given to the employee at the time the handbook is distributed; after it is signed, the statement should be put in the employee's personnel file.[17] The language should clearly express that it is the employee's responsibility to inquire about any uncertainty he or she may have about the meaning of any phrase or requirement set forth in the handbook.

Disclaimer Clauses

Many lawyers feel that the best solution to the problem of having enforceable rights created by the handbook is to include a disclaimer stating that the handbook is not a contract and can be changed at any time, at the discretion of the company. Exhibit 7.7 is an example of a typical disclaimer.

If **disclaimers** are desired, they are more likely to be sustained in a court if the language is highlighted so it is conspicuous and clear.[18] In addition to the preceding language, other factors should be considered to close loopholes and prevent a disclaimer from being challenged. These include:

1. The disclaimer language must be clear, conspicuous, and easily understood.
2. The at-will language must appear in other documents, such as application forms and job offer letters.
3. There must be unambiguous evidence that the employee has received the disclaimer, read it, and understands it, and is required to ask questions if it is not understood.
4. Subsequent employer action and communications with the employee must establish that the employee is treated as an at-will employee.

Whether a disclaimer is legally enforceable often depends on the court. In *Castiglione* v. *Johns Hopkins Hospital*, 517 F.2d 786 (Md. App. 1986), the court held that a disclaimer renders the handbook only a statement of the intent of

I, _____ (Social Security number), have read, understand, and have in my possession the company's policies and procedures. I agree as a condition of employment to follow the policies in the handbook; and if there is at any time something that I do not understand, I agree to ask a company representative. I further understand that this signed statement will be a permanent record in my personnel file.

EXHIBIT 7.6   Employee Confirmation Statement

> This handbook [or manual] is designed to familiarize you with the conditions of employment that the company expects you to follow. The conditions stated herein are not intended to be and do not constitute a contract of employment.
>   *or*
>   This manual [or handbook] is not intended to and does not constitute a contract between the company and its employees.

EXHIBIT 7.7   Sample Disclaimer

the employer. This is the law in at least 26 states, so long as intent is clearly shown. However, a sizeable minority of state courts take a different view. Sometimes these courts are concerned with the superior bargaining power of the employer, and will not enforce the contract without evidence of the employee's understanding of, and agreement with, the disclaimer clause. In *Helle* v. *Landmark, Inc.*, 742 N.E.2d 765 (Ohio 1984), the court held that a disclaimer would be disregarded if oral promises were made later. Sometimes a disclaimer will not be enforced where it has the effect of waiving statutory rights, such as workers' compensation or discrimination claims.

As is readily apparent from the foregoing cases, disclaimers are not an absolute assurance that there will not be exposure to a lawsuit. Less exposure would result from eliminating the disclaimer and writing the handbook in such a manner that its provisions were enforceable against the employee. There is also an employee relations problem with disclaimers. It certainly strains the company's credibility at the orientation program to go over the provisions of a handbook that is discretionary for the company but mandatory for employees. This may also expose the company to union organization, since the employee may feel little protection from company policies that may be changed at will. A disclaimer clause in written material may have negative connations to employees, but from an attorney's perspective it is a means to avoid liability.

Audit of a Handbook

A handbook should be reviewed at least once a year. If it has not been revised for the last three years, major changes are very likely to be in order. The review of the handbook should be made, regardless of whether or not the state law may construe the handbook to be a legal contract. The legal principles followed in states that do consider a handbook as a contract are generally good personnel principles. If there is a procedure in a contract, the law says that you must follow it. It is poor employee relations to promise or agree to do one thing and then violate that promise or agreement.[19]

The basic principle to be followed in reviewing the handbook is to tell the employees what the organization expects of them, not what the organization is going to do for them. Any procedure in the handbook that is not being followed, or is not likely to be followed, should be eliminated. Handbook procedures should be guidelines for the supervisors to follow but should not be communicated to the employees as an enforceable right.

Handbook Messages

Most handbooks say too much. A handbook states the rules and regulations that the employees must follow, and the consequences if they are not followed. Progressive discipline clauses may create future difficulties in that management actions are constrained and options limited. Management can do many things without stating them in the handbook. A policy on absenteeism can be a guideline for management personnel, without being detailed in the handbook. Excessive detail causes the loss of flexibility in dealing with special situations. **Zero tolerance policies** prevent any judgment or options. A promotion policy can be instituted without mention in the handbook.

The Family Medical Leave Act requires that if an employer has a handbook, information regarding employees' FMLA rights must be included. If there is no handbook, the employer is required to post a general notice of FMLA protections and the procedures for filing complaints. This notice must be in a language in which employees are literate.

The handbook should not deal with benefits such as health insurance, vacations, holidays, and other matters that are addressed by federal or state laws. Certain required, detailed communications are out of place in the handbook. It would cause an exposure if the courts apply the handbook language to statutes that require different benefit language. Another reason for keeping the benefits provisions separate from the handbook is that benefits are subject to change and benefit provisions can be altered without diluting the basic value of the handbook. Benefits are expected to change from time to time and these changes may increase employee cost or reduce benefit levels. If management has the unilateral right to make such a change, it may compromise this right through equivocal statements in the handbook. Such statements may cause employee dissatisfaction and diminish the stature of the handbook.

A good handbook may not win any prizes in legal or human resources literature, but it will tell the employees, in unambiguous terms, what is expected of them and what will result if they take, or fail to take, certain actions. The handbook is a useful statement of an organization's position. It can be a better communication tool if it is written as if it were a contract.

PERFORMANCE APPRAISALS

The purpose of a performance appraisal is to clearly communicate to employees how their job performance is perceived by the employer and how it might be improved. Performance appraisals may also be used to express credit and recognition for a job well done as well as to document specific performance weaknesses. Straightforward appraisals are often conducted on at least an annual basis. These appraisals should be in writing and provide for a face-to-face employee review with the appraiser, allowing for feedback and an opportunity for the employee to submit written rebuttal.

Exposure with Performance Appraisal Plans

Superficial or disingenuous performance appraisals lack legitimacy and may result in a legal exposure. This is particularly true if they are used to make an employment decision regarding a member of a protected class. Performance evaluation is subject to external audit in the same manner as any other employment program. Under present court decisions, a rating system that depends on subjective criteria, measuring personality traits rather than behavior or results, is worse than no system at all. When allegations are made that a rating system is discriminatory, the employer must defend the methods used. If they prove to be subjective, the defense becomes difficult. An example of what can happen when subjective appraisals are used is the case of a black engineer employed by General Motors. The plaintiff filed a class action lawsuit alleging that GM was using a discriminatory performance appraisal system. As a result of the appraisal system, there was an adverse impact in the selection of candidates for promotion.[20] Court decisions reinforce the view that the failure to correct faults in a subjective system invites litigation, legal costs, and possible penalties.

Reasons for Failure of Appraisal Systems

Most appraisal systems fail because the rater is not trained to rate *behavior,* and instead rates personal characteristics. Raters may be influenced by their own prejudices, or those of management. Common rater failures include:

1. Rating all performance on one impressive performance or failure incident.
2. Allowing one particular trait that the rater objects to influence the overall rating.
3. Utilizing only extreme ratings, either excellent or unacceptable.
4. Relying on recent events instead of performance for the whole rating period.
5. Avoiding conflict or justification by giving only satisfactory appraisals.
6. Comparing the ratee with self or being influenced by how the performance affected the rater's own situation.
7. Failing to inform the ratee what activity is being appraised, and how it is to be measured.
8. Not rating results or behavior, but instead using subjective factors such as cooperation and attitude.
9. Failing to give proper feedback.

Judicial Review of Performance Appraisals

It took judicial action to force many organizations to examine their performance appraisals and question whether they accurately measured performance on the job. For years the courts have considered performance appraisals to be a legitimate management right and function. However, federal antidiscrimination laws have forced the courts to review this position. In doing so they found that many performance appraisals were subjective in nature.

One of the first appellate courts to scrutinize performance appraisals was the Fifth Circuit in New Orleans. In this case the employer's appraisal methods were found unrelated to performance on the job, but rather to trait characteristics. The court stated that where the appraisal is used to make an employment decision, or an adverse impact is shown, the appraisal methods must be validated by performance.[21] Here, promotions were dependent almost entirely on a favorable recommendation by the immediate supervisor, who used subjective evaluations of job performance as a basis for these recommendations. Subjective evaluations permitted the supervisor to exercise race discrimination in the promotion process. It was clear that evaluations were based on judgments and opinions, with no evidence of identifiable job performance criteria.

Generally speaking, the courts are quick to reject appraisal systems that are subjective and not related to job performance. In another case, the court held that unless written guidelines are used by the raters, or they are otherwise trained in the standardized method of appraisal, the process is invalid.[22] There is little disagreement among the courts that subjective appraisal methods are in violation of Title VII. However, an appraisal method is bound to have some subjectivity. This is recognized by the courts, which have approved some subjective methods in hiring if they are based on objective standards. In one instance a subjective oral interview was given to applicants for an electrician's job. There was also a requirement that the applicant meet a valid objective test standard or have eight years' experience as a journeyman. The court found that the subjective oral interview was not discriminatory, as long as objective criteria of certain experience or skill tests were also used.[23] From the rationale of this case, it would appear that if an objective standard for performance is established, and subjective reasons for failure to meet that performance standard are given, the appraisal method would be valid.

Need to Change Performance Appraisals

If the employer does not validate performance appraisals, the courts will, on a case-by-case basis, do so. In *Allen* v. *City of Mobile*, 466 F.2d 1245 (5th Cir. 1972), cert. denied, 411 U.S. 909 (1973), the court said that the performance rating system was discriminatory and prescribed another performance rating system. However, there is no assurance that the judicially prescribed method of appraisal has any more validity or would serve a more useful purpose for promotion than the employer's system.

Another court followed the *Allen* case, ordering a rating system that would ensure that minorities and nonminorities would be equally graded. The federal district court prescribed the performance appraisal as an alternative to the one that it struck down. However, it was not a validation method that could be applied to other factual situations. A 1990 study by Field and Holley investigated the basis for court rejection of certain performance appraisal systems. They found that the courts consistently rejected appraisal systems as invalid if no specific instructions were given to the raters, appraisals were trait oriented rather than behavior oriented, or job analysis was not used in developing the content of the rating form.[24]

Recommendations for Validating Appraisal Plans

An initial consideration in an employee evaluation system is to agree on its purpose without confounding performance appraisal with pay issue. The objective is to improve employee performance. In the evaluation of a performance appraisal procedure, the first step is to eliminate all criteria based on personality traits. The next step is to determine whether any relationship exists between what the appraisal procedure measures and job performance. Key considerations in a valid performance review include:

1. The level of performance expected of the employee, expressed in quantitative terms to the extent possible, and clearly communicated to the employee
2. Criteria that will determine whether or not the employee met job expectations
3. An audit of the effectiveness of training of those doing the rating
4. Personal conduct as employee meets a standard
5. The use of uniform standards and rating methods

Removing Subjectivity from Appraisal Results

The courts have held that unless performance appraisals are objective and measure performance, they cannot be used to make employment decisions when members of the protected class are involved.[25] A performance appraisal program is objective if it contains the following elements:

1. The rater states what is expected of the employee in the form of job standards, based on assigned responsibilities. The employee must understand what part of the job is being appraised.
2. The rater evaluates and discusses performance (coaches) during the evaluation period. The employee must be told how she or he is doing and not be surprised at appraisal time.
3. Written ratings are supported by specific examples or observations of behavior related to the job. These observations should be made by the rater and be continual.
4. If the rater cannot observe continually, the opinion of others who use the employee's services may be used.
5. The rater appraises results, not effort or personal characteristics. The only proper subject for performance appraisal is productive behavior that produces results.

Steps in Developing a Valid Procedure

1. Rater meets with ratee to discuss:
   a. Job responsibilities
   b. Standards to be met during the rating period
   c. A work plan to achieve and maintain that level
   d. The method used to evaluate performance under the work plan
   e. The standardized form to be used in the evaluation process (see Exhibit 6.3)
   f. How the evaluation results will be used (salary review, for promotion or for training only, etc.)

2. Ratee makes a self-assessment of strengths and weaknesses and what he or she feels is needed to achieve the improvements. This is not communicated to anyone, except that it was done. This can be helpful, but it is not essential.

3. Rater monitors performance during the review period, communicating unacceptable performance, praising superior performance, and modifying the work of the ratee, if necessary. This is an ongoing procedure that communicates the progress toward achieving results to the ratee.

4. Rater states the reason for conclusions on the form and analyzes the ratee performance as to why the expected standards were exceeded or not met. Rater prepares for meeting with ratee.

5. Rater meets with ratee and discusses the evaluation of the ratee's performance and develops a plan for improvement through formal training or on-the-job exposure, if appropriate. (The evaluation should be no surprise to ratee if progress reports were made.)

6. Rater explains to ratee how the report is going to be used, in accord with what was discussed in the meeting at the beginning of the review period.

7. Rater has the next level of supervision review the process. This eliminates the charge of bias, fixes responsibility for compliance, and ensures that rating will be done.

EXHIBIT 7.8 Valid Performance Appraisal Procedure

Suggestion for a Judicially Acceptable Appraisal Plan

The appraisal form should be determined by the job category and the purpose for which the rating is to be used. Exhibit 7.8 shows a suggested procedure that considers all the decisions of the courts, and at the same time would serve to evaluate performance while improving the effectiveness of the ratee.

Performance appraisals have enjoyed extensive application in both public and private employment, but the decisions of the courts place some of these programs in a precarious position. Basically, the objection is that the appraisal does not measure actual job performance. The courts are in complete agreement that, when a member of a protected class is involved, a subjective, nonstandardized system cannot be used as a nondiscriminatory reason for treating one person differently from another. Faulty appraisals contribute to liability when there is an allegation that an antidiscrimination statute has been violated.[26] An appraisal that is defective also contributes to liability in any lawsuit when it is used as basis for an employment decision.

RECORD KEEPING

It is common practice for employers to keep individual records on each employee. These records are commonly called *employee records* or *individual personnel files. Employee records* are defined as records that contain initial application forms, results of physical examinations, interviewer's notations, test scores, periodic appraisals, transfers and promotions, disciplinary actions, releases and rehirings, wages, salaries, taxes paid, contributions, and similar items.[27] It is highly important that everything about the employee be included in individual file. Some attorneys believe that the personnel file is the first line of defense in litigation. The purpose of personnel records is to record information about an employee obtained during the course of employment. The records put the employee on notice that there is documentation of his or her activities while employed. It also permits an audit of whether addresses are up to date, whether beneficiaries are current, and other necessary personal employee data are accurate. Documentation for purposes of discrimination charges, unemployment compensation determination, and arbitration is an essential element of a case.

When considering whether to record or retain a fact, always ask the question, "For what purpose was the fact recorded and is it necessary to retain it?" Important arbitrations, discrimination or harassment complaints, unemployment compensation, and court decisions are often lost because the employer was unable to produce the proper evidence to substantiate a fact. Some practitioners believe that separate subject matter personnel files should be kept for each employee. They suggest a general file, job performance file, medical file, I-9 forms, and a closed file containing all letters of references, records of investigations, or other confidential matters. The justification often given for the separation of files is that sensitive information would not be given to outsiders, and information will not be disclosed inadvertently. Furthermore, the person reviewing the file would not be able to consider irrelevant material that may be damaging in litigation or in other employee relations problems.

The reason given by proponents for keeping everything in one file is the chance that, when segregated, relevant information may be missed; and an employee problem is seldom categorized according to the way the data are filed. Data in one file may not offer a solution to a particular problem unless all the files are reviewed. The ADA specifically requires that medical information be separate from a general file. Most access statutes do not permit employees to review the entire file.

Statutory Requirements to Retain Certain Records

There are statutory requirements stating that an employer must keep records on an individual employee. These requirements often change, so regulations must be periodically reviewed. The antidiscrimination laws, OSHA, IRCA, FLSA, ERISA, HIPPA, and ADA require that relevant information be available for investigation purposes and to ensure the proper administration of the laws.

The Immigration Reform and Control Act of 1986 (**IRCA**) requires employment records to be kept for three years, or one year after termination, whichever is later. The Act imposes a fine up to $1,000 for failure to keep the necessary records. The unique part of the requirement is that the person responsible for keeping the records can be personally liable.[28]

Under the Employee Retirement Income Security Act (**ERISA**) of 1974, records must be kept for not less than six years after the filing date of the documents. When the documents are changed, the six years start over again. Under ERISA, it would be advisable to keep all current records and their respective changes. Regulations promulgated by the agencies responsible for enforcing the antidiscrimination statutes have established record-keeping retention policies. The employer should comply, because the records may become the proof that an employment decision was legally made.

Record retention requirements are also indirectly found in the COBRA.[29] COBRA provides for the right of employees to purchase continued health-care coverage for a period of time between 18 and 36 months following a qualifying event that results in termination of coverage under a group policy. The Health Insurance Portability and Accountability Act (HIPPA) of 1996 serves to enable the bridging of coverage of a plan participant from one plan to another. If COBRA benefits become exhausted, an employee is leaving an HMO service area, the financial limits of a plan are reached, or a person becomes ineligible for coverage, HIPPA provisions enable the possibility of enrollment in a new plan. Other provisions also credit previous active enrollment to overcome exclusion periods for any pre-existing condition impediments in a new plan.

Regulations require that upon termination and/or health-care plan cancellation, the plan administrator (Third Party Administrator or the employer) provide the employee with evidence of participation in their previous plan in the form of a **Certificate of Coverage** for use in the new enrollment.[30] This form is the instrument permitting bridging or providing "**portability**." Application to a subsequent plan may require doing so under a special enrollment provision. Under the HIPPA amendment to ERISA, the plan administrator can be held personally liable up to $100 per day for failure to give notice of the right to be covered, or the court can grant such other relief as it may deem proper. This result is considerable personal liability for the plan administrator.

The HIPPA provisions require that covered entities, health-care providers, health plans, and health-care clearinghouses maintain medical records for six years, Medicare records for five years, and records for two in the event that a patient dies.[31] The legislation requires that the individual is to have access to her or his records and the provider is accountable for any inappropriate disclosure. A single violation may only result in a $100 fine, but violations due to negligence or willful violation without correction can carry fines of up to $50,000 under the Health

Information Technology for Economic and Clinical Health Act (HITECH) amendment of 2009.[32] Many states have adopted more stringent privacy requirements addressing the security of a citizen's personal health information.

Under HIPPA, information users are to assign a Privacy Officer to administer data safeguards, including standard formats for encrytion of electronic transmissions, staff training, and disclosure records. There are authorized releases for public research and law enforcement purposes. Preventive compliance action should include appropriate accountability statements in third-party agreements and routine auditing.

Under Title VII of the Civil Rights Act, job applications, resumes, payroll records, and employee personnel files must be kept for a minimum of six months or until disposition of a pending legal action.[33] Employers of 100 or more employees are required to file the EEO-1 report annually; this gives an inventory of employees by race, ethnic group, disability, sex, job category, and salary. Unions with 100 or more members must file an EEO-3 report, and records must be kept for one year after the report. Private employment agencies have not been subject to the Title VII record keeping or reporting requirement, except in their capacity as employers.

Government contractors, under Executive Order 11246, do not have a specific record-keeping requirement, except to make all their records available for compliance review. Under the Rehabilitation Act of 1973 and CRA 91, contractors and subcontractors must retain complaints or action taken for one year. The same rule applies for contractors under the Vietnam Era Veterans Readjustment Act of 1974.

The Equal Pay Act of 1963[34] requires that employees' records concerning wages, hours of work, and other terms of employment (including exempt-status employees) be kept for two years. Records supporting employment decisions under the act must also be kept for two years. The Age Discrimination in Employment Act of 1967 requires employment records, including the employee's personnel file, to be kept for one year. However, payroll information and information relating to name, address, birth date, and job category must be kept for three years. Under the Fair Labor Standards Act, records must be kept for three years. If a lawsuit is commenced, all relevant records must be retained for the duration of the lawsuit. If a discrimination claim is filed, the records must be maintained until final disposition of the claim.

Record Retention as a Personnel Policy

Proper practice in the areas of discipline, performance appraisals, skills inventories, and so on, requires the human resources practitioner to go beyond what the law requires in the area of personnel record keeping. Which records the employer should maintain is a policy as well as a legal question—except the employer must keep all records pertaining to a charge or a complaint from the date it is filed. The employer should have records to show that company policy and procedures are complying with the law. The employer should audit personnel records at least every three years and destroy irrelevant, immaterial, or damaging records, if not required to keep them. It is also advisable to separate certain records that you are required to keep, noting a destroy date. This policy will give stature to the records you retain, but not subject damaging records to the subpoena process in the event of a lawsuit.[35] Positive human resource administration and space limitations dictate that only those records that are useful should be kept.

Other Statutory Requirements of Disclosure

Records are the property of the employer, but certain statutes require the employer to disclose specific information for certain reasons.[36] This is usually to enable a government regulatory agency to carry out its function of enforcing the law. Under most statutes, the statutory requirement disclosure must be made upon request. The burden is on the party who requests to show that he or she is entitled to the information. Often the disclosure of employee information causes an employee relations problem, so the employer may take the position that it is better to be ordered to disclose than to do it voluntarily.

Under the NLRA, the employer is required to provide certain information. Often, a certified labor organization will request information on an employee or group of employees. The information requested must be relevant to the collective bargaining agreement and must be necessary in order for the union to represent the employee properly. This includes representation in grievances and arbitration as well as collective bargaining. The information requested must concern wages and working conditions and protect the collective bargaining relationship. The NLRB and the courts have given a liberal interpretation to this general principle. However, if the information requested relates to matters not within union jurisdiction, or is of individual concern, it can be rejected.[37]

Another statutory requirement to release limited employee information comes from a regulation promulgated under the authority of OSHA. This statute states that an employer must give access of the records to employees, or their representatives, and to other employees who are exposed to toxic and hazardous substances, when requested.[38] The person requesting the records must show a need and have professional qualifications to interpret the information requested. The regulation requires the medical records on exposure to toxic substances to be kept for 30 years. The employee must be informed, at the time of hiring and each year thereafter, that such records are available.

As in other areas under antidiscrimination laws, if employee information has a disparate impact on the categories of individuals being protected, it is unlawful. The information cannot be used for making an employment decision unless a business necessity can be shown. This does not mean that background investigations are prohibited, but it does mean there must be a nondiscriminatory use and purpose for such information. When a charge is broad and includes several allegations, information must be furnished for all the allegations. If the charge is properly worded, the agency has considerable latitude in seeking information. In this type of charge, the employer has less opportunity to refuse information, and the defense of relevancy must be used with discretion.

Disclosure Rights of Public Employees

Federal employees are protected by the Privacy Act of 1974.[39] The act requires federal agencies to permit employees to examine, copy, correct, or amend employee information in their files. If there is a dispute on the accuracy of the information or what is to be included, an appeal procedure is provided. The act prohibits, with certain exceptions, the disclosure of information to outsiders without written consent of the employee to whom the information pertains. The agency has no obligation to inform the employee that the information exists, except to publish it annually in the *Federal Register*.

Almost all states have enacted comprehensive privacy acts for the public sector. Other state legislatures have not gone quite as far as a comprehensive plan, but have imposed certain restrictions on disclosing employee information in the public sector.

Although the Federal Fair Credit Reporting Act[40] regulates the activities of consumer reporting agencies, it also affects the disclosure of information by the employer, when the employer engages a consumer agency to make an investigation. The employer, when using a consumer agency, must inform the employee that an investigation is being made as to his or her character, general reputation, personal characteristics, and mode of hiring. If the employee so requests, the employer must provide a complete disclosure of the nature and scope of the investigation.

The Freedom of Information Act (FOIA) states that where a federal agency maintains a system of records, on request, any individual or representative may gain access to that record if the proper authorization is shown by the representative.[41] The FOIA further provides that an individual or representative may request amendment to the record; if refused, adversary proceedings to determine the facts are triggered. Such proceedings are subject to judicial review.

The stated purpose of the Freedom of Information Act is to require the information to be released, and to inform the public; it is not for the purpose of benefiting the litigants in a lawsuit. The rules and regulations incompliance with this purpose are promulgated with emphasis on disclosing information to the public.

There are exceptions under the access act. The federal agency may promulgate challengeable rules if revealing personnel records will obstruct the agency's enforcement function. If the right of disclosure is doubtful, the courts normally rule in favor of disclosure. Medical records are exempted under FOIA, but under certain conditions they can be revealed under Section 552(a) of the act.

CASE 7.1

Maternity Leave

Ann Cassidy had worked in the mortgage department at Republic Bank for a little over two years. She was expecting her first baby and planned to be out on maternity leave after having the baby in late October or early November of 2009. She planned on using some of her vacation and sick time to be paid for a portion of her leave and to take FMLA leave for the remainder. Cassidy's supervisor, Linda Lopez, supported this plan and had already planned for and scheduled the mortgage department to accommodate Cassidy's proposed leave.

The bank employs 50 people and uses a rolling year for purposes of the FMLA. Cassidy was a full time employee and had worked 1,950 hours in the past year. She proposed to take 12 weeks of leave. However, just before she took her leave, Cassidy noticed in the Employee Handbook that the definition of a "year" for FMLA was not specified. She assumed that it was a calendar year since the bank followed a calendar year for all of its fiscal calculations. She then asked her supervisor if she could take a few additional weeks of FMLA leave into 2010. Lopez agreed to let Cassidy take a total of 18 weeks of FMLA time, a portion in 2009 and the remainder in 2010. However, the HR Vice President rejected this request as being contrary to bank policy and refused to make an exception in Cassidy's case. She noted that past FMLA leave for other employees had always been on a rolling year basis.

Can the bank accommodate Cassidy's request? Should it? Why or why not? ▨

CASE 7.2

New Employee Communication

A family of entrepreneurs owns a local convenience store, a tire store, and two restaurants. The manager of each of these stores enjoys his or her independence and latitude in decision making. Finance and accounting systems are relatively standard but other procedures vary. Each unit is considered a profit-making (or not) enterprise. A matriarch/CEO who visits the businesses on occasion and is the final authority on all matters of policy and procedure provides oversight for all of the locations.

The CEO learned of a successful lawsuit by an employee of another company in which an employee handbook played a role. She hired a personnel service firm to survey the new hire materials used in the family businesses to ensure no such threat existed in her group of enterprises.

What are the common provisions that should be expressed and those to be avoided in new hire materials and meetings?

Should the employer have a common handbook for all of its enterprises? ▨

CASE 7.3

Expensive Oversight

Gwen had worked for the city for 18 years before she developed an irregular heart beat. She took medical leave for several weeks and was released to return to work by her doctor. Instead, Gwen chose to retire at age 53 and was honored at a retirement luncheon. The city manager called the payroll services firm and left a message to remove Gwen from the payroll.

Three months later Gwen's husband called the city manager very upset. He told the manager that he had to take Gwen to the hospital on Saturday night. The couple had been trying for several hours to be admitted to the hospital when Gwen experienced serious heart failure and was placed in intensive care. The Admitting Office told Gwen that she had no insurance coverage, which had elevated her problem.

What might result from an investigation of this problem? Did the city fail to provide a required notification? What are the likely consequences? ■

CASE 7.4

Performance Evaluation

During the recent economic downturn, an employer implemented several cost-cutting measures. One of these cost-cutting activities involved reducing employee headcount. Each time a reduction was needed, the managers were asked to evaluate the employees on their team. This was referred to as a "top grading exercise." The company decided to keep top performers regardless of their current job function. If an employee was a top performer, but her or his job was no longer necessary, the employee would be able to remain employed, but might be required to perform a new role within the department or transfer to another department.

It was easy to identify the poor performers the first few times the exercise was performed. However, it became more and more difficult each time. At the conclusion of each top grading exercise, the Human Resource department, the managers, and attorneys would review the list to ensure there were no potential legal issues. The assessment was done at group level and an individual level. The individual level assessment would compare each person on the reduction in force list to their peer group.

The employee management selected during the current reduction in force 60-year-old Kathleen, a woman who had worked for the company for approximately 27 years and had been demoted for poor performance approximately 6 years ago. She could no longer handle the job requirements after an ERP implementation. She was transferred into the Accounts Payable department as a clerk. However, her computer skills did not allow her to perform the same tasks as the other clerks. As a result, Kathleen was assigned the task of opening and sorting the mail and matching invoices. She acted more as an administrative assistant to the accounts payable department than an actual clerk.

The company has an annual evaluation of all employees in addition to the plan just described. Employees are evaluated on a standardized 5-point "Likert-type" evaluation scale. Kathleen's last evaluation was "meets expectations," numerically a 3 on the 5-point scale. The evaluation was conducted based on her meeting the expectation of opening and sorting the mail, not on entering invoices and resolving issues. Kathleen did not necessarily do a poor job; however, her very limited skills restricted the tasks she could perform. In addition, she was not efficient and would not make an effort to take on additional work, even though she was not busy for the entire day. A "meets expectations" was generous grading for Kathleen, as she was not efficient and would often prolong certain tasks to fill up her day.

What potential exposures does the company risk if it terminates Kathleen as a result of the top grading evaluation?

Does the annual evaluation system potentially compromise the top grading evaluation? Explain. ■

Summary

This chapter consolidates and reviews an often-underappreciated aspect of human resource law. The federal government mandates record keeping about employees. Information security demands, as well as communications to employees about imposed federal policy and benefit plan notices, are ever increasing the obligations and liabilities of employers. For example, HIPAA requires a medical records officer in those firms dealing with personnel health files. Hard copy records need security provisions and access control, and vulnerability is compounded with heavily developed electronic databases.

Courts and state statutes have imposed extensive employee education requirements concerning harassment, and the primary responsibility for FMLA leave communication and administration rests on employers. These requirements implicate significant staff work responsibility and often result in contracts with third-party administrators. Normal employee communications represent legal risks. The chapter specifically addresses the common vulnerabilities in employee handbooks such as unintended commitments and compromises of an at-will employment condition. It also considers how carefully selected content and disclaimers can prevent lawsuits following employee terminations.

Key Terms

COBRA(Consolidated Omnibus Budget Reconciliation Act)   185
FMLA (Family Medical Leave Act)   185
WARN (Worker Adjustment Retraining and Notification Act)   187
harassment   187
negligent training   188
hostile environment   188
disclaimers   196
zero tolerance policies   198
IRCA (Immigration Reform and Control Act)   202
ERISA (Employee Retirement Income Security Act)   202
Certificate of Coverage   203
portability   203
medical records officer   209

Questions for Discussion

1. What types of communications to employees does the federal government require of employers?
2. Discuss desirable as opposed to undesirable handbook content.
3. Identify and discuss the various functions of handbooks from the employer's perspective.
4. Under what circumstances have the courts invalidated employee performance appraisals?
5. Identify three employer policies that should be published and widely distributed.
6. What two policies does the federal government require to be published?

7. Identify handbook content that can help prevent legal exposure.
8. Identify handbook content that might encourage adverse legal actions.
9. What steps should an employer follow in a harassment investigation?
10. What requirement does the employer have under federal law when it anticipates a major layoff of employees?
11. Identify four disclaimers or caveats utilized both in handbooks and on application forms.
12. Identify at least four federal posters that are required to be placed prominently in the workplace where employees can read them.

Notes to Chapter 7

1. *Crotty* v. *Dakotacare Administrative Services, Inc.,* No. 05-3798 (8th Cir. 2006).
2. *Alcorn* v. *Keller Industries, Inc.,* 27 F.3d 386 (9th Cir. 1994).
3. This does not apply to the job security of the employee.
4. Me. Rev. Stat. Ann. Tit. 26 § 807(3) requires employers of 15 or more to conduct harassment training for all new employees; Vermont "recommends training and the range of consequences for harassment.

5. See also commissions, laws, or regulations in Connecticut, Rhode Island, Texas, Colorado, Florida, and Vermont.
6. A good discussion of negligent training is found in J. Fenton, W. Ruud, and J. Kimbell,

"Negligent training suits: A recent entry into the corporate negligence arena," *Labor Law Journal,* (June 1991).

7. R. Kearney, "The unintended hostile environment: Mapping the limits of sexual harassment law," *Berkeley Journal of Employment and Labor Law,* 25, no. 1 (2004): 87–127.

8. *Baker* v. *Weyerhaeuser Co.,* 903 F.2d 1342 (9th Cir. 1991). Also *Spicer* v. *Virginia,* 66 F.2d 705 (4th Cir. 1995).

9. *Guess* v. *Bethlehem Steel,* 913 F.2d 463 (7th Cir. 1990).

10. Burtch, "Risks in interviewing the sexual harassment client," *American Journal of Trial Advocacy,* 17 (1996): 56.

11. See *Neville* v. *Taft Broadcasting Co.,* 42 FEP Cases 1314 (W.D.N.Y. 1987) (one sexual advance insufficient).

12. V. E. Hauck and T. Pearce, "Sexual harassment and arbitration," *Labor Law Journal,* 43 (January 1992): 31, discusses arbitration in sexual harassment cases.

13. *Radtke* v. *Everett,* 471 N.W.2d 666 (Mich. 1991); also *Kay* v. *Peter Motor Co.,* 483 N.W.2d 481 (Minn. App. 1992).

14. *Horkan* v. *U.S. Postal Service* EEO Appeal No. 1976837 (2000).

15. See also *EEOC* v. *Mt. Vermon Mills,* 58 FEP Cases 73 (BNA) [D.Ga. 1992], otherwise reported only in Westlaw.

16. See W. Hartsfield, *How to Write Your Employee Handbook.* Madison, CT: Business & Legal Reports, Inc., 1991. Section 110–1104.

17. *Crain Industries Inc.* v. *Cass,* 810 S.W.2d 910 (Ark. S.Ct. 1991).

18. *McDonald* v. *Mobil Coal Producing, Inc.,* 820 P.2d 986 (Wyo.1991).

19. Federal courts agree that "an employee handbook or other policy statement creates enforceable contractual rights if the traditional requirements for contract formation are present." *Duldulao* v. *Mary of Nazerath Hospital Center* 115 Ill. 2d 482 (1987). Also *Hohmeier* v. *Leyden Community H.S. District 212,* 954 F.2d 451 (7th Cir. 1992).

20. This case was settled out of court.

21. *Rowe* v. *General Motors,* 457 F.2d 348 (5th Cir. 1972).

22. In *Borer* v. *Hanes Corp.,* 715 F.2d 213 (5th Cir. 1985), the court found objective standards and dismissed an age discrimination charge.

23. *Hamilton* v. *General Motors Corp.,* 606 F.2d 576 (5th Cir. 1979).

24. Cited in D. Rosen, "Appraisals can make or break your court case," *Personnel Journal,* 71, no. 11 (November 1992).

25. *EEOC* v. *Mississippi State Tax Commission,* 873 F.2d 97, 99 (5th Cir. 1989).

26. *Norris* v. *Hartmax Specialty Stores,* 913 F.2d 253 (9th Cir. 1990).

27. Dale Yoder, *Personnel Management in Industrial Relations,* 6th ed. (Englewood Cliffs, NJ: Prentice Hall, 1970).

28. See H. Frye and H. Klasko, "Immigration compliance Guide (1991). Bureau of Immigration and Naturalization," 425 I St. N.W., Washington DC 20536.

29. 29 U.S.C. §§ 1161–68.

30. 701(e); 29 CFR 2590.701–705.

31. Public Law 104–191.

32. M. Halloway and E. Fensbolt, "HITECH: HIPPA gets a facelift," *Benefits Law Journal,* 22, no. 2 (Autumn 2009): 88.

33. *Capello* v. *FMC Corp.,* 50 FEP Cases (BNA) 1157.

34. 29 U.S.C. 206 et al.

35. See *Ramsey* v. *American Filter Co.,* 772 F.2d 1303 (7th Cir. 1985), where damaging notations on the applicant form cost the employer $92,500.

36. Under *University of Pennsylvania* v. *EEOC,* 850 F.2d 969 (3rd Cir. 1988), regulatory agencies have broad subpoena powers.

37. *NLRB* v. *Holyduke Water Power Co.,* 788 F.2d 49 (1st Cir. 1985).

38. 29 CFR Part 1910.20 and 29 CFR Part 1913.10.

39. U.S.C. § 552(a), 5 CFR 297.101.

40. 15 U.S.C. § 1681 et seq.

41. 5 U.S.C. § 552(a)(1) (FOIA).

42. J. Fenton, Jr., "Negligent hiring and retention doctrine adds to human resource woes," *Personnel Journal,* 69 (April 1990): 62–73; also *Garcia* v. *Duffy,* 492 So.2d 435 (Fla. App. 2nd Dist. 1986) for a good discussion of a negligent hiring cause of action.

43. Negligent hiring and retention is a common law action. See Restatement of Torts Section 213 (1958).

44. *Harvey Freeman & Sons* v. *Stanley,* 384 S.E.2d 682 (Ga. App. 1989).

45. *Abbot* v. *Payne,* 457 So.2d 1156 (Fla. 1984).

46. *Tallahassee Furniture Co.* v. *Harrison,* 582 So.2d 744 (Fla. App. 1st Dist. 1991).

47. *Slaton* v. *B&B Gulf Service Center,* 344 S.E.2d 512 (Ga. App. 1986).

48. *Pittard* v. *Four Seasons Motor Inn,* 688 P.2d 333 (N.M. App. 1984).

49. "Negligent referral: A potential theory for employer liability," *Southern California Law Review,* 64 (1991): 1645; also A. Ryan and M. Lasek, "Negligent hiring and defamation," *Personnel Psychology,* 44 (Summer 1991): 293–391.

50. In *Welch Mfg. Co.* v. *Pinkerton's,* 474 A.2d 436 (R.I. 1984), the court held that a police record and contacting two former employers was not enough. In *Burch* v. *A&G Associates,* 333 N.W.2d 140 (1983), the court said that a taxicab company has a higher duty to investigate than other employers. However, in *Evans* v. *Morsell,* 95 A.2d 480 (Md. 1978), the court said there was very little duty to check on a bartender. See also *Kassman* v. *Busfield Enterprise, Inc.,* 639 P.2d 353 (1981).

51. For further reading, see R. Jacobs, "Defamation and negligence in the workplace," *Labor Law Review* (September 1989): 52.

52. For a good discussion on negligent hiring and retention, see W. J. Woska, "Negligent employment practices," *Labor Law Journal,* 42 (September 1991): 605; also *Hutchinson* v. *McDonald's Corp.,* 110 S.Ct. 57 (1989).

53. D. Gregory, "Reducing risk in negligent hiring," *Employee Relations Law Journal* (September 1988): 34.

54. A good discussion of negligent training to relieve exposure is J. Fenton, William Ruud, and J. Kimbell, "Negligent training suits: A recent entry into the corporate employment negligence arena," *Labor Law Journal,* 42 (June 1991): 351.

55. R. L. Lansing, "Training new employees," *Supervision Management* (January 1989): 16–20.

CHAPTER 8

Collective Bargaining in the Private Sector

CHAPTER OUTLINE

Discontent with the NLRA

Mutual Obligation to Bargain in
    Good Faith

Administration and Enforcement
    of Labor Agreements

Union Duty of Fair Representation

Use of Economic Weapons: Strikes and
    Lockouts

Use of Arbitration in Dispute
    Resolution

Pay Equity and Collective Bargaining

P rivate-sector collective bargaining in the United States began with the passage in
1935 of the Wagner Act or National Labor Relations Act (amended in 1947 by the
Taft-Hartley Act and 1959 by the Landrum-Griffin Act). This act provided protection to private-sector employees to form and join labor organizations for the purpose of
engaging in collective bargaining over terms and conditions of employment. A basic
premise of the original legislation was to create a balance in **bargaining power** between
employers and employees.

Negotiations history since 1935 has amply demonstrated that the original goal of
the Wagner Act to equalize bargaining power between employers and employees was
not realized and continued to be a subject of expressed concern to the U.S. Congress in
1947 when it passed the Taft-Hartley Act. The stated purpose of the Taft-Hartley Act was

to provide orderly and peaceful procedures for preventing the interference by
either (employees or employers) with the legitimate rights of the other.

The passage of the Landrum-Griffin Act in 1959 was not intended to further balance
relative bargaining power between employers and labor organizations. It was specifically passed to eliminate certain corrupt practices of identified unions and create a Bill

of Rights for union members to guarantee all members equal rights of participation in internal union affairs.

To administer the NLRA's mandated secret elections to determine an exclusive representative and enforce the unfair labor practices listed by the act, an independent agency was created: the National Labor Relations Board (NLRB).

DISCONTENT WITH THE NLRA

The National Labor Relations Act (NLRA) was born in an era of economic turmoil. Its original passage was hotly contested legislation, as were its modifications in 1947 and 1959. Attempts to amend the act in 1976 died in a senate filibuster. Renewed demands for change in the statute developed great strength prior to, and immediately after, the presidential election in 2008. These demands concentrated on three central issues and gained national prominence as the economy sank into recession in the later part of 2008:

1. A desire by the union movement to counter the significant decrease in private-sector union membership experienced since 1970, resulting in only approximately 8 percent of the private-sector workforce being unionized in 2008.
2. Declining job opportunities available for American workers allegedly due to rapid increases, particularly in the 1990s, of free trade agreements.
3. Allegations by unions of increasing outsourcing of American jobs by employers seeking lower cost labor in low-wage countries.

MUTUAL OBLIGATION TO BARGAIN IN GOOD FAITH

The NLRA states that both employers and unions must bargain in **good faith** and that failure to do so is an unfair labor practice.

Alleged violations must be submitted to the NLRB for investigation and possible prosecution. Violations are difficult to prove, however, as there are few specific behaviors other than an outright refusal to meet and negotiate at reasonable times and places or a refusal to negotiate with regard to a subject considered by the NLRB to be a "mandatory subject of bargaining," which triggers a ruling by the NLRB of bad faith bargaining.

A common allegation of bad faith bargaining historically has been one of "surface bargaining."[1] This allegation centers not on the fact that one party refuses to meet and negotiate but rather generally alleges that although a party is willing to meet at reasonable times and places, it refuses to engage in substantive bargaining in good faith with intent to reach an agreement.[2] Such allegations generally fail as the NLRB has repeatedly noted that a party need not agree to proposals or make a concession to prove good faith bargaining.

Only a highly skilled negotiator has the ability give nothing or very little and not be charged with bad faith bargaining or accused of surface bargaining. Often, there is a very fine line between bad faith bargaining and simply refusing to agree in part or at all to a proposal. There is no legal definition of bad faith bargaining or good faith bargaining because the NLRB relies on a case by case basis for its decisions.[3] The board evaluates the total conduct of the parties at the bargaining table as the source for its decisions, as do courts in their review of the board's decisions on review. When the NLRB does find that a complaint from a party of bad faith bargaining is valid, it will issue a cease and desist order against the offending party. Such order does not, however, generally represent a significant problem for the party at fault. The order merely causes a cessation of a given strategy by the offending party.

A refusal by a party to bargain about certain subjects can bring into question whether the subject involved is considered by the NLRB a "mandatory," "permissive," or "illegal" subject of bargaining.[4] *Mandatory* bargaining subjects are wages, hours, and terms and conditions of employment. A refusal to bargain over these subjects is a per se violation of the act. *Permissive* subjects are virtually any subject not defined as an illegal or prohibited subject of bargaining. *Illegal* subjects include such issues as a closed shop or issues that would cause a violation of the federal Fair Labor Standards Act or equal opportunity legislation. The NLRB can order a party to negotiate about a mandatory subject or order the cessation of an attempt to bargain about an illegal subject. It cannot, however, order a party to bargain about a permissive subject.

Bad Faith Bargaining

If a union is certified by the board, the employer is required by law to deal exclusively with that union as a bargaining agent for the employees. Sometimes an employer may desire to reward a superior employee with a bonus or wages above the contract rate. If this is done without the union's consent, it is bad faith bargaining. In plain language, the rule is that no side deals are permitted with union-represented employees. Other conduct that supports a strong inference of bad faith bargaining includes failing to give management representatives sufficient authority to bind the employer, refusal to sign an agreement already reached, withdrawal of concessions previously granted, and delaying tactics. One of the problems of dealing with the NLRB in bad faith bargaining cases is that the only remedy for the unfair labor practice is a cease-and-desist order, not a signficant liability for the employer found guilty of bad faith bargaining. The board has created stronger remedies if the employer is engaged in flagrant bad faith bargaining. In one instance, the union was seeking a union shop clause.[5] The board, in an attempt to remedy the violation, ordered the company to include a union

shop provision in the agreement. On appeal, the Supreme Court said that such action was beyond the intent and scope of the act. Congress never intended to give the board power to compel a union or the employer to agree on any contract provision.[6]

Bad faith or surface bargaining charges usually come before the NLRB when the union does not want to **strike** but the company will not accede to its demands.[7] The union hopes to force the company to bargain by filing an unfair labor practice charge.[8] Union leadership strategizes that the employees will be more willing to strike or that the employer will accede to a few more demands if it is found guilty of bargaining in bad faith.

Bargaining over Permissive Subjects and the Application of Bargaining Power

From a practical standpoint, whether a party will or will not negotiate about a permissive subject will depend on the relative bargaining power of the parties. The many years of collective bargaining history both before and after the passage of the NLRA have clearly shown that the results of collective bargaining can be explained by the measured relative bargaining power of the parties—the relative cost of agreement versus disagreement.[9] History also shows that the relative power of the parties is not static. It changes continually over time based on a number of factors—economic, political, social, technological, legal, and geopolitical. Whether or not a party will negotiate over a permissive subject and the results of the bargaining on a permissive subject as well as on **mandatory subjects** will be determined by the relative bargaining power of the parties and their willingness to exercise it in the short run.

The exercise of bargaining power in the short or intermediate run can provide a labor organization or employer significant benefits until the identified factors change sufficiently to diminish, cancel, or modify the bargaining power. From a union standpoint, the U.S. automobile industry is an example of bargaining power diminished. From 1950 to the mid-1980s, the "big three" companies—General Motors, Ford, and Chrysler—built and maintained dominance in the U.S. automobile market. The United Auto Workers (UAW) union was able to utilize its perceived bargaining power to wrest from the companies an enviable level of wages and benefits.[10] However, a combination of factors substantially destroyed that perceived bargaining power and forced a significant decline in the level of wages and benefits within a period of less than one year in 2008 and 2009. A large part of the decline in the UAW's bargaining power stemmed from its inability to organize the workers at the plants built and operated in the southern United States by foreign automakers, which operated with substantially lower labor costs than the organized "Big Three." This economic disability of the Big Three was exacerbated by the economic recession of 2008–2009, which threatened them with bankruptcy and necessitated federal money subsidies to General Motors and Chrysler.[11] The federal money was given with strings attached. The strings forced the companies and the UAW to make significant concessions so as to enable the companies, in the government's opinion, to become competitive on their own.

A common subject of discussion by observers of collective bargaining in the United States in recent years has been the rapid decrease in unionized jobs due in part to American companies outsourcing jobs to other countries with lower production/servicing costs. Such outsourcing of jobs has increased the bargaining power of many U.S. employers, as it creates fear on the part of American workers that if their demand for increases in wages and benefits is strongly pursued, the company may outsource their jobs to low cost countries. Such outsourcing, combined with employer

resistance to organization accounts, is at least in part responsible for the decline in the union density of the private-sector workforce to approximately 8 percent.

To combat this continuing decline in the percentage of the organized workforce from 1975 through 2009, unions promoted legislation that would ease their ability to organize new members. Most of this proposed legislation was rejected by Congress. Accordingly, unions concentrated their efforts on the National Labor Relations Board by filing complaints alleging unfair labor practices on the part of employers during organizing drives.

However, beginning in 2008, the unions made a significant effort to advance the Employee Free Choice Act (EFCA). This proposed legislation, commonly known as EFCA, would amend the NLRA so as to permit a union to by-pass secret ballot elections and certify them as exclusive representatives based solely on signed authorization cards. Under this proposal, a union would need only to show that a 60 percent majority of potential bargaining unit members had signed authorization cards requesting union recognition. Although employers, through their organizations, almost uniformly opposed this proposed legislation, unions will be compelled to continue their efforts to make progress on such legislation. This is especially true given the report in early 2010 issued by the federal Bureau of Labor Statistics indicating that private-sector union employment hit a record low in 2009 of 7.2 percent—down from 7.6 percent in 2008. By contrast, government employment unionization rose from 36.8 percent 2008 to 37.4 percent in 2009.

THE EXTENT OF THE BARGAINING PROCESS

The NLRB has defined mandatory, permissive, and illegal subjects of bargaining. However, employers are regularly faced with economic and marketing decisions that will impact their production plans, both in volume and location, during the life of their labor agreements. The decisions made bring into question whether to close or phase out some of their physical facilities, to subcontract some work performed by their employees, to cease the provision of a benefit not negotiated but voluntarily provided, or to cease some operations in the United States and open operations in another country. The decisions made often raise the issue of whether an employer can unilaterally change working conditions that will have substantial impact on employees in subject areas where the labor agreement is silent.

The frequency of such issues has historically caused unions to file complaints with the NLRB, demanding the board to force employers to bargain about decisions that will have a significant impact on employees' jobs and terms and conditions of employment. The remedies sought attempt to either block the employer's implementation of such decisions or to provide restitution to employees after the employer's actions. The normal reaction of employers against a union unfair labor practice charge designed either to prevent an employer action, or to compensate employees for an employer action, was that they had fulfilled their legal duty to bargain in good faith. Therefore, employers were free to exercise their management rights to do what they believed they needed to do to operate their enterprise with regard to subjects in the area where the labor agreement was silent.

As a result, the NLRB determined to institute definitive guidelines to resolve such questions. The basic procedure used by the board was to examine the question of whether the action of the employer resulted in an economic impact on the employees. If the answer to that question was yes, the employer action potentially required negotiations. A frequently cited example is the subject of **subcontracting** of work. Employers often find that another

employer or an independent contractor can perform certain required work at lower cost or more expeditiously than its unionized workforce. When an employer took such action and placed the employees performing the work on layoff, the action was challenged by the union before the NLRB. The trial examiner and the NLRB agreed that the decision by the company to subcontract was an economic one and not based on union animus. The decision held, however, that the company had the obligation to bargain the decision. The Court agreed and said the subject of subcontracting was a mandatory subject of bargaining and ordered back pay for the employees.[12] Had no layoffs of employees been involved in the subcontracting, no mandatory discussion would have been ordered.

The Court's decision in *Fiberboard* v. *NLRB*, 379 U.S. 203 (1964), consisted of a three-part analysis:

1. The subcontracting of work performed by employees fell within the literal meaning of the language of the NLRA citing "terms and conditions of employment."
2. Finding subcontracting a mandatory subject of bargaining provides substantiveness to the purposes of the NLRA by "bringing a problem of vital concern to labor and management within the framework established by Congress as most conducive to industrial peace."
3. Other employers in the same industry have considered subcontracting as a part of the established network of mandatory subjects of bargaining.

Justice Potter Stewart, in concurrence, indicated that subjects that "lie at the core of entrepreneurial control" and decisions about "the commitment of investment capital and the basic scope of the enterprise" are not mandatory subjects of bargaining.

Essentially, the landmark *Fiberboard* decision outlined the framework for determining mandatory subjects versus management rights (permissive) subjects. Under this framework, the Court indicated that management decisions that lay at the heart of the viability and continuance of the enterprise were exempt from the obligation to bargain even though such decisions significantly impacted the terms and conditions of employees. This economic impact rule is not universally followed, however. If the NLRB believes that the subject has been traditionally considered a "management prerogative," a unilateral action having impact on employees may not be challenged by the NLRB even if a union complaint is filed. When a company, for economic reasons, closed part of its operation, the Court held that the employer was required only to bargain the effect of the decision and not the decision itself.[13] The Court reasoned that the economic burden placed on the employer in continuing the operation outweighed a benefit gained over labor management relations by the bargaining process. However, such action would be a violation of the Worker Adjustment and Retraining (WARN) Act. Under the Worker Adjustment and Retraining Act (WARN, 29 USC. Sect. 2101 et. seq), the employer must give 60 days' notice to employees and governmental agencies before closing the plant and laying off employees.

The board extended the balancing test analysis to a situation where the employer would transfer or relocate bargaining unit work to a nonunion facility during the term of the contract. The board held that this was not unlawful if the employer satisfied the obligation to bargain under the contract (the contract was silent on the issue). If the parties were bargaining over the relocation, the only requirement before relocating was that the parties had to be at an impasse in bargaining before the employer could relocate. But, when a company subsidized in-plant food services by an independent caterer, the court held the company must bargain over prices. The court affirmed the board's position that food services are "terms and conditions of employment" under Section 8(d) of the act. If the employer had not subsidized the food services, it would probably not have had to bargain over prices. A subsidy is a benefit to the employees, and price affects the amount of the subsidy; therefore, it is a working condition.[14]

Another frequent issue is in the benefit area, such as Christmas bonuses or turkeys given at Thanksgiving or Christmastime. This situation arises when the company has a profitable year and gives a Christmas present to the employees (turkey, ham, fruit). Next year profits are down, so the firm decides not to gift the employees. The general rule in this case is that if the benefits are intermittently given with no consistency, they are considered gifts. If they are unilaterally skipped after consistently being given, regardless of conditions, the courts reason that they are compensation that must be bargained over.[15] If turkeys and hams were discontinued without bargaining with the union, the board held that they were too minimal to be considered wages. In other cases, benefits are not determined minimal, depending on their monetary value.[16]

Whether a particular subject is bargainable or not is important to the parties. For this reason, the NLRB and the courts continue to hear a reasonable number of these cases. The company does not have to agree that a subject is bargainable, but the union can legally strike over a bargainable demand. Once the employer consistently grants a benefit such as a Christmas bonus, it may not be able to stop the benefit. Although this additional compensation was not bargained for by the union, the union can bargain over whether or not it must be continued.[17]

ADMINISTRATION AND ENFORCEMENT OF LABOR AGREEMENTS

After an agreement is negotiated, employers have accepted that they are compelled to comply with the **grievance** and **arbitration** procedure in the contract. However, they have maintained the view they should be free to make unilateral decisions in subject areas where they made no agreements and they had bargained in good faith over the mandatory subjects of bargaining. Unions fundamentally disagree with this concept. Unions believe that employees are the critical element to the success of any enterprise and accordingly should be involved in any employer decision involving employees' continued employment and their terms and conditions of employment broadly defined.

The NLRB, the courts, and the arbitrators in grievance decisions[18] have continually attempted to find a viable balance between these conflicting philosophies. In 1960, three cases, known collectively as the "Steelworkers Trilogy," were heard by the Supreme Court.[19] In all three cases, the issue was whether the company had to arbitrate an issue not covered directly in the labor agreement. The Supreme Court held that a labor agreement cannot cover every situation, but that the employee has certain rights not specifically stated in the agreement by virtue of the employer–employee relationship. This became known as the *common-law-of-the-shop* theory. This was expanded by arbitrators into the **past practice** rule of labor agreements. This rule usually applies in arbitration cases where the agreement is silent concerning a particular practice. Arbitrators have also ruled that the prior practice of the parties can be used as a guide to interpret intent when contract language is ambiguous.

Past Practice

The rule followed by most arbitrators is that a past practice is a part of the contract unless the contract clearly states otherwise.[20] The courts have continued to follow the Steelworkers Trilogy cases and have said that a past practice is an integral part of the contract.[21] The past practice concept has been followed into nonunion situations. In discrimination cases, the court or agency looks to past practice to

determine whether members of the protected class are treated differently.

The definition of a *binding past practice* has generally been defined as a practice that has been in existence for a reasonably long time; has occurred frequently as a clear, consistent, and accepted way to deal with a recurring situation in the work place; and is known and accepted by both union and management. Some arbitrators will require the union to demonstrate that they have been damaged by the change or cessation of the practice.

Changing a Past Practice

The process for the change of an existing past practice has become routine. The party desiring a change must communicate the desire to change a described past practice to the other party together with a statement of a willingness to bargain about the desired change. The reason for the desire for change should be communicated along with the anticipated effects of the change on both parties. If the desired change involves a change in the existing labor agreement, the new or replacement language should be cited. If no agreement is reached through negotiations, the party desiring the change should wait until negotiations for a new agreement begins.

Discrimination Because of Union Activity

It is unlawful to discriminate against employees because of their union membership or support of a union attempting to organize. Allegations of discrimination based on anti-union animus, unlike other discrimination claims, are handled exclusively as Unfair Labor Practice charges by the National Labor Relations Board. The board has the remedial authority to reinstate workers with back pay if it finds that a discharge was due to activity protected by the National Labor Relations Act. Decisions of the NLRB may be appealed to the federal courts.

UNION DUTY OF FAIR REPRESENTATION

The Supreme Court in *Steele* v. *Louisville & N R. Co.*, 323 U.S. 192 (1944), determined that a union had a concomitant obligation to its right of exclusive representation granted by the NLRA. This obligation is to fairly represent all members of its bargaining units. The Court ruled that a union's **duty of fair representation** applied to every action a union took in dealing with an employer in negotiations, grievance processing, its operation of an exclusive hiring hall, and its enforcement of union security provisions in the labor agreement. In the years since 1944, the courts have adopted a somewhat deferential attitude in examining unions' decisions challenged as a breach of their duty of fair representation. They have taken into consideration the fact that unions operate on a majority vote mandate as a matter of practicality and survival. Unions must make compromises in their negotiations and grievance settlement processes that inevitably favor some groups or individuals over others to attain an overall benefit of the majority of unit members. Thus, the courts have consistently ruled that a union breaches its duty of fair representation only when it acts arbitrarily, in bad faith, or discriminatorily. Therefore, the courts generally have supported union decisions when they have perceived that such decisions were based on reason and practicality even when the court finds the decision to be wrong. Representative of this court tolerance can be found the *O'Neil* case cited earlier.[22] Unions have been less fearful of an unfair representation challenge from a bargaining unit member since the *O'Neil* case.

The courts' grants of latitude in challenges by unit members of a union's duty do not extend to instances where the union has been found to fail to represent all of the interests of unit members impartially. A union may therefore refuse to file or process a grievance for a number of reasons as long as the union believes the reasons are valid. It cannot, however, refuse to process a meritorious grievance because of hostility or indifference toward a unit member, because of a member's political action within the union, or because the grievant is a non-union member.

The employer must be aware that for an employee to successfully file a fair representation lawsuit against the union he or she must also file a lawsuit against the company. Typically, the employee will allege wrongful discharge or collusion with the union on the part of the company. Both company and union can wind up together at the defendant's table in court. For this reason, if for no other, the employer has an interest in preventing fair representation actions and avoiding exposure.

Employee Rights under the Weingarten Doctrine

The court in *NLRB* v. *J. Weingarten, Inc.*, 420 U.S. 251 (1975), enforced the rights of employees as provided by Section 7 of the NLRA. The court concluded that the employee who reasonably believes an investigatory interview will result in disciplinary action is seeking "aid and protection" against a perceived threat to his or her employment security. According to the Supreme Court, four conditions must exist for the **Weingarten** Doctrine to apply:

1. The employee must request a representative. Employee silence is a waiver.[23]
2. The employee's right to request representation as a condition of participation in an interview is limited to where the employee reasonably believes the investigation will result in some kind of disciplinary action. (This would include a mere warning.)
3. The exercise of the right may not interfere with legitimate employer prerogatives. This means that management's

investigative process can't be interfered with. Management determines the rules of the interview process but must permit a representative to be present.[24]

4. The employer has no duty to bargain with the representative who is attending the interview. However, the representative has the right to participate in the interview. The employee may consult with his or her representative prior to and during the meeting.[25]

Litigation over whether the doctrine applies is a useless exercise. The same result can be obtained by other investigative means. The employer can cancel the interview at any time and make a decision on the available facts or continue to investigate by other methods. There has been considerable litigation as to the remedy when a violation is found. The majority rule is that reinstatement is allowed only when a prima facie case for reinstatement can be established. If concerted activities are not present, there will be no reinstatement. If these reinstatement requirements do not exist, then a cease-and-desist order is the proper remedy for a violation. If the employee would have been discharged for just cause, there can be no reinstatement, even though the doctrine was violated.[26] The violation of the doctrine does not have serious consequences. Under the labor agreement, there would be more serious problems than violation of the doctrine if the employee was not discharged for just cause.

Extension of Doctrine to Nonunion Employees

The NLRB originally took the position that the Weingarten Doctrine does apply to nonunion employees. The board stated that this would be contrary to the exclusivity principles of the NLRA. In other nonunion situations, the exclusivity principle is not applied. The court in *Slaughter* v. *NLRB, 876 F.2d 11* (3rd. Cir. 1989), agreed with the board and enforced the board's order.

The employer who refuses representation to a nonunion employee could have exposure to litigation, as board policy has changed over the years, even though the most recent ruling by the Board excludes unrepresented employees from Weingarten coverage.[27] The best policy would be to allow the representation under the conditions of the Weingarten Doctrine or not have the interview at all. To trigger litigation over a matter that can be resolved by some other means would appear to be ill advised.

USE OF ECONOMIC WEAPONS: STRIKES AND LOCKOUTS

Unions have the legal right to strike and employers have the right to **lockout** under specified conditions after an agreement terminates and there is a bargaining impasse over mandatory subjects of bargaining. Strikes and lockouts are not permitted to force agreement on permissible subjects of bargaining. As mentioned earlier, this prohibition, however, does not prevent parties with overwhelming bargaining power from forcing negotiations on permissible subjects, and is commonly seen in negotiations. Also common in negotiations is the fact that a threat of a strike or lockout by a party with overwhelming bargaining power is more effective in winning concessions than the actual use of these weapons.

The law permits an employer to hire replacement workers during an economic strike.[28] If the replacements are temporary, returning strikers return to their jobs immediately after the conclusion of the strike. If the replacements are permanent, the striking employees are placed on a preferential hiring list.[29] After they have given an unconditional request for reinstatement to the employer, they have the right to return to their jobs or substantially equivalent work as vacancies occur since economic strikers are considered by law as employees. The employer must give notice of recall to all qualified strikers on the preferential hiring list prior to hiring new employees.[30]

An employer can also hire replacements during an employer lockout over an economic impasse but not if the employer has engaged in unfair labor practices.[31] In *Labor Board* v. *Brown*, the Court referred to *Mackay Radio*, stating the respondents, who were members of a multiemployer bargaining group, locked out their employees in response to a whipsaw strike against another member of the group. They and the struck employer continued operations with temporary replacements. The NLRB found that the struck employer's use of temporary replacements was lawful under *NLRB* v. *Mackay Radio & Telegraph Co.*, 304 U.S. 333 (1938), but that the respondents had violated 8 (a) (1) and (3) of the NLRA by locking out their regular employees and using temporary employees to carry on business.

The Circuit Court of Appeals of the Tenth Circuit disagreed and refused to enforce the board's order. The court further indicated that the board and the Court of Appeals agreed that the case was to be decided in light of its decision in the *Buffalo Linen* case, *Labor Board* v. *Truck Drivers Union*, 353 U. S 87 (1957). There, the court sustained the NLRB's finding that, in the absence of a specific proof of an unlawful motivation, the use of a lockout by members of a multiemployer bargaining unit in response to a whipsaw strike did not violate either 8 (a) (1) or 8 (a) (3) of the act. The court stated that, although the lockout tended to impair the effectiveness of the whipsaw strike, the right to strike "is not so absolute as to deny self-help by employers when legitimate interests of employees and employers collide. . . . The ultimate problem is the balancing of the conflicting legitimate interests." The decision in this significant case demonstrates the continual effort by the board and the courts to attempt to balance the power of unions and employers in the negotiation process.

Belknap v. *Hale*

In the leading case of *Belknap, Inc.* v. *Hale*, 463 U.S. 491 (1983), the Supreme Court allowed the terminated replacements to bring a cause of action in a state court if they were promised permanent jobs when hired as strike replacements. This ruling opened the door for the employer to offer permanent jobs during the strike that could not be changed through bargaining. Belknap applies only when the replacements have been clearly offered permanent jobs. This gave the employer a strong bargaining position before the strike. The union would threaten a strike and the employer would say, "Go ahead, and we will hire permanent replacements." The threat of replacements to sue for breach of contract is assigned great weight by union negotiators. Union members, knowing they may not get their jobs back, are accordingly reluctant to strike. The use of replacements had for years been seen by the employer as not being effective. The *Belknap* decision is now used as a threat in bargaining that can be carried out. Employers have also discovered that an increasing number of employees will cross the picket line rather than lose their jobs to replacements.[32] Further, the employer has discovered that replacements can be trained in a short time for skilled jobs.

To further strengthen the employer's bargaining position, one court has held that replacements can be used for a legal lockout.[33] The lockout itself was not anti-union and it was not destructive of employee rights so long as no anti-union action was taken. Strikers on a preferential hiring list do not retain their seniority when they return to work. They cannot be placed above the employees who refused to strike.[34] The use of replacements does not mean that the union has lost its majority status.[35] The board has reaffirmed its position that when in doubt about the union's majority status, the employer can take a poll to find out. This poll can be taken even when the employer has no objective evidence to justify withdrawal of recognition.[36] Often, when union members return to work during the strike, the union will invoke provisions of the union constitution and fine the members. To avoid this, members crossing the picket line give notice to the union that they wish to be "financial core" members. The NLRB in *Carpenters Local* 470, 277 NLRB No. 20 (1985), held that this was lawful so long as the dues were tendered by the members. They could return to work without being fined.[37]

The use of replacements will be a continuing employer stategy to respond to a strike threat. When a strike occurs, the permanent replacements may be effective in bringing striking workers back to the job. As a result of *Belknap* v. *Hale,* the use of a strike to force economic demands has had diminished effectiveness.

Restrictions on Strikers' Conduct

The right to picket during a strike is protected by the NLRA, although the act does not expressly say so. It is inferred from the right to engage in concerted activities or other mutual aid and protection under Section 7. This right is conditional. The strike must be lawful and picketing must be peaceful.[38] Picketing in an unlawful strike can result in the strikers losing their employment status. They will not have the right of recall when the strike is over. Examples of an unlawful strike would include picketing for a closed shop, a secondary boycott, or picketing for the purpose of inducing the employer to enter into a "featherbedding" arrangement. Picket line violence can also result in denial of reinstatement rights. Violence during a strike can take several forms other than physical contact. Insulting language directed at the employer (a threat of bodily harm has been held to be violence and a reason to deny reinstatement).[39] Verbal threats to a

nonstriker that his family will be harmed are also sufficient to deny reinstatement.[40]

It is not necessary to be an employee of the facility being picketed to engage in picketing. Section 2(9) of the act defines a labor dispute to include "any controversy regardless of whether the person stands in proximate relation of employer and employee." This means that a union can utilize professional pickets or volunteers if it so desires. As a practical matter usually the pickets are either employees or members of the union employed elsewhere.

Enforcement of a No-Strike Clause

The National Labor Relations Act permits the employee to enforce the labor agreement against the union and the employer.[41] It also permits the union to sue the employer, and the employer to sue to enforce the labor agreement.

Enforcement of Labor Agreement

The employer's enforcement of a labor agreement against a union is most common where the union authorizes a strike in violation of a no-strike clause. Labor unions can enforce an agreement against the employer by bringing a lawsuit in federal court. Prior to *Groves* v. *Ring Screw Works, Ferndale Fastener Div.,* 111 S.Ct. 498 (1990), the only way the union could enforce a labor agreement was to go on strike. Under the Norris-La Guardia Act of 1932, the courts are prohibited from granting injunctions for strike activity. But where there is a no-strike clause, the question is whether it can be enforced in view of the Norris-La Guardia Act. Until 1970, no-strike clauses could not be enforced because the Supreme Court held that the Norris-La Guardia Act superseded the contractual no-strike clause.

However, in certain situations, the court held that a no-strike clause can be enforced provided the labor agreement contains a mandatory grievance adjustment or arbitration clause. The court reasoned that a no-strike clause is a trade-off for an arbitration clause; therefore, the union must arbitrate rather than go on strike.[42] In subsequent cases, the court has made it clear that the presence of an arbitration clause is a prerequisite to issuing an injunction to enforce a no-strike clause.

When employees went on strike in sympathy with other employees from another company, the court held that such a strike could not be enjoined. The strike was not over a dispute of the employer in the labor agreement but in support of others not subject to arbitration.[43] This case reaffirms the court's position in the Boys Market case that the decision is narrow. The Norris-La Guardia Act is by no means dead.

USE OF ARBITRATION IN DISPUTE RESOLUTION

A grievance arbitration procedure culminating in binding arbitration has been adopted by employers and unions as the preferred method of resolving disputes that arise during the life of a labor agreement. Over the years, since passage of the NLRA, the parties have concluded that arbitration is a more pragmatic and economic method than work stoppages or threats of work stoppages of settling differences over the interpretation of language in their agreements and resolving employee discipline issues. Almost all agreements now contain binding arbitration as the final step in their grievance procedures as a trade-off with unions for unions' acceptance of a no-strike provision in the contract.

The Steelworkers Trilogy

A number of Supreme Court rulings have demonstrated the Court's preference for grievance arbitration as the favored method of dispute resolution for the settlement of contract disputes. In 1957, the Court ruled that if a labor agreement contained binding arbitration as the final step in the grievance procedure, the employer was legally bound to submit unresolved grievances to arbitration.[44] In 1960, the Court made three landmark decisions on the same day involving the United Steelworkers of America—decisions commonly referred to as the Steelworkers Trilogy. Two of these cases involved the issue of whether employers with grievance procedures culminating in binding arbitration in their labor agreements can refuse to arbitrate if the grievance lacks merit or involves a subject not covered by the agreement. On the first, the Court ruled that in determining whether a grievance should be subject to arbitration, the courts should not look at the merits of the case because that is the role assigned to the arbitrator.[45] On the second, the Court ruled that unless the subject of the grievance is explicitly excluded from arbitration by the language of the agreement, it is subject to arbitration.[46] These cases are frequently cited as demonstrating the importance the courts place on the utilization of grievance arbitration for the resolution of disputes during the life of a contract.

The third case involved a different issue: Whether the courts can/should be utilized to review and overturn grievance arbitrators' awards. The Court's answer was no. It stated that courts cannot overrule an arbitrator's award as long as it "draws its essence from the collective bargaining contract."[47]

The *Collyer* Doctrine

The right to arbitrate a dispute under a labor agreement arises only out of the agreement between the employee representative and the employer. The NLRB takes the position that whenever possible it will defer to arbitration, provided the parties agree to arbitrate and the interpretation of the contract is the basis of the dispute. This NLRB position is known as the *Collyer* Doctrine based on the board's decision in *Collyer Insulated Wire*, 192 NLRB No. 150 (1971). In this case, the NLRB ruled that it would defer all cases to arbitration that could be settled under the labor agreement. The board, however, may not defer all disputes to arbitration under the *Collyer* Doctrine because the issue in dispute must pertain to the interpretation or application of a labor agreement. The *Collyer* Doctrine presents an economic plus for employers and unions as it provides a reasonably fast and cost-efficient way to resolve disputes in addition to giving the parties the ability to settle disputes without arbitration.

Determination of Arbitrability of Disputes

When unions and employers disagree over the issue of whether a matter is "arbitrable"—that is, appropriate for arbitration—the economic tendency is to proceed to arbitration rather than court for a decision. In 1986, the Supreme Court in *AT&T Technologies* v. *Communications of America*, 475 U.S. 643, 648 106 S.Ct. 415, reaffirmed the Steelworkers Trilogy principles and indicated that reliance on arbitration rather than strikes has served the labor relations community well. Under this decision, the parties are directed to send matters of procedural **arbitrability** to the arbitrator. However, the courts retain jurisdiction to decide matters of substantive arbitrability (whether or not the subject matter of the dispute is appropriate for arbitration).

The Court summarized its views on arbitration in the labor relations arena in the form of three principles: (1) arbitration is a matter of contract and a party cannot be required to submit to arbitration any issue the party has not agreed to arbitrate; (2) arbitrability of the subject matter of a dispute (substantive arbitrability) is "undeniably" an issue for judicial determination; and (3) in deciding a question of arbitrability, the courts will not to rule on the potential merits of the underlying claims. The merits are reserved for determination by an arbitrator. The Court thus reaffirmed that in the absence of an express provision excluding a specific issue from arbitration, "only the most forceful evidence of purpose to exclude a claim from arbitration can prevail."

Enforcing and Vacating Arbitration Awards

Arbitration is not a judicial process. No standard rules or procedures are consistently followed. Individual arbitrators are not bound by the decisions of other arbitrators. Accordingly, although prior arbitration decisions may be persuasive, they do not establish legal **precedent**. Rather, arbitrators pride themselves in their ability to make decisions that reflect their individual competence and judgment. In 1974, the Court in *Alexander* v. *Gardner-Denver*, 415 U.S. 36, clearly stated that whether the parties agreed to arbitrate an issue was a judicial question. However, in April of 2009, the Court appeared to overturn that decision in 14 *Penn Plaza LLC* v. *Pyett et al.*, 556 U.S. ___ (2009), discussed earlier. The Court held that nothing in the NLRA that provides for collective bargaining agreements on behalf of bargaining unit members, or in the ADEA, forbids unions and employers from utilizing arbitration to resolve statutory discrimination claims.

The fact that most labor agreements do state that all issues involving the interpretation/application of the labor agreement will be submitted to arbitration serves the parties well in avoiding the expense of litigation. Law enters into arbitration when an arbitration award is challenged. In either an enforcement or review determination proceeding, courts are not allowed to evaluate the arbitrator's decision on the merits (see *Steelworkers* v. *Enterprise Wheel and Car*). There are, however, certain limited grounds permitting an arbitration award to be vacated by the courts. A party seeking to vacate an award may bring a statutory action to impeach.[48] In either type of judicial proceeding, the court may be required to review the award to determine whether it should be enforced. The court may decide not to enforce an arbitration award because the dispute was not arbitrable (again, see *Steelworkers* v. *Enterprise Wheel and Car*); the award does not draw its essence from the labor agreement;[49] the award violates public policy[50]; or incompetence or fraud was involved.[51] Some courts will vacate awards for gross defects in procedure or rationality.[52]

The three most compelling reasons to overturn an award are: (1) the arbitrator exceeded his or her authority under the labor agreement, (2) the award is contrary to the clear and unambiguous language of the labor agreement, and (3) the award is contrary to public policy. The Supreme Court in overturning the arbitration award in. *Enterprise Wheel* stated that the arbitrator "may, of course, look for guidance from many sources, yet his award is legitimate only so long as it draws its essence from the collective bargaining agreement." The Court stated there was no authority in the contract that permitted rehiring of workers with unsatisfactory work records. The Court further stated that the arbitrator exceeded his authority under the agreement, "although the interpretation of the contract is none of our business."[53]

Another reason for overturning an arbitration award is if an arbitrator substitutes the arbitrator's judgment for that of the parties to the contract. This situation may be evident when a contract limits the right to challenge a disciplinary action after the facts are determined. In *Riceland Foods* v. *Carpenters Local 2381*, 737 F.2d 758 (8th Cir. 1984), the arbitrator improperly mitigated the discipline for a rule violation. The contract stated that the arbitrator was limited to determining if the rule had been violated and not whether the discipline was proper.[54] Arbitration awards have also been vacated by the courts where the award is deemed to be contrary to public policy. The basis for refusing to enforce such an award is found in *W. R. Grace and Co.* v. *Rubber Workers Local 759*, 103 S.Ct. 2177 (1983), where the Supreme Court held that the courts may not enforce any collective bargaining agreement that is contrary to public policy.[55] As public policy is difficult to define in specific terms, considerable difficulty can be experienced in defining it in any particular circumstance. Nevertheless, arbitration awards have been found contrary to public policy. For example, a truck driver's discharge was overturned by an arbitrator and the driver reinstated where the driver was discharged for drinking alcohol on the job.[56] Other awards where discharges were overturned by arbitrators and the courts found such actions contrary to public policy can be seen in previously cited *U.S. Postal Service* v. *Postal Workers,* where an arbitrator reinstated a discharged employee because he paid back money he had stolen; in *Carpenters Local 1478* v. *Stevens*, 743 F.2d 1271 (9th Cir. 1984), where the award was deemed contrary to the principles of labor law, and in *Newsday* v. *Long Island Typographical Union No. 95*, 915 F.2d 840 (2nd Cir. 1990), where the court held that reinstating an employee guilty of sexual harassment was contrary to public policy.[57]

The courts have been clear in confirming the judgment of the *Trilogy Court* that arbitrators should not be second-guessed by the courts—see *United Paper Workers* v. *Misco*, 108 S.Ct. 363 (1987), where the Court agreed with the arbitrator that there were insufficient facts to warrant a discharge. However, the courts have also stated repeatedly that awards that are contrary to clear and explicit public policy will be subject to judicial review while efforts to vacate based on a vague or generalized notion of public interest or policy will not succeed.[58]

Discharge Arbitration

The most common issue in arbitration under the contract is discharge.[59] It is in discharge cases that the arbitrator may exceed his or her authority set forth in the labor agreement. This is especially true where those agreements allow only the arbitrator to determine the facts and not determine whether the penalty justifies the offense. It is desirable for both parties to include in the contract a clause to limit the authority of the arbitrator if they wish to prevent an arbitrator for substituting their judgment for that of the employer. The parties to a labor agreement can include a clause to limit the arbitrator's authority to set aside a penalty when just cause has been established.

For example:

The following offenses are deemed sufficient cause for discharge, and are subject to arbitration only to determine the facts of whether the offense was committed. Once the facts are established, the arbitrator shall have no authority to reduce the penalty imposed. [List might include such offenses as possession of firearms or drugs, theft, sleeping, and violation of certain safety rules.]

First offenses for which discharge is imposed are violations that the employer considers serious. These offenses should be specified in the collective agreement, and all employees should be forewarned that committing these offenses will lead to immediate termination of employment.

The union in *S. D. Warren*[60] argued that the case was controlled by the *Misco* decision. In *Misco*, the company did not specifically reserve the right in the labor agreement to discharge for a rule violation. However, in *S. D. Warren,* the contract allowed only the arbitrator to determine the facts and then decide whether or not the company had just cause to invoke discipline. The penalty was reserved to the company. Unions are not ordinarily interested in keeping undesirable persons employed any more than the company is, although the union's view is often influenced by internal politics. Some unions will argue that they will be charged with a

failure of fair representation if they do not vigorously defend every discharged employee irrespective of the merits of the case. This is not the case as the *O'Neill* decision demonstrated.[61]

There is always the possibility that the employee will file a fair representation charge with the NLRB when the decision of the union is not based on a contract clause or its interpretation. Since arbitrators' decisions are difficult to overturn, the parties' best approach is to limit their authority in the labor agreement.

It has become somewhat more common in recent years for the courts to overturn arbitration awards[62] than at any previous time since the *Steelworkers Trilogy* cases in 1960. However, less than half of the awards that were contested in the last three decades have been reversed by the courts. Although both companies and unions will doubtless contine to appeal arbitration awards, the success of such appeals is rare.

Problem-Solving/Interest-Based Collective Bargaining

Interest-based bargaining as a viable alternative to traditional share bargaining has been adopted by unions and employers in various industries that have felt the need to move away from the adversarial approach to negotiations. The strategy has been steadily encouraged by both state **mediation** services and the Federal Mediation and Conciliation Service since the late 1980s as a more effective and productive strategy for settling contract disputes. Interest-based bargaining does not generally represent a total change from traditional adversarial negotiations. Rather, it represents an effort, by the advocates, to determine where the parties have common interests that they should pursue as well as more efficiently identifying the issues that will be adversarial.

Although many unions and employers remain committed to traditional adversarial negotiations, the economic realities accentuated by the 2008 recession, coupled with the continued loss of jobs in the United States to countries with lower wage and benefit costs, have led many unions and employers to conclude that the U.S. economy has entered into a new and different economic phase. Accordingly, more parties to the collective bargaining process have been convinced that a comprehensive recognition by employers and unions of their joint interests is vital for their future economic survival and progress.

PAY EQUITY AND COLLECTIVE BARGAINING

Interest-based bargaining would likely become more popular if federal legislation mandating that labor unions and employers observe new standards that promote pay equity between men and women is adopted. A bill passed in the U.S. House in 2008 called the "Paycheck Fairness Act" is before the Senate in a somewhat different form but written to accomplish the same basic goal: pay equity between men and women based on relative job value and market pay information. The House Act (H.R. 1338) states its purpose as: "To Amend the FAIR LABOR STANDARDS ACT of 1938 to provide more effective remedies to victims of discrimination in the payment of wages on the basis of sex, and for other purposes." The political fate of this proposed legislation is uncertain. Some observers are convinced that Congress will pass legislation resulting in a pay equity law that will force both employers and unions to deal with the problem of negotiating labor agreements that provide for greater equity in the relative wage rates between men and women based on both measured job value and market wage structures. The effort by employers and unions to meet statutory pay equity obligations would likely result in a further encouragement of the parties to engage in interest-based bargaining.

CASE 8.1

Changing the Bargaining Power Equation

In the fall of 2008 the International Association of Machinists and Aerospace Workers struck the Boeing Company for 57 days. The strike was the union's fourth strike within a 20-year period. Both the company and the union indicated that the primary issue was the company's outsourcing of work. The company stated it would offer no job guarantees and would not agree to any restrictions on its ability to continue to outsource work. The union indicated that it wanted at least the chance to bid against outside vendors on all work set to be off-loaded. The strike ended when the union gained a contract provision that provided the opportunity for the union to bid against outside vendors and the company retained the right to choose which vendor would have the right to do the work.

Boeing indicated that the strike convinced the company that it needed to find production sites for its operations other than the Seattle area of Washington State in the future—particularly as it progressed with work on its "Dreamliner" project. In the middle of 2009, Boeing found itself two years behind schedule on the 787 Dreamliner project and began looking for another production site in the southern United States where unions were allegedly weaker than those at its production facility in Everett, WA.

The union considers the company's consideration of another production facility to be a direct threat to its historic bargaining power regardless of whether the production facility is built in the South or in another country. The union has continued to oppose the company's plan to consider other geographic areas for production particularly since Boeing has been gradually moving some of its operations from the Seattle area for a number of years. Boeing's defense operations are located in the St. Louis area, and in 2001, Boeing moved its headquarters to Chicago. Additionally, the city of Seattle and the state of Washington have expressed concern since Boeing in 2009 employed approximately 74,000 persons in the Washington State.

The Boeing Company's planning as to where it will located production and office facilities is symptomatic of considerations by many companies as to where they will choose to locate their operations in the world economy of the 2000s and beyond. Although the unions representing employees in a given location are of course immediately concerned for the workers they represent, the challenge indirectly concerns the very existence of individual unions and geographic area of the country.

Questions for Consideration

1. Is the geographic location of a private-sector company's operations a mandatory subject of bargaining under the definitions of good faith bargaining by the NLRB? Should it be?
2. If a company determines to establish a production/operating facility in another geographic area of the

United States, should the employees hired in the new location be included in the bargaining unit in the existing location? (Give your answer on the basis of (a) the new employees in the new location perform essentially the same work as the employees in the existing unionized location and (b) they perform entirely different tasks.)
3. Is the process of establishing more production/operating facilities in different geographic areas a way for a company to diminish a union's bargaining power? Is the threat by a company to so do a beneficial strategy for an employer?
4. What are the strategies a union should/can adopt to persuade a company from establishing new geographic area of operation in the United States? Outside the United States? ■

CASE 8.2

When More May Be Too Much

The United Automobile Workers of American (UAW) had practiced the traditional goals of the American labor union movement well for more than 60 years when the twenty-first century began. The union had effectively lifted hundreds of thousands of workers associated with the traditional American automobile industry into comfortable middle-class status. The only adjudged failing of the UAW appeared to be its limited lack of success in organizing the transplanted foreign auto makers' workforces. As a result, in the 1990s, the total cost package of wages, benefits, and work rules of the "Big Three" companies of General Motors, Ford, and Chrysler were estimated to be up to two and a half to three times the total economic package of the workers in the "foreign transplants" producing in the United States. The economic toll of the difference began to be felt by 2002–2003. General Motors, for example, began to run its automobile production operations at a loss beginning in that period.

The Ford and Chrysler companies also began to operate at a loss shortly after General Motors, and by the beginning of the 2007–2008 economic recession all three companies admitted to the public that they were experiencing significant economic difficulty. The acknowledged problem for all three companies was their total cost of labor relative to that of the foreign transplants particularly at a time of low sales volume.

The U.S. government offered the three companies economic assistance in the form of loans to aid them

through their economic crisis with conditions. The conditions stated essentially were that they were to achieve reduced labor costs through negotiations with the UAW, and that without success in that effort the government would do nothing to prevent their bankruptcies. The government message indirectly to the UAW was for the union to agree to substantial labor cost reductions—particularly with regard to health insurance benefits for retirees. The UAW's bargaining power position relative to the three companies had been achieved in large part by its strategy of threatening a strike against "a chosen target company" in order to put it in a non-competitive position while the other companies produced product.

General Motors and Chrysler welcomed the loans; Ford did not. However, all three were able, under threat of the federal government to allow bankruptcy of the American automobile industry and the potential of the loss to the UAW of almost, if not effectively all, of its members' jobs, to successfully rework their labor agreements. These concessionary agreements significantly reduced labor costs and fulfilled the government's demand to achieve approximate parity with the labor costs of the foreign transplants.

Questions for Consideration

1. The U.S. government mandate tied financial help to the traditional automobile companies with a requirement that

the companies renegotiate their labor agreements to essentially equalize labor costs with the foreign transplants. Did this mandate represent a change in the government's traditional legal stance of hands off the results of "good faith negotiations" under the NLRA, Sections 8 (a) (5) and 8 (b) (3)?

2. When should "for the good of the public" considerations, if ever, negate the results of collective bargaining "in good faith"?

3. Should the fact that the Ford Company did not accept federal loans have exempted the UAW from the necessity of having also to lower its historic contractual gains and accept the requirement to modify its contract cost to approximately equalize labor costs with the foreign transplants?

4. Under what circumstances in the future should the U.S. government inject its interpretation of public-interest requirements on private and/or public collective bargaining results reached through "good faith negotiations"?

5. Does the fact that the U.S. government owns a majority of General Motors place the company under the federal Civil Service Statute? ■

CASE 8.3

The *Fiberboard Paper Products* Case and Nonmandatory Subjects of Bargaining

The Ace Electronics Company has determined that it is at a competitive disadvantage based on its costs of production in the northeastern United States and needs to move its production facilities over time to a lower cost location. Thus, it announced to its union, which represents its production employees, that it will relocate its production facilities and close its Northeast facility over a period of one year. During that year the company will build a new plant in the southern United States to produce product together with two other plants the company operates in the South. The company's two other plants are non-union organized. During the year, production employees who voluntarily leave their job will not be replaced. The existing labor agreement will last for two more years.

The union demands that the company begin negotiations concerning the "effects" of the pending plant foreclosure, citing the ruling in *Fiberboard Paper Products Corporation* v. *NLRB*, 379 U.S. 203 (1964), requiring that an employer bargain about the nonmandatory subject of the effects of a plant closing on the bargaining unit employees. The company refuses to enter into negotiations, stating that because the employees have been notified of the impending closing a year in advance, they will have the opportunity to find another job within the year period provided and/or apply for a job at the new plant or at one of the two other plants presently operating in the South. Thus, the company need only negotiate at the end of the year with those employees, if any, who have not voluntarily left the employment of the company.

Questions for Consideration

1. Should the union drop its unfair labor practice charge and wait until the end of the year to attempt to negotiate the effects of the plant closing on those who do not voluntarily leave during the year or gain satisfactory employment at one of the company's other plants, or should the union pursue the charge to gain satisfactory results for those who have no desire to leave during the year or seek work in another state?

2. How do you think the NLRB will rule based on the legal precedent and the facts as described in this situation?

3. Do you believe that the company should agree to bargain with the union so as to ascertain the union's positions on the effects of the plant closing? If so, might the company bargain to an impasse and then institute its plant closing under the legal philosophy expressed in *NLRB* v. *Katz*, 369 U.S. 736 (1962)?

4. Given the facts of the situation, how would you assess the relative bargaining power of the company and the union in collective bargaining if the company decides to agree to enter into negotiations as the union demands? ■

CASE 8.4

Defining a Collective Bargaining Impasse

Read the facts with regard to *Taft Broadcasting*, 163 NLRB 475, 478 (1967), with regard to unilateral changes by an employer and the decisions of the NLRB and Court. Then answer the following:

1. Determine whether you agree with the determination of the NLRB in this case or you agree with the ruling of the Court.
2. How you believe the company could have acted under the circumstances to make the decision it did to implement unilaterally within the NLRA's definition of good faith bargaining in Sections 8 (a) 5 and 8 (a) 1?
3. Did you believe an impasse began when the union took a strike vote and authorized a strike?
4. Did the company make a mistake when it rejected the union's offer to have its members continue to work despite the strike authorization under the terms of the old agreement?
5. Do you agree with the board's statement quoted by the Court that there is "no fixed definition of an impasse . . .

which can be mechanically applied to all factual situations (*Dallas General Drivers*, 355 F.2d at 845). It considers a number of factors, including bargaining history, the good faith of the parties in negotiations, the length of negotiations, the importance of the issue or issues as to which there is disagreement" or do you believe such statements are too vague to be determinative?

6. Evaluate the Court's quote that "163 NLRB at 478 also supports a finding of no impasse. If either negotiating party remains willing to move further toward an agreement, an impasse cannot exist: the parties perception regarding the progress of negotiations is of central importance to the Board's inquiry" and quoting the board in *Saunders House* v. *NLRB,* 719 F.2d 683 (3rd Cir. (1983), cert. denied, 466 U.S. 598,104 S.Ct. 2170, 80 L Ed.2nd 544 (1984) (impasse finding "often depends on the mental state of the parties"). By this quote, is the Court encouraging the NLRB and the courts to try to determine the mental state of the parties in determinations of impasses? ◼

Summary

This chapter examines the legal obligation imposed on private-sector employers and unions to bargain with each other in good faith for the purpose of reaching agreements on terms and conditions of employment. The original National Labor Relations Act and its subsequent amendments and its administration by the National Labor Relations Board and the courts made substantial efforts to create a balance in the bargaining power between employers and unions. The historical evidence clearly suggests that those

efforts failed. On the contrary, the actual use of the economic strike and lockout weapons of the parties, coupled with the ability of private-sector employers to threaten to relocate their operations to lower-cost geographic areas, has effectively rendered strikes and lockouts ineffectual in many situations. Furthermore, the ability of unions to exercise their economic power where the employer has no ability to relocate operations has resulted in significant bargaining power imbalances and economic abuses.

Key Terms

Questions for Discussion

1. What was the purpose/need for passage of the National Labor Relations Act in 1935 and did it fulfill its purpose?
2. Did the NLRA need to stipulate that the parties bargain in good faith and attempt to define that term?
3. What impact has the NLRB and courts had in their attempts to generate approximate equality of bargaining power between employers and unions, and have the results been worth the attempts?
4. Has the imposition by the courts of the necessity to observe past practices of the parties under a contract been beneficial or harmful to the collective bargaining process?

5. Has the union duty of fair representation been difficult for unions to manage consistent with their obligation to proceed to represent what they perceive to be the majority will?
6. How should the law deal with threats by private-sector employers to abandon all or parts of their domestic operations for overseas locations if their unions fail to make appropriate economic concessions?
7. Should the NLRA be modified to prohibit strikes and lockouts in favor of arbitration of negotiations impasses or redefine good faith bargaining to require interest-based bargaining?

Notes to Chapter 8

1. For a further definition of *surface bargaining*, see *Atlanta Hilton and Tower*, 271 NLRB 1600 (1984).
2. *Air Line Pilots Association* v. *O'Neill*, 111 S.Ct. 1127 (1991). See also S. Estreicher, "Collective bargaining v. collective begging," *Michigan Law Review*, 93 (1994): 511.
3. In *ALPA* v. *O'Neill* the union was charged with bad faith bargaining, a charge upheld by the court.
4. *NLRB* v. *Wooster Division of Borg-Warner Corporation*, 356 U.S. 342 (1958).
5. The union shop is a contract provision that requires all new employees to become members of the union within a certain period after hiring, typically 30 days.
6. *H. K. Porter Co.* v. *NLRB*, 397 U.S. 99 (1970).
7. Employer's bargaining position was not bad faith bargaining: *Cincinnati Newspaper Guild* v. *NLRB*, 938 F.2d 284 (D.C. Cir. 1991).
8. When the employer is found guilty of an unfair labor practice, the board requires that a notice be put on the bulletin board that the employer has been found guilty to assure employees that in the future the firm will follow the law.
9. Neil W. Chamberlain and James W. Kuhn, *Collective bargaining*, 2nd ed. (New York: McGraw-Hill), 1965, p. 170.

10. J. Budd, "The determinants and extent of UAW pattern bargaining," *Industrial and Labor Relations Review*, 45 (April 1992).
11. Chrysler was ultimately forced into Chapter 11 and a shotgun marriage with Fiat.
12. *Fiberboard Paper Products Corp.* v. *NLRB*, 379 U.S. 203 (1964).
13. *Dubuque Packing Co.*, 303 NLRB 386 No. 66.
14. *Ford Motor Co.* v. *NLRB*, 441 U.S. 488 (1979).
15. *NLRB* v. *Wonder State Mfg. Co.*, 344 F.2d 210 (8th Cir. 1965).
16. Benchmark Industries, 270 NLRB 22 (1984).
17. For further references and details on the employer's duty to bargain, see Leonard E. Cohen, "The duty to bargain over plant relocations and other corporate changes: Otis Elevator v. NLRB," *The Labor Lawyer*, 1, no. 3 (Summer 1985); "Proceedings of the Industrial Relations Research Association, spring 1985 meeting," *Labor Law Journal*, 36, no. 8 (August 1985); Brian K. Brittain and Brian P. Heshizer, "Management decision bargaining: The interplay of law and politics," *Labor Law Journal*, 38, no. 4 (April 1987): 220.
18. *Textile Workers Union of American* v. *Lincoln Mills*, 353 U.S. 448 (1957).
19. *United Steelworkers of America* v. *Warrior and Gulf Navigation Co.*, 363 U.S. 574; *United Steelworkers of America* v. *Enterprise Wheel*

and Car Corp., 363 U.S. 593; *United Steelworkers of America* v. *American Mfg. Co.*, 363 U.S. 564 (1960).

20. For discussion of past practice in arbitration, see Alan Ruben (Ed.), *Frank Elkouri and Edna Elkour: How arbitration works*, 6th ed. (Washington, DC: Bureau of National Affairs, 2003), Chap. 12.

21. *Norfolk Ship Building Corp.* v. *Local 684*, 671 F.2d 797 (4th Cir. 1982).

22. *Air Line Pilots Association* v. *O'Neill*, 111 S.Ct. 1127 (1991).

23. *Prudential Insurance Co.* v. *NLRB*, 661 F.2d 398 (5th Cir. 1981).

24. *Manville Forest Products Corp.*, 269 NLRB No. 72 (1984).

25. For the role of union representatives in employee disciplinary interviews, see *N.J. Bell Telephone* v. *Local 827 IBEW*, 308 NLRB 32 (1992).

26. This was first decided by the board in *Taracorp Industries*, 273 NLRB No. 54 (1984) and reaffirmed in *Communication Workers of America* v. *NLRB*, 784 F.2d 847 (7th Cir. 1986).

27. *Epilepsy Foundation of Northeast Ohio*, 331 NLRB No. 92 (2000). The board held that *Weingarten* applied to non-union workers. However, in *IBM Corp.*, 341 NLRB No. 106 (2004), the board reversed its position and held that *Weingarten* does not apply to non-union workers.

28. *NLRB* v. *Mackay Radio and Tel. Co.*, 304 U.S. 333 (1938).

29. This does not deny employees the right to return to their jobs if they have not been replaced. *American Linen Supply Co.* v. *NLRB*, 945 F.2d 1428 (8th Cir. 1991).

30. *NLRB* v. *Fleetwood Trailer Co.*, 389 U.S. 375 (1967); *Laidlaw Corporation.*, 171 NLRB 1366 (1968) enf'd 414 F.2d 99 (7th Cir. 1969), cert. denied, 397 U.S. 920 (1970).

31. *Labor Board* v. *Brown*, 380 U.S. 278 (1965).

32. The McDonnell Douglas and Hormel strikes and strikes in the airline industry are good examples.

33. In *Local 825 Operating Engineers* v. *NLRB*, 829 F.2d 458 (3rd Cir. 1987).

34. *Trans World Airlines* v. *Independent Federation of Flight Attendants*, 109 S.Ct. 1225 (1989).

35. *NLRB* v. *Cortin-Matheson Scientific*, 110 S.Ct. 1542 (1990).

36. *Texas Petrochemicals Corp.*, 296 NLRB 136 (1989), rem. and mod. 923 F.2d 398 (5th Cir. 1991).

37. *NLRB* v. *Local 54 Hotel and Restaurant Employees*, 887 F.2d 28 (3rd Cir. 1989).

38. In *General Indust. Empl. Union Local 422* v. *NLRB*, 951 F.2d 1308 (D.C. Cir. 1991), an unlawful strike was converted into an economic strike.

39. *Clear Pine Mouldings, Inc.*, 268 NLRB No. 173 (1984).

40. *Newport News Shipbuilding and Dry Dock Co.* v. *NLRB*, 738 F.2d 1404 (4th Cir. 1984).

41. *Sinclair Refining Co.* v. *Atkinson*, 370 U.S. 195 (1962).

42. *Boys Market* v. *Retail Clerks Union*, 398 U.S. 235 (1970).

43. *Buffalo Forge Co.* v. *United Steelworkers of America*, 428 U.S. 397 (1976).

44. *Textile Workers Union of America* v. *Lincoln Mills*, 353 U.S. 448 (1957).

45. *United Steelworkers of America* v. *American Manufacturing Co.*, 363 U.S. 564 (1960).

46. *United Steelworkers of America* v. *Warrior and Gulf Navigation Co.*, 363 U.S. 574 (1960).

47. *United Steelworkers of America* v. *Enterprise Wheel and Car Corp.*, 363 U.S. 593 (1960).

48. Uniform Arbitration Act § 7.7, U.L.A. § 114, RLA § 3 First (q). 45U.S.C. § 153. First (q) (1982).

49. *Miller Brewing Co.* v. *Brewery Workers Local 9*, 793 F.2d 1159 (7th Cir. 1984).

50. *Paperworkers* v. *Misco*, 484 U.S. 29, S.Ct. 364, 374 (1987).

51. *Union Pacific R.R.* v. *UTU*, 3 F.3d 255 (8th Cir. 1993).

52. *Mailhandlers* v. *USPS*, 751 F.2d 834-843 (6th Cir. 1985).

53. *Miller Brewing Co.* v. *Brewery Workers*, 739 F.2d 1159 (7th Cir. 1984).

54. See also *Devine* v. *Pastre*, 732 F.2d 213 D.C. Cir. 1984); *Morgan Services* v. *Local 323*, 724 F.2d 1217 (6th Cir. 1984).

55. See also *First Options of Chicago, Inc.* v. *Kaplan*, 514 U.S. 938 (1995).

56. *Meatcutters Local 540* v. *Great Western Food Co.*, 712 F.2d 122 (5th Cir. 1983).

57. See also *Stroehmann Bakeries* v. *Local 766 International Brotherhood of Teamsters*, 969 F.2d 1436 (3rd Cir. 1992). *Chrysler Motors Corp.* v. *International Union, Allied Industrial*

Workers of America AFL-CIO Local 793 959 F.2d 685 (7th Cir. 1992).

58. *W. R. Grace and Co. v. Rubber Workers Local 79, 103 S.Ct., 2177 (1983).*

59. Federal Mediation and Conciliation Service, Arbitration Statistics, report that over half of all referrals for a panel are for discharge disputes.

60. *S. D. Warren Co. v. United Paperworkers' International Union, AFL-CIO, 846 F.2d 827 (11th Cir. 1988).*

61. See also *Walk* v. *P.I.E. Nationwide*, CA6 No. 90-2097 (1992), where a grievant was discharged after failing a drug test.

62. See *Lee* v. *Chica*, 983 F.2d 889 (8th Cir. 1993).

CHAPTER 9

Public-Sector Labor Relations

CHAPTER OUTLINE

Legal Framework in Public-Sector
    Bargaining

Defining Bargaining Power

Differences in Bargaining Practices in
    the Private and Public Sectors:
    Practices and Court Decisions

Effect of Collective Bargaining
    and Contract Arbitration
    Decisions

Collective bargaining in the private sector of the United States began uniformly with the passage of the National Labor Relations Act (NLRA) in 1935. Collective bargaining in the public sector developed haphazardly and unevenly for employees in different states and their political subdivisions. Public-sector unionization in cities and states can be dated back to the formation of a firefighter local formed in Chicago in 1901; however, the official recognized commencement of collective bargaining in states occurred in 1959 with the passage of a law providing for negotiations between unionized public employees in Wisconsin and its political subdivisions.

LEGAL FRAMEWORKS IN PUBLIC-SECTOR BARGAINING

Federal Framework

Limited collective bargaining for federal government agency employees was mandated by President John F. Kennedy through Executive Order 10988 issued in 1962 and became a statutory right with the passage of the Civil Service Reform Act (CSRA) in 1978.[1] The act established the Federal Labor Relations Authority (**FLRA**) to act in a manner similar to the National Labor Relations Board (NLRB) created by the National Labor Relations Act (NLRA). The FLRA provided protection for federal employees' rights to form, join, or assist any labor organization, or to refrain from such activities with free will, without fear of reprisal or penalty, and to engage in negotiations over specified subjects. The FLRA, through a general counsel, investigates and prosecutes complaints of unfair labor practices.

The Federal Service Labor-Management Relations Statute spelled out the general subjects considered mandatory for negotiations—as well as those that were considered management rights and those that could be negotiated at management's discretion. Wages were excluded from negotiations and continued to be exclusively set by the various agencies. **Strikes** were prohibited and no provision for **contract arbitration** over bargaining impasses was established. **Grievance procedures** were to be negotiated to cover adverse actions such as discharge from employment, demotion, and long-term suspensions. Excluded were such subjects as prohibited political activities, retirement, health insurance, and pay rates in addition to any area that the agency and union agreed to exclude. Binding arbitration was the only avenue for addressing those subjects covered by the grievance procedure.

A Federal Services Impasses Panel (FSIP) was created to resolve impasses between federal agencies and labor organizations representing federal employees stemming from negotiations conducted under the Federal Service Labor-Management Relations Statute and the Federal Employees Flexible and Compressed Work Schedules Act. Either party during negotiations may request the panel's assistance. On investigation, the FSIP may assert jurisdiction over the request and recommend or direct the utilization of resolution processes to resolve disputes, including the imposition of contract terms.

State and Local Government Framework

Many students of the progress of legislation establishing the legal frameworks for collective bargaining in state and local governmental units regard the **Civil Service Reform Act** as unrepresentative of a substantive piece of legislation. As of calendar 2010, collective bargaining for public employees (1) has a legal foundation in approximately one-half of the states, (2) is provided for specific employees in an additional 18 states, and (3) does not exist for any employees in 8 states.[2] Additionally, collective bargaining is provided for in some cities by local ordinances or laws such as in New York City. However, in those states that have passed legislation providing for collective bargaining for public employees, the scope of the legislation varies significantly.

The state laws providing for collective bargaining vary from little more than a one-page document in Wyoming—which provides minimum substantive guidance with regard to definitions of bargaining units, bargaining standards, or subjects of negotiations—to extensive documents in Wisconsin, Iowa, Minnesota, Florida, Washington, and many of the northeastern states—which include much of the language of the private sector NLRA.[3] The majority of states with public-sector bargaining laws prohibit strikes and stipulate that bargaining impasses must be resolved by arbitration (e.g., see statutes in Iowa and Wisconsin and the law providing for collective bargaining for New York City employees). In some other states, strikes by certain groups of employees whose services to the public are defined as non-essential/critical to the public interest are allowed under controlled procedures, whereas bargaining impasses involving critical employee groups must be resolved through arbitration.

It is noted that legislation has been repeatedly discussed in Congress since 2006 to provide for the establishment of collective bargaining rights for firefighters and police officers throughout the United States. Specific legislation introduced in Congress in 2008 would prohibit strikes by firefighter and police officer bargaining units. Bargaining impasses would be subject to mandatory arbitration. Although this legislation passed the House of Representatives, it appears that there is little support within the Senate or the Administration for passage at this time.

Because of the wide diversity in state and local bargaining laws, the precedent value/importance of administrative and court decisions involving these different laws does not have the significance that such decisions have under the NLRA or other federal legislation. For example, the U.S. Supreme Court decision in *Chicago Teachers Union* v. *Hudson*, 475 U.S. 292 (1986), is significant not because it involved a public employee union but rather because it involved federal civil rights statutes. Thus court precedent with regard to a single state's labor relations law rarely has relevance beyond the borders of that state.

DEFINING BARGAINING POWER

Observers and students of collective bargaining between employers and employee groups, as it has been practiced in various countries and societies over the last century, have attempted to develop a model that would allow objective outsiders and the parties involved in collective bargaining to be able to develop alternative strategies during the bargaining process and to predict outcomes in impasse situations. The constraint in such effort has been the assumption, regarded as necessary to any predictive model, that the parties in a collective bargaining relationship would act rationally in their own best economic, social, and political interests.

Many economists have concluded the most reliable predictor of collective bargaining outcomes requires measuring the relative

cost of agreement versus disagreement for the parties based on their stated final positions for settlement. A prediction of outcome could presumably be based on the assumption that during negotiations, the parties would continually evaluate their relative economic costs of agreement and disagreement based on their stated positions. Agreement could be predicted when the parties estimated that the relative **costs of agreement/disagreement** were equal.[4]

This theoretical structure failed to prove useful as a practical predictive tool for economists, employers, labor organizations, and observers in practice based on the following observations:

1. Labor organizations and management representatives demonstrated they generally failed to act rationally in their own best interests when they became emotionally involved during the negotiations process.
2. Accurate measurements of the costs of agreement and disagreement proved to be difficult to estimate.
3. Employers and labor organizations experienced significant difficulty developing workable predictions of short- and long-term cost estimates of agreement and disagreement and in coming to rational conclusions concerning their most appropriate strategies.
4. Cost of agreement/disagreement estimates required assumptions of conjectural interdependence concerning what actions might be taken by the other party based on actions taken by the first party. Such conjectural interdependence issues often froze the parties into inaction causing an unpredictable impasse.
5. The assumption that labor organizations were democratic organizations making decisions based on majority vote often caused employers to make inaccurate estimates of a labor organization's strategy alternatives.

The theory also proved to be unworkable when the parties were unable to measure the psychological dynamics created during the bargaining process for employees, labor organization leaders, and employers. Accordingly, labor organizations, employers, and students of collective bargaining have continually sought to develop a more practical and useful model of **bargaining power**. Accordingly, bargaining power can be estimated by answering the following questions:

1. How essential to the employer's operations are the employees involved in the bargaining?

   The assumption, based on years of evaluating bargaining outcomes, indicated that if the service of an employee group was critical to an employer's operations in the short run, the group would have substantial bargaining power. However, if analysis demonstrated that the employer had the ability to operate effectively for a reasonable period of time without the employee group, the employee group likely lacked sufficient bargaining power to substantially affect bargaining outcomes.

2. Are the services of the employees replaceable by the employer if the employees choose to strike?

   If the answer is yes, the employees will likely be unable to dictate bargaining outcomes by threatening to or actually withholding their services.

3. If the employees' services are critical to the employer's operations and are not replaceable, what are the relative costs of agreement/disagreement for the parties based on their assumed final bargaining positions? In the private sector, costs are measured primarily in economic terms. In the public sector, however, the relative costs of agreement/disagreement are measured by

their impact on broadly defined public opinion.

An examination of the potential political impact of a work stoppage in the public sector would be necessary by both the employer and the union in an attempt to determine the extent of and the nature of the public reaction to a work stoppage. An evaluation of strikes by public employees in various public jurisdictions amply demonstrates how greatly the public attitude differed from that anticipated by the parties in some strikes and how accurate the parties predictions were in others.

4. Do the parties, with reasonable accuracy, perceive the relative costs of agreement/disagreement based on anticipated final bargaining positions for the purpose of determining appropriate strategies?

   If one or both of the parties are not capable of perceiving, with reasonable accuracy, the relative costs of agreement/disagreement, they will not be able to make rational decisions as to how to proceed in their own best interests during the bargaining process or determine what strategy to utilize in the event of a bargaining impasse.

5. Are the parties willing and psychologically prepared to take action based on their perceptions of relative bargaining power?

   If one or both parties are not willing to take action during the bargaining process based on their **perceptions** of relative bargaining power, they will be unable to make decisions as to their best strategic alternatives and be frozen into inaction.

Although an analysis based on these questions added a useful and necessary psychological dimension to the bargaining power equation, it fell short with regard to generating useful predictions when human emotions overwhelmed the ability of those involved in the process to act rationally on the basis of facts objectively determined.

Assessing Bargaining Power in the Public Schools

Nowhere in the public sector is relative bargaining power more difficult to assess than in the public school K–12 setting due to the multilateral nature of the bargaining. The threat of an impasse that could close a public school system is guaranteed to elicit almost furious reactions from a broad spectrum of individuals and interest groups. Public-sector collective bargaining history since the 1960s demonstrates that the public will be more agitated and concerned with the possibility of a shutdown of their school system than any other threatened closure, including transportation. The threat of a closure of a public school system is not simply a threat of a denial of education and the probability of substantially higher costs to the public, it represents, for many working parents, an unscheduled interruption of a vital service—a daily place for the children when the parents are working. Thus, the family economics, the educational needs for the children, and the loss of a safe and supervised environment are simultaneously threatened.

The threat divides **public opinion** and brings forth heated debate. Older members of the community with no children in school tend to view the threat in largely economic terms; parents of children in their final higher education preparation period worry about the impact on preparation and eligibility to gain entrance into desirable institutions; parents of teenagers are concerned about what their children will do with too much free time with little or no supervision; and parents of young children are concerned with their caretaking. In sum, the local politics of a threatened teacher strike are diverse and generally bring forth strong feelings and inflammatory comments.

For both the members of a school board and the teacher bargaining unit, the threat of a stoppage creates a relative bargaining power conundrum: How can the relative costs of agreement versus disagreement be measured when the potential costs to the public are so diverse and represent an interwoven and confusing mixture of both economic and non-economic costs? In geographic areas where the costs of K–12 education are regarded as abnormally high and have in part pushed property taxes to levels regarded as unacceptable—such as the property **tax levels** in 2009 in New Jersey, widely reported to be the highest in the country—a cost of agreement that would increase tax levels would overwhelm any discussed cost of disagreement. Likewise, in 2009 in California, when the alternatives to the significant budget deficit were placed before the public for a vote, the alternative that would have raised tax levels in part to fund the public education system was soundly voted down.

By contrast, a private-sector employer facing a strike need only price the costs of a shutdown due to a strike based on fixed costs; the estimated loss of market in the short and long run; the potential loss of competitive advantage, if any, in the short and long run versus the short- and long-term costs of a settlement on the union's last offer before strike action. Additionally, for an increasing number of private-sector businesses in a world economy a solution not available for a public entity such a school district, is to relocate to a lower cost environment.

For a public school district in the 2000s, the cost of agreement versus disagreement computation is further complicated by the increased willingness of parents to move children to alternative schooling. For many, a movement to private, schools, or other school districts, when that option is available, can be evaluatedbased on both costs and the quality of the available\educational opportunities.

For teachers, the relative costs of agreement/disagreement also are not simply economic. Agreement on the school district's economic "final position" may mean a diminished income potential in both the short and long run perceived as below that required for a self-determined minimum standard of living. Yet, the proposition of a strike to change that outlook may or may not be successful as the teachers assess their bargaining power position. They also have to estimate the reaction of the district to wage and benefit costs above those estimated palatable to the district. How might the district act if it believes the costs of settlement are higher than that can be provided? What percentage of them might be laid off? What other cost-cutting methods, such as significantly larger class sizes or the closing of some schools, might be used? What percentage of parents will decide the additional costs of private school or charter school have become more attractive or tolerable and the resulting exodus then forces layoffs?

The calculations of the relative costs of agreement/disagreement must be made by *all* parties—school board members, teachers, and the district public and its subgroups—within a relatively short time within an atmosphere of division.

DIFFERENCES IN BARGAINING PRACTICES IN THE PRIVATE AND PUBLIC SECTORS: PRACTICES AND COURT DECISIONS

Practices

Bargaining in the private sector under the NLRA is bilateral between the employer's representatives and the labor organization's representatives. The representatives are required by law to bargain in good faith concerning the terms and conditions of employment defined by the National Labor Relations Board as mandatory subjects of negotiations. Failure to negotiate about

subjects designated as mandatory subjects of bargaining can be considered an unfair labor practice and pursued by the charging party through the NLRB.[5] Negotiations between the parties over subjects considered by the NLRB as permissive are common. The extent of bargaining concerning permissive subjects of bargaining is commonly determined by relative bargaining power. A party with sufficient bargaining power as defined herein can force negotiations on whatever issues it wishes to pursue.

By contrast, collective bargaining in the public sector is **multilateral** and routinely involves, in addition to the designated employer and labor representatives, undesignated elected officials at different levels of government, various public interest groups, and competing and cooperative pubic employee union groups. While the employer and labor representatives meet in formal negotiations, both employer and labor organization representatives routinely meet with and discuss their bargaining goals with other elected officials. The labor organization's objective is to convince influential elected officials to direct the employer's bargaining representatives to adopt positions favorable to the labor organization. The employer's representatives' objective is to convince elected officials at other levels of government to support the employer's positions. In political jurisdictions where labor is the dominate political power, such intervention with elected officials during bargaining essentially determines the employer's final positions. In jurisdictions where labor organizations have little political influence, the effectiveness of a labor organization's attempt to cause elective officials to influence the employer's bargaining representatives is negligible.

Further complications may arise during bargaining when different groups of a jurisdiction's elected officials discuss differing/conflicting proposals with subgroups of union officials. In some situations, a number of different elected officials may be in discussions with different factions of a labor organization or another labor organization with cooperating and/or competing interests concerning substantially different proposals for settlement.

Court Decisions

Chapter 8 outlined some of the practical and legal aspects of private-sector negotiations with regard to the duty of the parties to bargain in good faith; mandatory subjects of bargaining; enforcement of and challenges to collective bargaining and strikes; and the use of arbitration for dispute resolution of grievances. Although some of the numerous court decisions and administrative decisions cited are applicable in the public sector, many are not relevant given the significantly different legal framework between the private and public sectors and the lack of uniformity in public-sector collective bargaining legislation between the states with a legal foundation for public employee bargaining. For example, strikes in the private sector are generally allowed and the use by a private-sector employer of strike replacements is permitted. However, in states where public employee strikes are permitted, employees *not* on the permitted strike generally must continue to work and cannot refuse to cross picket lines. Accordingly, public employers are almost universally prohibited from hiring strike replacements.

Ability to Pay

When contract/interest arbitration is mandatory in the event of bargaining impasses in states providing for arbitration, the employer's **ability to pay** is a subject that arbitrators are required to consider in their decisions. Although the exact manner in which the arbitrator must consider the employer's ability to pay is usually not specified, an employer may be able to force a change or overtun an arrbitrator's award if

it can effectively argue that such obligation was fully considered. For example, in New York a 90-day period for appeal of an arbitration award begins with the issuance of an award; see *McRae* v. *New York Transit Authority*, 39 A. D. 3d 861.

A question that has often been asked by public employers is, what happens when the employer has no ability to pay (e.g., the employer is bankrupt)? In such a case, can the employer abrogate its labor agreements? In *City of Vallego* (E. D. CA, March 13, 2009), a bankruptcy judge held that the city had the authority to void its existing labor agreements while attempting to reorganize, stating that public workers do not enjoy the same protections Congress provided union employees in the private sector. Given the number of unionized public employers alleging during the economic recession of 2008–2010 that they can no longer afford to pay their financial obligations, the *Vallego* case will be carefully watched.

Aside from considerations of bankruptcy, the recession of 2008–2010 has demonstrated that public employers can cut employee costs by layoffs, by mandating time off on a periodic basis for certain employee groups, by forcing employees to choose between layoffs or wage cuts, by ceasing some operations, by curtailing operations on a rotating time basis, or by eliminating employee positions through reorganization of activities and/or terminations of programs.

Subjects of Bargaining

Legislation is quite specific in defining mandatory and permissive subjects of negotiations in some states such as Florida, Iowa, Minnesota, and Wisconsin. In other states such as Wyoming, essentially all subjects are negotiable and subject to mandatory interest arbitration in the event of bargaining impasse. The common purpose of defining mandatory versus permissive subjects of negotiations is to determine for arbitrators the topics that can be subject to arbitrator decision. A subject/issue that is not identified as a mandatory subject of bargaining (a permissive or prohibited issue) cannot generally be subject to arbitration decision.

Collective Bargaining Impasses

Collective bargaining impasses in states and cities generally must be resolved by contract/interest arbitration. In a few states where strikes by certain employee groups are legal, stipulated procedures outlined in the law must be followed.

Resolution by Strike Action

When a legal strike is threatened, its outcome can generally be predicted when the principles of the bargaining power model previously discussed are applied. The questions to be posed and answered are:

Are the employee group's services essential in the short run?

Is the employee group irreplaceable in the short run?

What are the anticipated relative costs of disagreement/agreement in political terms?

What are the perceptions of the parties concerning relative bargaining power?

What are the parties willing to do based on their perceptions?

The answers to these questions by the parties should predict with reasonable accuracy the outcomes of the actions taken by the parties.

If the employee group is providing a service vital to the public, if the employee group is not replaceable in the short run, if the cost of disagreement in the opinion of the political leaders is higher than the cost of agreement on the employee group's final position, and if the employee group perceives the above and is willing to take strike action to achieve demands, then the outcome will likely be determined in the employee group's favor.

Examination of the outcome of illegal strikes of public employees has demonstrated that when the questions above are answered in the employee group's favor, the employee group's demands will prevail and legal questions will be put aside in favor of getting the services vital to the public restored. See, for example, the outcome of illegal strikes by New York City transit employees.

An analysis of public school strikes demonstrates that parents who rely on the school to provide a place for their children to spend the hours stipulated by both classroom and other school activities tend to support teacher demands. These parents are apparently motivated by their own self-interest in maintaining free **child care**.

Resolution by Arbitration

The majority of states that have passed collective bargaining laws have determined that collective bargaining impasses are best resolved by arbitration. The states differ with regard to the procedures to be utilized to identify the issues that can be submitted to arbitration. In a very few states, (e.g., Wyoming) any issue not resolved by the parties through negotiations is subject to an arbitration decision. In other states, certain subjects reserved as employer rights are not subject to arbitration unless the employer has agreed to submit them to arbitration. There is no standard procedure specified by law in the states requiring arbitration of unresolved negotiations for either the identification of issues to be arbitrated or which issues identified as being in impasse are to be considered **arbitrable**.

Enforcement and Challenges to Contract (Interest) Arbitration Awards

Few states have indicated in their laws specific limitations on an arbitrator's ability to fashion a decision the arbitrator believes is an appropriate solution to the issues raised by the parties and that the state law has determined to be arbitrable. In virtually all of the states and cities that have passed collective bargaining legislation for public employees, there are legal frameworks available to the parties to enforce and/or challenge an award found to be inconsistent with the arbitrator's authority or inconsistent with public policy. Overwhelming legal precedent demonstrates that a successful challenge to an arbitrator's award is as much of an uphill climb in the public sector as a challenge to a grievance arbitrator's award is in the private sector.

Criteria Stipulated by Law for Contract Arbitration Awards

A number of states, such as Wisconsin, stipulate the definitive criteria that a contract or interest arbitrator must consider in making a decision. However, the criteria generally specified, if any, are broadly framed and cite such factors as cost of living, ability of the employer to pay, and terms and conditions in comparable public jurisdictions that arbitrators have wide latitude to fashion an award that will meet the requirements specified. An unusual criterion is specifically required by law for both negotiations and contract arbitration in Minnesota. In the late 1980s, Minnesota adopted a statute entitled the Local Government Pay Equity Act (LGPEA). This act states that all political jurisdictions of the state must:

1. Conduct a job evaluation of all of its employees periodically and
2. Consider the compensation paid to employees in comparable jurisdictions.

The act requires public jurisdictions to compensate employees primarily on the basis of the relative job values of the employer's job classifications and on the basis of the compensation paid by comparable employers. The law also requires contract arbitrators to consider this data in making decisions concerning employee compensation. The law became effective in 1990.

The Minnesota LGPEA had a significant impact on collective bargaining and contract arbitration in Minnesota. The act provided, in its statement of purpose, that it was intended primarily to raise the compensation of female employees relative to male employees working for Minnesota political subdivisions. Even a cursory review of published wage data for calendar 1987, the year the Pay Equity Act was passed, reveals that this stated goal has been met both through voluntary actions of the state's political jurisdictions and through collective bargaining and contract arbitration awards.

Although Minnesota is the only state to have enacted mandatory pay equity legislation, the act's stated philosophy of establishing pay equity for employees based on relative job classification values and compensation paid by comparable employers has had an impact on the compensation systems of public employers in other states. A rapidly increasing number of cities and counties in other states have been employing job evaluation/compensation firms to conduct job evaluation and comparable employer market studies. The results of these studies have allowed many public jurisdictions to develop employee compensation systems that enable them to demonstrate to current and potential employees that they have an equitable compensation structure. They apparently believe that being able to demonstrate to their employees that they have an internally equitable and market competitive compensation structure will also provide them with a comparative advantage in their efforts to recruit and hire well-qualified employees as well as potentially providing a basis for eliciting public support for their positions in the event of a strike.

EFFECT OF COLLECTIVE BARGAINING AND CONTRACT ARBITRATION DECISIONS

When collective bargaining laws were proposed in many states, legislators were lobbied by a wide variety of groups that opposed any law, supported a law that essentially duplicated the NLRA, proposed a law prohibiting strikes by all public employees, or argued for a law that allowed all public employees the right to strike. The result has been that laws were passed that provided a variety of the options listed. A variety of predictions were made as to the probable results of the various procedures for the settlement of impasses. The most common prediction with regard to mandatory contract arbitration of collective bargaining impasses when it was proposed by legislators for the resolution of bargaining impasses was that arbitrators would make determinations which would simply compromise the positions of the parties. This prediction was based on the assumption that arbitrators would make decisions on this basis partly to convince the parties and the public that the process of mandatory contract arbitration was the most practical method for the resolution of collective bargaining impasses and the avoidance of work stoppages.

Those who have made attempts to evaluate contract arbitration awards have neither confirmed nor refuted those predictions. Rather, reviews of the results of mandatory arbitration of collective bargaining impasses compared to the outcomes of legal strikes and voluntary settlements through negotiations appear to indicate no significant differences in outcomes. However, there appears to be little dispute that the most significant improvements in compensation for unionized public employees have been achieved through the use of illegal strikes, and that fact will likely continue in the future. Mention must also be made, however, that the illegal strike conducted by the federal air traffic controllers during the Reagan administration was a complete failure. All strikers were permanently fired. The firings succeeded because the workers were replaceable (see the bargaining power model previously discussed).

Techniques Used by Public Employers and Labor Organizations to Help Build Constructive Relationships

An increasing number of public employers and their respective labor organizations are attempting to find ways to build more productive and constructive working relationships. Some are engaging in a program differing from the usual exchange of demands/proposals by the parties and then proceeding to bargaining based on those proposals. Rather, they have elected to use a bargaining process commonly known as *interest-based,* or *integrative bargaining.* This type of negotiation involves no exchange of proposals. Instead, the parties identify for each other what they believe to be their primary interests in the relationship, explain why they have the identified interests, and demonstrate why they believe their respective interests can be effectively shared interests.

Some public employers and labor organizations have found such bargaining to be more productive for the development of constructive relationships and reaching agreements, and more satisfying to both parties. A number of public employers and labor organizations in the Seattle, Washington, area have reported such bargaining concepts to have worked well.

Increasingly, a substantial number of public employers and labor organizations have found that the establishment of joint Labor/Management Committees provides an opportunity for problems of joint concern. The meetings also provide the representatives with the ability to form stronger personal relationships and provide for more open and more productive negotiations.

Such committees cannot be regarded as a panacea or a replacement for normal collective bargaining. However, many employers and labor organizations have reported that participating in regular labor–management meetings have led to more constructive and cooperative bargaining relationships.[6]

CASE 9.1

Federal Case Study: The PATCO Strike of 1981

U.S. air traffic controllers represented by the Professional Air Traffic Controllers Organization (PATCO) were in engaged in protracted negotiations with the Federal Aviation Administration (FAA) in 1981. In June of that year the PATCO negotiators agreed to an FAA offer that was rejected by the membership. PATCO threatened strike action if the FAA offer was not enhanced. President Reagan stated that any controllers engaging in a strike action would be discharged because strikes against the government were considered illegal.

On August 3, 1981, PATCO began strike action. The FAA, together with other units of the federal government, had carefully prepared for strike action. Within a week after the strike began the FAA was operating within 70 percent of normal capacity utilizing nonstriking controllers, military controllers, retirees, and supervisors. Four hours after the beginning of the strike, President Reagan warned the strikers that they must return to work within 48 hours or face

termination of their employment. Some returned to work, but the 11,000 who did not were discharged.

Should PATCO have been aware of the preparations by the FAA and other units of the federal government and avoided a strike while continuing to bargain after the membership rejected the tentative settlement offer of the FAA?

Should President Reagan have provided written terminations postdated for a longer time than 48 hours for refusal to return to work as a final warning rather than terminating after 48 hours?

Should more controllers have stayed on the job rather than heeding the call to strike, given the President's warning of discharge?

Evaluate the relative bargaining power of PATCO and the FAA based on the model outlined in this chapter and outline the best strategic alternatives available to the parties. ■

CASE 9.2

State Case Study: Minnesota State and Professional Employees Strike of 2001

Frustrated by the positions held by the State of Minnesota concerning wage rate increases and the employer's share of the cost of health insurance benefits, almost 25,000 employees represented by the American Federation of State, County, and Municipal Employees (AFSCME) and the Minnesota Association of Professional Employees (MAPE) conducted a strike that lasted 14 days. In an attempt to gain the support of the public, the unions placed pickets espousing their positions and arguments for their positions along pubic highways, downtown streets, and shopping centers in addition to places in front of state and university buildings.

The state provided factual information to newspapers and television news about its offer on wage rates together with the amounts in dollars provided by the state toward employee health care. At the inception of the strike, a number of employees, estimated by the unions and the state to be up to 13 percent of the employees in the bargaining units eligible to strike, did not join the strike. As the strike progressed, additional employees on strike began to go back to work out of frustration that the public appeared to be more in in support of the state's positions rather than thst of the union.

The strike was settled after the state agreed to increase percentages in wage rates slightly and add a modest improvement in its health-care package. The unions' and the state's negotiators indicated that although no confrontations were reported between employees who work side by side who were eligible to strike but who continued to work and those who went on strike, managers would institute training programs to "handle the inevitable tension in the workplace." Governor Ventura said that the state would pay for the excess cost of the settlement above the state's initial position with "budget cuts and, if necessary, layoffs."

Should the unions have continued with the strike after they learned that 13 percent of those eligible did not join the strike action and additional persons returned to work during the strike?

Should the unions have returned to the bargaining table when public polls indicated the majority of the state's population supported the state's position?

Given the minor adjustments in the state's position that generated a settlement, should the state have moved to positions more acceptable to the unions' proposals before the strike to avoid the strike?

What would you suggest should be the content of the training to be provided by the state to employee groups made up of strikers and nonstrikers who must work together?

How should the state explain the additional costs of a settlement to the public above that which a majority of the public believed appropriate? ▪

CASE 9.3

Comparative Cities Case Study: Crafted Bargaining Units versus Wall-to-Wall Units

City No. 1 is an inner-suburb next to a large metropolitan city traditionally dominated politically by labor union-endorsed city council members and the mayor. The public works department was organized more than 25 years ago on a "crafted" basis (i.e., truck drivers were organized by the Teamsters Union; laborers by the Laborers Union; and equipment operators by the International Union of Operating Engineers). When a job is undertaken that involves a truck driver, a laborer, and an equipment operator, the crew must include three persons, because none of the individuals can perform the work belonging to a different union. This is the case even though the job may involve a minimum amount of work that one person who is able to drive a truck, do labor work, and operate a piece of equipment could easily perform.

City No. 2 is an outlying suburb approximately 25 miles from the metropolitan city. It enjoys a significantly higher assessed value per capita than the metropolitan city that has become populated over the years with low-income individuals living in subsidized housing while losing high-income workers to the outer suburbs. City No. 2's public works department was organized 10 years ago on a "wall-to-wall" basis by one union. All employees are trained from date of hire to perform all of the routine tasks involved in the department. Thus, when a task is performed requiring a truck, routine labor, and equipment use, one person performs all functions.

The relative costs of operation for between City No. 1 and City No. 2 are slightly more than triple, since often a supervisor/lead-person needs to be used when three persons are working together. City No. 1 has been keenly aware of the high cost of its public works operations relative to the costs incurred by the suburbs with wall-to-wall bargaining units relative to its crafted units. It is concerned that its wage rate and benefit structure is higher per person than the more affluent suburbs due to the labor union influence on its city council when collective bargaining is ongoing. City No. 1 has approached the unions repeatedly in an effort convince them to reduce the costs of operation without success.

Collective bargaining in the state takes place under a comprehensive law providing for the mandatory mediation and contract arbitration of bargaining impasses. The severe recession of 2008–2009 has convinced City No. 1 that it must reduce its operating costs for its public works department to approximately the same level as the outer suburbs.

Given the city's failure to convince the unions to modify their bargaining unit structure to reduce operating costs, what strategies would you recommend City No. 1's management use to try and reduce the costs of operation? Evaluate the following options:

a. Conduct a public information campaign demonstrating relative costs and relative ability to pay compared to suburbs.

b. Convince the council to bargain to an impasse and prepare for contract arbitration using cost comparisons with the suburbs on relative costs and ability to pay.

c. Convince the council to threaten layoffs sufficient to reduce operating costs unless the unions agree to reorganization of bargaining units and/or other means of reducing costs.

d. Options not listed above. ■

CASE 9.4

Hard Economic Times

The recession that began in late 2007, which was predicted by economists in both the private and public sectors to ease only slowly beginning in 2010, had (and continues to have at the time of this writing) significant impact on public-sector collective bargaining. Forty-seven states reported fiscal deficits for 2009. More than 10 states reported severe deficits requiring reductions in state employees both in numbers of employees and enumeration of employees. Thousands of cities and counties in many states also suffered substantial losses of revenue and were forced to reduce the number of employees, subcontract work performed by employees, and reduce wages and benefits.

Where the employees of the states and political subdivisions were covered by labor agreements providing for specific wage rates and benefits (including retirement), negotiations were necessary before changes could be made. Often the negotiations and the basis for the negotiations became headlines in local papers and in some cases national news. The headlines in many states concentrated on the level of wage rates, the size and magnitude of fringe benefits, and the amount of and the ease for eligibility of pensions for public employees—particularly in California and New York. This information created significant public anger when coupled with the information also provided as to the size and scope of the unfunded liabilities for public employee pensions in many states.

Generally the 2007–2009 recession prompted the public to more closely focus on labor costs in both the public and private sectors. The public concern with the labor and benefit costs in the traditional U.S. automobile companies, for example, forced the federal government to demand a lowering of these costs as a condition for public assistance to those prevailing among the foreign companies operating in the United States as non-union entities. Similar public demands have appeared in the public sector as states and cities asked their employees for reductions in wage rates and benefits when they began to be publicly discussed. In substance, the severe recession that began in late 2007 has had and will continue to have a lengthy and significant impact on collective bargaining in the U.S. economy. This is particularly so in the public sector where, for many years, the employees—unionized and nonunionized—have enjoyed sizeable gains in wages and benefits without general public knowledge and concern.

The relative bargaining power of the employers and the unions has definitively changed based on the increased public awareness of the labor costs and the basis for these costs. The collective bargaining results during 2009 amply demonstrated that fact—whether the results were derived from the bargaining table or through awards by arbitrators.

Will the economic hardships facing states and their political subdivisions encourage greater use of labor–management committees to develop replies to public concerns about employee costs?

Will the increased public concern about public employee enumeration, particularly benefit costs that are perceived to be overly generous, continue to increase pubic employer bargaining power?

Will and/or can the public employee unions convince their members to lower their expectations about future wage rates and benefit increases?

Will the propensity of public employers to subcontract work to the private sector continue as a source of lowering employee costs? ■

Summary

This chapter discusses the process of collective bargaining in the United States in the absence of a generally applicable legal framework that could serve to establish a set of uniform rules and guidelines. By contrast, the private sector and the federal public sector collective bargaining processes can be examined in terms of the impact of law and the processes developed under the law because of the uniformity of the statute. Compounding the difficulty of examining the processes of collective bargaining as it has evolved among states and local jurisdictions is the lack of a consistent measuring stick. In the private sector, the commonly used measuring stick for both employers and unions is short- and long-run economic costs.

However, in the public sector, the commonly used determinative for the formulation of strategies and actions appears to be public reaction and opinion in the short run. A present representation of this fact is the publicity now being given to the almost unbelievable problems only recently being discussed of the unfunded liabilities of states with regard to their public employee pension funds. The numbers in some states such as Illinois, California, and New York stated in billions clearly demonstrate the almost casual approach of many elected officials to long-run liabilities that are often not discernable to the public.

Key Terms

FLRA   233
strikes   234
contract arbitration   234
grievance procedures   234
Civil Service Reform Act   234

costs of agreement/
    disagreement   235
bargaining power   236
perceptions   236
public opinion   237

tax levels   237
multilateral   238
ability to pay   239
child care   240
arbitrable   240

Questions for Consideration

1. Should public employees have the right to organize?
2. Should any public employee group have the right to strike? If yes, which groups should have the right and which groups should not?
3. Is mandated contract arbitration a rational alternative to the right to strike?
4. What subjects should be considered mandatory subjects of bargaining; what subjects should be considered permissive; and what, if any, subjects should be considered non-negotiable?
5. Should all or any negotiated agreements be subject to public ratification votes by citizens of the jurisdiction and/or by the state of the jurisdiction? If yes, and the tentative

agreement is rejected, what process should be followed?
6. Should all public employee bargaining sessions/meetings—formal or informal—be open to the public and or televised?
7. Should union demands be published and/or distributed to the public of the jurisdiction for comment prior to the beginning of negotiations?
8. Should all public employment labor agreements be required to contain a grievance provision mandating binding arbitration of all grievances involving the specific terms and conditions of the agreement—of the voluntary past practices of the parties to the agreement?

Notes to Chapter 9

1. 5 U.S.C., Chapter 71.
2. These states are Arizona, Arkansas, Mississippi, New Mexico, North Carolina, South Carolina, Utah, and West Virginia. Colorado and Louisiana have legislation that covers only public-sector transit employees. A. Ruben, ed., *Elkouri and Elkouri: How arbitration works,* 6th ed. (Washington, DC: BNA), 2003, pp. 1371–1391. See also Kearney, *Labor Relations in the Public Sector.*
3. J. Lund and C. L. Maranto, "Public sector labor law: An update," in Dale Belman , Morley Gunderson, and Douglas Hyatt, eds. *Public sector employment in time of transition,* (Madison, WI: IRRA), 1996.
4. N. Chamberlain and J. Kuhn, *Collective bargaining,* 2nd ed. (New York: McGraw Hill), 1965, pp. 169–180.
5. *NLRB* v. *Wooster Division of Borg-Warner Corporation,* 356 U.S.342 (1958).
6. For further discussion see J. Kriesky, "Trends in dispute resolution in the public sector," in A. Eaton and J. Keefe, eds., *Employment dispute resolution and workers rights in the changing workplace* (Champaign, IL: IRRA), 1999, pp. 247–242.

CHAPTER 10

Avoiding Termination Litigation

CHAPTER OUTLINE

Property Rights Employment

Faulty Dismissals

The Discharge Process

Waivers or Releases

Defamation

E veryone employed by an organization will ultimately terminate their employment, so it should be no surprise that there are legal issues at the point of personnel exits just as there are at the point of entry. The departure from employment
can be voluntary, result from a job becoming unnecessary, or result from retirement
or dismissal (involuntary separation).[1] There are also federal (WARN, for example)[2]
and state laws applying to the notification of personnel about impending temporary
separation or layoff.

This chapter is devoted primarily to involuntary separations and claims that may
arise following termination of employment. Wrongful discharge issues are most common
in the private sector and where at-will employment relationships exist and/or where
due process is ignored. Claims surrounding unjust dismissals, commonly referred to as
wrongful discharge issues, are among the most common in human resource law.[3] Despite
marked differences in termination practices between the private sector and many of our
public organizations, the following are some common general views:

1. Despite at-will rights, it's advantageous to have a sound reason for any adverse
   personnel action, lest discrimination allegations surface.
2. Even where at-will law prevails, there are exceptions.
3. Dismissal should not be an event but a process.
4. If it's not imposed, it's still wise to embrace the concept of justice.
5. A reluctance to dismiss can be counterproductive and possibly harmful under the
   concept of negligent retention.
6. Preventing dismissals is usually preferable to suffering them.

7. There is often some threat of a discrimination allegation lurking in any discharge action.
8. Societal conditions suggest care, prudence, and fairness in terminations.

PROPERTY RIGHTS EMPLOYMENT

Most public employees through union contracts, civil service rules, legislation, tenure provisions, or other policies of the organization enjoy protected job rights. "Public sector employees are viewed as having a bona fide **property right** in their jobs once they have passed their period of probationary service."[4] One model of desirable public human resource policies and procedures states: "All county employees are permanent employees with a property right in their employment. Each . . . employee has a substantial expectancy of continued employment . . ."Again, those completing the **probationary period** will qualify for "permanent appointment."[5] The job rights thereby enjoy "indisputable **just cause**" in the face of discharge. To that end, dismissal procedures provide for *"due process."*[6] Both of these employee protection principles apply to "merit"[7] and "civil service" systems. Hallmarks of a merit system included tenure protection, the use of written competitive examinations, and a neutral administration.

Public-sector organizations, with or without a union contract obligation, commonly embrace **progressive discipline** as an element in due process.[8] Typically, when a transgression occurs, this involves a series of disciplinary steps including verbal admonishment by the supervisor; followed by more severe discipline, such as a written warning, for a repeated offense; and finally, other increasingly severe sanctions such as a suspension without pay, up to the point of discharge. Sometimes a **last chance agreement,** where the employee is provided with a final opportunity to correct his or her failings, is utilized as a last resort to rehabilitate a miscreant. Federal supervisors can be hesitant to initiate discipline or discharge proceedings because they are uncertain about just cause, dealing with contractual grievance procedures, possible discrimination charges, or being overturned by higher management.[9] A few organizations limit progressive discipline[10] and a few reject the obligation completely. Following this process an employee can be entitled to time to arrange defense, accusations in writing, hearings, and appeals.[11] Supervisors can be unwilling to spend the time and engage in the controversy for such duration with uncertain support from higher management.

The public has frequently expressed frustration with perceived misplaced protectionism and political reform efforts have met with limited success. One author postulates that career bureaucrats often think in terms of increments or "gradualism" versus the urgent pace in the private sector.[12] Bureaucratic "internal clocks" also conflict with executive political appointees who have time parameters in which to accomplish objectives.

There is little doubt that due process practices will reduce court cases. However, that doesn't apply to all public-sector employers. Recall that "each state civil service system is unique, featuring varying levels of civil service sophistication and continuing elements of patronage."[13] Sometimes "a department head may dismiss any employee for any reason."[14] The public sector also reduces the frequency of wrongful discharge legal actions with long periods of probation to test performance and compatibility. Six months of trial, which is often concurrent with training, is common, but probationary periods of a year are not unusual for police and other public health personnel.

Employers will often resort to so-called last chance agreements as an alternative to discharge. An employee who has reached the end of his disciplinary rope is granted one more opportunity to perform satisfactorily with the proviso that the employee waives any appeal rights that he or she might otherwise have, should he or she fails to comply with the employer's rules and regulations. Exhibit 10.1

is an example of a last chance agreement that the employer might offer to an employee as an alternative to immediate dismissal.

The risk of wrongful discharge lawsuits under at-will employment in the private sector contrasts with the good faith and fair treatment characteristic of the public sector. The differences in the extremes of the two principles are stark and contribute to the differentiation of two different management models. In the private sector, due process and just cause are valued as principles of justice. However, many managers view the appeal procedures through which just cause must be established as too time consuming and costly to commit to in writing.[15] They believe the attendant loss of productivity and efficiency to be unnecessary to achieve fairness and justice in the workplace.

Applied Definitions

Among thousands of organizations that commit to due process (the pursuit of justice) and good or proper cause (sufficient reason) procedures, a variety of expressions or actions are used in defining these terms. Be alert to potential miscommunication, as these terms are all not easily defined and may mean different things to different people.

Due Process Expressions

- To be informed of the transgression
- Time to correct behavior
- Time to prepare defense
- Representation (Assistance)
- Written charges
- A warning
- An opportunity to respond
- An appeal procedure
- Good (Just) cause
- A reasonable rule or standard
- Knowledge of the rule or standard
- Forewarning of the consequences of a failure
- Valid evidence of the offense
- An impartial decision maker
- A fair decision
- Progressive discipline

Reasons for Termination

Dismissals occur because individuals aren't compatible with the preferences or needs of the organization. People can be "released"

Employee Name _____

Union Name _____

Employer _____

For mutual consideration, the adequacy of which they each acknowledge, the above named parties hereby enter into this Last Chance Agreement, and agree as follows:

As an alternative to the employer seeking termination (discharge) for _____ (e.g., conduct unbecoming a (job title), excessive absenteeism, unsatisfactory performance), the union and the employer have agreed to enter into this Last Chance Agreement as a full, final, and complete settlement of this matter.

The company and the union acknowledge and agree that if ___(employee name)___ engages in any of the following conduct or fails to comply with or complete any one of the requirements specified below, this conduct or failure shall constitute "just cause" for his or her discharge from employment and under any relevant statutory protection.

EXHIBIT 10.1   Sample Last Chance Agreement

because of economic reasons without fault. The following material involves decisions where an individual is unsuitable because of conduct, performance, or violation of rules or expectations. Clarity in the motivation for discharge is important. Established rules, standards, and purpose should be definite enough for clear articulation for the "reason." If a supervisor takes discharge action, it will require evidence to substantiate a legitimate reason. Provided that proper steps are taken before the discharge, the decision can ordinarily be justified. The proper *method* can result in the least exposure to litigation; therefore, the process should begin well in advance of the discharge date.

Discipline or Discharge for Off-Duty Conduct

Legal jurisdictions differ on the impact of off-duty transgressions on one's employment status. It can be complex and controversial. When considering whether off-duty conduct can be just cause for discipline, the courts and arbitrators require that the employer establish a *nexus* between the conduct on which the discharge is based and the workplace. Factors considered include:[16]

1. The degree of damage to the employer's business or reputation.[17]
2. The effect on co-workers of the off-duty relationships or conduct.
3. The effect the off-duty relationship or conduct may have on the employee's on-duty performance and workplace efficiency.

In criminal cases, the possibility of a temporary suspension prior to judicial determination is a consideration if strong facts show that the employer's business could be adversely affected.[18] In all three factors, the main element is that there must be a connection between off-duty activity or conduct and the nature and characteristics of the employee's work.[19]

When Off-Duty Comes into the Office

Off-duty conduct begs the question of where the employee's right to privacy ends and the employer's right to intercede begins.[20] Employers are frequently frustrated when incidents involving male–female relationships intrude in the workplace. These problems are commonplace and often surface when an off-duty relationship ends badly or one of the persons involved terminates or is promoted. In *Hunt* v. *Mid-American Employees Credit Union,* 384 N.W.2d 853 (Minn. 1986), an intimate relationship existed between a secretary and a sales manager. The two went on a business trip and upon their return the employer discharged the secretary. She immediately filed a sex discrimination charge. The sales manager objected strenuously that there was a question of his loyalty, so he was also discharged. He filed a wrongful discharge suit based on the handbook. The employer successfully defended both charges but was exposed to a lawsuit, lost two good employees, and incurred large legal costs.

Social relationships should be discouraged when employees are hired, but care should be taken not to interfere with privacy rights. The employees should be informed of the hazard both to themselves and to the company. Clear and concise consequences should be communicated. If explanation of the rules and employer expectations are not sufficient, and discouragement does not work, the employer may want to consider stopping the relationship, as occurred in *Patton* v. *J. C. Penney,* 719 P.2d 854 (Ore. 1986), where the employee refused to stop dating a co-worker and was discharged. The court held, in stating that the employer's interest outweighs the employee's right of privacy, that this was not a violation of public policy or an invasion of privacy. In *McCluskey* v. *Clark Oil Refining Co.,* 498 N.E.2d 559 (Ill. App. 1986), the court upheld the discharge of an employee for marrying a co-worker, ruling that such a termination was not a violation of public policy. Generally, prohibitions against nepotism have been upheld.[21] In *Malone* v. *Eaton Corp.*, the court affirmed that a prohibition of romantic relationships between a supervisor and subordinate could be enforced.[22]

FAULTY DISMISSALS

Some dismissal actions are ill grounded. Too often there is no legitimate and valid reason to terminate an employee. Dismissals because of a pregnancy, a single garnishment action, and an attempt to retaliate against an employee or to force someone to quit (**constructive discharge**) are not deemed just cause in the eyes of the law and can result in embarrassment in addition to damages and legal fees. Employees who report illegal acts of their employer or complain about illegal treatment have protection against harassment or mistreatment, both on and off the job, under numerous federal and state laws. The Sarbanes-Oxley Act is a federal law that protects employees from disclosing inappropriate financial affairs of their employer. The Civil Service Reform Act (CSRA) prohibits **reprisal** against federal employees for "whistleblowing" or complaining. Defensive measures should intercept such actions.

In the simplest of terms, *constructive discharge* may be taken to mean that when an employee apparently quits, he or she has actually been compelled to leave because of some action by the employer. However, the law applies a special—and much more complex—meaning to the term. Black's Law Dictionary defines *constructive discharge* as "that which occurs when an employer deliberately makes employee's working conditions so intolerable that the employee is forced into voluntary resignation."[23] Although most courts have followed this legal definition, the first-line supervisor does not generally understand it. For this reason, a termination is often recorded as a voluntary quit when in effect it is a constructive discharge and the employee has the same

remedies under the law as if she or he had been discharged.[24]

Constructive Discharge under the NLRA

The original concept of constructive discharge typically involved a situation where the employer wanted to discharge an employee but was concerned about the possible legal/contractual repercussions. By making life on the job so miserable that the employee would quit, the employer expected to avoid the need to discharge. Among the first cases to reach the courts were those based on charges of unfair labor practices where the employer would have "evil intent or motive" because of union activity and would set up a plan to entrap the employee or coerce the employee to quit.

An early case involved an employer who learned that an employee was supporting a union drive; as a result, the employer became hostile toward her as a result. In retaliation, the employer altered the employee's method of pay—putting her on incentive rates when she was not even earning the minimum wage. She protested, but nothing was done and so she quit. The court ruled that she had been fired for union activity in violation of Section 8 (a) (3) of the National Labor Relations Act. The evidence in this case showed intent or programmed action to force the employee to quit.[25]

Court Determinations

Court determinations of what is intolerable are on a case-by-case basis at the discretion of the court. Probably the best example of constructive discharge without specific intent involves a plaintiff who was hired as a teller. At the time of hire, she was told that all employees were required to go to a staff meeting. At the first staff meeting she discovered that the agenda included a religious talk and prayer, both delivered by a Baptist minister. Being an atheist, she refused to go to the meetings.

The employer countered that she must attend staff meetings and that if she objected to the devotions she could "close her ears." She still refused. The employer asked for a letter of resignation, stating that she was not being fired. She charged that she was constructively discharged for reasons of religious discrimination. The court held that mandatory attendance at company prayer meetings imposed intolerable working conditions because attendance would have forced the employee to sacrifice her fundamental religious beliefs.[26]

After the enactment of antidiscrimination laws, the courts had to consider whether a violation of an antidiscrimination law created an unreasonable atmosphere sufficient to warrant a finding of constructive discharge. One of the most common situations where intolerable conditions are alleged involves inadequate or discriminatory salary increases. The charge of intolerable salary derives its legal basis from Title VII of the sex discrimination section.

One employee argued that she was constructively discharged because of intolerable conditions of sex discrimination. She had come to work for a company as a secretary and had worked her way up to the position of buyer. After 90 days as a buyer, she was given a requested increase but she was still making $130 per month less than the male person she replaced. Because of her disappointment, she quit and filed a charge of sex discrimination, alleging that she was doing the same work as males but was paid $130 less per month. The court cited the general rule that if the employer deliberately made conditions so intolerable that the employee was forced to quit, the employer was guilty of constructive discharge. The employer was liable for any illegal conduct involved, just as it would have been if it had formally discharged the employee. The court found further that the pay arrangement did show sex discrimination but that in taking the promotion the employee had agreed to work for less money. Under these conditions, the court in *Bourque* v. *Powell Electrical Manufacturing* found that a reasonable person would not have quit because of unequal pay.[27]

Other courts have followed the *Bourque* precedent in holding that there is no constructive discharge even though the condition that caused the resignation is found to be unlawful. The plaintiff must prove more. He or she must show that the unlawful condition created by the employer is so offensive that a reasonable person would have found it intolerable. Failing in this proof, the employee must continue working while seeking to remedy the allegedly unlawful practice. The employee is not required to show the employer's intent in order to prove constructive discharge, only that the employer knowingly permitted the condition to exist.[28]

The courts are consistent in finding that the conditions created by the employer must be more than disagreeable.[29] If the conditions are severe enough, for whatever reason, the court will find constructive discharge and will usually find that because of the intolerable conditions, intent can be assumed.[30] In deciding whether an intolerable working condition exists, the court determines whether a "reasonable person in the employee's position and circumstances would have felt compelled to resign." This was the rule in the *Bourque* case, and it is followed in most jurisdictions.

The issue in all these cases is not whether a particular employee feels that the job is objectionable, but whether a reasonable person in the employee's situation would have been compelled to resign. An employee's own subjective assessment of what is tolerable is not sufficient to lead to a finding of constructive discharge.

Harassment

The courts have also found that sexual harassment in the workplace may be sufficiently pervasive to support a finding of constructive discharge. The Court in *Pennsylvania State Police* v. *Suders*, 542 U.S. 129 (2004), found that a resignation not compelled by an "official act" of the employer may still constitute a constructive discharge, but that the employer is entitled to an affirmative defense to avoid vicarious liability. Where an official act such as demotion, involuntary reassignment, or loss of pay is the apparent cause of the constructive discharge, no affirmative defense is allowed.

Demotion, Transfer, or Retirement

Official acts including transferring or demoting an employee can lead to a constructive discharge claim even if no harassment is present.[31] In such a claim, the transfer or demotion itself is alleged to be the intolerable condition. The reason for the action is alleged to be the unlawful act. Discrimination is often claimed at the same time to provide a statutory basis for the alleged violation. Although antidiscrimination statutes may be violated, courts will not find constructive discharge if the condition created by the transfer or demotion is not sufficiently severe.

In determining severity, the court will compare the new job with the employee's prior position. The comparison will consider differences in pay and benefits, day-to-day job conditions, increased travel requirements, and similar considerations. The courts will also consider the negative effect on the employee's prestige and whether the employee was embarrassed by the employer's action. In evaluating embarrassment claims, courts seek to determine whether the embarrassment would be daily and unavoidable and whether there was a radical change in job responsibilities sufficient to warrant embarrassment.

In constructive discharge cases, age discrimination is often the alleged legal basis for action. Lawyers prefer this approach because age discrimination cases are tried before a jury, and juries are more likely to be sympathetic to alleged intolerable conditions than are judges. In one such case the employee, a supervisor, was not performing her job up to standard and the employer gave her a choice between being retired and being transferred to a nonsupervisory position in the department that she formerly supervised. She chose retirement but then brought an age discrimination suit, stating that she was forced to retire. The jury agreed. The court found that there was sufficient evidence to allow the jury to find that the employee was constructively discharged.[32] The employer might have anticipated that when someone is transferred to a nonsupervisory position in a department that she formerly supervised, she would be forced to work with her former subordinates, which could create embarrassment and/or unbearable working conditions.

A transfer can sometimes result in a breach of an employment contract. An employer entered into a written agreement with an electrical engineer specifying that he would be employed as a manager of a department. The contract permitted discharge for "just cause." After a period of time, the supervisor of the employee attempted to reclassify him to the position of sales engineer. The engineer quit and sued for breach of contract. The court held the action of the supervisor to be a breach of contract.[33]

Resignation or Discharge

The clearest form of constructive discharge occurs when an employer tells an employee that she or he has an opportunity to resign, but that if the employee does not do so, she or he will be discharged (also called a *smoking gun threat*).[34] This is a common practice of employers, and the reason it is used is probably a misguided attempt to promote good employee relations by making a terminated employee more employable.[35] Whatever its effect on morale, the approach opens the door to litigation and sometimes to liability greater than would have been incurred if the employee had been discharged outright. This type of case is difficult to defend, as the courts often feel that the employer has threatened the employee even though the employer may have the right to discharge.

One employee had a written contract, but the school board asked for his resignation. He resigned and then brought action for breach of contract (*Knee* v. *School District No. 139 in Canyon City*, 676 P.2d 727 [Idaho App. 1984]). The court held that the mere request to resign is not enough to justify a finding of constructive discharge. Discharge must be stated as the alternative. The fact that he had a contract would lead one to believe that he could not be discharged. A different outcome resulted when an employee was told that she had the option of resigning or being discharged. She resigned and filed a claim for violation of a handbook provisions. The applicable state law considered the handbook to be a contract. The court not only found constructive discharge but also allowed punitive damages. The court said that the employer stands to gain from a resignation rather than a discharge because it will insulate itself from a wrongful discharge claim.[36]

An employer can be guilty of constructive discharge in encouraging early retirement. An employee who could either have taken early retirement or have been transferred under a reorganization program was told that it would be a waste of time to transfer if he preferred early retirement. He took early retirement and filed suit, alleging that he was coerced into this action. The court held that in order to be considered coercion in violation of the Age Discrimination in Employment Act, the alternative to early retirement had to be so intolerable that a reasonable person who wanted to continue work would have refused it.[37]

Prevention of Claims

Employers should not assume that constructive discharge cases are the exception rather than the rule. Employees—particularly in white-collar occupations—generally want to continue working and will resist being separated from their jobs. Exposure to charges of constructive discharge exists in every transfer, demotion, promotion, or termination, especially if the employee is approaching retirement age. Successful constructive discharge cases are on the increase, as the courts require less to find unreasonableness. Once intolerable conditions or an unreasonable alternative have been established, the courts do not expect the employee to continue working and will consider a voluntary quit as a constructive discharge.

An employer can take several steps to reduce exposure to constructive discharge claims. These include:

1. Educate the supervisors. This is probably the most important defense; the supervisor is frequently the one who seeks a way to make the employee quit.
2. Encourage the employee to accept the demotion or transfer rather than resign. Make sure that he or she understands that the action is not intended to result in termination.
3. If you do intend to discharge the employee, be honest and open with him or her and go through with the discharge rather than give the option to resign. The employee is less likely to feel that he or she was treated unfairly, and the judge or jury will be less suspicious if the matter does end up in court.
4. Beware of resignation; always ask for a reason. This prevents the employee from later raising allegations of constructive discharge. Courts give little weight to this technique.

Affirmative Action in Staff Reductions

Two competing exposures can be problematic. One discrimination charge resulted because the employer was trying to comply with its affirmative action obligation. In *Firefighters Local Union No. 1784* v. *Stotts*, 467 U.S. 561 (1984), a municipality laid off white firefighters out of seniority order according to a court-approved voluntary affirmative action plan. The layoff violated the seniority provisions of the collective bargaining agreement but maintained the balance of black and white firefighters set forth in the court-approved affirmative action program (51 cities had similar programs). The Supreme Court held that the seniority provisions of the collective bargaining agreement couldn't be ignored.[38] The *Stotts* decision also stated that the plan was inconsistent with the spirit and the letter of the antidiscrimination laws unless a lower court first ruled that discrimination existed. In *Stotts,* the lower court, without a trial, had determined that discrimination was practiced, but didn't provide a remedy because a voluntary agreement had been reached.

In the similar case of *Wygant* v. *Jackson Board of Education,* 106 S.Ct. 1842 (1986), the court majority found that past discrimination alone is insufficient cause to justify racial preference. It held that in order for a layoff procedure under an affirmative action plan to favor one race over another, there must be convincing evidence of prior discrimination as determined by a court.[39] The *Wygant* decision was very narrow, as the court in *Sheetmetal Workers Local No. 93* v. *City of Cleveland*, 106 S.Ct. 3063 (1986), said an employer may develop an affirmative action plan for hiring and promotion in the settlement of an employment discrimination charge. Here, the employer and union had violated the statute and entered into a court-approved settlement agreement to remedy the violation. The union also violated the settlement agreement. The court said the agreement was identical to a private out-of-court settlement. However, in another case the court held that those employees who were not directly affected could receive race-conscious relief.[40]

Avoiding Wrongful Discharge

An employer's exposure to allegations of wrongful discharge and the subsequent costs is ever present. Although the decision and process may be masterfully accomplished, an allegation, legitimate or not, is always a possibility. Accordingly, the employer must adopt a number of preventive policies, practices, and procedures, beginning at the time of hire. This is particularly true where no written due process commitments exist.

The best way to avoid costly wrongful discharge settlements is to use due caution in hiring and then communicate some understandings that the new employee acknowledges in writing. Selecting the right people, and avoiding those with a litigious bent, is an obvious first step. Background investigations that can minimize charges of negligence have been addressed.

Demonstrating Good Faith

If a day of "reckoning" in a court comes to pass, evidence of well intended, honest training, alternative job placement efforts and "doing unto others" might temper harsh penalties. If it doesn't count for anything, consider it a worthwhile employee relation's investment. In the meantime be sure some form of a declaration on the application is signed by the employee.

When the employment relationship between the employee and the employer is at-will and may be terminated at any time by either party with or without cause, a clause such as "I understand that false statements on my application will result in discipline" may be included. This statement supersedes all prior statements, either written or oral, as to terms and conditions of employment.

Establish At-Will Employments

Applicants typically agree to an employment-at-will relationship when completing an application form. Because employment at this point is still in the prospective, the applicant will usually not refuse to sign the form.[41] Employers who have the disclaimer in the application form find that it does not have a chilling effect on the applicant flow or is a barrier to obtaining good, qualified applicants.[42] Others feel that it puts the company in a negative position at the start of the employment period.

The courts will enforce an at-will clause in the applicant form and will usually hold that it is an expressed contract at the time of hiring. Where a handbook stated that discharge will be for just cause only and the employee was discharged after eight years, the court held that just cause had to be shown.[43] New York is a strong at-will state, but the court held that the clause in the application form was an expressed contract and removed the employee from at-will status. In addition to legal and employee relations, considerations when making a decision whether to include an at-will clause in the application form, it must also be considered whether it prevents subsequent charges. Some courts hold that although the application form clearly states one thing, a later statement in the handbook or a posted memo can modify the original statement.[44] A decision to include expressed contract language must consider future circumstances that may be troublesome. Sometimes it is better to say nothing.

A Complaint Procedure

A complaint procedure can be effective in reducing exposure to lawsuits in discharge cases. An employer-created grievance procedure can surface most of the perceived injustice in wrongful discharge allegations. However, it must be used the way it was intended. Often the restrictions or personalities involved in the procedure limit its usefulness; if this is the case, the restrictions or persons involved should be changed. The less formal the procedure is, with liberal time limits and no restriction on what member of management the employee can express a complaint to, the more it will be used. In *Meritor Savings Bank, FSB* v. *Vinson*, 196 S.Ct. 2399 [1986]), the employer was found guilty of sexual harassment. The complaint procedure was not utilized because the employee was required to report to the person responsible for the harassing behavior. Also, if a peer review or an impartial arbitrator is not provided for (assuming a non-union facility), and employees are not using the complaint procedure, serious consideration should be given to changing it.

Applying Just Cause

Public-sector organizations normally commit to just or proper cause for dismissal action. Private-sector firms are less willing to do so. An employer's policy or practice must be carefully considered and communicated to all employees. It must be applicable when a discharge occurs. The development of doctrines that create exceptions to the employment-at-will doctrine may encourage employees to file previously unthinkable claims for relief. The vague definition of "justice" by the courts may give employees license to pursue court action and discourage the employer from discharging anyone except in extreme cases. Employees will file lawsuits in almost any discharge case when just cause is not clearly evident. The first question that the court will ask is the reason for the discharge. If none can be clearly articulated, the reason alleged by the employee may serve as an exception to the at-will doctrine.

Seldom will a wrongful discharge suit succeed when the employer adopts a just cause termination policy. Employers should communicate to the employee the exact conditions that will cause severe disciplinary action or discharge. If just cause such as damage or disruption to the organization is evidenced, the courts have supported the discharge rather than rely on the common law exceptions. Exactly what constitutes just cause is decided on a case-by-case basis by arbitrators whose task it is to interpret labor agreements. However, in a non-union facility, just cause may relate more to general employee relations problems than to some external standard.

Fortunately, there are two court decisions that provide a logical definition of "just cause" in a non-union setting. In *Danzer v. Professional Insurers, Inc.*, 679 P.2d 1276 (N.M. 1984), the Supreme Court of New Mexico stated, "Termination for good cause is shown . . . in some causes inherent in and related to qualifications of the employee or a failure to properly perform some essential aspect of the employee's job function." Another court completed the definition, when in *Staton v. Amax Coal Co., Div. of Amax Inc.*, 461 N.E.2d 612 (Ill. App. 3 dist. 1984), the court, after reviewing the decisions on just cause involving arbitration under labor agreements, found that "just cause includes not only that conduct that an employee knows or should know is subject to discipline" but also where the employee's continuance in his or her position is in some way detrimental to the efficiency of the operation. The law and sound public policy recognize that there is good cause for no longer employing the person. Not all courts have adopted this two-part definition.[45]

If a court is presented with the fact that the employee was adequately informed, it is quite likely to find "just cause." In *Conner v. Fort Gordon Bus Co.*, 761 F.2d 1493 (11th Cir. 1985), the employee argued that just cause was only a pretext for discrimination. The court said it was just cause so long as the standard or policy violation was the basis for the discharge and the standard or policy was communicated to the employee before the violation.[46] On previous occasions, the employer had only issued reprimands for violations. The fact that the employer did not issue the reprimand, but discharged instead, doesn't mean the discharge was wrongful.

The just cause audit accordingly should determine the following when an employee was discharged: Was there a rule violation or poor performance? Was the employee knowledgeable before committing the act? In the case of poor performance, was there an opportunity to correct? In cases where the employer has been successful in defending just cause discharges, the employee often unsuccessfully alleges that she or he failed to understand the consequences of committing the act.

Implied Contract Vulnerability

An employer's procedures and practices can serve well or poorly, and can minimize legal exposure or create it. Aggressive recruiting and promotion can increase exposure to an implied contract. Promises made at the time of hiring, handbooks characterizing the company as a place of continuous employment, and salaries quoted as annual salaries, which may imply a contract of employment for one year, are all common statements that could result in an implied contract.[47]

Recruiting

Recruiting creates the most vulnerability when, in the interest of selling the company or promoting good employee relations, a certain commitment is made. In determining whether such a promise is an implied contract, the employee must show some reliance on the promise. One example would be a long-distance move where the employee left a secure job with a competitor and, at a later date, was discharged without cause, or where there was a reliance on a promise of a better opportunity that never materialized. Promises of this kind are not uncommon in aggressive employment activity. The reason that the job does not materialize or the employee is laid off may be legitimate, but the employee is still emotionally and financially harmed. In this situation, the courts can allow punitive damages.

One of the more definite statements from a court that adopted the implied contract approach is found in *Pugh* v. *See's Candies, Inc.*, 116 Cal. App. 3rd 311 (1981), where a vice president of employee relations of 32 years of service was terminated. When he asked why, he was told, "Look deep within yourself." The jury determined that length of service, a series of promotions and commendations, the lack of direct criticism of his work, and the assurance by his superior that, if he did a good job, his future would be secure, established an implied contract.[48] The company violated the contract by the discharge.

Quoting an Annual Salary

A common practice that can result in an exposure is quoting an annual salary in a job offer. This is a good selling point but it often backfires. An annual salary figure impresses the applicant because it looks much larger than a weekly or a monthly figure. The practice has caused unnecessary litigation. The courts consider how the employee reacts to the statement rather than the intent of the person who originated it. In *Berand* v. *IMI Systems, Inc.*, 8 IER Cases 325 (BNA 1993), the court, in reversing a long-established precedent, said that an employee expects to be employed at will when hired and an annual salary quote does not mean a one-year contract. The few state courts that have had the issue before them are split on whether a one-year contract is formed by quoting an annual salary.

South Dakota has a statute that says that when you quote an annual salary, it results in a contract for one year [S.D. Codified Laws Section 60(1)(3)].[49] This concept—that a contract is created by quoting a salary for a fixed period of time—is not the law in all jurisdictions. Only a few state courts have had the issue come before them. The problem in the use of annual salary is that it may create exposure to a lawsuit.[50] Although only a few courts have held that quoting an annual salary forms a contract for one year, there is no need to express compensation in that form if you can readily communicate in a different manner? Quoting a monthly salary does not create the same exposure. *Annual salary* is a term that should be deleted from the practitioner's vocabulary.

Interviewing Discipline

A promise made at the time of hiring can result in establishing a contractual relationship removing the applicant, once employed, from an at-will status. However, not every utterance of the employer is binding.[51] Secondary interviews can result in forming a contract. An employee can later allege the existence of a contract, and upon evidence of damages because a commitment was not fulfilled, there is a serious exposure to litigation.[52] Although the employer may have checklists and guidelines for interviewing, there is no assurance that they will be followed. An audit of process oversight can help assure management that proper instructions have been conveyed. The instructions to the interviewers should not be specific. It is sufficient if they are told that any promises made at the time of hiring will create an exposure to a lawsuit in the future in the event that those promises are not kept. Apart from the legal consequences, there is an employee relation's problem of working for an employer who does not keep promises.

Understandings with Strikers

When a strike replacement is recruited and is promised that the job will be permanent, a contract is created under the implied contract theory.[53] If the replacement worker is then terminated when the strike is over, she or he could sue in a state court for breach of contract. The outcome of such suits is dependent on state law. Replacement workers are often promised permanent jobs in order to recruit under strike conditions. When the strike is settled, the company may not be able to bargain away these implied contract rights. This weakens the union's desire to go on strike, because the recall rights and seniority of striking unionized employees may be jeopardized when permanent replacements are hired.

Handbooks and Policy Manuals[54]

Certain statements made in an employee handbook or a policy manual have been construed by the courts to be implied contracts. A Michigan court, in a leading case, held that guidelines and the supervisor's manual were an expressed contract.[55] The clauses that were especially troublesome stated that an employee could be discharged only for just cause and "could work until 65 as long as he did his job." In a companion case, the employee testified that he was promised at the time of hiring that he could work for the company "as long as I did my job." The court ruled that this statement created an implied contract that changed the at-will doctrine, even though it was an oral promise.[56]

One handbook stated that an employee would be discharged only for just cause. When hired, the employee signed an application form that stated that employment would be subject to the *Handbook on Personnel Policy*. Eight years later, the employee was discharged. The court held that the handbook was a contract and that just cause had to be shown. However, to reach this conclusion the court held that this was an expressed contract.[57]

One of the well-quoted cases following *Toussaint*, 292 N.W.2d 880 (Mich. 1980), on handbooks as implied contracts is the *Pine River State Bank* case. It involved a loan officer who was in default on his personal loan and had approved 56 out of 57 loans in violation of the loan policy. The discharge was held to be a breach of contract because the employer failed to follow the discharge procedure outlined in the handbook. This was true even though the employer was able to show a legitimate reason to discharge.[58]

The two Michigan cases and *Pine River* were subsequently accepted by several other jurisdictions and caused considerable concern on the part of employers. Many human resources departments became "gun-shy" and discarded their handbooks. As more and more states adopted the *Pine River* precedent, employers revised their employee handbooks and sought legal advice to avoid exposure. Since the views of attorneys on this matter vary significantly, advice is available for virtually every approach employers choose to take.[59]

A vast majority of the states hold that a handbook, and often a policy manual, is a contract, although some industrial states such as New York, Illinois, and Indiana still require a written employment contract before the at-will status can be changed.[60]

High-Risk Expressions

There is no substitute for a definitive choice of words that accurately reflects what is meant. If you don't mean it, don't write it. Many handbooks use such terms as:

"We reserve the right to . . ."

"Exceptions may be made for . . ."

"You have permanent employment."

"There is job security here."

"Fair treatment and the opportunity for promotion from within the company according to high moral standards . . ."

"Employees are classified as permanent, part-time, and temporary."

"We request" or "We encourage you to use this complaint procedure."

"These rules are guidelines" or "You are encouraged to follow them."

"We pay fair wages."

These are all boilerplate terms that can convey one meaning to the employees and another to management personnel. They are also often interpreted by the plaintiff's bar differently from what management intended. The problems arise when the courts accept employee arguments and award large monetary judgments for breach of contract. Under these circumstances, the employer must consider every clause in the employee handbook not only for its communication value but also for its potential legal consequences. One of the considerations in changing a handbook is the effective date of the change. Employment documents can be changed. However, to be sure to avoid exposure, the effective date of the change should be set for some reasonable time in the future. When working conditions are changed, the employee should be provided with sufficient time to find another position if he or she objects to the change.

The Job Offer Letter

Any offer of employment above a certain level should be in writing. The state of Minnesota requires any offer in public entities to be in writing. There are two reasons for this. The first is to avoid any misunderstanding of the conditions of employment. The second is to provide a mechanism to void any promises or implied conditions that the prospective employee may have inferred. The letter should contain a "zipper clause" to exclude any promises that may have been understood to have been made at the time of the interview so it is clear that such promises were not relied upon when accepting the position.

Exhibit 10.2 contains suggested language to be inserted in the job letter. The language should be as non-legal as possible but have the necessary elements for enforcement. When the employee reports to work, some written or at least oral assurance that the letter was understood should be recorded.

Employers communicate thousands of words to employees each year. Sometimes what is expressed can be interpreted in a way different than what was intended. A common protection for the authors is called a disclaimer. A disclaimer is basically a denial of responsibility to avoid a claim for what was written and may have been misinterpreted. Employers typically use disclaimers on application forms in offer letters, unofficial benefit descriptions, and employee handbooks. They serve a preventive purpose—protection from "spin" to achieve some unintended advantage to others. Often disclaimers contain management's pronouncement that employment is unequivocally at-will.

If disclaimers are used, they have a better chance of being enforced if the language is highlighted so it is conspicuous and clear.[61] Examples of disclaimer language include such phrases as:

"This offer letter is not, nor is it intended to be, a contract of employment."

"The handbook is not to be interpreted by the employee as a contract of employment."

"The employer retains the right to terminate its employees at any time for any reason not prohibited by law, and the employee can terminate at will."

"The employer retains the sole discretion to modify any and all provisions of

---

This job offer contains the entire understanding with respect to the conditions of employment. No other promises, agreements, or understandings, written or oral, not mentioned above shall be binding. No changes, additions, or modifications of this letter shall be binding unless they are in writing and signed by the parties.

EXHIBIT 10.2   Sample Job Offer Language

the handbook at any time for any reason." (This is often used but legally is not necessary.)

"The pattern of progressive discipline is subject to individual situations and its application is subject to management discretion."

In addition to the proper language, other factors are necessary to close loopholes to prevent a disclaimer from being challenged. For example, (1) the language must be clear, conspicuous, and easily understood; (2) any at-will language must appear in other documents such as application forms and job offer letters; (3) there must be unambiguous evidence that the employee has received the disclaimer, has read it, understands it, and is required to ask questions if it is not understood; and (4) subsequent employer action and communications with the employee must establish that the employee is treated as an at-will employee. See Exhibit 10.3 for a sample of a **handbook acknowledgment** by the employee.

Whether a disclaimer is legally enforceable often depends on the court. In *Castiglione* v. *Johns Hopkins Hospital*, 517 F.2d 786 (Md. App. 1986), the court held that a disclaimer makes the handbook only a statement of the intent of the employer. This is the law in at least 26 states, so long as intent is clearly shown. However, a sizeable minority of the courts takes a different view. Sometimes the courts are concerned with the superior bargaining power of the employer and will enforce the contract if evidence

of the employee's understanding of the disclaimer clause cannot be produced. In *Helle* v. *Landmark, Inc.*, 742 N.E.2d 765 (Ohio 1984), the court held that a disclaimer would be disregarded if oral promises were made later. Sometimes a disclaimer will not be enforced where it has the effect of giving up statutory rights, such as workers' compensation or discrimination claims.

As can be seen from the foregoing cases, disclaimers are not an absolute assurance that there will not be exposure to a lawsuit. Less exposure would result from eliminating the disclaimer and writing the handbook in such a manner that its provisions were enforceable. In this case, it would not be damaging if the employee attempted to enforce the handbook. If the language itself doesn't grant the employee any rights but is enforceable against the employee, it is difficult to see where there is reason to have a disclaimer and risk the exposure and false security.[62]

It is important that employees know about conduct that is unacceptable. A handbook could well express rules and regulations that employees must follow and the consequences if they are not followed. Progressive discipline clauses without escape caveats can be problematic and are to be avoided. Employees should be notified that serious violations of company rules or policy will result in immediate discharge. This information should be communicated to the employees in a way that will make certain that they know that there will be no warning or progressive discipline prior to

---

_____ I,
_____, have read, understand, and have in my possession the company's policies and procedures. I agree to follow the policies in the handbook, and if there is at any time something that I do not understand, I agree to ask a company representative. I further understand that this signed statement will be a permanent record in my personnel file.

EXHIBIT 10.3 Handbook Acknowledgment

discharge. These "sudden death" violations are limited to very serious offenses which should be specified.

Probationary Period Complications with At-Will Employment

The dictionary defines *probation* as applicable for one who is being tested: a trial or evaluation period. This definition is commonly applied in the public sector. Some courts have said that the term means more than a trial period. When used in a handbook or policy manual, it can be interpreted to mean that once the trial period has passed, the employee has a permanent job, and just cause has to be shown before he or she can be discharged. Private-sector employers who want no expectation of permanency among new hires frequently avoid probationary periods.

Case law has compromised dismissals without good faith and cause when a probationary period exists. Use of a probationary period can create an employment contract that will cancel the at-will doctrine. The use of the term *probationary period* often gives an employer a false sense of security. In the vast majority of legal jurisdictions, the at-will doctrine is upheld when the employer does not create a condition (as public organizations may do) that enables the courts to find an exception. The use of the probationary period creates such an opportunity. Courts have always upheld the right of the employer to discharge for poor performance. In this sense, the employee is always on probation.

There are other ways to communicate to the employee that the standard of performance is less rigorous during the first few months of employment. The standard of discipline, however, should be the same regardless of the length of employment. *Probationary period*, except as the term is used in labor agreements, is another term that private-sector practitioners may choose to avoid.

A labor agreement is an enforceable contract, and until the employee serves a normal probationary period, just cause does normally not have to be shown. Probationary periods under collective bargaining agreements do allow management to examine the performance of newcomers. Labor agreement provisions are one reason why the courts associate just cause with the probationary period in a non-union situation.

Swing Factors

Appraisal records can be helpful as written evidence of coaching efforts and the communication of standards and deficiencies. Records can serve as evidence of warnings and possible consequences. However, many appraisal reports are biased and subjective. They may also be unreliable because some supervisors take the easy path of submitting bland and uncritical appraisals. Courts are particularly sympathetic to an employee's cause where there is documented evidence that the employee had previously received subjective favorable performance ratings and a short time later was discharged for poor performance.[63]

Past practices are frequently a factor in discipline and discharge issues. Management actions in previous similar situations can support or contravene an action. Good counseling and disciplinary records are often a strength in public sector human resource management but less so in much of the private sector.

Contemporary management practices require the daily application of procedures and practices founded on substantive, measurable and legal standards. The degree of management's exposure to legal action in termination situations necessitates informed and disciplined supervisory practices that are consistent and uniform. Supervisors can routinely coach and salvage misplaced employees, follow discipline and discharge procedures, and see that established standards are met on a daily basis. Such performance represents effective management. Alternatively, a compassionate supervisor might tolerate an employee's marginal performance and document it as satisfactory rather than risk an argument. Performance standards may be unclear and applied inconsistently across departments or work units. These poor practices in some units are damaging because patterns of uniform and consistent practices and enforcement in the larger organization are disrupted.

THE DISCHARGE PROCESS

Employers thoroughly evaluate all the evidence before deciding to terminate an employee; however, when the decision is made, they often give little thought to the procedure. Even in today's litigation-prone society, most terminations are never challenged in court.[64] There continues to be a slight stigma to suing one's former employer. Generally, a discharged employee's decision to sue is not an easy one. Litigation poses fear of the unknown and the embarrassing prospect of airing a private misfortune in public. Most employees have never initiated a lawsuit and are reluctant to do so. However, legal service advertising and use of contingent fees have overcome some of this reluctance. Presumably the plaintiff's lawyer will assess the case before deciding to handle it. If the employee is angry enough, he or she can find a lawyer who will handle almost any claim.

Lawsuits Are Expensive

Throughout this chapter we have referenced exposure to lawsuits, because once the employee files a lawsuit, the employer usually loses, regardless of which side prevails on the merits. There is adverse publicity, lost time, and the distraction associated with having to defend a wrongful discharge. The lawyer must take a great deal of the employer's time in preparing for the case, because the employer is the only one who has all the facts that the lawyer must depend on to defend the case. This hidden management cost is in addition to the huge legal fees associated with a lawsuit. If the employer loses, usually it pays the fees for both sides. However, if the employer wins, it usually pays its own fees. Exposure to lawsuits can be minimized if the procedure recognizes that the less provocation generated, the less likelihood there is for a lawsuit.

Proper Discharge Procedure

There are certain requisite elements for a discharge procedure. The first essential element is that oversight of terminations should be assigned to one or two persons. It should not be solely in the hands of the first-line supervision. Discharge is no longer a routine task of telling an employee that he or she is fired. The discharge should be handled by someone who can monitor the case impartially and with due regard for the rights and feelings of both the supervisor and the employee. First-line supervisors are normally charged with getting the job out and may have little concern for legal requirements or the niceties of human relations.

The second element is that the procedure should be fair, firm, and business like. For the employer this means writing off an investment, and for the employee it means at least the temporary end of income and benefits. Discharge normally creates a sense of insecurity and perhaps shock and anger in the employee. The discharge procedure must consider the impact on the parties involved. It should not be a surprise to the employee.

A third element is that the reason for the discharge must appear reasonable from the employee's point of view as well as under the law. For example, an employer would not normally discharge an employee because of failure to greet people in the morning. The termination must be for something that a normal employer would act on or be prepared to justify, and appear to be of consequence to a reasonable person.

The fourth important element is that a proper investigation is conducted *before* disciplinary action is taken. An investigation should be made even when the employer thinks it knows the facts. There is nothing that will convince the employee of fairness, and receive more weight from a court than a thorough investigation and ability to articulate the facts.[65]

A vital element is preparation for the dismissal meeting. A number of things should occur; others must be avoided. More often than not, the merits are not as important as the manner of discharge. A judge or jury may "tune out" the facts of the discharge and hear only how the employee seemed to be treated. Preparation should include the following steps:

1. Develop a concise reason for discharge. It is important for the employee to logically understand why she or he was discharged. Obscure reasons "to soften the blow" will backfire.
2. Avoid inaccuracy. This fans the flame of anger more than any other factor. The most common misrepresentation is a charge of poor performance after a wage increase was given a month before. Inaccuracy indicates vulnerability, which in turn encourages seeing a lawyer.
3. Consider giving help. Give the employee a place to go (other than a law office).
4. Decide on all the severance details. There should be no ambiguities to negotiate.
5. Tell the employee who the decision makers are. If possible, the decision makers should participate in the discharge process.
6. Be brief and to the point. Lengthy dissertations usually sound weak and defensive and prolong the employee discomfort.[66] One can be sensitive and still not be defensive.

7. Offer some counseling service about finding another job to the degree it is well received. Outplacement service or advice on where the employee can sell his or her skills would be helpful and reduce anger and fright.
8. Answer the following questions:
   Is the deviation from the norm sufficient?
   Is the reason clear?
   Is evidence sufficient?
   Was help provided?
   Did the employee know the expectations and was he or she warned?
   Are there any risks to the action and can they be abated?
   Has the employee had a day in court?
   Is the process fair?
   Are pay and benefit matters resolved?
   Is COBRA notification prepared?
   Have privacy and discretion been provided?

Exit Interviews

An **exit interview** should be held in a place where there will not be an interruption, and upon conclusion, the employee can depart without undue attention. The discharged employee should be able to leave without needing to talk to other employees. The interview should be as private as possible. Only those who have a need to know should be told of the discharge. In *Bolton* v. *Department of Human Services*, 527 N.W.2n 149 (Minn. App.), Rev'd 540 N.W.2d 523 (Minn. 1995), the court held that **defamation** of character can occur by action. In *Bolton*, the employee was escorted out of the building after being discharged. This may be a minority opinion, but it shows how far the court will go to find an employer guilty of defamation of character. The exit interview should be structured so the employee leaves with dignity and without being emotionally upset. Violating the employee's sensibilities, conducting a meeting in view of an audience or otherwise belittling or humiliating an employee can lead to subsequent charges of defamation.[67] At the exit interview, the employee should be told what the employer's reply will be to reference inquiries, what position will be taken on unemployment compensation claims, and why.

Summary Discharges

Summary or *sudden death dismissal* refers to the nature of the offense more than the immediacy of the action. A discharge is an adverse action and therefore creates an exposure to a lawsuit. The employer should assume that the employee will challenge termination. A pre-discharge preparation reduces the likelihood that a termination will be challenged. There may be some question as to whether the act was committed, but even if the employer is sure of the facts, suspension pending further investigation is a good defensive move. This suspension should be of short duration. The employee should not be left in the dark any longer than necessary. One of the virtues of the suspension technique is that it forces management to investigate immediately. In the event the employee is exonerated, the employer should provide back pay for the period of the suspension.

The next step is to investigate all the facts that will establish a just cause for the discharge and to consider any legal problems of the discharge. An investigation should be well documented. Any evidence that the person was terminated for a reason that might be held to be contrary to public policy—such as refusing to commit perjury, whistle-blowing, refusing to be excused from jury duty, filing a workers' compensation claim, refusing to violate a professional code of ethics, or any other act that may be construed to have the public policy protection—should be considered.

The company's handbook or policy manual should be reviewed to determine whether there are any statements that indicate permanency status or if there is a permanent employee classification. If the document provides a discharge procedure, a determination that this procedure was followed should be made. All performance appraisals should be reviewed to determine whether there are any inconsistencies between the performance appraisals and the reason given for the discharge (record substantiation). Recruitment and selection procedures should also be reviewed to determine whether there have been any promises made as to job security, promotions, or termination only for just cause.

A determination should be made as to whether any statute has been violated. It should also be established that the reasons for the discharge have been established and that any rules that have been violated have been clearly communicated to employees. This may have implications for potential unemployment compensation claims.[68] Finally, if there are plans for a neutral party to review the evidence and process, preparation for management's presentation before the neutral should be anticipated.

An important consideration is determining what to tell the employee about the reason(s) for the discharge. Some attorneys advise not to give a reason. This is acceptable in most states under the at-will doctrine. However, if the employee files an unemployment compensation claim, a reason will have to be given. If one isn't given at the exit interview, the employee's version will be given to the unemployment claims representative and the employer will immediately be put on the defensive. The ambiguity can later be used in a wrongful discharge action to the detriment of the employer.

Information related to a dismissal is expected to be confidential. This includes the time and place of the meeting and explanations. The substance of a dismissal should never be discussed outside the company. See

Rue v. *K-Mart* No. 02531 Phila. 1995, 1997 WL 12 6045 - 6/16/1998.

WAIVERS[69] OR RELEASES[70]

Some companies feel that the way to stop all claims after discharge is to have the employee sign a release. This might certainly discourage a lawyer from taking a case where a release was signed, provided it was tightly worded and properly drafted. However, signed releases do not necessarily prevent litigation.[71] They are often challenged as not being completely voluntary nor completely understood, or because the employer has taken advantage of its superior bargaining position. They must be carefully drafted, and precautions must be taken to be sure that the employee fully understands what she or he is signing and that the language covers all claims that the employee might have, both present and future. In cases where the employer believes there to be some risk, agreements are drafted on a case-by-case basis. Large firms with a sizeable professional staff may have a standard procedure.

Agreements should be professionally prepared and cannot attempt to waive an employee's legal rights. They may require nondisclosure of company matters, no disparaging remarks, and the return of employer property. They may disclaim any wrongdoing by the firm. In exchange, the employee's consideration might be **severance pay,** outplacement service, benefits costs, or a reference letter.

Some states require a period of time to rescind the release after it has been executed.[72] Whether it is an agreement signed separately or a release at the time of termination, there is still an exposure if the employee feels that he or she was forced into it or is angry with the employer for how he or she was discharged.

This chapter may leave the impression that the discharge process is so complex that it is better not to start it but to live with the problem. The purpose of the analysis is to prevent exposure to lawsuits, not to stop discharges. Anyone can start a lawsuit, but most people are not predisposed to do so. Although winning in court can be satisfying, in the real sense "the horse is already out of the barn" when a claim is filed with a court or an agency. With careful, creative, sensitive procedures, objective performance appraisals, and proper discipline, most claims arising out of a discharge can be prevented. The courts and juries have indicated to employers that they will not interfere with the discharge process unless they do agree with the process or the employer's conduct. Juries tend to overreact when the discharge is not done in a humane way using the "reasonable person" standard.

The employer that believes that employment at will is a management right is challenging the discharged employee to test the doctrine and is exposed to litigation. The employer who modifies the discharge policy and procedures to protect against some exceptions to common law employment-at-will doctrine has considerably less exposure. Just cause policies along with other procedures should not be ignored.[73] The law makes one thing clear: The day has passed when a supervisor or a manager in an emotional state can walk up to an employee and say, "You're fired," and not be exposed to litigation.

DEFAMATION

Another exposure to lawsuits involving termination exists when employers make ill-considered or injudicious statements concerning former employees and the reason for which they were discharged. Legislation is in place to protect both parties in an employer–employee relationship. In addition to the assurance of the privacy of personal information and protections against harassment and physical injury, the protection of an individual's professional integrity is protected by legislation prohibiting defamation of character. In *Bolton* v. *Department of Human Services*, 527 N.W.2n 149 (Minn. App.), Rev'd 540 N.W.2d 523 (Minn. 1995), discussed earlier, the court held that the employer can communicate by action. In *Bolton*, the employee was publicly escorted out of the employer's premises after being discharged. This action created a potential exposure to a defamation claim.

A common law tort of defamation,[74] in the employment context, is most likely committed when the employer gives a false oral or written statement as to why the employee was discharged. In order to make out a claim of defamation, the plaintiff must prove that:

1. A statement has been made about him or her to another person.
2. It is false or given to someone who has no need to know.
3. It harms the reputation of the plaintiff by lowering his or her esteem or stature in the community or with other persons.[75]

There are several defenses to defamation: privilege (discussed at length in Chapter 12), no publication, truth, lack of defamatory meaning, opinion, and plaintiff consent The defense most often used in employment law is *privilege,* whether absolute or qualified. When the qualified privilege doctrine is violated, a defamation suit is the remedy. Once the court determines the privilege doctrine applies, the burden is on the plaintiff to show that the doctrine was violated.

Defamation "Per Se"

Ordinarily, when a person brings a defamation suit, the person must show an impairment of his or her reputation, loss of standing in the community or mental distress. In defamation "per se," whatever is said or written is presumed to be damaging, therefore no damages have to be proven. In order for a statement to be defamatory, it must be a personal attack on the plaintiff. A hearty disagreement with the plaintiff's views or a statement about an overly sensitive person is not defamatory. Depending on the circumstances, a plaintiff must have some "thick skin."

Disclosing Information to Co-Workers Who Have a Need to Know

One of the conditions of the doctrine of qualified privilege is that information be given only to those persons who have a legitimate business right to receive it.[76] This requirement goes to the very roots of the doctrine. The courts say that information about the reasons for the discharge of an employee should be released to other employees who have a reason to know. By so doing, the employer may prevent others from making the same mistake and also being discharged. Preventing acts that will result in discharge is in the public interest. The release of information about the reason for a discharge to employees who are not exposed to the opportunity to commit similar acts can be ruled to be defamatory.

The acquisition of one organization by another is commonplace in U.S. business culture. Frequently such combinations leave the merged organization with two persons for only one job. Although both may be competent, one has to go. In a fairly typical case, one company acquired another with an effective date on a Friday. On Saturday, three top executives were discharged. Over the weekend all other officers and department heads were called and instructed not to go to the office on Monday morning, but to attend a meeting at a nearby hotel at 8 o'clock on Monday. At the meeting, the officers and department heads were told why the three executives were fired. Only the top management was told. Other levels of management were excluded because they did not have the same need to know, since they would not be directly affected. By following this carefully thought-out procedure, the organization substantially reduced the risk of litigation. If all levels of management had been invited to the meeting, the organization would have been exposed to charges of defamation.

In *Benassi* v. *Georgia-Pacific,* 662 P.2d 760 (Ore. App. 1983), a general manager was discharged for allegedly having a drinking problem and using a "loud voice and considerable profanity." The employer called in all the employees and stated at a meeting, "I gathered you here to tell you why Mr. Benassi is no longer with the company. The man was drunk and misbehaving in a bar. The man had a drinking problem. Georgia-Pacific looks unkindly on this kind of conduct. It was not the first time. He had been warned." Mr. Benassi sued on the basis of this statement. The court found that there was an abuse of the qualified privilege doctrine because there was no reason to communicate to all employees in order to protect the interests of the employer.

The level of employees to whom information should be communicated should be carefully determined by the employer, taking into consideration the likelihood that the employee will benefit from the information. When an employee was discharged for falsifying company records, the employer told higher-level employees, as well as employees on the same or lower levels. In the resulting defamation suit, the court laid down the rule that communication was proper to all who have a need to know as well as those employees who would be directly affected by the discharge.[77] In this case, the court said that all employees to whom the information was communicated had a "need to know."[78]

Statements that Impute Crime

Statements that impute crimes are susceptible to a defamatory meaning as illustrated by the case of *Karnes* v. *Milo Beauty and Barber Supply Co., Inc.,* 441 N.W. 2d 565, 568 (Minn. Ct. App. 1989). In another case, an employee sued for intentional infliction of emotional distress, alleging that the employer initiated a drug investigation with a reckless disregard of whether or not the employee had committed the offense. The employer also communicated the information about the drug investigation to the narcotics unit of the local police department. The court found that the initiation of a drug investigation without a reason was outrageous conduct. Although the information was privileged, it was defamatory since the narcotics unit of the police department did not have a business right to receive it. See *Linebaugh* v. *Sheraton Michigan Corp.,* 497 N.W.2d 585, 587 (Mich. Ct. App. 1993).

Statements that impute crime are not always defamatory.[79] If properly made, they come under the qualified privilege doctrine, as in the case where an employer, based on a polygraph test, had reason to believe that the plaintiff was involved in vandalism. The statement of this fact was made only to other employees who had a need to know. The statement was protected by the qualified privilege doctrine.[80]

Giving False Reasons for Discharge

Many organizations make a practice of "softening the record" in the case of discharges. This avoids an adverse reaction on the part of the employee being terminated. It will also make him or her more employable. For many years it was common to avoid giving the real reason for discharge. A relatively innocuous reason such as "personality difficulties" or the more recent version, "a chemistry problem with the supervisors," was put into the record. If the statements are not damaging to the reputation of the employee, there is little exposure to charges of defamation.

Without Malice

If the false reason is damaging to the reputation of the employee, defamation is found. In *Lewis* v. *Equitable Life Assurance Society of the United States,* 389 N.W.2d 876 (Minn. 1986), the plaintiffs submitted an expense account after returning from a business trip. The employer considered it excessive, and requested them to reduce the amount. The employees refused, since the charges were legitimate. When they again refused, they were discharged. The reason given for the discharge was "gross insubordination." When they applied for employment, that reason was repeated to prospective employers. They could not find employment, so they sued their former employer for defamation. The court stated that the reason given was false, ruling that the employer should have known that the defamatory words would be repeated. Although the false reason was defamation, it was without **malice;** and so the privilege doctrine prevented damages from being awarded.

Defamation can result when a false reason for discharge is given through an interoffice communication. In one case, the reason stated in an interoffice memo was "failure to increase business as a major Project Sales Representative," which was untrue. Although the reason was communicated by memo only to the supervisor and CEO, the court held it was defamation, but without malice.[81]

It is a well-established principle that no liability results from releasing information about an employee or former employee to a prospective employer, so long as care is taken to follow the doctrine of qualified privilege. When exposure to liability is most likely to occur is in a situation where the information is released to persons who are not employers, or who do not have a business need to know.

A vice president of engineering was discharged. He alleged that Title VII was violated and that he was discharged because of his color. In preparation for the EEOC hearing, the employer allegedly told suppliers that the plaintiff was discharged because he was incompetent. The court said that such statements were not privileged, and an action for defamation could exist if the statements were false. The privilege doctrine does not extend to statements made to suppliers.[82]

Statements must be job related and without malice. When a former employer told a prospective employer that the plaintiff married another employee, causing the man to have mental breakdown, the court found this defamatory.[83] The court found that accusations of dishonesty or theft, even if indirect, were defamatory.

Guidelines to Prevent Exposure for Defamation

In all the cases where the court found defamation, the employer either made some assumptions without foundation or knowingly made malicious or false statements. There is a big difference between stating that you no longer have confidence in a person and calling her or him a liar. The fact that the qualified privilege doctrine has some restrictions does not mean that it cannot be used. The courts have indicated to the employer that it should be used, and when used properly, the employer is protected from any liability. The bottom line is whether the statement was intended to be damaging to the reputation of the employee or was factual, without malicious intent. If the effect of a statement was damaging to the reputation of the employee, without malice, there is no defamation. The term *poor performance* is often used as a matter of convenience, and is troublesome if the employee does not actually have poor performance.

In order to avoid exposure to defamation lawsuits, the employer should have a well-defined termination policy that prevents managers and supervisors from discharging prior to establishing cause. They should be trained to state the facts without adjectives that may imply malice or bad faith. The employer has the responsibility to train thoroughly the managers and supervisors in the use of the qualified privilege doctrine, or instruct them not to comment at all.[84] Often it is the attitude toward the person, not the truth of the statement, that influences the court. For this reason, the immediate supervisor or someone directly involved should not give a reference. In any policy on disclosure of employee information, consideration must be given to the employee's right to enjoy a good reputation as well as the employer's concern to employ qualified and desirable people. The employer must also be concerned with the welfare of other employees. Any policy should not discourage reference information, but must be drafted in a way that reflects a real concern for both the employee's privacy and the employer's need to know.

The following provisions are designed to accomplish this goal. Only certain designated and trained persons should be permitted to release information. These persons should be trained in the legal requirements of disclosing employee information. The practice of allowing the supervisor to disclose reference information over the telephone should be eliminated. Except for dates of employment, all requests for information should be in writing. Since information should be given only to persons who have a reason to receive it, this cannot be ascertained over the telephone. Sometimes former employees seek information under disguise of a prospective employer. Requiring the request to be made in writing will eliminate this problem. The employee should be required to consent to the release of the information requested. Although the courts hold that this is not needed, it is convenient to have this consent when the employer is being sued by an employee who consented to the release. In one situation where the employee was a member of an association, the court said that he had consented to the written cause of his dismissal through his membership. The Restatement of Torts puts it this way: "Moreover, one who agrees to submit his conduct to investigation knowing that its results will be published, consents to the publication of the honest findings of the investigators."[85]

It is also good employee relations to get the employee's consent; the employee receives some satisfaction in exercising the right to determine whether certain information should be released. For example, the employee may not want disclosure of an address to a mother-in-law but may want full disclosure of all information to the promoter of an exclusive club.

Employee personnel files should be released within the company only to those who have a job-related reason to know it. Only that information in the file that is not challengeable as to its validity and pertains to the stated purpose of the inquiry should be released. Information should be put in the employee's file only if it is truthful and there is a job-related or business need for it. Particular attention should be paid to records kept by persons outside the personnel office. Collecting irrelevant or inaccurate information adversely affects the quality of the relevant information, as well as causing problems. Information should be collected from reliable sources. Hearsay and subjective evaluations should be avoided. Employee access to the file should be permitted, but the file should be thoroughly reviewed. Knowledge of such information as comparative evaluations, mental problems, investigative interviews, and physical conditions could do more harm than good to employee relations.

When an employee disagrees with the information in the file, the disputed statement should be put in the file without comment, in the event it becomes material. The procedure should detail what, to whom, by whom, and under what limitations the information should be disclosed. Tell the employee, at the exit interview, what reference you will give to a prospective employer when asked. The employer should refrain from giving information about prospective performance on a specific job. This is often subjective and is not predictive of how the applicant will perform on another job. Also, always express any information on performance as an opinion, with a reservation. The employer should be wary of giving information for background or future reference. If the recipient is not a prospective employer, the qualified privilege doctrine may not apply. It is also difficult to predict how the information will be used. This is one method to get information for union organizing purposes, for a sales mailing list, or for a sales contact.

If a practice or procedure contains most of these provisions, the employer not only will be exchanging information for the public good but will also be able to select qualified and desirable applicants objectively while enjoying good employee relations. These provisions will also eliminate exposure to charges of negligent hiring and negligent retention. The law does not restrict disclosure of employee information, but does encourage it. An employer policy or practice that respects the privacy of the employee but gives prospective employers certain accurate and nonmalicious facts will prevent unwanted litigation.

CASE 10.1

A Questionable Discharge?

In August of 2007, the employee, a 25-year-old female, answered a newspaper advertisement and accepted a full-time clerical role at an hourly wage with health-care benefits available after 90 days of employment. The employee had previous continuous employment of at least three years with no history of involuntary discharge or performance issues. The employer, a small corporation, employed 25 workers who manufactured and sold chemical products. The company was managed by the founding individual (president), his spouse (vice-president), and a close friend. No formal human resources, legal, or accounting functions existed in house and no documented human resources policies or procedures were communicated or available to employees. The company and employees did not engage in collective bargaining.

The president delivered a satisfactory performance appraisal to the employee with a corresponding $1.50 per hour raise in January of 2008. The employee, at that time, declined health insurance coverage. In November of 2008, the employee submitted a vacation request form to the vice president for signature. She also requested two hours to be taken the following day. The vice president approved and signed the form and returned a copy to the employee. During this exchange, the employee told the vice president that the vacation time was for a prenatal doctor visit.

The next day, during a routine meeting between the president and the employee, the president placed the original vacation request form in front of the employee and accused the employee of forging the vice president's signature approval. The employee denied the accusation and the discussion escalated to shouting. The employee left the office without permission for the remainder of the day—two hours prior to closing.

The next morning, the employee returned and worked the full day with no reference to the incident. The employee arrived at work the following morning to find that her office had been locked. The vice president told the employee that she had quit, therefore she should leave the building. The employee calmly denied quitting, took a seat in the lobby, and indicated that she would work from there if her office was unavailable. The employer called the sheriff, who escorted the employee from the building. The employee did not pursue unemployment benefits and found other employment within 30 days.

Does the employer have an exposure for terminating the employee? Explain.

Does it make a difference that the employee was an employee at will?

What potential liability does the employer have for compensation?

Could this be viewed as a constructive discharge?

Is there an FMLA issue? ■

CASE 10.2

Termination Decision

County Road Supervisor Shirley noted the absence of one of her crew members one morning and so sent the crew out one man short. A few hours later the missing crew member arrived at the garage with the explanation that he had stopped to vote and there was a long line. All the other employees had left and Shirley was irritated and demonstrated no patience with the employee. She had planned to vote after work and anticipated no problems at the polling place.

Shirley was aware that the county could dismiss an employee at any time for any reason, and this particular employee, even after two years as a county employee, was marginal and had a poor attendance record, although he had never even been counseled about his attendance. Shirley therefore sent him home with the comment, "We'll call you if or when we want you back."

Should Shirley initiate termination action? Discuss the steps she should follow.

Do you anticipate any problems if she decides to terminate the employee? ■

CASE 10.3

The Uncertain Supervisor

The department manager left the office early on Friday afternoon with instructions to one of the supervisors to terminate a certain probationary employee at the end of the day when the employee returned from his worksite. The employee had worked for five weeks and his probationary period was to expire the following week. The manager didn't anticipate that the supervisor would have any problems because she had terminated another probationary employee in the past.

The manager was surprised to receive a phone call from the supervisor that evening informing him that she hadn't dismissed the employee and that he would be returning to work on Monday. The supervisor told him that the employee had acted in a very confident manner and demanded answers to several questions that the supervisor was unprepared to answer. These questions included: "What about my severance pay? Will I be paid for unused vacation? Are you going to deny my unemployment claim? When do I get to see my personnel records?" Finally, the supervisor told the manager that the employee had demanded his final paycheck immediately.

What responses should the supervisor have provided? What course of action should the manager take? ■

Summary

This chapter begins with an overview of the forms of employee terminations. The only federal statute referenced is WARN, a law intended to provide advance notice to employees marked for job loss. The chapter considers dismissal situations with an array of risks based on common law, and employer actions available to avoid dismissal litigation. Dismissals are often traumatic and can result in anger, which is one of the reasons employee legal actions are common.

The public sector often makes provision for a proprietary right to a job, and other employee protections are typically in place through contracts, statutes, and historic civil service procedures. At all levels of government it is common to find precise discharge stipulations based on just cause and due process, a lengthy period of job trial (probation), and an appeal procedure often with third-party resolution. In the private sector there is still reliance on the common law principle of at-will, which permits discharge at any time for any reason. The occasional expedient or thoughtless action mistakenly based on the premise of at-will employment can also result in legal charges of discrimination, defamation of character and/or breach of contract.

Key Terms

due process   248
property right   249
probationary period   249
just cause   249
progressive discipline   249
last chance agreement   249

nexus   251
constructive discharge   252
reprisal   252
handbook acknowledgment   262
exit interview   265

defamation   266
severance pay   267
malice   270

Questions for Discussion

1. Discuss the differences between public- and private-sector dismissal practices. To what extent are these practices impacted by collective bargaining?
2. What procedures or policies might an employer consider to avoid exposure to charges resulting from involuntary separations?
3. Why might supervisors be reluctant to dismiss employees?
4. Give an example of a faulty dismissal.
5. What is the intent of the federal WARN legislation?
6. Describe any experiences you have had related to employment terminations.

7. How might a defamation of character charge result from a dismissal?
8. How might a breach of contract charge result from a dismissal?
9. Explain just cause and due process.
10. What is progressive discipline? What are the dual purposes of progressive discipline?
11. What is a constructive discharge? A retaliatory discharge?
12. Is there a standard procedure for dismissal at any place that you have been employed? Describe the procedure.

Notes to Chapter 10

1. The terms *terminate* ("to end") and *separate* ("to disconnect, remove") are often used interchangeably, but *terminate* is more absolute and suggests discharge and dismissal. *Removal* is also commonly used in public service to denote involuntary termination. A temporary release, expected to be temporary, is normally termed a *layoff*. The British use the term *redundancy*. The employee is made "redundant" by lack of suitable work.
2. 29 USC § 2101 et. Seq. 20 CFR Part 639.
3. Laureen B. Edelman, Steven Abraham, and Howard S. Erlanger, "Professional construction of the law: The inflated threat of wrongful discharge," *Law and Society Review,* 26 (1992): 47.

4. David Patton, *Human resource management: The public service perspective* (New York: Houghton Mifflin 2002), p. 360.
5. S. Seldon, Human resource practice in state government," *Public Administration Review,* 61, no. 5 (September/October 2001): 599.
6. See the process in the *Lake County Personnel Manual,* Lake County, Ill. 2/9/1999.
7. *Merit System Principles,* 5 U.S.C. § 2301 (2006).
8. Mohave County, AZ, *Merit System Rules* 5/2/94 Article 7 Corrective Action, Rule 701 Discipline A (1), p. 1. "Generally, disciplinary measures begin with a less severe action and become increasingly severe if

new offenses occur. In some cases, however, even in the absence of prior disciplinary action, a particular offense may be so serious in nature as to warrant immediate dismissal or suspension."

9. "Federal supervisors and strategy: Human resource management," U.S. Merit Systems Protection Board, June 1988, Ben Erdzeich, p. 8.

10. "A program of progressive discipline will be followed unless individual circumstances merit otherwise." *Skagit County Personnel Policy and Procedures Manual*, Sept. 12, 12.2.

11. *Bishop v. Wood*, 42 6 U.S. 341 96 S.Ct. 2074 48 L.Ed.2d 684 (1976).

12. S. Stillman, *Public administration: Concepts and cases* (New York: Houghton Mifflin, 2000).

13. David Patton, *Human resource management: The public sector perspective* (New York: Houghton Mifflin, 2002), p. 54.

14. Procedures Manual, Dorchester County, SC 7-7-97.

15. For an analysis of litigation costs, see James Nimoricht and Franz Piegeon, "The costs of wrongful discharge costs," *Journal of Individual Employee Rights*, 11, no. 1 (2003–2004): 39–51.

16. See K. M. Hallman, "Invasion of privacy in protection against sexual harassment: Co-employee dating and employer liability," *Columbia Journal of Law and Social Problems*, 20 (1993): 45.

17. Conduct must have adverse effect; see, for example, *Conway, Inc. v. Ross* 627 P.2d 1029 (Alaska 1981).

18. For a good reference on criminal conduct outside the workplace, see Steve Bergsman, "Employee conduct outside the workplace," *The human resources yearbook, 1992–1993* (Englewood Cliffs, NJ: Prentice Hall, p. 8.13). Also *Hall v. Gas Cons. Pr. Co.*, 842 F.2d 101 (8th Cir. 1988).

19. C. Woolsey, "Off-duty conduct none of employer's business," *Business Insurance*, 26 (February 17, 1992): 10–11; M. Finneran, "We're from the government, we're here to help you," *Business Communication Review*, 22 (January 1992): 74–75. Also see R. Massingill and D. Petersen, "Legal challenges to no fraternization dates," *Labor Law Journal*, 46 (July 1995): 429–435.

20. See Hallman, "Invasion of Privacy."

21. *Planer v. Cash and Thomas Construction Co.*, 908 F.2d 902 (11th Cir. 1990).

22. *Malone v. Eaton Corp.*, 1999, U.S. App. Lexis 18514 (8th Cir. 1999).

23. *Black's law dictionary*, 6th ed. (St. Paul, MN: West, 1990), p. 863.

24. *Kass v. Brown Boveri Corp.*, 488 A.2d 242 (N.J. Super. 1985).

25. *J. P. Stevens & Co. v. NLRB*, 461 F.2d 490 (4th DCir. 1972).

26. *Young v. Southwestern Savings & Loan Association*, 509 F.2d 140 (5th Cir. 1975).

27. *Bourque v. Powell Electrical Manufacturing Co.*, 617 F.2d 61 (5th Cir. 1980).

28. *Goss v. Exxon Office Systems Co.*, 747 F.2d 885 (3rd Cir. 1984).

29. *Fraze v. KFC National Management Co.*, 492 F. Supp. 1099 (M.D. Ca. 1989).

30. See *Cockrell v. Boise Cascade* (10th Cir. 1986).

31. *Alicia Rosado v. Garcia Santiago*, 562 F.2d 1143 (1st Cir. 1988).

32. *Cazzola v. Codman & Shurtleff, Inc.*, 751 F.2d 53 (1st Cir. 1984).

33. *Kass v. Brown Boveri Corp.*, 488 A.2d 242 (N.J. Super. 1985).

34. In *Staggs v. Blue Cross of Maryland*, 486 A.2d 798 (Md. App. 1985), two salespersons were permitted to resign rather than be discharged. The court held this was constructive discharge per se. Also *Cockrell v. Boise Cascade* (10th Cir. 1986).

35. *Humana Inc., v. Fairchild* 603 SW 2d 918 (Ky. App. 1980).

36. *Gages v. Life of Montana Ins. Co.*, 668 P.2d 213 (Mont. 1983).

37. *Toussaint v. Ford Motor Co.*, 581 F.2d 812 (10th Cir. 1978).

38. The courts will usually uphold bona fide seniority systems when they conflict with discrimination claims.

39. In *City of Richmond v. J. A. Croson Co.*, 109 S.Ct. 706 (1989), the court struck down a city minority set-aside award plan for public contracts, because it favored one race over another although there was a racial imbalance. This case has been followed in layoffs, promotion, and hiring, except for federal

government programs. However, the Supreme Court reversed this in *Adarand Constructors Inc., v. Pena,* 115 S.Ct. 2097 (1995).

40. *Local 28 of Sheetmetal Workers* v. *EEOC.,* 106 S.Ct. 301 (1986); also *Cunico* v. *Pueblo School District No. 60,* 917 F.2d 431 (10th Cir. 1990).

41. Experiences of employment managers are that an applicant will sign anything and remember nothing at the time of hiring.

42. R. Hilgert, "Employers protected by at-will statements," *The Human Resources Yearbook, 1992/93* (Englewood Cliffs NJ; Prentice Hall), p. 818. See also *McKennon* v. *Nashville Banner,* 66 FEP 1192 (1995).

43. *Weiner* v. *McGraw-Hill,* a443 N.E.2d 441 (N.Y. 1982).

44. *Thompson* v. *Kings Entertainment Co.,* 653 F.Supp. 871 (E.D. Va 1987). For an opposite view, see *Leathem Research Foundation of CUNY,* 658 F.Supp. 651 (S.D. N.Y. 1987).

45. Rebecca M. Guerra, "Comment: Oral contracts to fire for good cause only. Courts putting the cart before the horse," *Baylor Law Review,* 47 (1995).

46. Communication in this context is best described by a situation where an employer had to get 100 percent participation in order to have a group life insurance program. One employee would not sign; the supervisor talked to him but could not convince him; the plant manager tried without success. They reported to the president that they could not put the program in. The president talked to the employee and said, "Sign up or you are fired." The employee signed. The supervisor and plant manager were bewildered. They asked the employee why he signed when the president talked to him but refused when they tried to get him to do so. The employee's reply was, "Nobody explained it to me before."

47. M. R. Wallace, "Employee manuals as implied contracts: The guidelines that bind" (comment), *Tulsa Law Journal,* 27 (1991): 263.

48. F. Vickory, "The erosion of the employment-at-will doctrine and the statute of frauds: Time to amend the statute," *American Business Law Journal,* 30 (May 1992): 97–122. Also see Axel R. Granholm, *Handbook of employee termination* (New York: John Wiley & Sons, 1991), p. 19.

49. In *Goodwyn* v. *Sencore, Inc.,* 389 F.Supp. 824 (D.S.D. 1975), the court held that an annual salary formed a 1-year contract. This was before the statute was adopted.

50. In *Tipton* v. *Canadian Imperial Bank of Commerce,* 872 F.2d 149 (11th Cir. 1989), the court rejected the concept. Some courts will reject but hold that annual salary is an inducement to accept the job.

51. *Dumas* v. *Kessler & Maguire Funeral Home,* 380 N.W. 2d 544 (Minn. App. 1986).

52. *Bower* v. *AT&T Technologies,* 852 F.2d 361 (8th Cir. 1988).

53. *Belknap, Inc.,* v. *Hale,* 103 S.Ct. 3172 (1983).

54. Only implied contract law will be discussed here. The writ___ handbook is given in detail in Chapter 12.

55. *Toussaint* v. *Blue Cross and Blue Shield* 292 N.W.2d 880 (Mich. 1980); also *Bullock Michigan,* 444 N.W.2d 114 (Mich. S.Ct. 1989) employee-at-will state.

56. *Ebling* v. *Masco Corp.,* 292 N.W.2d 801.

57. *Weiner* v. *McGraw-Hill,* 443 N.E.2d 44. However, in *LeNeave* v. *North American Life* 854 F.2d 317 (8th Cir. 1988), the court held that language did not always imply a contract.

58. *Pine River State Bank* v. *Richard I*—333 N.W.2d 622 (Minn. 1983).

59. See John D. Combe, "Employee handbooks: Asset or liability?" *Employee Relations Law Journal,* 12, no.1 (Summer 1986): 4–17.

60. *Enis* v. *Continental Ill. Nat. Bank & Trust,* 5872 F.Supp. 876 (N.D. Ill. E.D. 1984); *Mead Johnson and Co.* v. *Openheimer,* 458 N.E.2d 668 (Ind. App. 1 Dist. 1984). See *Fleming* v. *Kids and Kin Head Start,* 693 P.2d 1363 (Ore. Appl. 1965) for majority rule.

61. *McDonald* v. *Mobil Coal Producing, Inc.,* 820 P.2d 986 (Wyo. 1991).

62. See "The use of disclaimers to avoid employer liability under employee handbook provisions," *Journal of Corporation Law,* 12 (Fall 1986): 105. For the opposite view, see "Unjust dismissal of employees at will—Are disclaimers a final solution?" *Fordham Urban Law Journal,* 15 (1987): 533–565.

63. Some courts hold that failure to evaluate performance accurately is proof of discrimination: *Vaughan* v. *Edel,* 918 F.2d 517 (8th Cir. 1990) (minority opinion).

64. It is estimated that there are more than 100,000 discharges for which damages could be collected if the employee sued.

65. See William E. Hartsfield, "Suggestions for investigating employee misconduct," *The Practical Lawyer* (March 1, 1985): 11.

66. This is advisable in communicating other misfortunes. Sometimes the reaction isn't what is expected. The author once told a spouse in a brief and to-the-point statement that her husband was killed in a work-related accident an hour before. Her reply was, "How much do I get?"

67. *Uebelacker* v. *Ancom Systems, Inc.* 80 Ohio App. 3d 97, 608 NE 2d 858, 8, IER, Cas. 1992.

68. Discharge unemployment compensation appeals have been lost because members of management give different reasons for the discharge. See *Flanigan* v. *Prudential Federal Savings & Loan Association*, 720 P.2d 257 (Mont. 1986), where three managers all testified to different reasons for the termination in a wrongful discharge case.

69. To relinquish a legal right.

70. To release from liability, to abandon a claim.

71. See *Pratt* v. *Brown Machine Company*, 855 F.2d 1225 (6th Cir. 1988).

72. Minnesota Statutes Section 363.031 allows 15 days to rescind after the agreement has been signed by both parties.

73. Michael D. Fabiano, "The meaning of just cause for termination when an employer alleges misconduct and the employee denies it" (Note). *Hastings Law Journal*, 399 (1993).

74. To prove defamation, the statement must be false, unprivileged, and negligent on the part of the publisher. There must also be damages to the plaintiff.

75. *Stuempes* v. *Parke, Davis & Co.*, 297 N.W.2d 252 (Minn 1980). Also see W. Keeton, *Prosser and Keeton on torts*, 5th ed., Sect. 111 (1984), p. 774; Restatement of Torts, Sect. 558 (1977).

76. *Hutchinson* v. *McDonald's Corp.*, 110 S.Ct. 57 (1989).

77. If the person can do something about the situation, he or she has a need to know, according to most courts.

78. *Hodges* v. *Tomberlin*, 319 S.E.2d 11 (Ga. App. 1984).

79. *Gillson* v. *State Department of Natural Resources*, 492 N.W.2d 835, 843 (Minn. Ct. App. 1992). The statement "the readers should ask themselves if they would want a female relative to spend the night with [the sexual harassment offender]" was not defamatory "per se."

80. *Larson* v. *Homet Aluminum*, 449 N.W.2d 1172 (Ind. App. 3 Dist. 1983).

81. *Frankson* v. *Design Space International*, 394 N.W.2d 140 (Minn. 1986); also *Banas* v. *Matthews International Corp.*, 502 A.2d 637 (Pa. Super. 1985). The court in *Rouly* v. *Enserch Corp.*, 835 F.2d 1127 (5th Cir. 1988), took the opposite view.

82. *Medina* v. *Spotnails, Inc.*, 591 F.Supp. 190 (E.D. N.D. Ill. 1984).

83. *Marshall* v. *Brown*, 190 Cal. Rptr. 392 (Cal. App. 1983).

84. A $250,000 award could have been avoided if one person had been designated and trained in qualified privilege doctrine: *Sigal Construction Corp.* v. *Stanbury*, 586 A.2d 1204 (D.C. App. 1991).

85. Restatement of Torts, Sect. 583 (1938), p. 221.

CHAPTER 11

Alternative Dispute Resolution

CHAPTER OUTLINE

Growth of Alternative Dispute
    Resolution

Selection of the Process

Mediation and Arbitration

Settlement

Court Enforcement of ADR

T he legal approach to the resolution of employment disputes is for the complainant to initiate the litigation process by filing a lawsuit in the appropriate jurisdiction. However, there are other means of resolving problems that arise within the employment relationship that may be more efficient and satisfying to the parties. Alternative dispute resolution (ADR) includes a variety of processes that are designed to assist the parties in resolving disputes without resorting to the court system. Most scholars and practitioners recognize that these processes result in quicker and cheaper resolution than going to court. In a speech nearly 150 years ago to a law school class, Abraham Lincoln encouraged the use of alternative means of resolving disputes. He said, "Discourage litigation. Persuade your neighbors to compromise whenever you can. Point out to them how a nominal winner is often a real loser—in fees, expenses and waste of time."[1] The reasons cited by Lincoln have not changed. The cost of litigation has increased dramatically in recent years and litigation in employment disputes has become more complex, often involving multiple witnesses and substantial documentation. Litigation also involves discovery and lengthy investigation. This may preclude parties with legitimate claims from pursuing those claims since a part of what they recover in a judgment could be required to pay their own legal fees. Even in contingent fee cases, one party or the other is typically required to pay all or some of the costs. Costs are sometimes negotiable but may require difficult and prolonged negotiation.

    Those who choose ADR typically desire a quick settlement of the dispute, particularly if there is a need to preserve an ongoing relationship between the parties.

Litigation in today's environment is unlikely to result in quick settlement, even if the matter in dispute can be stipulated by the parties. While litigation is pending, the participants will likely be compelled to rehash the events leading up to the dispute, and often find it difficult to go on with their lives with a lawsuit pending. A long discovery process also works against quick settlement. The old maxim "Justice delayed is justice denied" may be applicable without settlement or other speedy resolution of a dispute. Long delays also cause a loss of faith in the court system. Alternatively, there is a fear on the part of some individuals that ADR will result in less satisfactory outcomes than litigation leading to a reluctance to waive legal resolution in a court of law. This is often caused by lack of knowledge and inexperience with the ADR process. As the parties gain experience and education, these obstacles are usually removed.

GROWTH OF ALTERNATIVE DISPUTE RESOLUTION

Two Chief Justices of the Supreme Court provided impetus to the increasing use of ADR. Chief Justice Warren Burger favored diverting appropriate disputes to alternative tribunals, particulary arbitration. In 1976, Burger convened a national conference to consider possible judicial reforms in response to criticism of, and substantial dissatisfaction with, the administration of justice. This conference was known as the "Pound Conference" in recognition of a speech by Roscoe Pound before the American Bar Association in 1906 calling for judicial reform.[2] The ABA Committee on Dispute resolution subsequently recommended that three pilot programs be established to test alternative methods to dispute resolution. This conference signaled the beginning of the modern ADR movement.[3]

Burger's support for arbitration and other forms of alternate resolution was continued by Chief Justice William Renquist. The Renquist Court issued a number of decisions that supported the arbitration of employment disputes and, in the process, overturned prior decisions limiting the scope of arbitration. Although arbitration had been accepted by the Court where provided for by collective labor agreements in the 1960 Steelworkers Trilogy,[4] its use was upheld in a number of cases heard by the Renquist Court where employees had signed individual agreements that provided for arbitration.[5] For example, in 1991, the Court compelled the arbitration of an EEOC charge under the ADEA where the plaintiff had signed a pre-employment agreement containing a broad arbitration clause.[6] The same court also struck down a prior **precedent** excluding the enforcement of employment contracts under the **Federal Arbitration Act** in *Adams* v. *Circuit City,* 122 S.Ct. 1302 (2001).

Alternative Dispute Resolution programs supported by the courts have expanded rapidly in the past 30 years. Today over 25 percent of the federal district courts and half of all state courts have adopted either mandatory or voluntary arbitration programs. Additionally, 51 federal district courts have court-annexed mediation and/or summary jury trials as ADR options.[7]

Over the past decade the demand has increased for low-cost alternative dispute resolution as an alternative to litigation. Countless cases have been brought in federal and state courts involving the Federal Arbitration Act, arbitration, mediation, and other forms of ADR. The American Arbitration Association, a private provider of neutral services in business and industry, reported a dramatic increase in inquiries from parties seeking alternative, cost-saving dispute resolution services during the recent economic crisis. The Finance Industry Regulatory Authority (FINRA), which administers both investor and employment arbitrations in the financial services industry, reported a 54 percent increase in case filings in 2007–2008.[8] Part of the growth of ADR has been fostered by the legal system, either by judicial direction or as a result of dissatisfaction with the court system. Judges may order parties to participate in summary jury trials or to arbitrate claims pursuant to court rules or in accordance with existing employment arbitration clauses. Some judges may require the parties to attempt mediation before setting a trial date. Other parties have voluntarily chosen ADR because of the expense, inflexibility, and excessive delay of the court system.

Disputes that arise in the private sector may be placed before a mediator or arbitrator of the parties' choosing on an *ad hoc* basis or referred to private ADR service providers who offer a wide range of dispute resolution options from mediation to private judging.[9] Public-sector disputes may also be handled informally or referred to private service providers but are often submitted to a state arbitration or mediation agency. In the federal sector, the Civil Justice Reform Act of 1990, 28 U.S.C., requires every federal district court to adopt an alternative dispute plan for civil matters. The Administrative Dispute Resolution Act of 1990, 5 U.S.C., requires all federal agencies to develop policies on the voluntary use of alternative dispute resolution.[10] Both the Americans with Disabilities Act (42 U.S. 12 *et al.*) and the Civil Rights Act of 1991 (42 U.S.C. § 1981) encourage the use of ADR procedures, including mediation, to resolve employment disputes. In the federal sector *ADR* is an umbrella term for a variety of conflict management and dispute resolution processes designed as an alternative to litigation or administrative adjudication.

It should be noted that the increased use of ADR has not necessarily meant the exclusion of attorneys from the dispute resolution process. Although ADR is often perceived as a layman's forum, lawyers frequently represent or advise the parties to a dispute and may be required to enforce awards or settlement agreements in court.

Forms of Alternative Dispute Resolution

Mediation is a process of voluntary negotiation with the assistance and guidance of a neutral third party. Mediation typically involves a single mediator but can involve multiple mediators working together or separately. The process is both informal and flexible, allowing the mediator to utilize his or her persuasive and compromising skills. The mediator is not called on to make a decision but rather to inform the parties through the introduction of outside information. Presumably the introduction of information together with the mediator's expertise will enable the parties to reach a settlement on their own.

Arbitration is a process that can be binding or nonbinding in terms of the arbitrator's final decision. The term *arbitration* normally refers to binding arbitration (the parties agree in advance to be bound by the decision of the arbitrator), whereas *nonbinding arbitration* is usually called "advisory arbitration" or "**fact finding.**" Arbitration is less structured than court procedures, and is much faster. It also permits the arbitrator to fashion a nonstandard remedy that is tailored specifically to the dispute. In the nonbinding variety of arbitration, the parties may select the neutral themselves from a variety of sources. In binding arbitration, the parties often use an outside agency such as the American Arbitration Association, the Federal Mediation and Conciliation Service, or a state agency to administer the process and provide a list of qualified third-party neutrals.[11]

A hybrid version of mediation and arbitration is known as **Med-Arb**, a contraction and combination of the terms *mediation* and *arbitration*. It allows the neutral(s) to first attempt to mediate the dispute and, if unsuccessful in enabling the parties to reach agreement, to issue a binding award resolving the issues still outstanding at the conclusion of the mediation stage.

A **mini-trial** is a forum that utilizes procedures similar to those in a court presentation. It combines facilitated negotiation with mediation and provides for an abbreviated presentation of the case before a panel of decision makers, one of whom serves as a neutral chair. The decision rendered (usually by the neutral) is either binding or may be used for further settlement discussions.

A **summary jury trial** is an alternative procedure where the parties present expedited evidence to a mock jury that is selected either by the parties or impaneled by a judge. The mock jury provides the parties with an advance assessment of what a regular jury might do. Accordingly, the opinion rendered is advisory (nonbinding) and is typically used for further discussions toward settlement.

A **moderated settlement conference** is a process wherein the parties present an expedited version of their case to a panel of neutrals (usually retired judges or arbitrators). These neutrals preside over judicial process and render a binding opinion. This opinion can also be used in further settlement discussions.

Neutral fact finding or **early neutral evaluation** (ENE) allows the parties to select a neutral(s) to issue a report or finding regarding a complex issue. The report can be binding but usually is nonbinding. A variation involves the use of an **ombudsman**. Some companies have created ombudsman postions that can provide employee advocacy, mediation, or fact finding, depending on the nature of the dispute. Recommendations of the ombudsman are intended to provide the company with an unbiased perspective on the dispute.

Private judging allows the parties to select a neutral (usually a retired judge or arbitrator) to preside over the process and make a decision. The decision is usually binding and the parties give up control of the case.

Some of these processes operate within the traditional legal system as public tribunals, whereas others are private actions independent of the courts. Any of these processes can be used, depending on the nature and facts of the dispute. What names are given to the technique selected and the procedures that are used depend on the parties.

SELECTION OF THE PROCESS

Mediation and arbitration are used commonly in the United States and Canada but are rarely utilized elsewhere in the world. Some companies have used alternative dispute resolution in international disputes, particularly in Canada, Great Britain, and France. It should be noted that, unlike the United States, many countries have created special labor or employment courts for resolution of employment disputes.[12]

The ADR process selected depends on the parties and the facts of the case. Mediation is the most popular with arbitration running a close second.[13] The selection of the right process depends in part on the parties' objectives. The most important question in selecting an ADR process is: Will it lead to the resolution of the dispute or to a settlement? When settlement is desired, ADR is often more efficient than litigation. A study of the U.S. Department of Justice's use of alternative dispute resolution between 1995 and 1998 found a 65 percent rate of settlement with ADR compared to a 29 percent rate of settlement with traditional litigation.[14]

Although ADR is not always successful, most users report satisfaction with it and use alternative processes wherever possible.[15] Aside from judicial referral, the main reasons that parties choose ADR are to maintain flexibility, reduce costs, and save time. Other motivating factors include maintaining the relationship between the parties, avoiding a precedent-setting decision or resolution, avoiding the technicalities of the legal process. and handling sensitive disputes internally. Alternative dispute resolution is most likely to be effective in routine cases where the involvement of top management is presumed to be unnecessary. This is not to suggest that top management should not be involved. On the contrary, line managers must monitor the process and be involved in all decisions, especially in settlements. Most users are satisfied with the result if the process is entered into voluntarily, but when involvement is involuntary, particularly in employment arbitration pursuant to a pre-hire contract, employee users are much less satisfied. When employees have agreed to arbitration provisions that require them to waive their right to sue the employer over any dispute arising out of the employment relationship, they may well feel coerced and dissatisfied when these disputes arise.[16]

Prior to selecting an unfamiliar alternative dispute resolution process, it is advisable to consult an attorney or an ADR service provider to familiarize the parties with the process and ascertain that there are no hidden legal issues related to the dispute. This is particularly true of arbitration when the award is final and binding on the parties. Placing a legal issue before an arbitrator can result in a ruling that is inconsistent with settled case law, or worse, a misinterpretation of a statute. Such rulings are difficult to change because of the extremely limited grounds for appealing an arbitrator's award.[17]

Taking a hard-line position in alternative dispute resolution is likely to jeopardize the outcome in nonbinding ADR procedures. By design, these processes involve negotiation and require flexibility and the ability and willingness on the part of both parties to counter propose and compromise. A successful ADR doesn't just happen—it requires preparation. The neutral and the respective parties and their representatives are all a necessary part of the process. Alternative dispute resolution makes possible the use of creativity in a way that litigation or compulsory binding arbitration cannot. All nonbinding processes involve some form of mediation, but all are not as flexible. Mediation can be used in conjucntion

with litigation before a suit is filed, in pre-discovery, after the trial, or in any other stage of the legal proceedings.

MEDIATION AND ARBITRATION

Mediation

Mediation is defined as a structured process in which the parties to a dispute or conflict negotiate its resolution with the assistance of a neutral party. Because of its cooperative, problem-solving nature, mediation is helpful in identifying and articulating serious concerns that might otherwise be dismissed, derogated, or, more likely, left unexpressed and unresolved. The focus of mediation and mediation training is to shift from the usual emphasis on an adversarial method of problem solving to a cooperative approach toward conflict management. Mediation's popularity is related to its nonbinding nature, since the parties are free to walk away if the direction of the mediation session or the outcome prove to be unsatisfactory to either party. In some cases mediation is not advised, particularly where legal issues and precedents are important or where the application of the law is undisputed and a motion for summary judgment is likely to be granted.

There are seven stages of mediation: (1) introduction, (2) problem determination, (3) summarization, (4) issue identification, (5) generation and evaluation of alternatives, (6) selection of approriate alternatives, and (7) settlement. These stages are not necessarily conducted in sequence, as the mediator has the flexibility to separate issues, meet privately with each of the parties, and move to whatever stage of the process he or she deems appropriate.

An integral component of mediation is training. Mediation training often involves the use of case simulations and role playing. Two trainees play the roles of opposing disputants, each having been assigned certain attitudes, positions, goals, and negotiating techniques/styles. A third trainee, acting as the mediator, is provided with very limited information regarding the dispute. The trainer provides guidance to the two trainees acting as opposing disputants.

An advantage of mediation over other methods of dispute resolution is that all decision-making authority remains with the disputants. The parties are in the best position to make their own creative settlements and are accordingly more likely to support and sustain any settlement. They must take care to choose an appropriate and experienced mediator. Successful mediators have the training and skills to be an impartial neutral and the ability to deflect hostility and criticism. A good mediator establishes rapport very early in the session. He or she meets with the parties early to discuss various issues and relates some of their own background so that the parties may identify with and confide in the mediator. Unless an element of trust is established, the mediator will have little chance of success. Co-mediators are often considered when several issues are involved or one party feels that it is important to have a neutral with a similar racial, ethnic, or protected class background. Often the parties want a second opinion. This is especially true when it is difficult to reach agreement on the selection of a single mediator.

Mediation is normally voluntary and either party is permitted to withdraw and thereby terminate the mediation without consequences, but when the court has *ordered* the mediation of a dispute, the failure of a party to appear or participate in the proceedings may subject that party to court sanctions.[18]

Mediators have minimal duties to the parties insofar as their professional standards are concerned. Under these standards attorney mediators have six distinct duties:

1. To describe the process and costs (if any) of mediation before the parties reach a final agreement to mediate.
2. To protect information learned in the mediation process.
3. To be impartial.
4. To assure that the parties make decisions based on sufficient information and knowledge.
5. To suspend or terminate the process whenever continuation would harm one or more of the participants.
6. To advise the participants to obtain legal review prior to finalizing any agreement or settlement.

One criticism of mediation is that the parties may not be aware that the role of the mediator is primarily to effect a settlement. He or she is not necessarily interested in whether the settlement is fair and equitable to both parties, or even that the settlement is advantageous to either party. If the parties can be persuaded to agree to a settlement proposal, even a poor settlement proposal, the mediator's job is finished. Further, mediators have relatively little liability for their work on behalf of the parties. Whereas the Society of Professionals in Dispute Resolution and the American Bar Association have both established minimal criteria or ethical standards for mediators, it would be necessary for a complaining party to show that a mediator was negligent in the performance of his/her duties or responsibilities to one of the parties and that he or she thereby caused damage to the party.

There is relatively little case law involving the enforcement of agreements to mediate or the enforcement of settlements reached through mediation. Enforcement in these instances would have to be based on a written agreement and could only be enforced under contract law. The lack of case law in this area may well be the result of the high degree of voluntary compliance with mediated procedures and settlements.

Arbitration

Arbitration is a formal, quasi-judicial process utilizing a neutral chair who presides over a structured hearing and serves as both judge and jury. A common variant is known as *tri-partite arbitration*, where each of the parties selects a representative to serve on a board of arbitration, and those two representatives select a neutral chair.[19]

The respective parties present their positions to the arbitrator by examining witnesses, offering documentary and physical evidence, and making closing arguments, either orally at the hearing or through post-hearing briefs. The crux of the process is the accumulation and presentation of relevant evidence and argument. The arbitrator will issue a decision or award, usually in writing, following the hearing.

When the arbitrator finds that one of the parties has been damaged by the other, he or she will order a *make-whole remedy*.[20] Ordinarily, arbitrators are not empowered to award punitive damages.[21] The decision of the arbitrator is final and binding on the parties. However, arbitrators have no enforcement power so the prevailing party may be required to seek enforcement through the courts. Although the courts permit appeals from the awards of arbitrators, the grounds for appeal are limited and appeals are rare.[22] Appeals to the court are limited because arbitration is conducted under a different legal doctrine than is standard litigation. While **stare decisis**, the basis of our legal system, relies on precedent-setting appellate decisions by superior courts, arbitration functions under the doctrine of **res judicata**, which does not permit appeals on the merits of a dispute and confines the applicability of an arbitrator's award to the specifc facts of that dispute. Although one arbitrator's award may be persuasive to another arbitrator in a similar case, there is no legal precedent in arbitration.

Because arbitration is final and binding, it has the advantage of resolving a dispute quickly while avoiding litigation. After an arbitration award has been made, mistakes or errors of law will not affect its enforceability. However, arbitration also requires the parties to give up control and decision-making authority over the dispute. As a result, it is important for the parties to select an arbitrator who is both experienced in the process and knowledgeable of the area of dispute. Lists of qualified arbitrators are provided by the private American Arbitration Association, the Federal Mediation and Conciliation Service, and many state agencies.

SETTLEMENT

Agreement or settlement is the goal of every alternative dispute resolution process. Settlement is often desired because it represents a consenual resolution that the parties can presumably live with in the future, and can be tailored to the parties' specific needs or to unique situations. However, in nonbinding processes, settlement cannot always be attained. If no settlement is reached, the process can be very costly as the parties still may have to litigate. Another negative result is that the relationship between the parties is often further damaged. Mediation requires disclosing facts that ordinarily would not be disclosed. If one of the parties reveals confidential information and there is no settlement, then the relationship may deteriorate. Some obstacles to settlement are poor communications, different views of the facts or the law, and external pressure from the employer, a constituent, or a personal relationship. An unsuccessful ADR can create an adverse situation that does neither party any good.

In any human endeavor there is always the possibility of failure. In ADR, if there is no settlement the process may still be worth the effort. If ADR fails, then the parties can still go to court to seek resolution. After ADR, the issues will be narrowed, the witnesses will be better informed, and there is still the possibility that the dispute can be settled before or during litigation. It is also possible that another ADR method, such as a mini-trial, can be attempted. The court proceedings can start from there. Scheduling for the discovery process starts at the unsuccessful meeting. All of these factors will save management time and legal fees if and when the parties go to court. The time and money invested in ADR will have been well used.

When a settlement is reached, the neutral should not let the parties leave the room until a settlement agreement is drafted. This essential document should state the issues and how they were settled. Later, a more definitive document can be drafted. The original agreement should state clearly who is agreeing to what, when, and how. Wherever possible, the disputants' wording should be used. It should be signed by all parties.

The final settlement agreement is a definitive document. It is more specific than the initial agreement in that it sets times and deadlines. It is a balanced document that is positive and provides for resolution of any future disputes that may arise out of the settlement. This document is drafted as a contract and is a legal document. In this respect the definitive agreement differs from the agreement signed at the process session. It states that the neutral has no obligation or authority to further protect the interests of the parties and that the signing could affect the legal rights of the parties. (The settlement cannot violate public policy.) The process is stated to be voluntary or that it was ordered by a judicial body. The parties agree to a voluntary settlement or that the decision was binding on both parties.

The settlement agreement should include specific waiver of any right, statutory, or common law that is inconsistent with what was agreed on. It is advisable that the parties consult an attorney before signing. Often an attorney will draft the definitive agreement but not necessarily the initial settlement terms.

COURT ENCFORCEMENT OF ADR

The courts have become increasingly friendly toward alternative dispute resolution in the last 20 years, specifically with respect to arbitration where the arbitrator's award is final and binding and forecloses further litigation. Generally speaking, the role of the court is limited to confirming or vacating arbitration awards, although there are limited circumstances under which an award may be returned to the arbitrator for clarification.[23] Encouragement of ADR reversed a long-standing antipathy on the part of the courts toward the arbitration/arbitrability of statutory claims.[24] In 1987, the Supreme Court decided *Shearson/American Express* v. *McMahon*. This decision not only upheld the arbitrability of claims arising under federal statute (the Securities Exchange Act of 1934) but also noted that the historical case law and precedent reflecting judicial hostility toward arbitration have been rejected.[25] The court's endorsement of arbitration in *Gilmer* v. *Interstate/ Johnson Lane Corporation,* cited ealier, was extended to claims arising under the Age Discrimination in Employment Act in 1991. This decision effectively opened the door for the utilization of all forms of ADR in employment disputes in nonunion settings. Before *Gilmer,* it was unclear whether any form of private agreement could require the arbitration of a statutory employment discrimination claim. In *Williams* v. *Katten, Muchin & Zavis,* 837 F.Supp. 1430 (N.D. Ill. 1993), a federal district court affirmed the report and recommendation of a magistrate who applied *Gilmer* to require arbitration of statutory discrimination claims under an employment agreement.

The incentives have never been greater to use a procedure to settle a dispute out of court. It is not uncommon for one lawsuit involving a wrongful discharge to cost more than $100,000. Court decisions have suggested that ADR will be fully accepted by the courts. Judicial attitudes about ADA have changed drastically since *Alexander* v. *Gardner-Denver,* 415 U.S. S.Ct. 36 (1974).[26] The vast backlog of cases, the availability of arbitrators to resolve statutory claims, and Congress's intent that statutory claims do not have to be resolved in judicial forums are probably the reasons for this change. It would appear that the courts have concluded that a plaintiff does not sacrifice any legal rights when he or she agrees to an alternative forum and is merely substituting that forum for a traditional adjudication in front of a judge and/or jury.

A recent backlash against arbitration in financial disputes arose in 2009 when Minnesota's attorney general brought suit against a private arbitration service. The state alleged that parties to many commerical contracts requiring arbitration of all disputes between the finance provider (credit card company, installment loan provider, etc.) were coercive and that the arbitration service was apparently biased against consumers.

The matter was settled out of court when the arbitration service agreed to withdraw from the compulsory arbitration agreements. However, the lawsuit apparently caused the American Arbitration Association to stop handling commercial credit arbitrations and Bank of America to rescind its mandatory arbitration clauses.

The strong trend of recent cases is to give the widest possible role to alternative dispute resolution procedures in the employment context. In view of the costs that can be incurred even in successfully defending against a lawsuit, as well as the uncertainties inherent in the ever-expanding availability of jury trials and punitive damages, most employers should at least consider whether adopting some form of alternative dispute resolution would be appropriate. A formal ADR program may not be appropriate for all employers. The nature of the workforce, experience with claims, willingness to abide by procedures that will be considered fair, and many other issues need to be considered before adopting ADR.

CASE 11.1

Mediator Liability

Mary was employed by a small cellular phone provider as a sales representative. When she was hired she signed an employment agreement specifying that she would submit any dispute arising out of her employment with the company to arbitration. She developed serveral commercial accounts resulting in the sale of multiple cell phones and service contracts. Once developed, Mary earned an adequate income servicing these accounts and renewing them. However, her employer became concerned that Mary was not aggressively soliciting new business and so reassigned some of Mary's large accounts to another sales representative.

Mary objected to the loss of her largest accounts but was unable to persuade the company to reverse the work assignment. Consequently, she was forced to seek new business but was only minimally successful in doing so. When her revenues (and accordingly her income) dropped, she was counseled about her job performance and warned that she could be terminated if her numbers didn't improve. Uncomfortable with the requirement to arbitrate, Mary proposed to the company that they attempt to mediate their differences and the company agreed.

The mediation was successful. Mary was permitted to resign, the negative comments about her job performance were expunged, she waived her right to arbitrate the dispute, and received a monetary settlement from the company. However, after receiving the settlement Mary began to have second thoughts. She became convinced that the mediator had failed to fully inform her of her rights and had obtained and inadequate monetary settlement. She felt that the mediator could have obtained a better settlement for her.

What remedies might Mary have against the mediator? What exposure does the company have to a lawsuit? ■

Adhesion Contract

Harry was a recent honors graduate of City University with a major in Technology and Computer Science. He obtained an interview with Big Systems, a large manufacturer of systems hardware and peripherals. Big Systems was Harry's first choice and he immediately canceled his other interviews when the recruiter from Big Systems told him that he had been selected for the position he was seeking. However, when he reported to complete his employment paperwork, Big Systems Human Resources Director advised Harry that Big Systems had an arbitration provision in its employee handbook that required employees to submit "any and all" disputes arising out of their employment to arbitration if they could not be settled informally between the company and the employee.

Harry wanted the job but didn't like the idea of waiving his right to sue. When he objected, the HR director told him that he could "take the offer or leave it" if he didn't agree to the arbitration provision. He was further told that he was expected to be at work the following morning and that he could not complete his employee sign-on until he signed the arbitration agreement.

What are Harry's options?
Can the employer enforce the arbitration requirement?

Summary

This chapter traces the development of alternative dispute resolution methods in response to demands for reform of the American justice system. These methods were designed to replace litigation with cheaper and speedier adjudication of disputes. It briefly describes several techniques that disputing parties may utilize to resolve conflicts and discusses mediation and arbitration, the two most popular ADR processes, and considers how mediation and arbitration have been accepted by the courts. The chapter also addresses settlement through ADR and court enforcement of awards.

Key Terms

Precedent   279
Federal Arbitration
   Act   279
Mediation   280
Arbitration   280
Fact finding   280

Med-Arb   280
Mini-trial   281
Summary jury trial   281
Settlement conference   281
Early neutral evaluation
   (ENE)   281

Ombudsman   281
Stare decisis   284
Res judicata   284

Questions for Discussion

1. What is the difference between binding arbitration and advisory arbitration? Why do some consider "advisory arbitration" to be a misnomer?
2. Under what circumstances might the parties select ADR as opposed to litigating a dispute?
3. What is the role of the lawyer in ADR procedures?

4. Why do many employers who are not unionized require their employees to sign pre-employment arbitration clauses?
5. Why are settlements much more common when using ADR than they are in litigation?
6. What was the role of the Pound Conference in encouraging ADR?

7. Why is ADR likely to be effective in resolving discrimination complaints?

8. What are the advantages/disadvantages of utilizing ADR when an employee challenges discipline or termination?

9. Why is arbitration considered to be the most powerful ADR mechanism?

10. Why have the courts limited appeals of ADR settlements and awards?

Notes to Chapter 11

1. See B. Cogan, "Alternative dispute resolution and judicial immunity: A potential retail pitfall?" *Labor Law Journal* (November 1994): 772.

2. Katherine A. V. Stone, *Private justice: The law of alternative dispute resolution* (New York: Foundation Press, 2000,) p. 3.

3. C. Menkel-Meadow, "What will we do when adjudication ends? A brief intellectual history of ADR," *UCLA Law Review,* 44 (1997): 1613.

4. *United Steelworkers of America* v. *American Mfg. Co.,* 363 U.S. 564 (1960); *United Steelworkers of America* v. *Warrior and Gulf Navigation Co.,* 363 U.S. 574 (1960); *United Steelworkers of America* v. *Enterprise Wheel and Car Corp.,* 363 U.S. 593 (1960).

5. M. LeRoy and P. Feuille, "Judicial enforcement of predispute arbitration agreements: Back to the future," *Ohio State Journal on Dispute Resolution,* 18, no. 249 (2003).

6. *Gilmer* v. *Interstate/Johnson Lane,* 500 U.S. 20, 1991.

7. Stone, p. 4.

8. D. Lipsky, "Workplace arbitration in the current economic crisis," *Dispute Resolution Journal,* 64, no. 1 (February 2009): 7–9.

9. Jacqueline M. Nolan-Haley, *Alternative dispute resolution* (St. Paul, MN: West, 1992).

10. T. Nabatchi, "The institutionalization of alternative dispute resolution in the federal government," *Public Administration Review,* 67, no. 4 (July/August 2007): 646–661.

11. See Deloitte & Touche Litigation Services, 1993 Survey—MN, CLE 40 Milton St., Suite 101, St. Paul, MN 55104-7094.

12. Most other countries have curtailed employment-at-will by statute. Some utilize their regular courts to resolve employment disputes, whereas others have created labor/employment courts.

13. For a good article on the selection process see "Fitting the forum to the fuss: A user guide to selecting an ADR procedure," *Negotiation Journal* (January 1994).

14. American Arbitration Association, "Study compares U.S. Department of Justice's use of ADR and litigation" *Dispute Resolution Journal,* 63, no. 4 (November, 2008): 8.

15. See Goult study, "Future of worker-management relations," 1995.

16. K. Stone, "Mandatory arbitration of individual employment rights: The yellow dog contract of the 1990's," *Denver Law Review,* 73, no. 1017 (1996).

17. Federal Arbitration Act, 9 U.S.C. § 10(a). See also: *First Options of Chicago, Inc.,* v. *Kaplan,* 514 U.S. 938 (1995).

18. *Raad* v. *Wal-Mart Stores, Inc.,* 1998 WL 272879 (U.S.D.C., D. Neb. 1998).

19. System Boards of Adjustment under the National Railway Labor Act provide for multiple member boards of arbitration equally appointed by labor and management with a neutral chair. Decisions are by a majority vote.

20. *United Steelworkers* v. *Enterprise Wheel and Car Corp.,* 363 U.S. 597 (1960).

21. *Mastrobuono* v. *Shearson Lehman Hutton, Inc.,* 514 U.S. 52 (1995).

22. For a discussion of the court's role in the review of arbitration awards, see D. Arnavas, "Alternative dispute resolution: Getting it right the first time." *Contract Management,* 48, no. 8 (August 2008): 19–28.

23. *Hall Street Associates LLC* v. *Mattel,* 128 S. Ct. 1396 (2008).

24. *Wilko* v. *Swan,* 346 U.S. 427 (1953); *Southland Corporation* v. *Keating,* 465 U.S. 852 (1984); *Rodriques de Quijas et al* v. *Shearson/American Express, Inc.,* 490 U.S. 477 (1989).

25. *Allied-Bruce Terminix Companies, Inc. et al.* v. *G. Michael Dobson et al.,* 513 U.S. 265, 115 S.Ct. 834 (1995). Also see *Shearson/American Express* v. *McMahon,* 482 U.S. 220 (1987).

26. See *14 Penn Plaza LLC* v. *Pyett,* 556 U.S. (2009) discussed in Chapter 2.

CHAPTER 12

Human Resource Issues in the Twenty-First Century

CHAPTER OUTLINE

Management Malpractice Issues

Privacy in the Workplace

Changing Composition of the Workforce

Globalization and Immigration

Future of Human Resources Management

There can be little doubt that the law as it applies to the management of human resources will continue to change as the courts interpret existing statutes and legislatures create new laws to regulate the employment relationship. Not only has employment-at-will been challenged through breach of contract actions alleging wrongful discharge, but employers have been increasingly compelled to respond to tort actions alleging that the employer has engaged in outrageous conduct or has intentionally inflicted emotional distress on an employee. Human resources management in the twenty-first century has witnessed, and will continue to witness, changes in antidiscrimination laws, complaints of workplace harassment, and courts willing to hold individual managers personally liable for their treatment of employees. Further, as noted in Chapter 8, there will be increasing pressure to amend the National Labor Relations Act to make it easier for employees to organize and negotiate collective bargaining agreements.

Human resources managers will also be required to respond to a changing workforce that brings to the job a different set of values and expectations. These changes in the workforce will be exacerbated by the contentious argument over immigration policy and the status of noncitizen workers.

MANAGEMENT MALPRACTICE ISSUES

One of the more recent legal concerns confronting managers is court application of the concept of **malpractice** to the workplace. Malpractice suits have not been uncommon for medical and legal professionals, and have also resulted from soured business relationships, but they are relatively new to human resources management. The concept of management malpractice in dealing with employees is different from that in business conduct. The term *malpractice* refers to conduct that is not necessarily negligent or incompetent but includes behaviors that are unacceptable in American society. The court in *Belanoff* v. *Grayson*, 471 N.Y.S.2d 91 (A.D. 1st Dept. 1984), characterized it as "conduct that exceeds all bounds usually tolerated by society."

Management malpractice may occur when an employer uses what it believes to be an effective means of correcting what it views as unacceptable conduct on the part of employees. The methods used by management to make certain that such employee conduct will not recur may be construed as malpractice. A problem arises when it is determined by a court that the methods or techniques used are not acceptable to society. What may seem legitimate conduct to management may not be deemed as acceptable to society as determined by a court.

To prevent malpractice in management it is first necessary to know what types of behaviors and actions, and their legal consequences, could be deemed malpractice. Management malpractice includes conduct that has serious consequences for an employee's personal or physical well-being. This area of potential managerial liability is small, but it has grown, aided by other expanding areas of employee rights. The courts have taken the position that the employer–employee relationship carries with it certain legal obligations. This position is supported by statutes as well as the common law. For example, the National Labor Relations Act requires the employer to refrain from certain activities affecting the employee's right to act in concert with other employees and to join, or refrain from joining, a union. Financial protection for job-related injuries is provided under the workers' compensation laws of the various states. The Equal Pay Act requires employers to give equal pay for equal work without regard to gender, and Title VII prohibits an employer from making any employment decision based on race, color, religion, disability, nationality, or gender. The Age Discrimination in Employment Act and its amendments, and the Americans with Disabilities Act also prohibits discrimination based on age and physical disability respectively. All of these statutory rights have strengthened the view that an employee has a property right in his or her job. This view has been accepted to the detriment of the common law employment-at-will doctrine. The result has been to limit management prerogative in hiring and firing and to increase the exposure to malpractice suits.

The erosion of the at-will doctrine has been accompanied by a change in employee attitudes. Formerly, a disgruntled employee may have grumbled for a while, complained to his or her co-workers, possibly looked to a union for help, or even quit. Today, employees readily utilize the various agencies established to hear complaints such as the Department of Labor, the NLRB, the EEOC, or a union. Alternatively, they may turn to an attorney and initiate a private lawsuit. Plaintiffs in these cases often receive large monetary awards through the jury system or are paid by the employer to settle the matter. In some instances the employer will feel compelled to settle a meritless suit simply to avoid publicity, court costs, and defense attorney fees.

Malpractice Lawsuits

Almost all malpractice suits are actions in tort. They differ from the breach of contract suits common in wrongful discharge cases in that they are more serious offenses. The successful prosecution of malpractice action requires a showing of extreme action by the defendant employer and typically results in the award of higher damages than in a wrongful discharge action. Malpractice actions frequently involve a claim for emotional distress. In these cases it is usually necessary to show intent on the part of the employer. In other malpractice actions the courts only require evidence that the plaintiff was injured by the defendant's unreasonable conduct.

A form of management malpractice is where the employee alleges intentional infliction of emotional distress. This is sometimes called a *contemptuous tort* and is a common allegation in discharge cases. In this type of case the employee alleges that the employer's conduct was intentional, reckless, and contrary to what a civilized society should tolerate. The effect on the employee must be severe but what "severe" means is typically defined by a jury on a case-by-case basis. In one case, an employer refused to allow an employee to take a tranquilizer while the employee was being questioned about a theft. The court held that this was intentional infliction of emotional distress where the employer had knowledge of the employee's nervous condition.[1] When an employer ridiculed, threatened, humiliated, and sexually harassed an employee, the court found a tort of outrageous conduct.[2] When an employer demoted a manager to janitor and otherwise set out to humiliate the employee, the jury, with court approval, awarded $3.4 million for infliction of emotional distress.[3]

Wrongful Conduct but Not Malpractice

An example of a case where the employer's verbal comments were not severe enough to be considered malpractice is *Moye* v. *Gary,* 595 F.Supp. 738 (S.D. N.Y. 1984). In this case a supervisor called an employee a "fag" and a "poor woman." Similarly, in *Morrison* v. *Sandell et al.,* 466 N.E.2d 290 (Ill. App. 1983), a co-worker put human waste in a file drawer that the plaintiff was about to use. The court held that this conduct was inappropriate but

not severe enough to create emotional distress and was an "isolated incident that lacked duration." Another example of conduct found not severe enough to find emotional distress and management malpractice is *Vinson* v. *Linn-Mar Community School District,* 360 N.W.2d 108 (Iowa 1984). An employer was found guilty of defamation of character by malice and mistruths, for which damages were awarded, but the court held that this was not an act that was "atrocious and utterly intolerable in a civilized community." The employee complained of:

- Embarrassment because of his wrongful discharge when he had to tell acquaintances that he was unemployed.
- Sleeplessness at night worrying about employment.
- Unsteady nerves.
- Depression most of the time.
- Fear of social contact with his friends.
- Fear about meeting financial obligations.
- Stress compelling him to visit a physician as well as a psychologist.
- Loss of self-confidence when meeting prospective employers.

The court did not consider these effects severe enough to maintain a claim of intentional infliction of emotional distress for the wrongful discharge. It held that the law intervenes only when the employer's action is "so severe that no reasonable man could be expected to bear it."[4]

Another case involved an employee who refused to stop dating a co-worker. The discharge caused severe distress. The court held that the discharge was not severe enough to warrant an action for emotional distress.[5] This rule was also adopted in Missouri, where the employer—before the discharge—said, "Dammit, you've done it again," and commented that she "doesn't know a goddamn thing." The employer's conduct at the time of the discharge was alleged to cause the plaintiff suffering in the form of severe mental pain, anguish, embarrassment, stomach problems, and loss of sleep. The court noted that the employer's conduct, although not above reproach, could not be characterized as so extreme and outrageous as to be considered a tort. It further held that employees must necessarily be hardened to a certain amount of rough language and other action that is inconsiderate and unkind. Although the plaintiff suffered mental stress, it was not sufficient to allow recovery.[6]

The successful prosecution of an emotional distress claim requires the plaintiff to show more extreme action by the defendant than in other malpractice cases. In supporting an allegation of emotional distress it is usually necessary to show intent, but in other malpractice actions the courts only require that the plaintiff was injured by the defendant's unreasonable conduct.

PRIVACY RIGHTS IN THE EMPLOYMENT RELATIONSHIP

The protection of a person's privacy is a common law right that has been protected by the courts for many years.[7] The Restatement (Second) of Torts Section 652b states:

One who intentionally intrudes, physically or otherwise, upon the solitude or seclusion of another or his private concerns is subject to liability to the other for invasion of his privacy, if the intrusion would be highly offensive to a reasonable person.

This principle has been used in a wide variety of situations.[8] In police investigations, the officer must be careful not to invade the privacy of the accused. For example, the Supreme Court held in *Eisenstadt, Sheriff* v. *Baird*, 405 U.S. 438 (1972), that it is an invasion of privacy to question another person about her or his marriage and sex life, since these are fundamental rights entitled to privacy protection.

On the issue of abortion, one court has held that a state statute prohibiting it is an invasion of privacy.[9] Various state laws that require safety measures such as the wearing of helmets by motorcycle operators have, on a case-by-case basis, been held to be an invasion of privacy. In many situations, the plaintiff will claim emotional distress, caused by invasion of privacy. An uninvited intrusion into a person's solitude or seclusion may also provide for an invasion of privacy claim.[10] This is a common argument in drug and alcohol testing, as well as other areas.

In sum, then, invasion of privacy claims are found in all walks of life.[11] The employer can ask personal questions about personal matters, only so long as they are business related and reasonably executed.

Technology and Training

We take technology as a part of our daily lives. It is the very fiber of our society. We get up in the morning and turn on the television or computer for the news. From that time on, we are often dependent on technology to navigate our lives. In the job market, technology has caused many persons to be retrained. Training to run information systems is constant. Training in technology is the most popular subject in corporate training programs. This training has more influence on the success of the organization than ever before. Workers are not only expected to know their craft but are also expected to apply it technically. Without a doubt, we have gone from an industrial era to a knowledge era. The weekday edition of the *New York Times* contains more information than the average seventeenth-century person was likely to come across in a lifetime. Technology has created a whole new vocabulary with such words as *Internet, bits, bites, blog, tweet*, and so on. All are now a part of our constantly changing, new vocabulary.

Technology and Privacy

Email, voice mail, and other technical devices have caused a legal confrontation in the common law doctrine of the invasion of privacy.[12] In a lawsuit in federal court, a manager sued McDonald's Corporation for monitoring and taping his voice mail messages. According to the lawsuit, the messages contained intimate exchanges with a co-employee with whom the manager was having an affair. The manager alleged his employer secretly recorded the messages and played them to his wife, possibly violating federal and state wiretapping laws and the **Electronic Communications Privacy Act**. The manager argued that he had an expectation of privacy in the communications because he accessed his voice mail with a confidential code. This case helps define the contours of appropriate employer monitoring of electronic communications such as email and voice mail systems. As technology becomes increasingly common in the workplace, further challenges to employer monitoring are certain to arise.[13] In summary, the summary can ask personal questions about personal matters, so long as they are business related and reasonable.

There is pressure on state and federal levels of the government to pass legislation to protect various privacy rights of the employee. Protection by statute is necessary, since under the common law, the employee in the employer–employee relationship has fewer rights than as a citizen. As the court said in *United States* v. *Blok,* 188 F.2d 1019 (D.C. Cir. 1951), it was a violation of privacy under the Fourth Amendment for the police to search the employee's desk, but it would have been proper for the supervisor to do so.

Many believe that the legal scales are weighted too heavily toward the employer. The greatest exposure to litigation over the privacy rights of the employee are in the areas of drug and alcohol testing; record keeping, particularly medical records; psychological and honesty testing; and communication on discipline.

Employer Invasion of Privacy

Under the common law, employer invasion of privacy usually occurs when the employer commits some act that damages the employee's right to enjoy a good reputation. Public disclosure of true facts could be an invasion of privacy.[14] An example is disclosure by the employer of information about an employee's drinking habits, a positive AIDS test, or failure of a drug test. The plaintiff must prove that these facts are highly offensive and are not of legitimate concern to the public, in order to recover under tort law.[15]

The public not only includes persons unrelated to the employment situation, but it also includes supervisors and others closely related to the employment situation who have no reason to know. A flight attendant directed her private physician to supply her employer with information concerning her medical condition. Based on this information, the employer's medical examiner waived weight limits imposed for appearance regulations and applicable to her job. The information supplied included details of contemplated gynecological surgery. The employer's medical examiner disclosed this information to her male supervisor and to her husband. She sued the employer for invasion of privacy. The court found that it was an invasion of privacy to disclose the information to her supervisor and her husband. The supervisor had no authority to act on the data disclosed, and her husband "faced no problem involving his own well-being or emergency care for his spouse"; therefore, neither recipient had a need to know.[16] The court allowed compensatory damages but denied punitive damages, as there was no evidence of malice. Unless malice can be shown in privacy cases, the court will not allow punitive damages.[17] In a related case, the court held that a consultation between the company physician and the employee's personal physician concerning an employee's illness did not constitute an invasion of privacy. Employer conduct was motivated by concern for the employee, when the information related to a requested leave of absence.

Rights in Public Sector

Employees in the public sector have more rights than those in the private sector, since they are protected by the Fourth Amendment of the Constitution. When a police officer was discharged for living with a married woman, the court said this was an invasion of privacy. However, if the private life of the employee affects the job, the court will find that the job requirements will override the privacy right.[18] In *Potter* v. *Murray City*, 760 F.2d 1065 (10th Cir. 1985), cert. denied (1985), the discharge of a Utah police officer was upheld when he was practicing plural marriage in violation of a Utah statute.

As discussed in Chapter 2, the courts have found, with increasing frequency, that certain types of sexual harassment are an invasion of privacy. To avoid liability under privacy law, the court must find the plaintiff had a reasonable expectation that the employer's action would cause damage to the employee's reputation.

Use of Polygraph Tests

The use of polygraph tests and other forms of lie detectors is one way for employers to stop or decrease property losses.[19] This may or may not be an effective way to control losses, and it involves a certain degree of exposure. One of the human resources practitioner's most important tasks is to determine the facts when a job applicant is alleged to be dishonest. Applicants may not always seek specific jobs for wages, but for the opportunity to embezzle, steal, sell company secrets to competitors, or have other dishonest intentions. For many years the use of a lie detector test has been an available, but controversial, method of detecting dishonesty.

Employee Polygraph Protection Act

The **Employee Polygraph Protection Act** of 1988 was passed by the Congress "to prevent the denial of employment opportunities by prohibiting the use of lie detectors by employers involved in or affecting interstate commerce."[20] The act restricts the use of mechanical or electrical devices to determine the veracity of an employee's statements. If the results are used for the purposes of rendering a diagnostic opinion regarding the honesty or dishonesty of an employee, it is illegal.[21] The employer is prohibited from requiring, requesting, or even suggesting to any employee or prospective employee to take any type of lie detector test. The act further prevents the employer from using or threatening to use any of the results of a lie detector test in making an employment decision. The act is enforced by the Secretary of Labor, who has promulgated rules and regulations under the act. The secretary has also prepared a summary of the act to be posted by each employer in conspicuous places on its premises. This is usually in the employment office or where employees normally come with problems, such as the personnel office.

If an employee is discriminated against for refusing to take a test, or for testifying that another employee or prospective employee was discriminated against, the act will protect such an employee from any employer's adverse action. The Secretary of Labor has investigative powers and can conduct a hearing. Violation of the act has a civil penalty of not more than $10,000. The amount is determined by the Secretary of Labor, who can go to court to collect the fine or have an employee reinstated. An employee may file a lawsuit within three years after the alleged violation. The act provides for attorney fees for the prevailing party. Waiver of employee rights and procedures under the act is specifically prohibited.

Sections 7 and 8 of the Employee Polygraph Protection Act provide for very broad exemptions that are important to note.[22] Under Section 7, all employers in the public sector are exempt, including consultants, experts, or contractors employed by the federal government when performing any counterintelligence function. Under Section 8 of the act, certain employers in the private sector are also exempt. If there is an ongoing investigation involving an economic loss or injury, the test can be used. It has a specific exemption for investigation of drugs. When the polygraph test is used under Section 7 or 8, the results must be used only as supportive evidence. It could be argued that most present uses of the polygraph test are exempted under these sections, except for pre-employment testing.[23]

The act restricts disclosure of the results to the examinee, the employer who requested the test, or any court or governmental agency. The examinee may, in writing, permit disclosure to any other person.

The special preemption provision of the act in Section 10 provides that no state or local law, or collective bargaining agreement that is more restrictive than the act, will be preempted. As a practical matter, most state laws are less restrictive, so the result of the act will be to preempt them, except under the exemptions, which are subject to extensive court interpretation.[24]

The act is void in the situation where the employee offers to take the test without a request from the employer. This is a common occurrence for which a great deal of case law has been developed.[25] The employer has a choice of not using a polygraph test at all, or being exposed to litigation. For the employer who still feels it is important to use the test, a policy or procedure that conforms to federal

and state law should be developed. However, any polygraph policy should be reviewed by an attorney.

Recommended Policies for Polygraph Testing

When it becomes necessary to obtain evidence about the suspected dishonesty of an employee, the first consideration must be which techniques are allowed by federal and state law. Some states restrict the use of electronic devices in varying degrees, whereas others have no restrictions. Both the polygraph test and search are means of obtaining evidence to determine guilt or innocence. If it is permitted by state and federal law, there is no reason why the polygraph test cannot be used. Not only is it a method of obtaining evidence, but exposure of employees to the test may have a chilling effect on employee dishonesty. The human resources practitioner should always consider the possible effects of the use of the polygraph on employee relations. An atmosphere of unwarranted suspicion may cause more harm than the test results can cure; refusal is not an admission of guilt.

A policy or guideline regarding the use of the polygraph test might include the following provisions:

1. The polygraph test can be used in pre-employment screening where the applicant is being considered for a position of trust or one that requires handling a large amount of cash from customers (bank teller, safekeeping department of a hospital, and so on) under the exemptions of the federal statute.
2. If used, it will not be the sole qualifying or disqualifying factor in a pre-employment evaluation but be supportive of other information.
3. For current employees, a rule should be established to require that a voluntary test be only supportive in determining the facts, that an employee be a suspect

before the test is given, and that there is no other way to determine the facts.

4. The polygraph test will always be used in combination with other techniques.

5. Passing or failing the polygraph test will not be considered by itself to be conclusive nor will the refusal to take the test, but in both situations the presumption of innocence or suspicion of guilt may be affected.

6. Results of the test will not be disclosed, except to those who have a right to know, or where a written release is given by the examinee.

Employer Right of Search and Seizure

The employer–employee relationship must be distinguished from a person who might be engaged in criminal activity. The U.S. Supreme Court on numerous occasions has restricted search and seizure under the Fourth Amendment.[26] Surveillance by the police is restricted to what is observable. The court allows various techniques to make evidence observable, such as trained dogs, "beepers," flashlights, and so forth. The law, as it relates to search in the criminal sense, is in place.[27] In a police–citizen confrontation, the search of lunch boxes would be a violation of Fourth Amendment rights. However, workplace search situations are different. The employer has a legitimate interest in protecting its own property and that of other employees.

Fourth Amendment Protection in the Public Sector

Would it be proper for a supervisor of a public employer to search an employee's desk when the public employee has the protection of the Fourth Amendment? The court in *O'Connor* v. *Ortega*, 107 S.Ct. 1492 (1987), said a reasonable search is permitted, but left it up to the trial court to determine what is reasonable. In *O'Connor*, the employee had been placed on administrative

leave from his hospital job pending investigation of a charge of work-related misconduct. While on leave, his office was searched, including his desk and files. Work-related information and several items of personal effects were taken from his desk, only to be used later in an adverse administrative hearing. The employee claimed that the purpose of the search was to obtain evidence for the hearing, but the employer argued it was designed to inventory state property. The employee sued the persons making the search.

The court, in a 5-to-4 decision, said that public employers must be given wide latitude to enter offices and should not be subject to probable cause requirements, as are police officers. The standard applied was the same as in the private sector—one of reasonableness. The court said what is reasonable is decided on a case-by-case basis. Justice Scalia wrote a separate opinion, stating any work-related search is reasonable, regardless of how private or public the employee's office may be. Even where the employee has the protection of the Fourth Amendment, his or her office may be searched. This decision gives both the public and the private employer considerable authority to make searches in the workplace.

Limitation of Searches by Labor Agreement

Privacy matters are seldom included in labor agreements, because the parties choose to bargain about them on a one-by-one basis. The usual practice is that the company makes a rule; if the union feels that it is unreasonable, they challenge it through the grievance procedure. If the matter is not settled, it then goes to arbitration.

Generally speaking, arbitrators have given management the right to search employees and their private property, and have permitted disciplinary action when the employees refuse. The basis for this position is that employment can be conditioned upon compliance with reasonable rules. The employer also has a legitimate right to prevent theft not only of property of the company but also the property of employees. As in any arbitration situation, there is always a minority view.[28] Although most arbitrators permit searches, they disagree widely on the treatment of evidence obtained in a search. Arbitrators also differ substantially on the right of the employee to refuse a search. A showing of probable cause is generally enough to support discipline for refusing to permit a personal search. An organization must not act in an unreasonable fashion and must have a reasonable basis for the search of lockers and offices of employees. Such a basis might be the fact that certain property of the organization is missing.[29] Some arbitrators require the organization to have a rule or demonstrate the existence of a past practice before they will uphold a search. One company changed its policy to require employees to purchase their own locks for toolboxes and use them for company and personal use. The arbitrator ruled that the company could not search the toolboxes after this policy change, although the arbitrator implied that they could have done so prior to the policy change.[30]

Most arbitrators consider a parking lot to be company property, especially if it is close to the work facility.[31] However, a rule to prohibit smoking in the parking lot is reasonable if there is evidence of potential negative health consequences or property

damage. It appears from arbitration decisions and the absence of court cases on searches and seizures, that if an employer has a probable cause to search the personal property of the employees in the workplace, including the parking lot, the search will be permitted.[32] This conclusion is in line with other case law and with the common law rule that the employee cannot refuse to answer questions because of possible self-incrimination, and must reveal any information that was acquired during the course of employment.

Recommended Procedures for Searches

In order for the employer to exercise the rights granted by the common law, it is necessary to establish a policy on searches, if exposure to invasion-of-privacy claims is to be avoided. Most courts will permit any reasonable search, especially if the employee is warned that it might happen. Several courts take the position that continued employment, after being warned that routine searches will be made, is implied consent. This prevents any lawsuit for invasion of privacy.[33] A policy on searches is shown in Exhibit 12.1.

There should be guidelines for the supervisors to follow, if exposure to privacy lawsuits is to be avoided. The guidelines should state the following:

1. The purpose of the policy is to protect company and employee interests.
2. Searches will be used only when there is legitimate reason to believe that

---

Effective _____ [at least two weeks], the company will implement procedures to improve security and to protect employees' property from theft and to obtain facts for accusations of theft of company property. All persons entering and leaving the company's premises will be subject to questions and a search as a condition of employment. The search may include lockers, parked vehicles, packages, purses, handbags, briefcases, lunch boxes, and all other possessions. Failure to cooperate will be considered a violation of this policy. Employees or others violating this policy will be treated accordingly.

EXHIBIT 12.1   Search Policy

pilferage is taking place. This includes employees' property as well as company property.

3. In all searches, personal privacy will be respected, but this consideration will not eliminate the search.

4. Searches, if possible, will be conducted away from other employees, on company time, and on company premises.

A search could be an invasion of privacy (defined as something highly offensive to a reasonable person) if not conducted for the purpose of obtaining facts. Often the person doing the search becomes abusive and acts with malice in the attempt to get the employee to admit the wrongdoing, and a suit for invasion of privacy results. In *K-Mart Corp. Store No. 7441 v. Trotti*, 677 S.W. 2d 632 (Tex. App. 1984), the court held that it was an invasion of privacy to search lockers when there was no warning that lockers would occasionally be searched. This decision may have been influenced by the fact that unreasonable search methods were used.

The law permits the employer to use all reasonable means to protect property, whether it be the company's or that of an employee, and all management has to do is exercise the rights that the law provides.[34]

Sometimes management takes the position that the way to prevent pilferage is to involve the law enforcement authorities. This can be a serious mistake. Law enforcement authorities need more proof of a violation than an employer does. All that the employer must show is that the company policy was violated, but the police need substantial evidence that the employee committed the act and violated a law. If the employer accuses, and the authorities fail to prosecute or the employee is found not guilty, the employer's employee relations efforts may have been dealt a severe blow. The second reason why the authorities should not be involved is that the employer's primary business is not improving society and removing all dishonest persons from the streets. The employer's concern must be work related, so the only penalty the employer would normally consider is discharge.

Most employees will accept the truth but are quick to challenge any falsehood. In the past, it was not what the employer had been doing that caused the lawsuits, but rather the poor execution of a policy or the handling of a situation that resulted in large awards. This caused some employers to become "gun-shy" in exercising their common law rights.

Common Law on Disclosure of Employee Information

Disclosure of information about employees is problematic; the subject became popular in professional literature and personnel textbooks in the 1980s.[35] Under present legal doctrine, personnel records (defined as all information about employees kept by an employer) are not confidential but are the property of the employer, to be used at its discretion. The employee can do little to stop disclosure.[36] The release of information about employees is largely controlled by the employer. The discretionary control of personnel records by the employer has often been considered by civil rights advocates, academics, and the general public as a potential unjust infringement on employee privacy.

The advent of antidiscrimination laws in the 1960s and 1970s imposed certain restrictions on the disclosure of information about employees. The upsurge in the interest of employee privacy and the recognition of individual rights by the judicial system have caused employers to become aware of the employee privacy problem inherent in the maintenance of personnel records. The employee privacy problem has two distinct facets. On one side is the need of the employer for data on the employee for benefit packages, job placement, promotion, and compliance with government information requests. On the other hand, employees have an interest in preventing unwarranted intrusions into their private lives. The human resources practitioner must become familiar with court decisions and statutes regarding disclosure of employee information. The use of a subpoena to obtain employee records is excluded from this discussion. Subpoeanas are issued only in legal or quasi-legal proceedings, and human resource practitioners have little alternative but to comply with a lawfully issued subpoena.

Restrictions under HIPPA

The release of employee health records may be severely limited under the Health Insurance Portability and Accountability Act if the employer is deemed a covered entity under the Act. This can occur if the employer sponsors its own health plan, provides health care directly to employees, or sponsors a prescription drug card. The Act is intended to facilitate the exchange and protect the privacy and security of health information. Under HIPPA the employer can only release employee health information subject to a court order or under subpoena supported by a court order.[37]

Leave records and the education records of employees are excluded from coverage under the HIPPA restrictions. State law restrictions vary and may provide further limitations.

Right of Employee to Review Own Records

It is a well-established principle of common law that information obtained by the employer about an employee, relating to the employment relationship, is the property of the employer. This includes the request of the employees to see their own records.[38] Some states have passed laws requiring the employer to give the employees access to

their own records.[39] Those states that require disclosure in the private sector usually permit the employer to remove certain information before disclosing the file to the employee. These statutes should not be confused with the Freedom of Information Act (5 USC Sect. 552), which requires federal agencies to disclose information about agency activities to the general public.

Many employers, both large and small, have adopted policies allowing employees restricted access their own records, apart from any statute. They argue that denying an employee access to such records is not good employee relations. Those companies allowing employees to see information from their own files have a policy that the employer can remove certain information that it chooses not to disclose. Normally the policy does not define the information that may be removed. Determinations are made on a case-by-case basis. Information that could possibly be withheld from the employee might include consideration for promotion, the fact that an employee is suspected of violating a rule and therefore must be watched, and the scheduled elimination of the job, or that of the supervisor.

Exposure to Liability in Reference Requests

The employer has no obligation to grant requests for disclosure of personnel records to anyone, unless required by statute. At the same time, almost nothing can prevent voluntary disclosure by the employer. If the employer wants to cooperate with the local law enforcement agencies or with the Federal Bureau of Investigation (FBI), it may do so. If the employer chooses not to do so, the law enforcement agency can obtain this information only by subpoena.

If the employer decides to reveal information in the personnel file that is detrimental to the employee, the employee may seek damages under certain conditions. This kind of lawsuit usually occurs when information that invades privacy under the common law is revealed to the public. *Public* is generally interpreted by the courts to mean a small group of people. If information is revealed to only one person, regardless of the seriousness of the injury, the employee likely has no basis for a tort action.[40]

Under the common law of privacy, public disclosure of embarrassing private facts about a person is an invasion of that individual's interest in acquiring, retaining, and enjoying a good reputation. The violation of this interest is called *defamation*, which includes libel and slander.[41] Common law invasions of privacy occur where the employer discloses information, such as a medical condition or drug abuse, to someone who has no business need to know, as in *Bratt* v. *IBM,* 785 F.2d 352 (1st Cir. 1986).[42] Liability for this tort usually arises when an employer communicates information that is injurious to the reputation of an employee or former employee to a prospective employer or a credit agency. Since nothing prevents an individual from filing a lawsuit, one might say that every time an employer discloses adverse information about an employee to a prospective employer, this is an exposure to a lawsuit.

Protection by the Qualified Privilege Doctrine

Exposure for a lawsuit is greatly diminished by the common law doctrine of **qualified privilege**. This doctrine protects the employer when revealing information about former or present employees. The qualified privilege doctrine can protect from defamation liability, but often an innocent statement related to job performance can create a serious exposure. When an employer told an executive search agency that a former employee was a homosexual, no malice was involved. The employer had no liability, but nonetheless paid almost a million dollars in legal fees.[43]

Privilege is defined in the Restatement of Torts as:

> the modern term applied to those considerations which avoid liability where it might otherwise follow. . . . In its more common usage, it signified that the defendant has acted to further an interest of such social importance that it is entitled to protection, even at the expense of damage to the plaintiff. He is allowed freedom of action because his own interests or those of the public require it, and social policy will best be served by permitting it.

This definition of privilege has been applied to employee records. The courts have taken the position that the public good is best served by a free exchange of information between the prospective employer and former employer as to work habits and performance. When an employee falsified production records and the employer told other employees about it, the court said that the employer was justified in that it would discourage other employees from committing the same act.[44] However, this immunity from liability, when disclosing adverse injurious information, is not without limitations; an employer must take certain precautions if liability is to be avoided.[45]

Requirements of the Privilege Doctrine

As a general rule, the courts will allow an employer to give information about a former employee that may be defamatory, if such information is in the interest of the requesting employer and the public. The giving of information must protect that interest.[46] This is called a privilege that the courts will protect, but it is not without conditions.

1. The information must be given in good faith. In a case where a supervisor accused an employee of starting a

competitive company and repeated other office rumors which he failed to substantiate, the court awarded $19,000 in punitive damages.[47] Punitive damages are the damages that compensate above actual loss and are punishment for evil behavior.

2. The information given must be limited to the inquiry. Asking about work habits does not require revelation of facts about personal life, or information about union activities.[48]

3. The statement must be given under the proper occasion and in the proper manner. If given at a cocktail party or while playing bridge, an otherwise proper statement could be construed as invasion of privacy or libelous.

4. The information must be communicated to the proper parties and not the general public. In one case, an inquiry was made by an aunt, uncle, and spouse as to an employee's whereabouts. The reason given for the inquiry was that he was accused of misappropriating company funds. The court said that it was not privileged because relatives had no job-related interest in receiving the information.[49]

5. Information requested must be related to the requirements of the job.

6. Information revealed must be true, or a reasonable effort must be made to seek the truth.

7. Information must be revealed without malice and bad faith.[50]

Reference checks run afoul of antidiscrimination laws only where it can be shown that the reference check was for a discriminatory purpose or information received was used in a discriminatory manner. If conclusions drawn from reference reports are biased, the result will be considered discriminatory or malicious. A minority applicant may receive a poor reference report because of poor performance on the job for a former employer. This does not necessarily mean that the applicant is unqualified for a different position and different employer. The reasons for poor performance must be considered; poor performance cannot always be used as a reason for not hiring a member of the protected class. Often, the prospective employer will ask if the former employee is eligible for rehire; if the answer is negative, the person will not be hired. Relying solely on this answer may indicate a discriminatory motive in refusal to hire if the applicant is a member of a protected class.

When the Privilege Is Lost

The most common reason for losing protection of the privilege doctrine is that the information is given out of malice. The presence of malice is a factual question determined on a case-by-case basis. In most situations the person disclosing knows whether or not it is malicious, since intent is usually present. In one case an employee was discharged under a company policy of automatically terminating everyone working a shift during which a cash shortage occurred. The plaintiff could not obtain employment elsewhere as the result of the termination. The court held that a qualified privilege existed; therefore, the employer was not liable unless the plaintiff could prove that there was malice. In finding that there was insufficient evidence of malice, the court said "actual malice requires proof that the statement was made with malice in fact, ill-will or wrongful notice." There was no evidence from which a jury could infer any motive founded on ill-will toward the plaintiff or a desire to harm her; it was merely an enforcement of a policy.[51]

Refusal to Disclose Reference Information

More than half of all employers have adopted a policy that information disclosed about former employees should be limited to verification of employment and the length of employment.[52] This policy may be considered the safest to avoid lawsuits. However, from the prospective new employer's point of view, it could result in the hiring of many undesirable applicants. Such a policy may also create ill will among former employees who are refused favorable references. An employer can reduce the risk of litigation to near zero, still maintain good recruiting practices, and maintain good employee relations by taking advantage of the qualified privilege doctrine.

The Legal Paradox

It is a legal paradox that the courts are granting immunity from prosecution by ruling that it is in the public interest to exchange information about employees in order to discourage the hiring of undesirable applicants; at the same time, many employers are unwilling to disclose because of the danger of being sued. Releasing information makes good sense, and will help convince the jury that the employer is dealing fairly with its employees. Large jury awards have caused employers not to give reference information except for dates of employment and job titles. This policy is intended to avoid exposure to litigation, but disregards the qualified privilege doctrine.[53]

Reliability of References

Some personnel administrators feel that the abolition of reference checks concerning performance would have no effect on hiring qualified persons, because reference checks are not a valid method of determining an applicant's acceptability as to performance. Reference requests regarding character are somewhat unreliable as to performance unless a personal, confidential relationship exists between the person requesting the information and the person disclosing the information. If a personal relationship exists, exposure is not usually present.[54]

The only absolute protection against being sued is to not provide any reference information. However, an employer who is interested in selecting qualified and stable applicants must obtain background information from some source. If no reference information is provided by prior employers concerning an applicant's qualifications or trait characteristics, then undesirable individuals or criminals may be hired. A subjective selection process is almost certain to run afoul of the antidiscrimination laws.

Invasion of Privacy

An intrusion on a person's right to seclusion is a tort. To prevail in this type of claim the plaintiff employee must show that the defendant intentionally intruded, physically or otherwise, on the plaintiff's private affairs or concerns. The plaintiff must also show that a reasonable person would find this intrusion offensive. In *Luedtke* v. *Nabors Alaska Drilling, Inc.*, 834 P.2d 1220 (Alaska 1989), the employer implemented a drug testing program. The plaintiffs refused to submit to urinalysis pursuant to the program and were terminated. They sued, claiming that the test was an intrusion on their privacy and accordingly their discharge was contrary to public policy. The court found that there is a sphere of activity in every person's life that is closed to scrutiny by others. The boundaries of that sphere are determined by balancing employees' and employers' competing interests. For example, an employer tested employees for drugs on an oil rig for health and safety reasons. This employer interest in maintaining a safe workplace superseded the employees' right of privacy.

The Civil Rights Act of 1991 places certain limits on the total amount of compensatory and punitive damages that an individual may recover. Some legal scholars argue that this applies to infliction of emotional distress. Others disagree maintaining that Section 102 of the act applies to intentional discrimination only. If there is a severe wrong the court likely will find a way to hold a defendant guilty. However, case law involving unlawful intrusion on privacy is relatively scarce. It is therefore difficult to determine whether the common law right to privacy constitutes a clearly mandated public policy.

Electronic Communications

The almost universal use of electronic communications has created both opportunities and challenges for employers. Email has largely replaced typewritten and handwritten memoranda, saving both time and paper. Employees can manipulate and analyze data through the use of computer programs, post information on websites, and access the Internet from their workstations, permitting time-saving research. However, the ready access to computers has created new problems for the employer, as few employees can resist the temptation to utilize the company's computer for personal business.

Personal email can be tolerated on a limited basis but is subject to abuse and is prohibited by many employers. More serious is the unauthorized use of the computer to search inappropriate websites or exchange emails containing attachments with offensive or illegal content. Employees have been discovered accessing and transmitting obscene and vulgar messages, downloading pornographic content, and even conducting an illegal betting pool using the employer's time and equipment. This unauthorized use can result in disciplinary action, lead to criminal prosecution, or expose the employer to a harassment charge.

One of the problems with instant electronic communication is that it often leads to ill-considered responses and comments. Intemperate emails may create internal problems and can result in the unauthorized communication of sensitive or confidential information. This is particularly true where employees post information on personal Facebook or MySpace pages or discuss and comment on internal matters on Twitter. For example, several professional athletes have been disciplined for "tweeting" about their teammates, coaches, and activities. Employers who fail to control these actions through policy risk exposure.

Sexual Harassment

Sexual advances are considered an invasion of privacy under certain conditions. Sexual harassment of all types has considerable potential exposure to lawsuits. In the *Eisenstadt* case noted earlier, the U.S. Supreme Court held that questions about an employee's marriage and sex life invade fundamental rights entitled to privacy protection. Questions about sex with an employee's husband, accompanied by sexual advances, also suggest an invasion of privacy for which damages would be determined by a jury, as was true in the case of *Phillips* v. *Smalley Maintenance Services,* 711 F.2d 1524 (11th Cir. 1983). The courts in these cases held that inquiring about a person's sex life, an act that the court viewed as creating a hostile work environment, is an invasion of privacy, whereas touching or other sexual advances (quid pro quo sexual harassment) may not be an invasion of privacy but would be a violation of Title VII.

Sexual harassment can be considered a tort. The tort occurs when the employee alleges that failure to submit to sexual advances results in emotional distress or is an invasion of privacy. The court explained the difference between statutory violation and the common law in *Lucas* v. *Brown & Root,* 736 F.2d 1202 (8th Cir. 1984). This case involved an employee who refused to submit to sexual advances and alleged that she was discharged for that reason. In dismissing a Title VII claim because it was not filed within the time limits, the court allowed the employee to recover punitive damages on the basis that the discharge was a violation of public policy. The court stated that "a woman invited to trade herself for a job is in effect being asked to become a prostitute." The court allowed damages for intentional infliction of emotional distress because "in light of the nature of the employment relationship and the power of the employer" punitive damages would be justified. The courts that allow recovery beyond Title VII for mental anguish and physical symptoms of distress state that back pay and reinstatement would not adequately compensate the employee. Under Title VII, the suit limitations of CRA91 as to punitive damages may apply. Mental anguish was allowed in *Holien* v. *Sears, Roebuck and Co.,* 677 P.2d 704 (Ore. 1984).[55] This decision effectively allowed a tort recovery in a wrongful discharge action.

In some situations the evidence will not sustain a violation of Title VII, but the employer still can be liable for sexual assault. Under CRA91 intent would have to be shown to prove a Title VII violation. A District of Columbia court in *Clark* v. *World Airways,* 24 F.E.P. Cases (BNA) 305 (D.C. of D.C. 1980), held that the evidence would not allow a Title VII action because the company president never made submission to sexual favors a condition of employment. However, there was sufficient evidence for a jury to find that the president had sexual relations with the plaintiff and while doing so he was serving his employer. The court found that the act was in the course of employment because the employer provided the opportunity for the offensive conduct and it was an outgrowth of the employment situation.

Not all courts will hold that sexual harassment is a tort. When a fashion director with high-performance ratings was discharged, allegedly for refusal of sexual favors, the court in *Wolk* v. *Saks Fifth Avenue, Inc.,* 728 F.2d 221 (3rd Cir. 1984), held that the remedy was under Title VII and

did not permit an action for tortuous conduct. Similarly, a Florida court found that mere sexual harassment conduct was not outrageous enough to allow an action for punitive damages.[56]

It is doubtful whether the result would be the same under CRA91 limits. A lawsuit can be filed under Title VII if intentional sexual harassment can be shown. In that case a jury trial and punitive damages (a monetary punishment for a wrong) would be permitted under Section 201 of CRA91. Punitive damages would be determined by a jury and are always greater than back pay. The common law action for a tort as a result of the sexual advances could also be asserted, and if the employee prevailed the remedy would be the same as under CRA91. If the sexual harassment involves the creation of a hostile work environmental as opposed to quid pro quo harassment, CRA91 applies.

The problem of sexual harassment in the workplace is not likely to be completely eliminated in the near future. Management's exposure to litigation very often will extend beyond Title VII. Not all courts agree that sexual harassment can result in a tort, but there is presently enough case law to make the exposure troublesome for the employer. Avoiding this exposure can only be addressed by adopting and enforcing a strict sexual nonharassment policy.

Individual Liability When Acting on Behalf of the Employer

A concern for all employer representatives is whether or not they can be held personally liable when acting on behalf of their employer. Because we are living in an era of legal scrutiny of all management activity, supervisors, managers, and human resources professionals are often afraid to act on behalf of the employer for fear of **personal liability**. In an unpublished survey of management personnel by the authors, respondents were asked whether they believed they could be held personally liable when acting on behalf of their employer. Almost 80 percent (incorrectly) thought that they could. Few knew the circumstances that might lead to personal liability.

Managers run the risk of personal liability in several different areas of activity, such as price fixing under antitrust laws, misuse of funds or company property, and conflicts of interest. Most directors of any organization, whether profit or nonprofit, have potential personal liability when acting on behalf of the organization. Officers of corporations are often asked to participate in community activities, which they often do on company time and company expense accounts. They could be held liable for their participation in these activities under certain circumstances. For example, many officers are exposed to information that makes them "insiders" for security transactions. Administrative management personnel, when participating in other areas of management activity, might be well advised to get legal counsel to protect their personal liability.

Corporate Veil Protection

The general rule is that a manager is not liable for mere mistakes—errors of judgment—when acting on behalf of the employer. The courts take the position that a **corporate veil** of immunity protects the manager from personal liability except for deceit or fraud. If deceit or fraud is present, the manager is usually liable.[57] There have been rare instances where egregious acts have caused the corporate veil to be penetrated. In these situations the courts found the manager individually liable to the employee when acting on behalf of the employer.[58] For example, when an employer co-mingled personal assets with corporate funds, failed to pay wages and benefits, and then dissolved the corporation, the NLRB held the owner personally liable.[59]

Liability of Company Officers

Unless an officer participates in deceit or fraud, the courts will not find individual liability. However, where corporate officers knowingly permitted the company to violate the Wage Payment and Collection Act to deny employees their wages, the officers were held individually liable for the unpaid wages when the company filed for bankruptcy. The court found in *Mullins* v. *Venable*, 297 S.E.2d 866 (W.Va. 1982), that the officers had a duty to see that the corporation obeyed the law.

As a general rule, the courts will inflict a greater degree of responsibility on officers than on other members of management. In a situation similar to the *Mullins* case, the corporate officers had a substantial interest in the corporation and were directly involved in decisions affecting the employees' compensation. They were held personally liable under the Fair Labor Standards Act for failure to pay minimum wages and overtime during the last week of existence of the corporation.[60] In considering the liability of an officer, the court will look to see if the officer was acting in good faith, within authority, and using the proper degree of prudence and diligence. In one case a manager attempted to hide assets to avoid back pay for wages due; the court said the corporation was the alter ego of the manager and held him personally liable.[61] Where corporate officers acting in behalf of the corporation caused damages by willful participation in fraud and deceit, they were held personally liable.[62]

A stockholder-employee asked to inspect the corporate books and was discharged instead. The court found the officer-director was personally liable for inducing the corporation to discharge the employee. The discharge was not for the benefit of the corporation.[63] The corporation was not held liable because it had a right to discharge under the employment-at-will doctrine. Normally, officers are not held personally liable for discharge. Most courts hold that it is within their supervisory duties to act on behalf of the corporation. In the case cited, discharging the employee was not the cause of liability, but refusing him access to the stockholders' list created a personal liability.[64]

CHANGING COMPOSITION OF THE WORKFORCE

There can be little doubt that the composition of the American workforce has become substantially more diverse over the past 30 years. This change is projected to accelerate. Changes in demographics, technology, and social trends will confront human resource practitioners with an environment very different from the one in which they began their own careers.[65] New entrants to the labor market will present diverse racial and ethnic backgrounds, technological skills, and values compared to those of current workers. The workforce participation rates of different segments of the population have also changed with the participation rates of white males declining and the rates for minority and women workers increasing.[66] Managers will need to recognize the changing nature of employee–employer relationships and create new job structures that facilitate flexible work patterns, innovative compensation structures, and a different type of career planning.[67]

The legal implications of the changes in the gender, race, religion, ethnicity, and national origin composition of the workforce are significant for human resources managers and practitioners. Particularly critical is the need for employers to deal with both the legal and cultural implications of the growing number of immigrant workers and their documentation status. Employers are also being forced to deal with employees whose sexual orientation compels them to seek accommodation in the workplace and request modifications in benefit plans to cover their domestic partners. Perhaps the greatest change is the emergence of distinct generational groups with different expectations about work and the workplace. This change has become increasingly important in human resources because of the graying and impending retirement of the Baby Boom generation—those workers born between 1946 and 1964 who comprise approximately 35 percent of the U.S. population and 25 percent of the workforce. Baby Boomers, particularly the older ones, share many expectations about work with their pre–World War II generational counterparts. They expected that the employer would establish the terms and conditions of employment, including hours, worksites, leave policies, and benefits and dutifully accepted what was offered. They also generally accepted the doctrine of employment-at-will but tended to believe that they were exempt from its most draconian application so long as they performed their work competently. And they expected long tenure with the same employer along with a concomitant loyalty to their employer. These expectations are not shared by so-called Generation X workers—those born between 1960 and 1980 who comprise 45 percent of the current workforce, or by their younger Millenial Generation or Generation Y co-workers born since 1980 who are expected to comprise 25 percent of the workforce by 2011.[68] Generation Xers and Millenials expect that their employers will accommodate their desire for **flexible work schedules**; alternative worksites, including work from home; unmarried partner benefits; and time away from work to care for children and aging parents. They also expect fair and equitable treatment, no doubt in part as a result of the antidiscrimination laws, but they do not expect long tenure or significant employer loyalty. They are more straightforward and self-reliant as opposed to team oriented, and are more concerned with work–life balance than their older, work ethic oriented counterparts. They also tend to perceive themselves as superior employees and expect positive feedback and financial rewards for meritorious performance.[69]

These changed employee expectations have led employers to adopt substantial modifications in working conditions and benefits and may well result in new legislation requiring employer response. In the past 10 years employers have increasingly offered flexible working arrangements and new types of benefits. Based on the Families and Work Institute's *2008 Study of Employers*, 79 percent of employers allow employees to adjust their arrival and departure times from work (up from 68 percent in 1998); 47 percent of employers allow employees to move from part-time work to full-time work and back again (down slightly from 57 percent in 1998); 52 percent of employers allow workers to work some hours from home (down slightly from 56 percent in 1998); and many employers have expanded employee assistance programs and initiated wellness programs.[70] Employers who have adopted these changes have witnessed improved employee morale, reduced absenteeism, and heightened commitment to organizational goals.[71]

Proposed health-care reform could result in employer mandates to provide health insurance for employees or, alternatively, could permit employers to eliminate increasingly expensive coverage.

Human Resources Practices to Consider

There should be little doubt that human resources practitioners will need to adapt practices and policies in response to the expectations of the new generations of employees, not only to maximize the performance of existing employees but also in the interest of employee recruitment and retention. Some considerations include:

1. To what extent are all generations of employees involved in hiring decisions?
2. Are members of all generations considered for promotion throughout the organization?
3. Do performance appraisals consider generational differences?
4. Does the company have a succession plan?
5. Does the company have an electronic communications policy?
6. Does the company offer career planning and retirement planning support?

GLOBALIZATION AND IMMIGRATION

As noted earlier, the racial and ethnic composition of the U.S. workforce has changed dramatically in recent years. These changes have been accentuated by immigration policies that have inconsistently restricted entry and indirectly encouraged unlawful immigration. As a result, the U.S. domestic workforce includes large numbers of undocumented workers. Immigration policy and its impact on employers as well as employees will likely be confronted by Congress sooner than later, but the outcome is uncertain.

National Origin Discrimination

Unlawful discrimination occurs when an employment decision is based on the national origin of the person adversely affected by that decision.[72] Although national origin discrimination under Title VII has not been common and case law is scarce compared to that for other protected classes such as race, religion, and gender, it can be troublesome.[73] National origin bias is unlawful in hiring and promotion. Lawsuits are subject to the same limitations applicable to race, religion, and gender. However, there is an additional requirement if the employee cannot speak English. To require the employee to do so is a violation of Title VII if knowledge of English is not required for successful performance of the job. However, a foreign accent is a legitimate reason for rejecting if the job requires the applicant to deal with the public.[74] Labor unions may be required to publish collective bargaining agreements in a foreign language in order to ensure adequate representation of their members when a large proportion of that membership speaks only a foreign language.

Discrimination because of national origin is unlawful if physical requirements such as height tend to exclude certain nationalities, unless business necessity can be shown.[75] National origin discrimination under Title VII is independent of citizenship status; an employer may refuse to hire noncitizens provided the refusal is applied to noncitizens of all national origins.[76]

Immigration Reform and Control Act of 1986

The Immigration Reform and Control Act of 1986 (**IRCA**; 8 USC 1324(a)) substantially limited the employer's ability to hire undocumented aliens. Prior to the act, it was not considered illegal to knowingly hire an undocumented alien. However, Congress apparently concluded that one way to stop illegal entry into the United States was to prevent the employer from hiring undocumented workers.[77] Accordingly, a substantial burden was placed on employers to determine whether or not a job applicant was legally entitled to work in the United States.[78]

The Immigration Reform and Control Act imposes sanctions not only on the employer but also on the individual within the company who knowingly hires an undocumented worker without complying with the statute. It is also unlawful to knowingly continue to employ an undocumented worker.[79] The Immigration and Naturalization Service (INS), which is responsible for enforcement, has issued regulations implementing the act at 8 CFR Sect. 274a (2). It is important that the employer maintain a copy of these regulations because they provide a reasonable guide for compliance.[80] The IRCA is not violated by a simple mistake in hiring. The employer must have failed to ascertain, or failed to make a reasonable effort to do so, that an employee was not authorized to work in the United States.[81]

Verification of Employability

The employer must obtain sufficient documentation from the prospective employee, before hiring, that the applicant is authorized to work in the United States. The documentation must reasonably appear to be genuine. A passport, certificate of citizenship, naturalization or resident card (green card), valid work authorization card, or birth certificate would establish employment authorization. A driver's license or a state-issued ID card would only establish identity, and further documentation of authorization to work, such as an unexpired work permit or a Social Security card, would be required. A list of acceptable documents appears in Exhibit 12.2.

Both the applicant and the employer are required to fill out an I-9 form. The employer is required to inspect the applicant's part and make certain that the questions answered on the I-9 form appear to be accurate. Verification is required for all applicants, not just those believed to be aliens.[82] Hiring without verification may constitute harboring an alien and be in violation of the law. The failure of the employer to comply with verification requirements will create an exposure to a fine under the terms of the statute. Indeed, the courts have held that the employer is required to discharge immigrant workers immediately if it is clear and indisputable that they are not authorized to work.[83]

Employee Eligibility Verification

The most recent attempt to enhance immigration and border security enforcement is a Department of Homeland Security (DHS) program known as **e-Verify**. It is a voluntary, Internet-based program that allows employers to electronically verify information a worker

LIST A	LIST B	LIST C
Documents that Establish Both Identity and Employment Eligibility	Documents that Establish	Identity Documents that Establish Employment Eligibility
OR		**AND**
1. U.S. Passport (unexpired or expired)	1. Driver's license or ID card issued by a state or outlying possession of the United States provided it contains a photograph or information such as name, date of birth, gender, height, eye color, and address	1. U.S. Social Security card issued by the Social Security Administration (*other than a card stating it is not valid for employment*)
2. Permanent Resident Card of Alien Registration Receipt Card (Form I-551)	2. ID card issued by federal, state, or local government agencies or entities, provided it contains a photograph or information such as name, date of birth, gender, eight, eye color, and address	2. Certification of Birth Abroad issued by the Department of State (**Form FS-545 or Form DS-1350**)
3. An unexpired foreign passport with a temporary I-551 stamp	3. School ID card with a photograph	3. Original or certified copy of a birth certificate issued by a state, county, municipal authority, or outlying possession of the United States bearing an official seal
4. An unexpired Employment Authorization Document that contains a photograph (Form I-766, I-688, I-688A, I-688B)	4. Voter's registration card	4. Native American tribal document
	5. U.S. Military card or draft record	5. U.S. Citizen ID Card (**Form I-197**)
5. An unexpired foreign passport with an unexpired Arrival–Departure Record, Form I-94, bearing the same name as the passport and containing an endorsement of the alien's nonimmigrant status, if that status authorizes the alien to work for the employer	6. Military dependent's ID card	6. ID Card for use of Resident Citizen in the United States (**Form I-179**)
	7. U.S. Cost Guard Merchant Marine Card	
	8. Native American tribal document	7. Unexpired employment authorization document issued by DHS (**other than those listed under List A**)
	9. Driver's license issued by a Canadian government authority	
	For person under age 18 who are unable to present a document listed above:	
	10. School record or report card	
	11. Clinic, doctor, or hospital record	
	12. Day-care of nursery school record	

Illustrations of many of these documents appear in Part 8 of the Handbook for Employers (M-274)
Form I-9 (Rev. 06/05/07) N Page 2

EXHIBIT 12.2   Lists of Acceptable Documents

presents by accessing information maintained in databases by the Social Security Administration and the Department of Homeland Security. Although the program is voluntary, a rule proposed by the federal government would make use of e-Verify mandatory for federal contractors. The rule would affect over 165,000 contractors and approximately 4 million workers.[84] This rule was included in Executive Order 13465 (Bush) in June of 2008.

Implementation of the rule was suspended in late 2008 due, in part, to a lawsuit for injunctive relief filed by business groups. However, the Obama Administration began enforcement of the rule on September 8, 2009. The rule requires all federal solicitations and contracts over $100,000, lasting for a period of 120 days or more, to do the following:

1. Enroll in e-Verify.
2. Use e-Verify for all new hires in the United States.
3. Use e-Verify for all workers assigned to the contract.
4. Include a provision in certain subcontracts for commercial or noncommercial services and construction that are over $3,000, and last for a period of more than 30 days , requiring use of e-Verify.[85]

Contractors may also reverify all existing workers hired after November 6, 1986, the enactment date of IRCA, whether or not they are assigned to the federal contract. Such action is likely to draw a legal challenge since e-Verify was designed to cover only new hires.[86] The Department of Homeland Security indicated that it will not enforce the Bush Administration plan to force employers to fire workers who can't resolve a mismatch between their Social Security number and the employer's payroll data.

Supply items, including food, purchased through federal contract is generally exempt from e-Verify requirements. Higher education institutions, state and local governments, and companies engaged in

surety performing pursuant to a performance bond are also exempt but may choose to verify new hires assigned to a federal contract.

No-Match Notification

The Social Security Administration can trigger enforcement of IRCA through a *no-match letter,* a notice that informs both employers and employees that the names and Social Security numbers listed on the employer's W-2 report do not match Social Security Administration (SSA) records. Workers normally receive the no-match letters but the employer is also notified when the employee's home address is incorrect or if at least 10 percent of the total number of names reported were no-matches. Unfortunately, no-match letters can result from errors in the Social Security database and not necessarily from worker error or falsification. Employers who wrongly terminate authorized workers upon receipt of a no-match letter can be subject to liability state or federal employment laws. Employers should therefore afford employees who receive no-match letters a reasonable opportunity to resolve the no-match question before terminating the employee.

Penalties

Penalties are in the form of a fine ranging from $250 to $2,000 per undocumented worker hired. If there is a second violation, the fines are increased from $250 to $3,000. A pattern and practice of hiring undocumented workers or a complete disregard for the act could result in a criminal violation, which permits up to $10,000 in fines *and* six months in prison. The employer is required to retain employment records for three years or one year after termination, whichever is sooner. Failure to do so carries a fine of $1,000.[87] The wording of the statute indicates that the enforcement provisions leave little room for discretion.[88]

The employer may also be liable for back wages or overtime violations because all workers, regardless of their immigration status, are protected by the provisions of the Fair Labor Standards Act and state wage and hour laws. In one case, an employer failed to pay prevailing wages to undocumented construction workers who performed work on a public contract project. The court held that immigration status is irrelevant to claims for unpaid prevailing wages.[89] Undocumented workers are also protected under all discrimination statutes (Title VII, ADEA, Equal Pay Act, ADA) but the Supreme Court has ruled that they are not entitled to back-pay remedies under these statutes.[90] Such workers may also be protected under state wrongful discharge statutes and are entitled to unpaid leave to resolve employment authorization problems.[91]

Employers may attempt to raise the immigration status of workers either during discovery or in litigation of employment discrimination claims. However, employers should be aware that the Court of Appeals for the Ninth Circuit has prohibited such inquiries and barred retaliation against the claimants.[92]

Discrimination Provisions of IRCA

The Immigration Reform and Control Act (Sect. 102) provides a remedy for discrimination based on nationality in the same manner as Title VII, but it is broader, since it covers employers with three or more employees. (Title VII applies only to employers with 15 or more employees.) When requiring identity, the employer must be cautious not to appear to use nationality as a factor in the hiring decision. Specifically, the employer may not favor one nationality over another but may give preference to U.S. citizens.[93] If the INS adopted the EEOC position, verification requirements would force the employer to justify the reason for asking certain questions. Requesting place of birth was a "red flag" under EEOC rules, but it may be necessary for verification under the statute. The courts

have held that undocumented workers are protected by other statutes.[94]

To avoid a violation, the employer should verify all applicants and any present employee whose authorization is questionable. The employer must have complete documentation or be able to demonstrate a good faith effort to determine the employee's status. The penalties for violation are severe fines, rather than reinstatement with back pay, as under Title VII. The fear that foreign-looking applicants and those with accents may not be authorized must be confirmed by the employer. To avoid national origin lawsuits under IRCA, the employer should do the following:

1. Review the recruiting and selection procedures. The emphasis in the past has been on other forms of discrimination, and nationality has often been overlooked.
2. Audit supervisors' practices to be assured that they are not treating one ethnic group differently from another. Many individuals have subjective prejudices against an ethnic group that are often based on past experience.
3. Tolerate an accent unless it interferes with the job. Sometimes an accent will cause prejudices that result in discrimination charges.
4. Have a broad harassment policy that includes all members in the protected class, not just related to sex.
5. Require employees to speak English only when necessary.
6. Be sure height and weight requirements are necessary for the job.
7. Treat lawful aliens who are in process of becoming U.S. citizens the same as U.S. citizens.
8. Permit nationality discrimination allegations in your complaint procedure. If it is properly established, an employee will use the procedure rather than a regulatory agency if he or she believes it is fair.

The Immigration and Reform Control Act is not to be confused with the Immigration Act of 1991, which deals with U.S. immigration policy regarding skilled workers.

Immigration and Customs Enforcement

Following the 9/11 terrorist attack, the federal government stepped up immigration enforcement through multiagency workplace inspections targeting noncitizens in the workplace. Since 2006 this work has been carried on primarily through Immigration and Customs Enforcement (ICE) in an initiative known as Secure Border Enforcement (SBI). The SBI was a multiyear initiative of the Bush Administration both to secure America's borders and reduce unlawful immigration. In an effort to enforce the employer sanctions provisions of IRCA, ICE can conduct random or targeted investigations of employers, including review and inspection of I-9 documents. Employers' hiring practices have also been investigated by Immigration and Customs enforcement. Before initiating such an investigation ICE requires a lead and articulable facts that would provide reasonable suspicion that IRCA is being violated. "Articulable facts" might include a high concentration of undocumented workers in a geographic area, the industry or type of employment involved, and the inability of workers to speak English. However, investigations cannot be based on subjective impressions or the individual bias of an enforcement officer.[95]

Employers are to be provided with at least three days' notice prior to an inspection, but ICE does not need a warrant to conduct an I-9 audit or an inspection. Refusal or delay in presenting the I-9 Form may be deemed a violation of the law.

Immigration Reform

Immigration reform continues to be an intractable issue before Congress. There can be little doubt that the Immigration Reform and Control Act of 1986 failed to achieve its objectives, but finding a consensus on new legislation has been elusive. Unions have consistently opposed increasing visas for foreign-born workers and support limitations on new immigration together with strict enforcement against future illegal immigration. Alternatively, employers have supported visas for highly skilled foreign workers and permits for agricultural workers. Furthermore, a large segment of the general public opposes amnesty for workers who entered the country illegally. Congress had hoped to have a new immigration reform act in place by the fall of 2009.[96] Its failure to do so is as much an indication of the complexity of the problem as it is of lack of political consensus. Given the recent history of immigration reform legislation and the disparate positions of business, labor, immigrant groups, and the remainder of the electorate, it appears likely that only compromise legislation will survive—legislation that is unlikely to resolve the contentious issues of immigration policy and employment rights for immigrant workers.

FUTURE OF HUMAN RESOURCES MANAGEMENT

There are a number of current issues in human resources management that twenty-first century practitioners will be required to address. Foremost is the role of human resources in leadership and decision making. In many organizations human resources is viewed as a staff function and is afforded only a limited role in strategic planning and the allocation of personnel. Too often the HR department becomes involved with an employee complaint only after it has matured into a problem or a lawsuit has already been filed. As has been repeatedly suggested in this book, avoidance of exposure is critical to preventing litigation and its significant costs. Human resource managers familiar with the legal environment concerning prohibited discrimination, compensation requirements, employee privacy rights and labor relations can be invaluable in guiding a company through potential legal pitfalls. However, they can only do so if they are involved in both the development and implementation of policies and are consulted before an exposure is created.

Leadership from the human resources area of a company will be essential as employers are faced with new civil rights legislation and changing court interpretation of existing legislation. Such leadership will also be required in creating innovative compensation practices to comply with the various statutory requirements discussed in earlier chapters. Perhaps no issue will be as contentious as the changes to the National Labor Relations Act proposed by the Employee Free Choice Act (EFCA). Although there is wide agreement that our basic labor law needs reform, there is little agreement as to what that reform should look like. Proponents of EFCA would make it easier for workers to organize and gain a first collective bargaining agreement, but others would prefer deregulation of employment through repeal of the NLRA and a return to a free market model based on employment-at-will. Implicit in this debate is the question of whether or not U.S. unions are still necessary or relevant in the new global economy.

Some would argue that the demand for unionization has declined as unions have failed to respond to the needs of a changing workforce and employers have become more responsive to worker concerns. Certainly the increase in worker-protective legislation described in this book has made unions less relevant in some respects by establishing minimum wages and working conditions for most workers. Alternatively, others would argue that a continuing demand for unionization has been masked by strenuous, often hostile, and sometimes unlawful, employer opposition to union organizing efforts. Although the demand for union representation may not have declined, union density in the private sector clearly has. The result has been what some have called a "**representation gap**" where no one, other than the employer, articulates the needs and desires of the vast majority of workers.[97] Indeed, based on recent surveys it would appear that approximately one-third of currently nonunionized workers would favor having a union in their workplace and that labor unions, long in disfavor in terms of public approval, are now viewed favorably by a majority of respondents.[98] Human resources managers will be required to respond to worker demands for representation, whether it be through traditional labor–management relations and collective bargaining or through some alternative form of employee involvement and participation in decision making.

CASE 12.1

The Angry Employer

Jake Schultz was the owner and president of Schultz Distributing, a regional beer distributor in the Midwest. His major competitor, Budd Brands, was another large distributor that handled competitive brands of beer. Budd Brands and Schultz Distributing were located within a mile of each other in a city of 30,000. Jake was the son of the distributor's founder and anticipated passing the presidency on to his son Bill, who worked as the office manager of the company. Jake

was a paternal but authoritarian employer with a quick temper and often had angry outbursts when his directions were not followed. Kathryn Freese was the company's second in command and held the position of sales and distribution manager. The company handbook included a disclaimer that Kathryn was an employee at will.

Kathryn Freese recognized that, with Bill Schultz waiting in the wings, she had virtually no opportunity for promotion or an ownership share in the company. Further, she had little use for Bill, who she considered to be lazy and incompetent. She was therefore interested when Bradford Budd, the president of the rival distributorship, approached her about going to work for Budd. One Friday Kathryn took the afternoon off, ostensibly to go golfing, and met with Budd. She was observed by one of the Schultz drivers having lunch with Budd. The driver immediately reported this event to Jake and Bill.

Jake was outraged at what he considered to be Kathryn's disloyalty and immediately conducted a search of Kathryn's office, including her computer and files. When he was unable to find a current sales summary in Kathryn's office, he concluded that Kathryn had taken it with him to share with

Budd. At the close of business on Friday Jake called a meeting of all employees and told them that Kathryn had been discharged for theft and dishonesty. He then had the locks changed on the office and had all of Kathryn's files and personal items placed in locked storage room. Jake then prepared a summary discharge letter accusing Kathryn of lying, disloyalty, and theft and then sent it to Kathryn's home by certified mail. He also sent a blind copy of the letter to Bradford Budd.

Does Schultz Distributing have an exposure to an invasion of privacy or a defamation claim?

Is Jake protected by a corporate veil or the qualified privilege doctrine? Could his conduct be deemed malicious? ▪

CASE 12.2

Discrimination or Immigration Law Exposure?

Jose Ruiz, a Nicaraguan national, came to the United States in 1980. He obtained a social security card and became a lawful permanent resident of the United States in 1990. He was hired by Upstate Shipping as a warehouseman in 1995 after presenting a green card and a social security card. In 2005, the company learned that U.S. Immigration and Customs Enforcement (ICE) planned to inspect their I-9 records. Accordingly, the company initiated an investigation to verify the validity of its employees' social security numbers. In doing so it discovered that Ruiz's social security number and the social security numbers of several other employees apparently did not match.

Upstate Shipping decided to require all the employees with questionable social security numbers to provide additional documentation of employment eligibility. When Ruiz presented his naturalization certificate, the employer suspended him and

told him he could not return to work until he received a different social security number. Ruiz argued that the original social security number was his but the employer rejected his argument and revealed that it had discovered that someone else had used that number for both employment and credit purposes. Accordingly, Ruiz was effectively discharged.

Does the employer have potential liability under Title VII? Why or why not?

How would the employer respond to a charge that its decision to suspend Ruiz and subsequently terminate him was a pretext for racial or national origin discrimination?

Does the employer have potential liability under IRCA? Why or why not?

Did the employer commit an unlawful immigration-related employment practice? ▪

Summary

This chapter addresses many of the issues facing the human resource field today. Human resources management in the twenty-first century has, and will continue to witness, changes in antidiscrimination laws, complaints of workplace harassment, and courts willing to hold individual managers personally liable for their treatment of employees. There will be increasing pressure

to amend the NLRA to make it easier for employees to organize and negotiate collective bargaining agreements. Human resources managers will also be required to respond to a changing workforce due to immigration and globalization. Other issues such as privacy, freedom of information, search and seizure in the workplace, and HIPPA are discussed.

Key Terms

Malpractice   289
Electronic Communications
   Privacy Act   293
Employee Polygraph
   Protection Act   294

Qualified privilege   300
Personal liability   304
Corporate veil   305
Immigration Reform and
   Control Act   308

e-Verify   308
Representation gap   313

Questions for Discussion

1. What is the difference between management malpractice and wrongful conduct? Give an example of each.
2. What exposure to legal action does an employer risk if it chooses to monitor the email received by an employee on his or her company computer?
3. The *Potter* v. *Murray* decision limits the privacy of employees when it affects job performance. Do you agree with the court's decision and ruling? Why or why not? Are there exceptions to this?
4. You are a HR manager, and your boss, Lauren, comes to you suspecting her assistant is stealing money from the company. Lauren would like a polygraph test conducted to see if her assistant is actually stealing from the company. What do you need to consider before conducting the polygraph? Are there considerations that are not part of your legal obligation?
5. William, the owner of Bert's Delivery, receives a phone call about a former employee, Kevin. Kevin recently left his position at Bert's Delivery and is applying for a new job at Gary's Drivers. William is asked to provide information about Kevin and his work performance. What should William consider before providing information and feedback to Gary's Drivers? Is William obligated to say, or not say, anything?
6. What are the differences between the right of the employer to search employees' lockers or desks in the private, as opposed to the public, sector?
7. What is the "Qualified Privilege Doctrine"? How may this privilege be lost?
8. What are the advantages and disadvantages of the e-Verify system? As a manager, how would you decide if this was a good tool for your business?
9. As an HR manager, list three ways you can best support your business and employees, given the recent and anticipated changes to the workforce.
10. Under what circumstances can employees be held personally liable when acting on behalf of the employer?

Notes To Chapter 12

1. *Tandy Corp.* v. *Bone*, 678 S.W. 2d 311 (Ark., 1984).
2. *Wing* v. *JMB Management Corp.*, 714 P.2d 916 (Colo. App. 1985).
3. *Wilson* v. *Monarch Paper Co.*, 939 F.2d 1138 (5th Cir. 1991).
4. *Eklund* v. *Vincent Brass and Aluminum Co.*, 351 N.W.2d 371 (Minn. App. 1984).
5. *Patton* v. *J.C. Penney Co.*, 719 P.2d 854 (Or. 1986).
6. *Rooney* v. *Super Markets, Inc.*, 668 S.W.2d 649 (Mo. App. 1984).
7. Keeton, W., D. Dobbs, R. Keeton and D. Owen Eds. *Prosser and Keeton on Torts*. 5th ed. (1984).
8. See D. Warren and L. Brandeis, "The right to privacy," *Harvard Law Review*, 4 (1990): 193.
9. *Roe* v. *Wade*, 410 U.S. 113 (1973).

10. See "Snoops put a strain on employee loyalty" (editorial), *Business Week* (January 15, 1990): 91; also J. Rothfeder and M. Galen, "Is your boss spying on you," *Business Week* (January 15, 1990): 74–75.

11. R. Machsun and J. Monteleone, "Insurance coverage for wrongful employment practice claim under various liability policies," *Bus. Law*, 68 (1994): 49.

12. M. Levy, "The electronic monitoring of workers: Privacy in the age of the electronic sweatshop 14 *Legal Ref.Serv.Q.* 5 (1995).

13. See D. McCartney, "Electronic surveillance and resulting loss of privacy in the workplace," 62 *Lmke L. Rev.*, 8J9 (1994).

14. Where a city ordinance requires the employee to sign an affidavit the court held to be invalid.

15. Restatement (2d) of Torts Sect. 652E. See also A. Richman "Restoring the balance: Employer liability and employee privacy, *86 Iowa Law Review* 1337 (May 2001).

16. *Lewis* v. *United Airlines*, 500 N.E.2d 370 (Ohio App. 1985).

17. This is important, because if punitive damages can be shown, a jury trial is allowed under the CRA91 amendment to Title VII.

18. *Soraka* v. *Dayton-Hudson Corp.*, 1 Cal.Repr. 2d 77 (Cal. App. 1st Dist.).

19. Elliot Lasson, "How good are integrity tests?" *Personnel Journal*, 71 (April 1992): 35.

20. Public Law, 100–347, 102 Stat. 646 et seq. 29 USC 2001 et seq., CFR Part 801 1991 is a revision.

21. Pencil-and-paper dishonesty tests (sometimes called *employee theft proneness tests*) are permitted. The real purpose of these tests is to get the facts on a theft.

22. Testing for drugs is exempt. *O'Brien* v. *Papa Gino's of America*, 780 F.2d 1067 (1st Cir. 1986), is still good law.

23. 29 CFR Part 801 allows private employers to give polygraph tests in jobs where a large amount of cash is acquired from customers.

24. For reference on state laws, see *State by state guide to human resource laws* (New York: Panel Publishers, 1993).

25. *Kamrath* v. *Suburban National Bank*, 363 N.W.2d 108 (Minn. 1985).

26. This is different from entrapment, which is not allowed: *Jacobson* v. *United States*, 112 S.Ct. 1535 (1992).

27. *Smith* v. *Maryland*, 422 U.S. 735 (1979); *Texas* v. *Brown*, 103 S.Ct. 1535 (1993).

28. *Higher Market, Inc.*, 97 LA 92 (Prasyzich 1991).

29. *B.F. Goodrich Chemical Div.*, 709 LA 326 at 329 (Oppenheim 1978).

30. *Kawner Co.*, 86 LA 297 (Alexander 1985).

31. *Hess Oil Virgin Islands Corp.*, 93 LA 580 (Chandler 1989).

32. For arbitration cases on searches, see Frank Elkouri and Edna A. Elkouri, *How arbitration works*, 4th ed. (Washington, DC: Bureau of National Affairs, Inc., 1985), pp. 790–791.

33. *Faulkner* v. *Maryland*, 564 A.2d 785 (Md. 1989).

34. A search is reasonable if the measures adopted are reasonably related to the objectives of the search and there is no excessive intrusion considering the nature of the misconduct being investigated: *O'Connor* v. *Ortega*, 107 S.Ct. 1492 at 1503 (1987).

35. D. J. Duffy, "Privacy v. disclosure: Balancing employee–employer rights," *Employee Relations Law Journal* (1982): 594–609; Phillip Adler, Jr., Charles Parsons, and Scott B. Zolke, "Employee privacy: Legal and research developments and implications for personnel administration," *Sloan Management Review* (Winter 1985): 17; William Petrocelli, *Low profile—How to avoid the privacy invaders* (New York: McGraw-Hill, 1981), p. 112.

36. *Cort* v. *Bristol-Meyers*, 431 N.E.2d 908 (Mass. 1983).

37. *Beard* v. *City of Chicago*, N.D. Ill., No. 03-C-3527 (2005).

38. G. A. Abramson and E. J. Lyons, "Protection of employer's records from disclosure to employees, government agencies, and third parties," *Labor Law Journal*, 41 (June 1990): 353–363; A. Hartstein, "Rules of the road in dealing with personnel records," *Employee Relations Journal*, 17 (Spring 1992): 673–692.

39. At least 15 states have passed such laws, including but not restricted to California, Pennsylvania, Illinois, Delaware, Michigan, Minnesota, New Hampshire, North Carolina, Oregon, Tennessee, Utah, Wisconsin, and Vermont.

40. *Biderman's of Springfield, Inc.,* v. *Wright,* 322 S.W.2d 892 (Mo. 1959).

41. *Prosser & Keeton on torts,* 5th ed., Hornbook Series (St. Paul, MN: West, 1984), p. 771. See Chapter 11 for a full discussion of defamation.

42. See Suzanne Cook, "Invasion of privacy—A 1984 syndrome," *Industrial Management,* 29, no. 5 (September–October 1986): 18–21.

43. *Boehm* v. *American Bankers Insurance Group, Inc.,* 557 So.2d 91 (Fla. App. 3rd Dist. 1990).

44. *Ponticelli* v. *Mine Safety Appliance Co.,* 247 A.2d 303 (R.I. 1968).

45. For additional information on this privilege, see Jack Turner and Terry Esser, "Reference and background checks: Myth and fact," *Human Resources Management Ideas and Trends,* no. 36 (Chicago: Commerce Clearing House, April 1983); E. Dube, "Employment reference and the law," *Personnel Journal,* 65, no. 2 (February 1986): 87–88.

46. For a good explanation, see *Circus Circus Hotels* v. *Witherspoon,* 657 P.2d 101 (Nev. 1983). Also see *Humphrey* v. *National Semiconductor Corp.,* 18 Mass. App. 132 (1984).

47. *Calero* v. *Del Chemical Corp.,* 228 N.W.2d 737 (Wisc. 1975).

48. *Sindorf* v. *Jacron Sales,* 341 A.2d 856 (Md. 1975).

49. *Stewart* v. *Nation-Wide Check Corp.,* 182 S.E.2d 410 (N.C. 1971).

50. *Bolling* v. *Baker,* 671 S.W.2d 559 (Tex. App. 4 Dist. 1984). The employer stated that the discharged employee was a liar and not trustworthy. Although this was revealed only to other employees, the court found the privilege doctrine was violated by statements made with malice and reckless disregard for the truth.

51. *Haldeman* v. *Total Petroleum, Inc.,* 376 N.W.2d 98 (Iowa 1985).

52. See Janet Swerdow, "Negligent referral: A potential theory for employer liability" (note), *Southern California Law Review,* 64 (1991): 1645.

53. Refusal to give information to avoid one kind of a lawsuit often creates another kind of a lawsuit.

54. This is one advantage in being active in local professional associations.

55. See also *Ball* v. *Cracking Good Bakeries,* 777 F.2d 1497 (11th Cir. 1986), where the court allowed a claim for malpractice. Also see *Ford* v. *Revlon, Inc.,* 734 P.2d 580 (Ariz. 1987), and *O'Connell* v. *Chasdi,* 400 Mass. 686 (Mass. 1987), where the court found emotional distress in sexual harassment complaints.

56. *Ponton* v. *Scarfone,* 468 So.2d 1009 (Fla. App. 2 Dist. 1985).

57. J. J. Manna, "Personal liability under the Civil Rights Act of 1991: Piercing the corporate veil." *4 Temp.Pol.& Civ.Rts.L.Rev.* 339 (1995).

58. *Emmert* v. *Drake,* 224 F.2d 299 (5th Cir. 1955).

59. *Las Villas Produce,* 279 NLRB No. 120 (1986).

60. *Donovan* v. *Agnew,* 712 F.2d 1508 (1st Cir. 1983).

61. *Donovan* v. *Burgett Greenhouses, Inc.,* 759 F.2d 1483 (10th Cir. 1985).

62. *Lentz Plumbing Co.* v. *Fee,* 679 P.2d 736 (Kan. 1984).

63. See also Restatement (Second) of Agency, Sect. 439 (1958).

64. Also *Nordling* v. *Northern States Power Co.,* 465 N.W.2d 81 (Minn. Ct. App. 1991).

65. B. O'Leary and B. Weathington, "Beyond the business case for diversity in organizations," *Employee Responsibilities and Rights Journal,* 18 (November 2006): 283–292.

66. R. DeCicio, K.. Engemann, M. Owyang, and C. Wheeler, "Changing trends in the labor force: A survey," *Federal Reserve Bank of St. Louis Review* (January/February 2008): 47–62.

67. D. Vaishampayan, "Responding to the changing workforce," *Strategic HR Review,* 5, no. 6 (September/October 2006).

68. The Conference Board projects that 64 million skilled workers will be eligible to retire by 2010. According to the AARP, by 2014, one-third of the workforce will be over age 50.

69. Consider Garrison Keillor's reference to the fictional Lake Wobegon, "where all children are above average." See also L Lofton, "Different generations, different expectations mean HR challenges," *Mississippi Business Review,* 29, no. 48 (December 2007): 17, 25.

70. E. Glinsky, J. T. Bond, and K. Sakai, *2008 national study of employers.* Families and Worklife Institute (May 2008).

71. N. Lockwood, "Work/life balance: Challenges and solutions," *HR Magazine*, 48, no. 2 (2003): 2–10.

72. *Butros* v. *Canton Reg. Transit Authority*, 997 F.2d 196 (6th Cir. 1992).

73. It is more difficult to show hostile environment under national origin: *Daemi* v. *Church's Fried Chicken*, 931 F.2d 1379 (10th Cir. 1991).

74. *Fragrante* v. *City & County of Honolulu*, 888 F.2d 591 (9th Cir. 1991).

75. For a good discussion of language problems as they relate to nationality discrimination, see Eric Matusewitch, "Language rules can violate Title VII," *Personnel Journal* (October 1990): 98.

76. *Fortino* v. *Ousar*, 950 F.2d 389 (7th Cir. 1991).

77. The Act has caused considerable litigation, is difficult to enforce, and has been only marginally successful in preventing illegal entry.

78. The 1990 amendment relaxed some of the problems created by orginal act.

79. *Mester Mfg. Co.* v. *INS*, 879 F.2d 561 (9th Cir. 1989).

80. The INS also has a handbook (revised) that gives instructions on how to complete I-9 form.

81. *Furr's* v. *INS*, 976 F.2d 1366 (10th Cir. 1992).

82. In *Food International Corp.* v. *INS*, 948 F.2d 549 (9th Cir. 1991), the court held that failure to check the signature on a Social Security card according to INS handbook for filling out I-9 form did not establish willful intent to violate the act. However, in *El Rey Sausage, Inc.,* v. *INS*, 925 F.2d 1153 (9th Cir. 1991), the same court required intent.

83. *Hoffman Plastic Compounds Inc.,* v. *NLRB*, 122 S. Ct. 1275 (2002).

84. The rule amends 48 CFR and appears in the Federal Register at 73 FR 67651-705 (November 12. 2008).

85. 73 FR.

86. Illegal Immigration Reform and Immigration Responsibility Act of 1996, enacted as Division C of the Defense Department Appropriations Act, 1997, Pub. L. 104-208, 110 Stat. 3009-659 (1996).

87. This is an unusual provision. Most statutes requiring record keeping do not provide for a penalty when the statute is violated.

88. To allow more skilled immigrants to enter the United States, Congress passed the Immigration Act of 1991.

89. *Reyes* v. *Van Elk, Ltd.*, 148 Cal. App. 4th 604 (2007). An appeal was denied by the California Supreme Court.

90. *Hoffman Plastic Compounds, Inc.,* v. *NLRB*, 122 S. Ct. 1275 (2002).

91. *Incalza* v. *Fendi North America Inc.*, 479 F.3d 1005 (9th Cir. 2007).

92. *Rivera* v. *NIBCO Inc.*, 364 F.3d 1057 (9th Cir, 2004). The Supreme Court declined to review.

93. In *Patel* v. *Quality Inn South*, 846 F.2d 700 (11th Cir. 1988), the court held that an undocumented worker had the protection of the Fair Labor Standards Act.

94. This is the rule in all jurisdictions: *Rios* v. *Enterprise Association Steamfitters Local 638 of U.A.*, 860 F.2d 1168 (2nd Cir. 1988); *EEOC* v. *Tortilleria "La Mejor,"* 758 F.Supp. 585 (ED. Cal. 1991).

95. *Nicacio* v. *INS*, 797 F.2d 700 (9th Cir. 1985).

96. S. Gamboa, "Schumer: Immigration bill to be ready by Labor Day," Associated Press, July 8, 2009. found at http://truthout.org/070909E?

97. Brian Towers, *The representation gap: Change and reform in the British and American workplace* (Oxford: Oxford University Press, 1997).

98. Richard B. Freeman and Joel Rogers, *What workers want* (Ithaca, NY: ILR Press, 1999). Peter Hart Poll, 2007.

APPENDIX

GLOSSARY

Ability to pay A commonly used term in public sector negotiations by employers and unions to justify their bargaining positions as being within or beyond the financial resources available to fund a union proposal—generally a meaningless argument given the difficulties inherent with regard to the public financing of any given expenditure by a public employer relative to the employer's overall financial picture.

Accommodations Adjustments or changes to a job or worksite which will permit a handicapped individual to perform the essential functions of a job.

ADA (Americans with Disabilities Act). 1990 statute that prohibits employers from discriminating against "qualified" individuals based on a disability and, in some instances, to provide "reasonably accommodation" Amended by the ADA Amendments Act (ADAAA) of 2008.

ADAA The Americans with Disabilities Amendments Act of 2000.

ADEA (Age Discrimination in Employment Act). 1967 statute that prohibits employers, unions, employment agencies and apprenticeship/training programs from discriminating on the basis of age.

Affirmative action A remedial action initiated by an employer to improve work opportunities for protected classes considered to have been denied employment opportunities because of past discrimination.

Applicant pool The group of applicants for a particular job or position.

Arbitrability Issues submitted to arbitration may or may not be legally subject to an arbitration decision. When a question is raised as to whether an issue(s) is legally subject to a decision by an arbitrator, a determination may be made by a court or other appropriate/designated jurisdiction as to whether the issue(s) is subject to arbitration: ie: is the issue(s) arbitrable.

Arbitrable A dispute which is suitable for arbitration and has no substantive or procedural barriers.

Arbitration The use by unions and employers of a neutral third party to make a final and binding decision as to the outcome of a dispute. Arbitration may be subject to court review as to both the decision and arbitrability of the issue(s).

Assessment center A process that evaluates job candidates based on multiple assessment techniques, standardized tests, and pooled judgments of the individuals doing the assessment.

Bargaining power A theoretical measure of the ability of an employer or union at a given time and place with regard to a particular dispute to determine which party has the ability to prevail. Bargaining power is defined in private sector disputes in economic terms and in the public sector in political/public opinion terms.

BFOQ (Bona Fide Occupational Requirement). Legitimate job related requirements or qualifications that an applicant must meet to be considered for employment.

Business necessity A legal defense based on legitimate employment requirements against charges of employment discrimination.

Certificate of Coverage A certificate issued by an insurance company indicating the existence and extent of coverage.

Change time Time required or permitted for an employee to don working clothes or a uniform, or to remove the clothes or uniform.

Child Care Services Services available to adults through public institutions or private entities to provide for general or specific care of children (age indeterminate). Primary educational services through the public school system serve as an important example of a specific child care service.

Civil Rights Act of 1991(CRA91). Statute amending and extending the provisions of the Civil Rights Act of 1964.

Civil Service Government employment exempt from patronage.

Civil Service Reform Act Title 5, U.S.C. Legislation passed by Congress in 1978 to provide statutory bargaining rights for federal employees.

COBRA Consolidated Omnibus Budget Reconciliation Act which provides up to 18 months of health insurance coverage for employees who lose their coverage because their employment terminates.

Comparable worth A compensation theory which asserts that comparable jobs should be equitably compensated.

Compensable time Work time for which an employee must be compensated.

Compensatory time off "Comp time" is balancing weekly hours to avoid premium pay. Time off in one work week cannot be used to offset extra hours in a different week. There is an exception in the health care industry.

Complaint When used in non legal context it is an employee's disagreement over a management policy or action concerning working conditions or wages. In a legal context it is an allegation of wrongdoing and a request for remedy.

Concerted activity Actions undertaken by a group of employees for mutual action verses an employer.

Constructive discharge Coercing or forcing an employee to resign.

Content validity Test validation based on the internal consistency of test items and the extent to which they appear to measure job requirements.

Contract arbitration The use of arbitration as a means of resolving negotiations impasses.

Corporate veil protection A legal doctrine that shields officers or agents of corporations from lawsuits.

Cost of agreement/disagreement Generally refers to the costs to be incurred by the employer and the Union in a strike or lockout situation with regard to a specific proposal or set of proposals measured in economic terms in the private sector and in public opinion/political terms in the public sector.

Cumulative trauma syndrome An injury that develops over time due to repetitive activity on a job.

Defamation A written or oral statement that has the effect of damaging the reputation or social stature of another person; defamation by slander is via the spoken word, defamation by libel is through printed material.

Defenses Arguments raised by a party in a lawsuit or arbitration proceeding.

Deposition A pretrial discovery procedure whereby testimony is given under oath outside of open court.

Disability A physical or mental impairment that substantially limits one or more of the major life activities such as hearing, walking, or working. This is often a permanent condition under the ADA but temporary under workers compensation regulation.

Disclaimer An express or implied denial of a right, privilege, or thing in question.

Discovery Procedures designed to reveal facts and proposed testimony prior to a trial so as to avoid surprise.

Disparate impact Discrimination that effects an entire class of workers.

Disparate treatment When an employee is treated less favorably than other employees in violation of a statute.

Diversity Differences or dissimilarities in personnel bases on their race, religion, sex, national origin, or age.

Drug-Free Workplace Act 1988 Statute covering Federal employees and contractors prohibiting workplace drug use.

Due process Legal proceedings and procedures designed to protect individual rights and liberties.

Duty of fair representation The duty of a union to provide good faith representation to all employees in a bargaining unit.

Early neutral evaluation (ENE). Alternative dispute resolution procedure involving submission of a dispute to a neutral for a report or finding.

Electronic Communications Privacy Act 1988 statute that limits the ability of employers to monitor the voice and e-mail communications of employees; amended in 1994 to apply to cellular phones.

Employee Polygraph Protection Act 1988 statute that prohibits private sector employers from using pre-employment lie detector tests or from discriminating against current employees who decline to take such tests.

Employee Retirement Insurance Security Act of 1974 (ERISA). Statute requiring minimum funding and other protections for employee pensions.

Employment-at-will A diminishing common law doctrine whereby an employee can be terminated for good cause or for no cause.

Enforcement Procedure to compel litigants to comply with the court decision.

Equal Pay Act 1963 statute prohibiting gender discrimination in compensation—wages and benefits paid to an employee for work performed.

Ergonomics The study of workers interacting with job demands and conditions such as repetitive stress injuries or cumulative trauma disorder.

Essential job function Those job duties and functions that an incumbent must be able to perform. See ADA.

E-verify A voluntary, internet based program that allows employers to electronically verify the citizenship/immigration status of their employees.

Executive order An order issued by a public chief executive officer, usually the President of the U.S. or a State Governor.

Executive Order 13058 A presidential Executive Order issued in 1997 that established federal workplaces as smoke free.

Exempt status Refers to employees exempted from coverage of the provisions of the Fair Labor Standards Act.

Exit interview Interview with a terminating employee designed, in part, to determine the reasons for the employee's departure.

Exposure An act or omission which may result in a lawsuit.

Fact finding A third party dispute resolution technique in which the neutral(s) issues a formal recommendation for resolving a dispute. This recommendation is not binding upon the parties.

Fair Pay Act 2009 statute extending the statute of limitations for filing civil rights action.

Federal Arbitration Act 1925 statute that provides for the voluntary arbitration of all disputes including procedures for hearings, awards and enforcement.

FLRA Federal Labor Relations Authority established in 1978 providing for the administration of collective bargaining for federal employees.

FMLA (Family Medical Leave Act). 1993 statute that entitles eligible employees to up to twelve weeks of leave in a twelve month period for qualifying personal and family medical issues. The Act was amended in 2009 to provide for certain medically related leaves for military personnel and their caregivers.

Garrity warning A warning, either verbal or in writing, that must be given to public employees informing them that anything they say during an employer's investigation hearing cannot be used against them in a court of law.

General duty clause Refers to the General Duty Clause of the OSH Act, Section 5(a)(1). Which states that "[e]ach employer...shall furnish to each of his employees employment and a place of employment which are free from recognized hazards that are causing or are likely to cause death or serious physical harm to his employees."

GINA (Genetic Information Non-discrimination Act). 2008 statute that prohibits discrimination based on a person's genetic information.

Good faith Actions that a neither arbitrary or discriminatory.

Grievance A complaint made by a union that a provision of a negotiated labor agreement has been violated or misinterpreted by the employer.

Grievance procedure A process outlined in a labor agreement providing for the handling of a grievance filed by an employee or union on behalf of an employee(s) alleging a violation of the requirements of the labor agreement or past practices of the parties under the agreement. A grievance unresolved under the procedure is generally referred to arbitration for resolution.

Handbook acknowledgment Signature indicating receipt of an employee handbook.

Harassment Giving an individual unwanted attention; intimidation.

Hazard abatement To alleviate, reduce, minimize the severity of, or remove a hazard.

Hostile environment A workplace characterized by discriminatory antagonism, opposition or harassment.

Impairment A physical or mental defect or disability. See ADA.

Implied contract An agreement absent a written contract which is construed by a court based on the behavior of the parties.

Independent contractor Independent contractor is an individual employed for a fixed period time pursuant to contract and is not considered an employee within the meaning of the Fair Labor Standards Act.

Interrogatories Written questions asked in a discovery procedure to a party having information of interest in the case.

IRCA (Immigration Reform and Control Act). 1986 statute designed to limit the ability of employers to hire undocumented aliens.

Job analysis The definition of a job based on its component requirements and responsibilities.

Just cause A standard used to determine whether or not an employee was properly disciplined or discharged.

Last chance agreement A conditional offer of reinstatement in which the employee agrees that any future transgression or violation of the employer's rules will result in immediate and uncontested discharge.

Lockout A withdrawal of the opportunity to work by an employee.

Loudermill Hearing A hearing public employees are entitled to prior to termination. A due process guarantee named for Cleveland, OH school employee James Loudermill.

Major life activity Activities such as walking, speaking and caring for oneself that are central to most people's daily lives.

Malice The intentional commission of an unlawful act; evil intent.

Malpractice Conduct that is not necessarily negligent or incompetent but is deemed unacceptable by society.

Mandatory subjects Items which the National Labor Relations Act requires employers and unions to negotiate.

Meal periods Normally 30 to 60 minutes of time for lunch during a work shift for which pay is not required so long as the worker is free of job obligations. Be attentive also to related stipulations in some states.

Med-Arb A hybrid dispute resolution procedure in which a third party neutral first mediates issues that can be resolved by negotiation, and then arbitrates those issues that cannot be resolved.

Mediation The utilization of a neutral third party to assist labor and management in negotiations in their attempt to reach a settlement.

Military caregiver Individuals who provide care to qualified military personnel under the Family Medical Leave Act.

Mini-trial An alternative dispute resolution procedure utilizing mediation that is similar to a trial in court.

Multilateral Collective bargaining in which there are more than two parties of interest. For example, most public sector bargaining involving an employer, a union, and a legislative body.

Negligent hiring Failure by an employer to exercise due care and diligence in hiring.

Negligent retention Where employer is aware of or should have been aware of an employees' dangerous propensity for violence or maliciousness (regardless of the cause) and did not do anything about it.

Negligent training Failure by an employer to properly and diligently train employees.

Nexus A relationship.

NLRB (National Labor Relations Board). An Independent federal agency created by Congress in 1935 to administer the National Labor Relations Act.

Older Workers Benefit Protection Act of 1990 (OWBPA). Statute protecting the pensions and other benefits of senior employees.

Ombudsman An individual, often a neutral party, who investigates complaints or grievances.

Outside salesperson An individual hired to sell merchandise away from the employer's place of business.

Past practice A term used to define a consistent mutually agreed to response by a union and employer over a period of time to a situation or condition. Courts and arbitrators consider a mutually agreed on past practice to be binding as a solution for same or similar situations.

Patronage The power to appoint to office or grant political favors.

Pay equity The notion that compensation should be equal for all similarly situated employees.

Perceptions The mental impressions of the extent of bargaining power by those involved in the negotiations process concerning their ability to achieve their proposals in the negotiation process though the use of different strategies—including strike and lockout.

Personal liability Liability that an individual employee rather than the employer incurs.

Portability The ability to transfer individual benefits from one employer to another.

Precedent A concept used by employers, union, and arbitrators indicating that decisions made in the past should be decisive in determining how decisions should be made in the future where the circumstances are the same or similar—related to the Term "Past Practice."

Probationary period Initial period of employment during which a new employee is considered to be temporary and has no expectancy of continued employment.

Progressive discipline The principle that discipline should be corrective, and not punitive, and that the severity of discipline imposed should be appropriate to the nature of the offense.

Progressive Era A period of time marked by progress and reform covering approximately the first twenty-five years of the twentieth century.

Property right A right based on a personal, tangible, intangible or real property interest.

Public opinion An attitude of a majority of a population on a stated subject or issue alleged to exist by an individual, group, or entity claiming knowledge of such attitude.

Public policy A specific statement of goals, objectives or requirements contained in legislation or court decisions that is generally applicable.

Qualified privilege The common law doctrine which permits employers to disclose truthful information about their employees.

Quid pro quo Something for something. As used in the text, fiving one thing of value to one person for another thing considered valuable to another person.

Reasonable accommodation An effort on the part of the employer to change methods to enable an employee.

Reasonable suspicion drug testing A test initiated by the employer's reasonable belief that an employee is impaired or under the influence of drugs.

Representation gap The numerical discrepancy between those employees who claim that they would like union representation and those who actually have union representation.

Reprisal Retaliate on against an employee.

Res Judicata A legal doctrine that deems each case to rest on its own merits and considers no precedent; the doctrine applicable to arbitration.

Rest periods Break periods in the workday.

Salary test A pay level ($) decision point which can be used to make a snap judgement on whether or not a position should be considered exempt from overtime regulations.

Settlement conference An alternative dispute resolution procedure in which the parties present an expedited version of their case to a panel of neutrals.

Severance pay Compensation given to an employee in lieu of wages at the time of separation (termination).

Sleep time Normally 5 to 20 minutes of free time in the first and second half of a work shift voluntarily granted by an employer including federal agencies that is considered compensable under regulations. Be attentive also to related stipulations in some states.

Standards Minimum requirements under the Occupational Safety and Health Act.

Stare Decisis A legal doctrine that bases lower court decisions on prior superior court decisions. See Precedent.

Strike A call by a union to members of its bargaining unit to cease work for an employer—the call may be for an indefinite time or a specific period of time. The members may or may not heed the union call.

Subcontracting Action by an employer to begin to utilize persons other than the employer's employees to produce goods or provide services.

Subpoena A court order directing testimony on a specific matter.

Summary jury trial Alternative dispute resolution procedure similar to a jury trial.

Summons A document that commences a civil action or proceeding that asserts jurisdiction, and requires an appearances or an answer.

Test validation Statistical procedure used to determine the validity of a test.

Title VII 1964 statute which undertakes to eliminate all employment discrimination based on race, color, religion, sex or national origin.

Tort When one person causes injury (physical or otherwise) to another, for which a court will allow a civil action.

Travel time Time required to travel to and from a job.

Undue hardship A requirement or accommodation that would place an excessive burden on an employer.

WARN Worker Adjustment and Retraining Act of 1989.

Weighted Application Blank (WAB). A structure method for determining which characteristics will predict job retention.

Weingarten A ruling of the U. S. Supreme Court which provides an employee with the right to union representation when confronted with a mandatory investigatory interview which the employee believes could result in disciplinary action.

WHD Wage and Hour Division of DOL.

Whistle blower A person, often an employee, that reveals illegal activity engaged in by an individual, employer or company.

Writ of certiorari A discretionary device used by the U.S. Supreme Court to choose cases it wishes to hear.

Wrongful discharge A discharge prohibited by statutory or common law.

Zero tolerance policies Strict employment requirements which allow for no deviation or exceptions.

INDEX